¡Viva el Español!

¡NOS COMUNICAMOS!

Annotated Teacher's Edition

Ava Belisle-Chatterjee, M.A.
Chicago School District 6
Chicago, Illinois

Marcia Fernández
Chicago School District 6
Chicago, Illinois

Abraham Martínez-Cruz, M.A.
Chicago School District 6
Chicago, Illinois

Linda West Tibensky, M.A.
Oak Park School District 200
Oak Park, Illinois

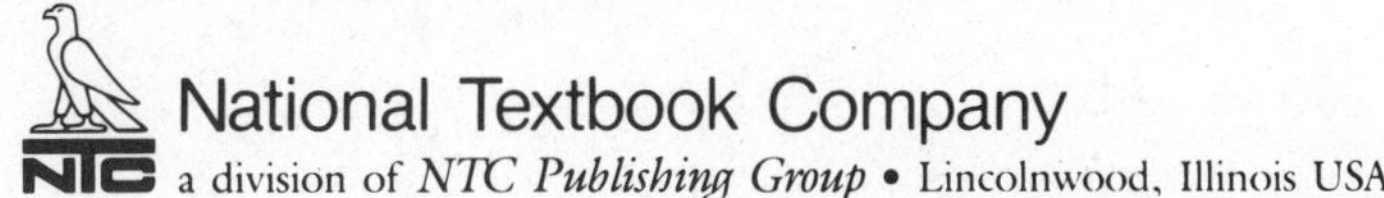

National Textbook Company
a division of *NTC Publishing Group* • Lincolnwood, Illinois USA

Acknowledgments

The authors wish to acknowledge the administration of Oak Park District 97 and 200 and Sabin Magnet School District 6 for their support and encouragement.

Project Director
Michael Ross

Project Editor
Marcia Seidletz

Content Editor
Minerva Figueroa

Production Editor
Mary Greeley

Design
David Corona Design

Design Assistant
Kim Meriwether

Production Services
Carlisle Communications Ltd.

Contributing Writers to the Textbook Series

Sandra Blake

Colleen Finnerty

Jill Ginsburg

Marcia Gotler

James Maharg

Elizabeth Millán

Robert Paral

Catherine Shapiro

Georgianne Urban

Marina Vine

Artists for the Textbook Series

James Buckley

Don Wilson

Fred Womack

Contributing Artists

Lisa Ansted

Tim Basaldua

Tony Colonna

a division of NTC Publishing Group
4255 West Touhy Avenue
Lincolnwood (Chicago), Illinois 60646–1975 U.S.A.

Printed in the United States of America.

9 0 KP 9 8 7 6 5 4 3 2 1

Testing program

Test Designers

Stanley W. Connell

Martha Lucía Torres

Test Consultant

Jean D'Arcy Maculaitis

Pilot Testing

Friedrich L. Jahn
Elementary School
Chicago Public Schools
Chicago, Illinois
Supervising Teacher:
Abraham Martínez-Cruz

New Sabin Magnet School,
District 6
Chicago Public Schools
Chicago, Illinois
Supervising teacher:
Zulma V. Meléndez

Consulting Educators

Diana Azcoitia
Bilingual Coordinator
Chicago Public Schools
Chicago, Illinois

Dr. Gladys C. Lipton
Coordinator of Foreign Language Workshops
University of Maryland Baltimore County
Catonsville, Maryland

Carmen Macías
Assistant Principal
Los Angeles Public Schools
Los Angeles, California

Dr. James Maharg
University of Illinois
Chicago, Illinois

Gloria A. Mariscal
Teacher of Spanish
Eastwood High School
El Paso, Texas

Denise Mesa
Spanish Teacher
Sabal Palm Elementary School
Dade County Public Schools
Miami, Florida

María A. Montalvo
Coordinator of Modern and Classical Languages
Albuquerque Public Schools
Albuquerque, New Mexico

Dr. Francisco J. Perea
Language Consultant
Austin Independent School District
Austin, Texas

Elsa Statzner
Spanish FLES Teacher
Longfellow Humanities Magnet School
St. Paul Public Schools
St. Paul, Minnesota

Preface

The *Annotated Teacher's Edition* of *¡Nos comunicamos!* forms the core of this innovative, lively program of Spanish as a second language. It contains all the information you will need to plan and implement the program during the school year. The following are some of the features of the *Annotated Teacher's Edition:*

- Introduction to the *¡Viva el español!* Spanish-language development program
- How-to section for incorporating the program components
- Sample daily lesson plan
- Detailed scope and sequence chart
- Unit-by-unit suggestions for presenting, reviewing, extending, and enriching instruction
- Exercise answers and suggestions printed directly on the pupil edition pages

Whether you are an experienced teacher or new to the foreign language classroom, this complete *Annotated Teacher's Edition* will help guide, refresh, and inspire you to make students truly say and mean *¡Viva el español!*

Contents

Unit Plans (continued)

Index to Charts and Figures

Introduction

Overview

¡Viva el español! is a six-level program for developing Spanish-language proficiency in students from the elementary grades through middle school and junior high. Consisting of complete teacher-resource kits—Learning Systems A, B, and C—and a comprehensive textbook series—*Converso mucho, Ya converso más*, and *¡Nos comunicamos!*—the *¡Viva el español!* program not only teaches language skills but also equips students with learning habits and skills that will aid them as they continue their studies in later years.

The Learning Systems

Designed specifically for young students, Learning Systems A, B, and C develop the language skills of listening, speaking, reading, and writing in a gradual, logical progression. Students participate in their language learning in a positive, nonthreatening environment, similar to the way in which children acquire their first language. To that end, each multimedia learning system provides components that encourage teachers and students to enjoy the Spanish learning experience.

The integration of the learning system components—puppets, full-color flash cards, stimulating cassettes of songs and activities, full-color posters, picturebooks, and filmstrips—is explained clearly and in detail in the Learning System A, B, and C *Teacher's Manuals*, which also describe the full use of the black-line masters in the *Resource and Activity Book.*

The Textbook Series

The *¡Viva el español!* textbook series—*Converso mucho, Ya converso más*, and *¡Nos comunicamos!*—has been designed both for those students beginning their Spanish studies (students with no prior Spanish language background) and for those students who have previously acquired some knowledge of Spanish either with the *¡Viva el español!* learning systems or by some other means. You will find a thorough discussion on how to use the textbooks with various target groups later in this Introduction.

The textbooks *Converso mucho, Ya converso más*, and *¡Nos comunicamos!* develop and refine language skills while they establish and promote basic language-learning skills through an enthusiastic, lively, and positive approach. The components accompanying the textbooks are carefully integrated to provide all the materials necessary for students' active participation while learning Spanish. In addition to the student textbook and this *Annotated Teacher's Edition*, the following components make up each level of the textbook series:

- Workbook
- Workbook, Teacher's Edition
- Teacher's Resource and Activity Book (black-line masters)
- Lesson Cassettes
- Exercise Cassette
- Song Cassette
- Testing Program (black-line master book of tests and audiocassette)

Goals and Key Features of the **¡Viva el español!** Textbook Series

Objectives

The overall objectives of the *¡Viva el español!* textbook series are to develop, reinforce, and refine proficiency in listening, speaking, reading, and writing. Through an essentially inductive approach, students will gain an understanding of how the language is structured and how they can use this knowledge to express their own needs and talk about the world around them. By developing and refining their skills of observation, students also acquire a basic understanding and appreciation of the diversity of cultures in the Spanish-speaking world.

Time Frame

Each textbook in the series—*Converso mucho, Ya converso más,* and *¡Nos comunicamos!*—contains sufficient instructional materials for a full academic year of stimulating thirty- to forty-minute class periods. Each regular unit of the textbooks contains sufficient materials for twelve days of interactive, hands-on learning, with evaluation on the last two days of the twelve. The elements of the textbooks, the time frame of a sample unit, as well as the Testing Program will be described in detail later in this *Annotated Teacher's Edition.*

Versatility of Instruction

The design of the textbooks enables you to target the lessons to the abilities and needs of your students. Whether your class is made up of students who are just beginning their studies or of students who have previously acquired some proficiency in Spanish—as well as any combination of the two groups—the multilevel approach of the exercises in the program gives you the flexibility to tailor your instruction to the specific needs of your students.

Three-level Approach

Both in the textbooks and in the workbooks of *Converso mucho, Ya converso más,* and *¡Nos comunicamos!*, exercises are provided at three different levels of difficulty. The degree of difficulty is indicated in the *Annotated Teacher's Edition* only, so that students are not aware that they are either not doing the most difficult material or are reviewing easy material. With this hierarchical system, you will know instantly the level for which the exercises are intended. The following symbols appear next to exercises on the annotated pages of the student textbook:

○ **Lowest level of difficulty.** These exercises consist of simple activities that require minimal manipulation of the language.

◐ **Average level of difficulty.** These exercises require some manipulation of the language within a communication context.

● **Highest level of difficulty.** These exercises require students to express their own preferences, feelings, and thoughts and often to interact with classmates, either in pairs or small groups.

Naturally, you may use any or all of the exercises regardless of level, according to the speed at which your students progress. Some students may progress quickly to the more difficult exercises, whereas others may need to complete the easy exercises for reinforcement or review. In short, the three-level approach has been devised to give you the flexibility you need to respond to the learning styles, abilities, and language-learning backgrounds of your students.

Another purpose of this three-level design is to allow students to focus on essential vocabulary and structures while practicing different language skills. Thus, you can control and vary the pace so that students get the practice they need to build a proper foundation in all the essential language skills.

By the end of *¡Nos comunicamos!*, the third textbook in the series, all students—whether they began their studies with *Converso mucho* or with the learning systems—should have mastered the equivalent of one-plus years of high school Spanish. It is anticipated that students who started with Learning Systems A, B, and C will demonstrate a greater degree of proficiency and fluency in Spanish than students who have not studied with the learning systems.

Communication Orientation

With all the activities and elements of the *¡Viva el español!* program, the emphasis is on communication. Throughout the program, lessons and units begin with the students' world and gradually spiral outward to the communities of the world. In concert with students' naturally developing awareness of their surroundings and the world at large, the vocabulary and language structures of each textbook enable them to express their own meanings as early as possible.

To encourage and develop students' ability to communicate, all exercises, regardless of the level of difficulty, are built around communicative situations. In addition, many of the exercises call for communicative interaction among students, either in pairs or in small groups. Examples of brief dialogues and conversations are provided as models for students to use in forming their own conversations. Thus, students may read or listen to an interaction as an example of how the vocabulary or grammar is used in real life; they are never required to memorize or parrot a dialogue. Communication in this sense is the application of language to express meaningful questions, responses, preferences, and opinions.

Methodologies

Throughout the *¡Viva el español!* program, communication and inductive learning are stressed. The various methodologies employed take into consideration different learning and teaching styles. Thus, *¡Viva el español!* uses an eclectic approach, bringing together the best aspects of many teaching methodologies while allowing you to use the methodology or style with which you feel most comfortable.

Foremost among the methodologies incorporated in *¡Viva el español!* are the Natural Approach and Total Physical Response methods, developed by Tracy Terrell and James Asher, respectively.

The Natural Approach and Total Physical Response methods approximate in the classroom, as much as is realistically possible, the informal environment of first-language acquisition. In doing so, they fulfill the objectives of second- or foreign-language education: to learn a foreign language in both its spoken and written forms and to use it actively in everyday life.

Asher, Terrell, and other researchers in the field of foreign-language teaching have shown that programs based on the processes of first-language acquisition result in greater retention and a greater ability to create new and meaningful messages. Equally important, foreign-language programs that incorporate these methods have generated a more favorable attitude among learners toward foreign-language study. One reason for the improved attitude is that both methods presuppose that foreign-language instruction should meet students' communicative needs. That is, foreign-language programs should help students acquire the vocabulary, phrases, structures, and eventually the grammatical skills appropriate to and useful in their everyday environment. When this has been accomplished, foreign-language study, like first-language acquisition, is considered to be meaningful, useful, and pleasurable.

The Natural Approach

The Natural Approach to second-language instruction has been implemented throughout the *¡Viva el español!* program. As employed in the program, this approach helps foster spontaneous, nonthreatening, and meaningful communication among students. The key to this approach is that second-language instruction in the school should attempt to parallel the manner in which children learn their first language in the home.

In contrast with traditional methods of second-language instruction, first-language acquisition is a low-stress learning process. It includes an extended period of listening, positive reinforcement, meaningful and effective communication, and a nonthreatening environment.

As children learn to speak at home, they first pass through relatively passive stages of learning in which their responses to the language of their caretakers consist first of physical reactions and simple utterances and later of the generation of complete, grammatical sentences.

Traditional second-language instruction in schools has often consisted of a teacher-centered environment in which beginning students are required to produce completely formulated, error-free responses to the teacher's questions. Also in many traditional classrooms, the actual use of the target language is only a small percentage of the total communication, relegated only to dialogues, readings, and exercises. Thus, students are expected to communicate in a second language to which they have actually received very little exposure. This unnatural atmosphere has often resulted in a high-stress environment and considerable student anxiety, both of which hinder language learning.

In the *¡Viva el español!* learning systems and textbook series, the numerous activities, lessons, and units all work together to maximize the students' willingness to communicate while providing a language-rich environment. Unlike the traditional anxiety-producing programs, *¡Viva el español!* eliminates the fear of failure. Students utter completely formulated sentences only when they are ready and are motivated to communicate meaningful messages. You, as the teacher, become the caretaker, model, and significant other in the second-language learning process.

Translated into practical terms, you, the caretaker, establish a learning environment with the following characteristics:

- Extensive use and examples of the target language in the classroom
- Continual positive reinforcement
- Stress-free correction of student errors through modeling and by example
- Meaningful communication through activities, such as learning games; short questions and comments about everyday activities; in-class recognition of birthdays, achievements, and other events important to students; positive comments on and display of students' work, etc.
- A nurturing and positive attitude toward students' efforts and toward the language itself and the cultures of which it is a part
- A stimulating, flexible agenda in which students are actively participating in the communication process throughout the class period

In short, you create a learning environment in which the language directly relates to the students and their surroundings and reflects their needs, interests, and everyday life.

Total Physical Response

Closely related to the Natural Approach is Total Physical Response (TPR). The TPR method promotes the use of nonverbal communication in the acquisition of a second language. As with the Natural Approach, this concept is based on the process by which a first language is acquired whereby children respond to their caretakers with appropriate physical actions.

As its name implies, the TPR method in the classroom involves a physical response to a command or direction to help students learn vocabulary and other concepts. Equally important, the physical response and activities help students retain what they have learned over time.

Generally, TPR is used most in the first stages of learning new words and language concepts, when the emphasis is on the development of listening comprehension and speaking skills. Following this method, students pass through a silent period during which they listen as you say the various TPR commands and then demonstrate the appropriate responses to those commands. Eventually, students indicate comprehension, not necessarily through speech, but by performing or carrying out the direction or command. Activities associated with TPR are ideal for children and adolescents because they take into consideration the short attention spans and need for physical activity that are characteristic of these age groups.

Typical TPR activities are set up in a four-step process. In the first step, the teacher gives the command and models it several times as students passively observe. Then, in the second step, students respond to the command as a group with the teacher still modeling the appropriate response. As the students' self-confidence increases and after they successfully carry out the commands as a group, the teacher begins the third step by giving commands to individuals. During this step, continued input through modeling is crucial in maintaining a low anxiety level among students. Finally, as students become more familiar with the commands, they are ready for the fourth step in which they give the commands to one another and even create their own variations.

In the Unit Plans section of this *Annotated Teacher's Edition*, you will find specific suggestions for integrating the Total Physical Response method into instruction.

Language Experience Approach

The Language Experience Approach (LEA), which is part of the Natural Approach method, parallels first-language acquisition in that it allows students to absorb the language effortlessly. LEA activities begin with the students' active participation in a student-centered, communicative, low-stress activity. Thus, LEA activities carry through and expand on the key elements of the *¡Viva el español!* program—namely, meaningful and comprehensible communication in a positive, language-rich environment.

Through LEA, students develop reading and writing skills by using language that relates to their own experiences. Normally, you would begin LEA activities relating to a lesson when students are in the final stages of internalizing the vocabulary and structures. At the final stage, students are comfortable with the new words and structures and are ready to use them freely in the course of a language experience.

A typical LEA activity may begin with a simple role-play activity, a skit, an interactive exercise, or even an in-class project or a class field trip. The activity continues under your guidance with a discussion of the language experience. Initially, this guidance may take the form of asking questions; the discussion takes the form of verbal responses. As students acquire more language, and more confidence in using the language, your role becomes one of facilitator or moderator of a discussion group.

As the discussion of the experience continues, you write key sentences on the chalkboard or on a transparency for students to read. From the outset, students are reading passages that are meaningful and comprehensible to them because they created the passages.

Once a passage, or coherent series of sentences, has been developed, students practice their reading skills first through choral readings and then through individual readings. Willingness to read aloud is enhanced when students know that others are reading with them and when they feel secure in the knowledge that their efforts, though not perfect, will be met with a positive, nurturing response from the teacher.

From reading aloud, students then progress to reading a neat handwritten or typewritten copy of the passage. This copy of the passage can be used for a number of activities. For example, it may be cut into sentence strips for students to put the individual parts or sentences back into a whole passage. The passage may also be used to create a "Big Book," in which students illustrate and assemble the sentences in a book form.

Big Book Activities

Big Book activities promote a positive sense of achievement in students. The Big Books themselves become concrete examples of the students' communication in the language which they can share with their peers and even take home to share with their families. Big Books also provide continual reinforcement. For example, they may be displayed and used for an in-class lending library or even as a special display in the school library. A Big Book review page may be attached to the back for fellow students to write their comments or reviews.

Many of the interactive exercises, as well as the situational story exercises, found in the textbook series can form the basis of LEA Big Books. Throughout *Converso mucho, Ya converso más,* and *¡Nos comunicamos!*, you will find many suggestions for incorporating Big

Book activities in the lessons. Students may convert an interactive classroom activity into a story or they may create graphs and charts from the numerous "in-class surveys" that appear in the exercise sections. Students may also build a story around one of the colorful photographs in the textbooks. In short, ample opportunities for LEA activities are provided in the textbooks to stimulate meaningful communication.

Functional-Notional Approaches

Built into the *¡Viva el español!* program are opportunities for students to begin learning and practicing simple functions, or tasks, of communication within the notions, or content categories, of instruction.

In *Converso mucho*, *Ya converso más*, and *¡Nos comunicamos!*, activities at the highest level of difficulty are often based on language functions such as gathering information, reporting, and expressing preferences and opinions. These simplified language functions tie in closely with the theme and grammatical content of the unit in which they are practiced. Students who participate in these activities are building the skills to perform concrete language functions within meaningful contexts. That is, they are acquiring the skills to perform communication tasks that naturally relate to their immediate world and interests.

As a result, the language functions and notions are consistent with the program's emphasis on meaningful and comprehensible communication that evolves naturally as students progress in their acquisition of a second language. *¡Viva el español!* is not centered on a functional-notional approach. Instead, it lays the foundation on which students may build their functional skills within meaningful content categories.

Experience—Using What Works Best

In summary, the methodologies, approaches, and techniques incorporated in the *¡Viva el español!* program have all been tempered by the practical, commonsense knowledge that has evolved during the many collective years of classroom and materials-development experience of the program's authors, contributors, and consultants. It is expected—and even hoped—that you will pick and choose from the suggestions and examples contained in this *Annotated Teacher's Edition* to tailor your Spanish-language program to the ages, backgrounds, needs, and abilities of your students. Young children and early adolescents will communicate to you whether a certain approach is working. The keys to a successful, stimulating language-learning environment are to use only what works and to inject variety and fun, mixed with the occasional surprise, into your classroom routine.

Components of the **¡Viva el español!** Textbook Series

Annotated Teacher's Edition

The teacher's editions of *Converso mucho*, *Ya converso más*, and *¡Nos comunicamos!* form the core of the program. In each *Annotated Teacher's Edition* (A.T.E.), you can find the information you will need to plan and implement a course of study over the school year, adapt the program to meet the unique needs of your students, carry out the daily lessons, enrich the language-learning experience, assess students' progress, and integrate the school's Spanish program into the home and community. The A.T.E. also contains a full-size reproduction of the student textbook with annotations for information, suggestions for extending and enriching the daily lessons, and the answers to exercises.

In the front section of the *Annotated Teacher's Edition*, you will find a discussion of the features and methodologies of the *¡Viva el español!* program; a complete scope and sequence chart, containing the unit-by-unit active vocabulary, points of grammar and language usage, and language skills, functions, and cultural topics; unit-by-unit plans, listing the materials and components you will need; suggestions for review, extension, enrichment, and informal assessment activities; and a resource section of games and activities and a reproduction of the ACTFL Proficiency Guidelines for the Novice and Intermediate levels.

Textbooks

The colorful student textbooks contain three preliminary lessons, thirteen regular units, three review sections, a final review unit, useful appendixes for reference, a Spanish-English glossary, an English-Spanish word list, and a general index. From the beginning of the school year, students should learn to use all the features of the textbook as tools in building their language skills. (The organization of the textbook will be described later in detail.)

Teacher's Resource and Activity Book

The black-line masters in the *Teacher's Resource and Activity Book* contain numerous black-and-white illustrations to enhance classroom activities and to save you time in searching for and preparing materials for the classroom. Each book of black-line masters is divided into seven sections:

1. **Panorama de vocabulario,** which reproduces in black and white the vocabulary section of each regular unit of the textbook
2. **Vocabulary Cards,** which contains individual illustrations of the vocabulary for use in TPR activities, as well as games
3. **Vocabulary Review,** which contains reduced illustrations of vocabulary groups on a single page
4. **Numbers/Letters**
5. **Maps,** which contains outline maps for extension and enrichment activities
6. **Game/Activity Pages**
7. **Tape Exercise Pages,** which are the written exercises that accompany the Exercise Cassette

In addition, a complete answer key to the Tape Exercise Pages is printed in the front of the *Teacher's Resource and Activity Book.*

Workbook

Each student workbook is correlated to the textbook lessons, units, and sections. Included in the workbooks are exercises to practice writing skills, reinforce the vocabulary and language concepts taught in the textbook, develop language-learning skills, and have fun with the language. As in the textbook, the activities and exercises in the workbook are provided at three levels of difficulty to meet the needs of students' learning styles and abilities.

Workbook—Teacher's Edition

The Teacher's Edition of the workbook contains the answers to exercises, the symbols that represent the degree of difficulty of the exercises, and suggestions for using and extending exercises. In addition, the Teacher's Edition contains a complete tapescript of the Lesson Cassettes and Exercise Cassette, as well as the music and lyrics of the songs recorded on the Song Cassette. The tapescript is designed to help you select the conversations and features of the audiocassettes that will enrich the listening comprehension experiences of your students.

Audiocassettes

The audiocassettes that accompany the *¡Viva el español!* textbook series fall into four categories:

1. Lesson Cassettes
2. Exercise Cassette
3. Song Cassette
4. Test Cassette

Lesson Cassettes

Recorded by native speakers of Spanish of varied ages and backgrounds, the Lesson Cassettes contain the vocabulary, pronunciation, and conversation sections of each regular unit of the textbook. Whenever a section of the textbook has been recorded on the Lesson Cassette, you will find the following symbol printed at the top of the page in your *Annotated Teacher's Edition:*

The Lesson Cassettes also contain conversations and features to provide students with additional opportunities to hear the language spoken by native speakers in simulated real-life situations. The conversations and features not only synthesize the vocabulary and grammar of each unit but also serve as practical examples of the language in use.

Exercise Cassette

The Exercise Cassette contains exercises that further students' practice in distinguishing sounds and in using the structures of the language. Some of the exercises have been designed for oral responses and others have been designed for paper-and-pencil responses on the Tape Exercise Pages found in the *Teacher's Resource and Activity Book.*

Song Cassette

The Song Cassette contains all the songs that are included in the Teacher's Edition of the student workbook.

Test Cassette

The Test Cassette accompanies the *¡Viva el español!* Testing Program, which is described in the next section.

Testing Program

The Testing Program for *Converso mucho, Ya converso más,* and *¡Nos comunicamos!* is made up of a black-line master book of tests and a Test Cassette. Not only does the black-line master book contain all the tests you will need throughout the school year, but also it provides a student progress chart for you to record each student's development of language skills, a complete discussion of strategies for assessing and evaluating students' abilities and, of course, an answer key. Recorded on the Test Cassette are listening comprehension activities that correspond to the Testing Program.

How to Use and Teach the **¡Viva el español!** Textbook Series

In this section you will find information about the organization of the textbooks, the purposes and uses of each section and subsection, general strategies and techniques, recommendations for structuring the lessons, and an explanation of how the components of the *¡Viva el español!* textbook series all work together to create an exciting, effective language-learning program.

Organization of **Converso mucho, Ya converso más,** and **¡Nos comunicamos!**

Preliminary Lessons

Each of the three textbooks begins with three preliminary lessons: *Primera lección*, *Segunda lección*, and *Tercera lección*.

In *Converso mucho*, the first textbook in the series, the three lessons begin with the basics of language learning—greetings, numbers, and classroom vocabulary. Through these lessons, beginning students are eased into second-language learning by simple, success-oriented vocabulary and exercises. Students who have already been exposed to Spanish will have the opportunity to review familiar vocabulary and structures and to learn some new words and expressions. This is accomplished through the formats of *Panorama de vocabulario* and the follow-up exercises (*¡Aprende el vocabulario!*), which will be described in detail later.

In the second and third textbooks in the series, *Ya converso más* and *¡Nos comunicamos!*, the preliminary lessons take the format of review sections. They serve as reminders and refreshers to reaccustom students to Spanish after the summer break. The brief conversations and activities in these lessons review and practice the important vocabulary and concepts of language from the preceding year.

Regular Units

Each textbook contains thirteen regular units that are made up of seven sections. The first section, or **Unit Opener,** is a colorful two-page spread of photographs that depict real-life examples of the topic of the unit. Before you begin a unit, you may have students practice their skills of observation and prediction by having them guess what the unit will be about. Following the unit activities, the same photographs may be used for informal assessment of the vocabulary and structures the students have learned, as well as for review and practice of previously learned vocabulary and language.

Throughout all the sections of the units, you will also find photographs that can be used to practice vocabulary and grammar, provide brief reading and writing activities, and serve as examples of everyday life in Spanish-speaking areas of the world. These photographs have been chosen primarily to give students practice in applying their language skills to describe real people and situations, as well as to sharpen their skills of observation.

Panorama de vocabulario. In this section, illustrations with their corresponding captions or labels serve as an introduction to the vocabulary of the unit. The vocabulary words and phrases are never translated into English on these pages. Instead, the *Panorama de vocabulario* section serves as a "picture dictionary" through which students associate the illustrations with the words and thus absorb the meanings.

Following the presentation of the vocabulary is *¡Aprende el vocabulario!*, a series of vocabulary exercises ordered by level of difficulty from lowest to highest. Each exercise is preceded by a communication context that provides the framework of the exercise and gives coherence and meaning to the individual exercise items. Often the actual instructions for completing the exercises are worded to give you the flexibility of doing them orally in class, assigning them as homework, or combining them for in-class and take-home practice. Most exercises contain one or more completed models of the exercise items so that students fully understand what is expected of them. [Beginning with *Unidad 5* of *Converso mucho* and continuing through *¡Nos comunicamos!*, the instructions to the exercises are given in Spanish. All of the terms in the instructions have been included in the Spanish-English glossary for student reference when completing at-home assignments.]

Los sonidos del idioma. To enable students to learn about the sound-letter correspondences of Spanish, the pronunciation section lists examples of words containing a particular sound or sound combination, followed by sentences in which the sound dominates. When used in conjunction with the Lesson Cassette, students can determine the relationship of the sound to its written equivalent.

Usando el español. Highlighted by a band of color at the top of the textbook pages, the *Usando el español* section presents the structure and grammar of Spanish using an inductive approach. By observing illustrations, reading the corresponding words or sentences, and answering guided questions, students are led to form conclusions about a given use or rule of language. Students also read examples of the language structure or function in sample questions (*Preguntas*) and answers (*Respuestas*). To help students who may not respond to an inductive approach, the language rule is given in the *Annotated Teacher's Edition* in simple, informal words that do not presuppose a knowledge of grammatical terms.

The exercises that follow each presentation (*¡Vamos a practicar!*) continue the practice and reinforcement of the language. As with other exercises, these are ordered by level of difficulty and may be used for both oral and written activities. Also, they are preceded by communicative contexts that give meaning and direction to the individual exercise items.

Each *Usando el español* section contains at least two presentations followed by exercises. The presentations and exercises combine the vocabulary of the unit with the grammar to provide a meaningful, logical, and coherent whole.

¡A conversar! In the illustrated conversation of this section, students will see how the vocabulary and grammar of the unit can be applied in real-life situations. The conversations incorporate humor with situations that relate to the interests of upper elementary, middle school, and junior high students. Carefully placed within the conversations are examples of unfamiliar words and expressions that are designed to help students develop the ability to guess meanings from context, to recognize cognates, or to practice their dictionary skills. Following each conversation is a set of comprehension/recall questions.

Beginning with *Unidad 3* in *Converso mucho*, students are asked personalized questions under the heading of *¡Conversa tú!* Through these personalized questions, students are encouraged to express their own observations and to use the language to talk about themselves.

Vamos a leer. In the textbooks *Ya converso más* and *¡Nos comunicamos!*, the conversation section alternates with *Vamos a leer.* In this section of short readings—which sometimes take the form of simulated real-life documents—the vocabulary and grammar of the unit come together to provide practice in and reinforcement of reading skills.

¡A divertirnos! In *Converso mucho* students have fun with the language through the brightly illustrated antics of two characters—Lolín and Joaquín. In *¡A divertirnos!* students encounter amusing situations and questions; find-the-missing-items activities, similar to popular games found in Spanish-language newspapers; and proverbs whose meanings they are encouraged to guess with the help of lighthearted illustrations.

In *Ya converso más* and *¡Nos comunicamos!*, this just-for-fun section features riddles, tongue twisters, short poems, and cartoons, in addition to proverbs and other activities.

La cultura y tú. The theme of each unit is carried through in the culture section. Related aspects of life in the Spanish-speaking world are depicted in photographs of schools, students, and daily-life situations, as well as simulated real-life documents, charts, and tables. *La cultura y tú* also reinforces vocabulary and structures of the unit within the context of culture.

Review Sections

Three review sections are interspersed throughout the textbooks to provide additional review and practice and to recombine and synthesize vocabulary and grammar in different contexts:

- *Primer repaso* follows *Unidad 3*
- *Segundo repaso* follows *Unidad 6*
- *Tercer repaso* follows *Unidad 9*

Each section focuses on the grammar and vocabulary taught in the preceding three units.

The activities in the review sections may take the form of brief conversations, which are recorded on the Lesson Cassettes; personalized questions; or simulated letters from pen pals. In addition, the review sections provide ample opportunity for students to create with the language, interact with fellow students, develop and refine their language skills, and practice the skills of language learning.

Unidad 14: The Final, Cumulative Review

The last unit of the textbook not only reviews *Unidad 10* through *Unidad 13* but also provides activities to practice the salient vocabulary and structures taught throughout the year. Following the same format as the three review sections, *Unidad 14* contains many varied activities that refine and practice the skills students have developed. For example, students may practice their reading skills or their creative use of the language or simply respond to questions based on an illustration or photograph. The same flexibility inherent in the review sections enables you to choose activities that will appeal to your students as well as respond to their different learning styles and abilities.

Using the Components of the **¡Viva el español!** Textbook Series

All the components accompanying *Converso mucho*, *Ya converso más*, and *¡Nos comunicamos!* have been designed to give you the basic tools you will need to implement a successful Spanish-as-a-second-language program. (For a description of each component, see pages T-11–T-14, "Components of the *¡Viva el español!* Textbook Series.")

Each regular unit of the textbook series has been structured to be covered over twelve class periods, given a multisection class-period framework. You may extend or shorten the time as needed, depending on the length of your class periods as well as on the learning styles and abilities of your students.

The chart on the following pages represents one approach to incorporating all the components in the *¡Viva el español!* program.

Abbreviations			
ATE Annotated Teacher's Edition		**LC** Lesson Cassette	
PT Pupil Textbook		**EC** Exercise Cassette	
W Workbook		**SC** Song Cassette	
TRB Teacher's Resource and Activity Book (Black-line Masters)		**T** Testing Program (Black-line Masters)	
		TC Test Cassette	

Unit Sections / Days	1	2	3	4	5
Panorama de vocabulario	Present 4–6 (6–8) words **TRB, PT**	4–6 (6–8) words **TRB, PT**	4–6 words **TRB, PT, W**	Practice **TRB, PT, W**	Practice **W, LC, TRB, ATE**
Los sonidos del idioma	Present **LC, PT**	Practice **LC, PT**			Practice (optional) **EC, TRB**
Usando el español			Present and practice 1st point **PT, W**	Practice **PT, W**	Present and practice 2nd point **PT, W**
¡A conversar! / Vamos a leer*					
¡Conversa tú!					
¡A divertirnos!	Present (fr. previous unit) **PT**	Present and practice **PT**			
La cultura y tú	Present (fr. previous unit) **PT**	Present and practice **PT**			
Review activities	Warm-up **ATE**	Warm-up **ATE**	Warm-up **ATE**	Warm-up **ATE**	Warm-up **ATE**
Extension and enrichment activities	**ATE, SC (TRB, W)**	**ATE, SC (TRB, W)**	**ATE, SC**	**ATE, SC**	**ATE (TRB, W)**

*In the textbooks *Ya converso más* and *¡Nos comunicamos!*, the *¡A conversar!* section alternates with the section *Vamos a leer*. *¡Conversa tú!* only appears in conjunction with the *¡A conversar!* sections.

6	7	8	9	10	11	12
Practice **W, ATE, TRB**	Quiz	Review **PT, W, ATE, TRB**	Informal assessment	Review	Test or review **T, TC**	Test or review **T, TC**
Practice (optional) **EC, TRB**					Test or review **T, TC**	Test or review **T, TC**
Practice **PT, W**	Practice **PT, W, TRB, EC**	Practice (game) **ATE, TRB**	Review (game) or quiz **ATE, TRB**	Review **PT, W, EC, TRB**	Test or review **T, TC**	Test **T, TC**
	Present **LC, PT**	Practice **LC, PT**	Practice **PT**			
		Present (1–2 questions) **PT**	Present (2–3 questions) **PT**	Practice or informal assessment	Practice	Test **T, TC**
					Present (optional) **PT**	Present (optional) **PT**
				Present **PT**	Present, practice **PT**	Assess
Warm-up **ATE**	Warm-up **ATE**	Warm-up **ATE**	Warm-up **ATE**	Warm-up **ATE**	Warm-up **ATE**	Warm-up **ATE**
ATE (TRB, W)	**ATE (SC, TRB, W)**	**ATE**	**ATE**	**ATE (LC, SC)**	**ATE (LC, EC)**	**ATE (LC, SC)**

General Strategies and Techniques

In this section you will find numerous suggestions for strategies and techniques to use in the *¡Viva el español!* language classroom. Different techniques and strategies may result in success at different stages of the learning process. Whichever suggestions you follow, it is wise to keep the following points in mind:

- Allow students to respond spontaneously. Requiring them to speak before they are ready may produce anxiety and actually impede their progress.
- If a strategy is successful, add it to the many strategies you use in the classroom. Adapt it, vary it, and enrich it; however, do not use it exclusively. Even the most tasty dishes become boring if they are the mainstay of your diet.
- If a strategy is not successful, drop it. What may work well with one group of students may not work at all with another group.
- Be sensitive to the emotional, as well as the cognitive, needs of your students. Very young students are often willing to engage in whimsical activities, whereas self-conscious early adolescents may not do something that may be perceived as foolish or silly.
- Provide continual constructive, positive feedback. Positive reinforcement may consist of a nod and a smile, a pat on the back, or an enthusiastic *¡Muy bien!* Students should be rewarded for doing their personal best as well as for achieving a standard of perfection.
- Use props, costumes, realia, and puppets in the classroom. Even older students sometimes find it easier to speak through a puppet

or to assume a character role because attention is then diverted from themselves. Especially during the awkward, vulnerable early teenage years, students may need the comfort of a psychological security blanket when learning something new.

Suggestions for Teaching Vocabulary

Total Physical Response (TPR) methods have proven to be effective in teaching vocabulary. Teachers who have used TPR in the classroom have reported extreme satisfaction with the results: students remember the vocabulary over long periods of time. In fact, with little prompting, students have recalled vocabulary quickly even after the summer vacation break.

In a beginning class, you may wish to devote the first several class periods of the school year to teaching the TPR commands themselves before the textbooks are distributed. During the school year, you may incorporate new commands into the daily lessons and combine commands in new ways to add variety and stimulate interest.

Setting the Stage for TPR

As early as the first day of class, you can teach some useful commands for TPR activities as well as classroom management. You may wish to begin by explaining that you will give yourself a command and that you will then carry out that command. The following sequence is recommended for presenting and modeling new commands:

1. Give yourself the command and then act it out. Repeat the procedure at least three times.
2. Give the command and act it out, with the entire class following along.
3. Give the command but do not act it out. Students respond on their own.
4. Give the command to small groups and individuals.
5. Have students volunteer to give the command to you and the class.
6. Have students give the command to one another in pairs or small groups.

Steps 5 and 6 may be carried out after students have exhibited willingness to speak and are ready to work independently. Students who have participated in the *¡Viva el español!* Learning Systems A, B, and C may make willing volunteers for the initial small-group activities.

During the school year, you may expand on the TPR commands by giving them in writing. To prepare students for reading commands—such as those given in exercise instructions in *¡Aprende el vocabulario!* and *¡Vamos a practicar!* sections of the textbooks—you may write the command on the chalkboard and point to it before following steps 1 through 3 of the TPR sequence. Then, volunteers may point to a command, say it aloud, and have the class respond appropriately.

Preparing to Teach Vocabulary

Each regular unit of *Converso mucho, Ya converso más,* and *¡Nos comunicamos!* begins with the vocabulary section *Panorama de vocabulario.* This section is reproduced in the *Teacher's Resource and Activity Book* (black-line masters). For the initial presentation of vocabulary, these black-line master pages may be made into transparencies for use on the overhead projector or enlarged on a photocopier and mounted for use as flash cards. Also included in the Vocabulary Cards section of the black-line master book are illustrations of the individual vocabulary words. These illustrations may be duplicated, mounted on heavy-gauge paper, and then laminated to become a classroom set of vocabulary cards. The effort expended in preparing these materials will be rewarded, as you will soon have a permanent set of classroom materials that will last for years. The illustrations may also be photocopied and distributed to students, allowing them to compile their own sets of vocabulary cards throughout the year.

Presenting the Vocabulary

Armed with your illustrations, you are ready to begin teaching vocabulary. It is recommended that an average of four or five vocabulary words be taught during one class period. Depending on your particular class, the number of words may range from a minimum of three to a maximum of eight.

In general, the following procedure may be used for presenting, modeling, and practicing new vocabulary:

1. Point to, touch, or hold up an illustration of the word (if practical, use the real object), and say the word. Repeat this step at least

three times (e.g., *La ventana. La ventana. Es la ventana. Ésta es la ventana.*).

2. Continue by asking a question to which students may respond either nonverbally or verbally. Repeat this several times, as in the following examples:

   Yes/no questions

   T: (*pointing to or touching the window*) ¿Es la ventana? ¿Sí o no? ¿Es la ventana?

   C: Sí. (*Students may also respond by nodding their heads.*)

   Either-or questions

   T: (*pointing to or touching the window*) ¿Es la ventana o es la puerta? ¿Es la ventana o es la puerta?

   C: La ventana. (*or*) Es la ventana.

3. Practice the vocabulary by using vocabulary cards and issuing TPR commands, such as the following:

   T: *Anita*, anda con la ventana.
   Diego, pásale la ventana a *Rita.*
   Inés, pon la ventana en mi escritorio.
   Susana, dibuja una ventana en la pizarra.
   Eduardo, borra la ventana.
   Juan, salta con la ventana. Dale la ventana a *Ricardo.*
   Alumnos, brinquen con la ventana.

4. After students have demonstrated their comprehension of the words, volunteers may take turns giving commands to the class, or students may work in small groups or pairs to practice the vocabulary.

As students progress throughout the *¡Viva el español!* textbook series, you may increase the amount of comprehensible input with each unit by incorporating previously learned vocabulary and structures into the presentation of new vocabulary. For example, when presenting the *tener* expression, *tengo calor*, you may combine the previously learned weather expressions with pantomiming techniques:

T: (*fanning yourself and wiping your forehead*) No hace viento. No hace frío. Hace calor. Hace mucho calor. (*pointing to yourself*) Tengo calor. Tengo calor. Tengo mucho calor.

By increasing familiar, comprehensible input, you help students to sharpen their listening skills and to derive meaning from context.

Useful Commands for TPR Activities and Classroom Exercises

abre / **abren** (open)

anda / **anden** (walk)

asómate / **asómense** (look out of)

borra / **borren** (erase)

brinca / **brinquen** (jump)

busca / **busquen** (look for)

canta / **canten** (sing)

cierra / **cierren** (close)

colorea / **coloreen** (color)

contesta / **contesten** (answer)

corta / **corten** (cut)

cuenta / **cuenten** (count)

da / **den** (give)

da / **den un saltito** (hop)

date / **dense una vuelta** (turn around)

di / **digan** (say)

dibuja / **dibujen** (draw)

dobla / **doblen** (fold; turn)

entra / **entren** (enter)

escoge / **escojan** (choose)

escribe / **escriban** (write)

escucha / **escuchen** (listen)

habla / **hablen** (talk)

levanta / **levanten la mano** (raise your hand)

levántate / **levántense** (stand up)

mira / **miren** (look)

muestra / **muestren** (show)

párate / **párense** (stand up; stop)

pasa / **pasen** (pass)

pon / **pongan** (put)

pregunta / **pregunten** (ask)

quita / **quiten** (take off)

recoge / **recojan** (pick up)

recorta / **recorten** (cut out)

repite / **repitan** (repeat)

responde / **respondan** (respond)

saca / **saquen** (take out)

sal / **salgan** (leave)

salta / **salten** (jump)

señala / **señalen** (point to)

siéntate / **siéntense** (sit down)

sigue / **sigan** (follow)

suma / **sumen** (add up)

tira / **tiren** (throw)

toca / **toquen** (touch)

toma / **tomen** (take)

trae / **traigan** (bring)

ve / **vaya** (go)

ven / **vengan** (come)

Suggestions for Teaching Grammar

The Inductive Approach

In *Converso mucho, Ya converso más,* and *¡Nos comunicamos!,* the inductive approach has been used primarily to teach grammar and language usage. With the inductive method, students first hear, see, and read specific examples of a point of grammar and then form a general conclusion about those points. For example, in the *Usando el español* section of each regular unit, students see illustrated examples of a part of speech, such as subject pronouns. First they look at the pictures, hear and/or read the words below the pictures, and then answer questions about what they have observed. Following this, they practice with examples of the part of speech used in context—usually through questions and answers. From their observations and practice with examples in context, students—under your guidance—draw conclusions or form simply stated rules about how that part of the language works.

When you present a new structure, supplement the presentation with as much comprehensible input as possible before students even open their textbooks. That is, begin the presentation with oral examples of the language structure. For example, when introducing *estudiar* with *-ar* verbs, pantomime or act out the activity while you talk to the students:

T: (*pantomiming*) Estudio mucho. Estudio en casa. Estudio en la escuela. También estudio en la biblioteca. No estudio mucho los domingos. Pero sí estudio los lunes, los martes, los miércoles, los jueves y los viernes.

By demonstrating a structure, you give students the opportunity to hear it used in context before they see it in writing. Also, by including familiar vocabulary and structures, students can experience the language passively with comprehension before they use it actively themselves.

After students have been exposed to the language structure, they are ready to begin forming conclusions about it. In the textbooks, have students observe the illustrations as you read the words or sentences below them aloud. Point out features in the illustrations that help convey the meanings of the words. Guide students in answering the questions posed in the text. [For quick reference, the answers to the questions are given on the annotated pages of the student textbooks.] After students have completed the presentation and have read or heard the examples of the structure in context, help them come to a conclusion about the language. By stating a rule of language in their own words, students are more likely to remember it. Once stated, these rules are to be remembered but not memorized and recited.

At the beginning of each *Usando el español* presentation in the *Annotated Teacher's Edition*, you will find a statement of the rule or point of grammar being stressed. These rules have been worded very simply, as they might actually be stated by the students themselves. The purpose behind these simplified statements is to avoid the excessive use of grammatical terminology. Students at this stage of their education may not know the parts of speech and the grammatical terms as they apply to their first language. Therefore, reliance on prior knowledge of grammar and terms has been eliminated.

Grammatical terms are introduced and defined as needed throughout the textbooks. Students should be aware of these terms, but they should not be expected to memorize them or define them as part of the assessment of their progress. It is more important that they incorporate the newly acquired information in their everyday communication than it is that they recite a rule or conjugate a verb.

An Alternative Approach

Techniques of inductive learning are not equally successful with all students. If your students demonstrate frustration with not being able to understand what is expected of them, you may wish to try a different approach. For example, you may reverse the process. That is, you may begin with the general statement about the language and follow up with specific examples of its use. In practical terms, you may present the rule first, encouraging students to repeat it or read it aloud. Or you may write the rule on the chalkboard and encourage students to write it in their notebooks. Then, from the rule you may progress to its application, as given in the illustrated examples, charts, and contextual examples of its use in the textbook.

It is more important to maintain a low-stress learning environment than it is to adhere to a specific technique of instruction.

If students have difficulty with a particular concept, do not spend an inordinate amount of time trying to explain it. The language is continually reinforced and reintroduced throughout the textbook series. For example, the singular forms of regular *-ar*, *-er*, and *-ir* verbs are presented and practiced in *Converso mucho.* They are reintroduced and reinforced in *Ya converso más* when students learn the plural forms of the verbs.

Suggestions for Developing Reading Skills

The spectrum of reading skills in young students may not be fully developed in their first language. Therefore, you may find yourself teaching some of the basic skills of reading as well as teaching reading skills in the second language. However, any approach to reading begins simply and develops gradually.

Reading as Support for Speaking and Listening

Beginning students need to become acquainted with the written language. Accent marks, punctuation, and sound-letter correspondences can begin early on. Just as children begin to develop reading skills by being read to while looking at the text of a book, beginning language students may also begin their reading development by associating sounds with their written equivalents. In short, reading begins as a support for speaking and listening skills.

Reading skills may develop from reading isolated words to reading complete sentences. You may start, for example, by having a student match word cards to vocabulary cards. Word cards may be made from 3" x 5" index cards with the word printed neatly on one side. These cards may then be used to match the written word to its vocabulary-card illustration, which is provided in the *Teacher's Resource and Activity Book.* This activity of passive reading is nonthreatening and parallels the acquisition of reading skills in the first language.

Gradually, in the security of a group, students may read the words aloud in choral reading activities as a class and in smaller groups, such as by rows. Then after they have practiced, you may ask volunteers to read the words aloud. As with speaking, individuals should read aloud only when they are ready. Following this approach, students may progress to reading the words in context and finally to reading complete sentences based on familiar material.

Once the sounds of the language have been related to the written forms of the language, you can begin to develop more sophisticated skills, such as guessing the meanings of unfamiliar words from visual and textual contexts and deriving meanings by recognizing cognates. Throughout the annotated pages of the student textbooks and in the specific Unit Plans in the front of the *Annotated Teacher's Edition,* you will find many practical suggestions for helping students to develop these skills.

Basic Reading Skills

Reading skills in Spanish may then progress to the broader, basic reading skills of skimming, scanning, reading for specific information, and reading for general meaning. It is important for students to realize that they do not have to understand every single word in a passage or simulated document in order to understand its general meaning.

Skimming

The reading skill of skimming—a quick, overall glance at a passage or selection—helps students understand the framework of the selection. For example, students may quickly skim a selection to determine that it is an advertisement, a questionnaire, a friendly letter, or a conversation between two people. Once they identify the framework, they consciously or subconsciously trigger information they have stored about that framework in their own language.

Scanning

Scanning, another reading skill, involves looking for specific pieces of information. For example, students may scan a friendly letter to find out who wrote it or they may scan a television schedule to find a particular program.

Students can incorporate these skills in their second-language reading by following your guidance. For example, before beginning to read a selection, you may ask students to state what the selection is. The activities in the *Repaso* sections and *Unidad 14* of the textbooks often lend themselves to practice in skimming and scanning.

Reading for Information

Reading for specific information may first involve scanning the selection to locate the information and then reading every word to understand the information itself. For example, in answering the *preguntas* following the conversation in the *¡A conversar!* sections, students may practice scanning the text to find key words and then reading the sentence or sentences carefully to find the information they need to answer the questions. As students progress in their language studies and as their reading encompasses Spanish-language newspapers, novels, magazines, and works of nonfiction, the skills of skimming, scanning, and reading for information that have been developed in their early studies will become increasingly valuable to them.

Reading for General Meaning

The skill of reading to understand the gist of a passage or selection most closely approximates the reading people do for pleasure. In this kind of reading, it is not necessary to understand every word nor to process the information for a specific purpose. Instead, it is more useful to comprehend the overall meaning as it advances the plot or relates to the character. Only when the student experiences difficulty in grasping that meaning is it necessary to isolate the barriers to understanding and then to solve the problem by looking up the troublesome words or expressions in the dictionary. At the beginning stages of reading, students may read a selection first for general meaning; for example, they may begin by quickly reading a friendly letter in a *Repaso* section. Then, as students answer the questions in the friendly letter or formulate their own questions for their "pen pal," they may read the letter again for specific information.

In many instances, you may discover that the basic skills of skimming, scanning, reading for specific information, and reading for general meaning have not been taught in the first language. You may then need to provide practice in developing the skills themselves in addition to applying those skills to reading selections in Spanish. Although time in the classroom is short, it is important to address the need to develop solid, basic reading skills in your students if they are to progress successfully from reading carefully controlled selections to reading lengthier, richer, authentic materials in the Spanish language.

The path is easier, of course, if students recognize that a skill they have practiced in a language arts class can be applied to their activities in Spanish class. At the beginning of the school year, you may wish to work together with the language arts teachers to determine the kinds of skills that can be applied in the second-language classroom as well as to exchange practical ideas for teaching and reinforcing those skills.

Suggestions for Teaching Writing Skills

The development of writing skills in the target language is similar to the development of reading skills. As students progress in writing, they may begin with isolated words, develop with complete sentences, and then flourish with directed or original compositions.

Beginning with Individual Words

Writing skills may begin in conjunction with learning new vocabulary. Once comprehension of the spoken word has been established, you may then combine reading and writing skills development. The following procedure is recommended for initial writing skills development:

1. Write the word (or words) on the chalkboard or on a transparency for the overhead projector.
2. Pronounce one word at a time and have the class repeat it.
3. Spell the word and have the class repeat it.
4. Spell the word and have the class write it.

Four to eight words is the most you should use in initial writing practice.

In the beginning, writing skills and speaking skills are closely linked. At first, students may copy or write words and sentences they have only practiced orally. In this way, writing is a controlled skill that depends on and reinforces speaking skills. Most of the exercises provided in *Converso mucho, Ya converso más*, and *¡Nos comunicamos!* may first be completed orally in class and then used as writing practice to support students' speaking abilities. Likewise, Language Experience Approach activities, such as producing Big Books, also reinforce speaking activities. These are controlled activities, yet they give students the sense that they are writing and creating their own materials.

Applying the Writing Process

As students develop in their first language, they learn that writing is a process. Initially they learn and practice skills of choosing a topic, identifying their audience, gathering information, and organizing the information. These activities form the prewriting process.

Once these skills have been practiced, students move on to the writing process itself. They develop their ideas by writing the information in a noncritical first draft, followed by a "cooling-off" period. Then they revise the first draft by reading it critically and by changing sentences and paragraphs according to the organization of their topic and the clarity of meaning of their paragraphs. They read the revised draft again to edit it, correcting errors they recognize such as misspelled words, incorrect subject-verb agreement, etc. The final step in the process is the preparation of a final, clean copy of their writing and a final proofreading to ensure that the text is as good as they can make it.

If students are just beginning to learn and practice these skills in their first language, it is unrealistic to expect them to produce error-free compositions in one sitting in their second language. Although it is not necessary to focus on the writing process in the second-language classroom, it is valuable to encourage students to incorporate the skills they are learning in their language arts classes into their Spanish-class activities. Again, your communication with the language arts teachers may result in better transference of skills into the second-language classroom as students' confidence and competence in writing increase.

Suggestions for Teaching Culture

Each regular unit of *Converso mucho*, *Ya converso más*, and *¡Nos comunicamos!* ends with the section *La cultura y tú.* In this section, students are introduced to aspects of everyday life in Spanish-speaking countries through photographs, charts, and simulated real-life documents. By observing the photographs and answering questions, students begin to formulate ideas about the diversity of Hispanic peoples.

La cultura y tú is simply an introduction. It should, by no means, be the sole point of integrating culture into the program. In the Unit Plans section of this *Annotated Teacher's Edition*, you will find suggestions and information that will help you incorporate cultural instruction in the daily lessons.

Cultures are not static. They change and evolve over time. Therefore, it is important to build the skills students will need to gather information, make observations, and formulate general and specific conclusions. It is also important to develop a nonjudgmental appreciation of the way of life of other people.

As students gain competence and confidence in communicating facts and opinions about their own world, they can develop an awareness of those same aspects of culture in the Spanish-speaking world. They can begin to recognize similarities and differences through observation. They can begin to experience how behavior is affected by culture through role-play activities, research projects, and interviews with native speakers.

In addition to the many photographs in the textbooks, it is recommended that you use maps, slides, and other visual aids to lay the foundation of basic skills and information. For example, students may need to learn first that geography and climate greatly affect how people live before they investigate a specific region of the Spanish-speaking world. Likewise, they may need to recognize first that in their own culture, life in a big city differs from life in a small town or rural area before they can appreciate the same differences in other cultures.

The following suggestions will help you to add variety to the teaching of culture in the classroom as well as to build skills that will aid students in understanding other ways of life.

- Use maps and globes to help identify areas of the world where Spanish is spoken—including in the United States. Whenever possible, have students locate specific countries and areas being discussed or depicted and then determine the relationship of that area to where they live.
- Show slides, filmstrips, and videotapes. Visual aids that relate to the theme of a unit can begin to make cultural information more concrete and meaningful. For example, with the increased prevalence of Spanish-language television programs, students may be exposed to aspects of the culture that previously would have required them to visit the culture. Practical examples of greeting and leave-taking, food, homes, family life, popular music—all may be depicted in programs broadcast on the Spanish-language networks.
- Invite native speakers to the class. As often as possible, it is recommended that you invite native speakers—neighbors, exchange students, business people—to interact with the students. Preparation for the visit may consist of presenting background information on the visitor, such as country and city of origin, having students research the country, preparing suitable questions for the visitor in advance, and so forth. Likewise, the visitor will need information about what the students are studying and the questions they will ask.

  Activities following the visit can include writing thank-you notes, conducting discussions about what the students learned, and assigning further research.
- Create a cultural environment. If you have your own classroom, you may display artifacts, create culture corners, and provide a "lending library" of resources and references for information

gathering. Through records, cassettes, and radio programs, you can expose students to the diversity of music in Spanish-speaking countries, from well-known folk songs to currently popular rock music and music videos.

Suggestions for Correcting Errors

Maintaining a nonthreatening, positive classroom environment and nurturing students' confidence in their abilities to communicate in the second language are the first requirements for successfully correcting students' errors. For many teachers who have been schooled in traditional methods of teaching, this means altering their own behavior patterns before they can effectively encourage linguistic accuracy in their students.

At one point or another, most people who have acquired a second language have experienced the frustration of trying to communicate a message while a well-meaning second person interrupts at every third or fourth word with corrections of agreement, verb tense, or pronunciation. The level of frustration rises to such a point that the message is lost, the speaker's confidence is shaken, and the corrections offered with good intentions are forgotten. Even worse, fear and reluctance to communicate in the second language replace the initial enthusiasm and joy at communicating a message.

This is not to say that errors should not be corrected. Making mistakes is a natural, inevitable part of the learning process. If left alone, they can convert into deeply ingrained bad habits. If corrected in a positive, nurturing way, they can be eliminated without creating anxiety in the learner.

Knowing What and When to Correct

In general, researchers have shown that teachers who select the errors to be corrected at the proper time can be more effective than those who correct by the interruptive reflex method.

In student speech and writing, it is important to correct errors that interfere with overall communication. That is, if an error makes a message unintelligible, it should be corrected. If an error creates a barrier to listening and reading, it should be corrected. In the literature on second-language instruction, these errors are called global errors, in contrast to minor, local errors. If a global error is made frequently, it is important to correct that error first, while temporarily ignoring a smaller error or slip within the same message.

Researchers have also shown that correction is effective at the time of practice, for example, while doing exercises that follow a pattern. Conversely, correction can have an adverse effect when given while students are earnestly communicating freely, for example, during paired interviews or conversations.

Knowing How to Correct

Guiding students to discover an error for themselves and to correct it on their own has generally proven more effective than supplying the correct answer or form for them. The following suggestions have been gleaned from the literature on techniques of error correction in the second-language classroom.

One approach to correcting through gentle guidance is to repeat what the student has said up to the point of the error. Often this will cue the student to recognize the mistake and then correct it alone.

S: Me duele las manos.
T: (*holding up two hands*) Hay dos manos. Me . . .
S: Me duelen las manos.

Another possibility is to provide an on-the-spot multiple choice, thus allowing the student to choose the correct response (e.g., *¿Me duele las manos o me duelen las manos?*). If the student has had sufficient initial input and modeling, he or she will be able to recognize the correct response and choose it.

You can also correct an error by supplying your own response to serve as a model (e.g., *A mí no me duelen las manos. Me duelen los pies. ¿Qué te duele a ti?*).

Students may make an error or fail to respond when they do not understand the question or do not fully understand what is expected of them. In these instances, you may rephrase or restate the question or provide additional models to clear up the confusion. A confusing word or expression can also be cleared up by either allowing the student to see it in writing or, if the phrase is familiar from oral work, to hear it spoken.

In summary, it is important to be sensitive to your students' affective as well as cognitive needs. Especially for early adolescents for whom peer approval is important, techniques that guide, nurture, and support yet correct their efforts without damaging their self-esteem are far more effective than those that are perceived as being humiliating. Sarcasm, impatience, and interruptive, reflex-action correction have no place in the *¡Viva el español!* classroom. The humiliation and anxiety experienced when students' every utterance is corrected improperly can be permanently harmful and not only reduce their willingness to speak but also destroy their enthusiasm for learning.

Your efforts in studying and applying the research on error correction in the second-language classroom will be rewarded in your students by their positive attitude and willingness to take communicative risks.

Suggestions for Structuring the Class Period

Spanish language instruction is far from standardized; the number of classes, length of class periods, and class size and composition are as varied as the schools in which they are offered. *¡Viva el español!* has been structured to provide flexibility and ease of adaptation to fit almost all needs of Spanish-as-a-second-language instruction.

Multisection Class Periods

A multisection class period allows the freedom to adapt activities to fit the structure of any situation. Each section of a class period serves to keep the routine familiar, yet interesting and stimulating, by virtue of the variety of activities.

- The **Warm-up** serves as a transition from the first-language environment into the target-language environment. It affords a brief period for students to "switch gears" and begin thinking and responding in Spanish.
- **Review** activities may act as reminders of material recently learned or of vocabulary and structures learned some time previously. These review activities may take the form of continuing games, "show and tell," brief role-play activities, pencil-and-paper puzzles, or even a rereading of a passage or conversation. Numerous suggestions for review activities are listed in the Unit Plans section of the *Annotated Teacher's Edition.*

- **Presentation** periods include the presentation and/or explanation of the core vocabulary, language structure, conversation, or culture concept corresponding to the appropriate section of the unit being studied.
- **Activities** time allows students to use the target language in varied situations, by completing exercises, interviewing classmates, preparing Big Books, etc.
- **Closing** activities briefly wrap up the class session.

The following skeletal daily lesson presents suggestions for allotting time for each section of a class period. It is expected that you will modify the times and activities to reflect your own classroom situation and instructional objectives.

Multisection Class Period

Time	Section	Activities
2–5 min.	Warm-up	Quick questions and answers (*¿Cómo estás? ¿Qué día es hoy? ¿Cuál es la fecha? ¿Qué tiempo hace?* etc.) Brief relay game, chain activity, song, etc.
5 min.	Review	Games Oral presentations; role-playing Audiocassette exercises TPR activities Paired or small-group activities
5–15 min.	Presentation	Learning activities corresponding to the unit being studied Introduction of vocabulary or language structures, etc.
5–15 min.	Activities	Textbook or workbook exercises Guided oral practice Games Paired, small-group, or large-group activities or projects Individual or small-group informal assessment Extension or enrichment activities/projects
3–5 min.	Closing	Riddles, rhymes, songs Summary of the day's lesson

The ¡Viva el español! Testing Program

Assessment and evaluation of students' progress in acquiring a second language play an important part in sustaining the enthusiasm for language learning generated during the instructional phases of the language program. The testing program of the *¡Viva el español!* textbook series has been designed and constructed to follow through with the purposes, goals, and objectives, as well as approach, of the materials in *Converso mucho, Ya converso más,* and *¡Nos comunicamos!*

In this section you will find information about the key principles of the testing program, the skills tested, the nature of the testing items, and recommendations for conducting and scoring the tests.

Components of the Testing Program

A complete, self-contained testing program accompanies each of the three textbooks in the *¡Viva el español!* series. For each level the program includes the following components:

- *Testing Program,* a black-line master book, containing a detailed description of the program, suggestions and instructions for testing, black-line masters of the tests, an answer key for all written and oral tests, a complete tapescript of the audio Test Cassette, and a Student Progress Chart.

- Test Cassette, a sixty-minute audiocassette corresponding to the oral testing section in the *Testing Program.*

The components have been designed within the standards of the latest testing methodology, bearing in mind that students react most favorably to materials that are appealing and applicable to real conversation and that you, as a teacher, need testing materials that are pedagogically sound and easy to prepare and score.

Key Principles and Concepts

A successful program of assessment and evaluation must be compatible with the instructional goals and objectives and the approach used to achieve them. A central concern in preparing the *¡Viva el español!* testing program has been the consistent and careful matching of the testing objectives with the teaching goals within the methodologies followed in the language program.

Key to the objectives of the *¡Viva el español!* textbook series is communication—that is, using the language at the active and receptive levels to express real needs and interests in order to function in and describe the communicator's everyday real world. Therefore, the challenge is to devise stimulating, practical testing materials that help students feel early on that the skills and language they learn in the classroom have real-life applications—that they are using real Spanish and not simply studying Spanish usage.

Evaluation Techniques

The evaluation techniques and design of the *¡Viva el español!* testing program are compatible with the Natural Approach and Total Physical Response methods that stress the use of interesting and relevant materials, comprehensible input, and intense observation and involvement from students. The design of the testing program will help you create a nonthreatening testing environment in your classroom—an environment that allows sufficient success to encourage low to average achievers, yet stimulate high achievers and students who are gifted in second-language learning.

The testing model has followed, in large measure, Kenneth Chastain's commonsense twenty-four "guidelines for classroom testing." These guidelines not only cover the preparation and administration of tests but also relate testing to classroom teaching methodology. The complete list of these useful guidelines follows:

1. Test objectives.
2. Test what has been taught.
3. Test all four language skills.
4. Test one thing at a time.
5. Weight the exam according to objectives.
6. Sequence the items from easy to more difficult.
7. Avoid incorrect language.
8. Make directions clear.
9. Prepare items in advance and prepare more than you need.
10. Specify the material to be tested.
11. Acquaint the students with techniques.
12. Test in context.
13. Avoid sequential items.
14. Sample fairly the material covered.
15. Allow sufficient time to finish.
16. Make the test easy to grade, if possible.
17. Go over the test immediately afterwards.
18. Help those students with problems to determine specific areas in need of improvement.
19. Test each concept only once.
20. Give credit for what a student knows.
21. Distinguish between recall and recognition tests.
22. Distinguish between discrete items and global items.
23. At some point in the learning sequence, the students should have to choose between various grammar structures.
24. Be prepared to incorporate new types of test items.

For a brief, but excellent, description of each of these guidelines, see Chastain's text, *Developing Second-Language Skills.**

Test Items

In keeping with current second-language testing methodologies, the test items themselves are almost entirely in Spanish. The use of English has been avoided so that students will not have to alternate between Spanish and English. On the other hand, test instructions to students are in English. In a testing situation, it is inappropriate and counterproductive to have students lose time and become frustrated trying to decipher instructions written in the second language.

Also, the tests follow the principle of "testing in context." They test sounds, vocabulary, and grammar within an environment of other sounds, words, sentences, conversations, paragraphs, and eye-catching drawings that suggest meanings. In short, the tests provide meaningful linguistic contexts in which students produce or match desired Spanish forms. All test items are designed to reinforce the original instruction presented in the textbooks.

The tests are comprehensive; that is, they represent a fair sampling of the content of the textbooks without going beyond the materials taught. Also, besides being accurate achievement tests designed to help you target your students' strengths and weaknesses with respect to your instructional objectives, they have the additional "exercise-sheet" function of providing another opportunity for your students to confirm or reinforce their knowledge when you return and review the tests with them.

*Kenneth Chastain, *Developing Second-Language Skills* (Chicago: Rand McNally, 1976), pp. 489–97.

Test Types and Objectives

The *¡Viva el español!* testing program features two types of tests: (1) a Placement Test to be administered at the beginning of the year and (2) Achievement Tests.

Placement Test

At the beginning of the school year, your students will probably fall into one of the following categories:

1. Absolute beginners
2. Novices (as defined by the ACTFL Proficiency Guidelines)
3. Students with three years of Spanish, using the *¡Viva el español!* learning systems
4. Students with some prior knowledge of Spanish from previous academic or real-life experience.

The Placement Test is designed to measure the language proficiency of students in groups 2, 3, and 4, giving you an accurate evaluation of each individual's current level of competence in Spanish. Since the instructional materials in the textbooks have been designed to accommodate all of the student groups listed above, the Placement Test makes no pass/fail distinctions. The test results, however, will provide scores that will enable you to compare your students' abilities and determine your teaching strategies.

The Placement Test consists of a series of short subtests for evaluating your students' language skills (listening, speaking, reading, and writing) and their mastery of the elements of language (pronunciation, grammatical structure, and vocabulary). Within each subtest, items are arranged from easy to difficult. The fact that the subtests are based on the ACTFL Proficiency Guidelines at the Novice and Intermediate levels provides you with a point of reference for determining your students' level of proficiency in the language skills. (For your information, the descriptions of proficiency for speaking, listening, reading, and writing at the Novice and Intermediate levels can be found in the Resource Section of this *Annotated Teacher's Edition.*)

Achievement Tests

Besides the Placement Test, there are eighteen Achievement Tests, including thirteen individual unit tests, a test for each of the three review sections, a mid-year test, and an end-of-year test. The Achievement Tests fully cover the skills and elements taught in the textbook and accurately reflect the content of the program. In other words, you will not have to adjust your teaching to prepare students for tests whose content and techniques differ substantially from those of the instructional program. While the main purpose of the Achievement Tests is to help you evaluate your students' progress in mastering the textbook materials, the tests can also serve as effective review activities when you return them and discuss them with your classes. The key goal of the testing program is to teach communication in context—not as an intellectual exercise nor as a reward or punishment. In a sense, the tests become another instructional tool in helping your students develop and refine their language skills.

The chart on page T–46 gives you an overview of how the testing program may be scheduled during the school year.

The ¡Viva el español! Testing Program

Days of Instruction	Instructional Content	Test
	First Semester	
		Placement Test
3–5	Primera lección	
3–5	Segunda lección	
3–5	Tercera lección	
12	Unidad 1	Unit Test
12	Unidad 2	Unit Test
12	Unidad 3	Unit Test
3–5	Primer repaso	Achievement Review Test
12	Unidad 4	Unit Test
12	Unidad 5	Unit Test
12	Unidad 6	Unit Test
3–5	Segundo repaso	Achievement Review Test
		Mid-year Test
	Second Semester	
12	Unidad 7	Unit Test
12	Unidad 8	Unit Test
12	Unidad 9	Unit Test
3–5	Tercer repaso	Achievement Review Test
12	Unidad 10	Unit Test
12	Unidad 11	Unit Test
12	Unidad 12	Unit Test
12	Unidad 13	Unit Test
10–12	Unidad 14	
		End-of-year Test

Skills and Elements Tested

The *¡Viva el español!* testing program evaluates listening, speaking, reading, and writing skills (the "linguistic skills").

Listening Skills Listening skills evaluated include the understanding of high-frequency statements, questions, and commands likely to occur in everyday conversations about common subjects. Students are also tested on their ability to discriminate sounds in meaningful contexts, to distinguish variations in stress and intonation patterns, and to understand basic structures, idiomatic expressions, and common words used in context.

Speaking Skills Speaking skills evaluated include the ability to respond to most routine statements, questions, and commands; to speak coherently using a vocabulary adequate for basic expression; and to discuss situations relevant to everyday life. Students are also tested on their ability to reproduce sounds, to employ appropriate stress and intonation patterns within a communication context, and to use words, idiomatic expressions, phrases, and sentences as they apply in common, real-life situations.

Reading Skills Reading skills evaluated include students' ability to understand most common expressions learned orally and to read nontechnical passages on familiar themes with the aid of references, such as the Spanish-English glossary in the textbook. Students are also tested on their ability to read familiar material with comprehension, as well as on their ability to read aloud, approximating correct pronunciation of sound segments and stress and intonation patterns.

Writing Skills Writing skills evaluated include students' ability to use basic constructions and vocabulary to communicate essential information relating to common, real-life situations. Students are also tested on their ability to write familiar material and simple dictations within the norms of Spanish orthography.

Elements The elements of language evaluated by the testing program are pronunciation, grammatical structure, and vocabulary.

Pronunciation The first element, pronunciation, has three separate components: sound segments, intonation patterns, and stress patterns. Students are tested on their mastery of these three components, that is, their ability to use them accurately in realistic contexts.

Grammatical Structure The second element, grammatical structure, has two main subdivisions: morphology and syntax. The testing program evaluates knowledge of Spanish morphology and syntax through test items in which students demonstrate their knowledge of pattern word formation and word order.

Vocabulary Testing of the third element—the vocabulary, or lexicon—includes measuring your students' active and passive vocabularies, as well as their understanding of content words, function words, and idioms.

Item Types

The *¡Viva el español!* testing program features an imaginative variety of test item types, including both recall (often called "production") and recognition items. Still, your students will be neither surprised nor confused by unfamiliar item formats because the testing program employs the same general concepts and item types as those found in the textbooks. The tests will enable you to objectively quantify your students' language skills and level of linguistic competence, using a mixture of written and oral item types that include fill-ins (letter, word, phrase, sentence); cloze items; multiple choice; true or false; matching; dictations; placing elements in logical order, or sequencing; rejoinders; naming objects; circling words, phrases, and drawings; among others.

Item formats used with the audio Test Cassette are largely multiple choice, true or false, and dictations, the latter progressively sequenced from letter to word to phrase to complete sentence fill-ins. These items test recognition of sounds, as well as students' ability to understand words, phrases, brief sentences, and segments of conversations.

Like the instructional exercises, each test section is classified according to degree of difficulty, using the same set of symbols that classify the exercises on the annotated textbook pages. The symbols represent the levels of difficulty from lowest to highest:

○ Lowest level of difficulty

◐ Average level of difficulty

● Highest level of difficulty

Generally speaking, recognition items such as true or false, matching, and multiple choice represent the low end of the scale, while production items requiring active—as opposed to passive—knowledge of the pronunciation, vocabulary, and grammatical structure of Spanish occupy the high end. No single item type, however, exists at any one level of difficulty, because each item type can be tailored to any of the levels of difficulty.

The symbols indicating degree of difficulty are found only in the teacher's answer keys, so students are generally not aware that they are working with items at a specific level of difficulty. Exceptions to this are the optional, starred items, which always represent the highest level of difficulty and are designed to challenge your most advanced students.

Conducting the Tests

Conducting classroom tests can resemble a balancing act in which you strive to preserve a nonthreatening atmosphere while you maintain students' enthusiasm for learning Spanish. The following key features of the testing program will help you achieve this goal:

- ▶ The familiar format of the Achievement Tests will build your students' confidence because students will recognize item types and pictures from their textbooks.
- ▶ The open, uncluttered appearance of the test pages, with a limited number of test items on each, enhances readability. Your students will feel a sense of accomplishment as they complete the pages in relatively short periods of time.

- The fact that the tests are not speed tests, which lessens student stress. Students have no need to "beat the clock" to finish a particular section.

In keeping with the concept of promoting mastery for all students, tests are not excessively "hard," but they do contain items at various levels of difficulty so that all students will be challenged.

Suggested time limits for the tests are generous (20–30 minutes) because the tests are essentially power tests, rather than speed tests. As power tests, they generally contain fewer, relatively challenging items and allow students sufficient time to complete the entire test—as opposed to speed tests, which usually feature a large number of relatively easy items but do not allow students time to finish. The technique of having students exchange test papers and score them immediately in class is recommended. By reviewing tests right after taking them, students receive immediate feedback on their errors and have a chance to master materials not yet learned. The *¡Viva el español!* textbook series tests are designed for easy correction, and they feature useful, authentic sentences suitable for oral exercises.

Scoring the Tests

The *¡Viva el español!* testing program permits you to analyze test scores accurately and to give your students sufficient feedback in the form of meaningful numerical grades and positive learning reinforcement. The Achievement Test scores are not designed to be punitive; rather, they serve as markers for past achievement and as points of reference for further improvement. All tests allow for a separate oral achievement subscore. The Placement Test answer key includes guidelines for interpreting student scores to determine level of proficiency.

Following is a suggested scoring scale for the Placement and Achievement tests.

Score	Performance
5	Excellent expression, almost no errors
4	Response executed well, but with noticeable errors
3	Communicates fairly well, but with many noticeable errors
2	Response understandable, but grossly erroneous
1	Practically incomprehensible
0	No response

A Student Progress Chart is provided in the *Testing Program* black-line master book. On this chart, you can record your students' test scores, your informal assessment comments, and notes on individuals' strengths, as well as specific language skills that need improvement.

Parent and Community Participation in ¡Viva el español!

Your students' parents or guardians and other members of the community can play a vital role in motivating students to learn and use Spanish and in reinforcing the importance of learning a second language and understanding other cultures. In this section, you will find suggestions for inviting parents to participate in the program, for increasing community awareness of the program, and for utilizing community resources.

Positive Parent Support

Laying the groundwork for parental participation begins with communication. It is equally as important to instill enthusiasm for second-language learning in the parents and members of the community as it is to foster and maintain enthusiasm in the students. At the earliest opportunity during the school year, you may share your program's goals and objectives with the parents, either at the first meeting of your Parent-Teacher Association or Organization or through an open letter to parents, inviting them to learn about the *¡Viva el español!* program.

Explain the goals and benefits of learning Spanish simply and clearly to establish realistic expectations. In addition, you should explain the methodologies used to achieve the goals of communication and proficiency in Spanish to help parents understand the different kinds of exercises, activities, and projects their children will be working on during the school year. It is likely that any experience the parents may have had with learning a second language involved the grammar-translation method, the audiolingual approach, or another traditional approach to second-language learning. Therefore, their idea of how to learn a language should be brought up to date. An explanation of the approaches used in *¡Viva el español!* may likewise ensure parental support of and participation in Spanish language and cultural experiences outside the classroom.

You may wish to make a formal presentation at a PTA/PTO meeting, beginning with an overview of the program and following up with a sample lesson, including TPR activities, games, and textbook exercises. You may conclude with concrete suggestions for what parents can do in the home and in conjunction with school activities. Underscoring the relationship of parent participation and student achievement may instill in parents an essential awareness of their importance in the second-language learning process. Attitudes toward other languages and cultures are learned in the home. Starting out with a clear understanding of the Spanish language program in your school and the *¡Viva el español!* textbook series can pave the way toward fostering positive attitudes in parents.

Parent-Generated Activities

Whether or not the parents know Spanish themselves, they can do many things at home and with the school to encourage their children's interest in learning Spanish and to generate support for your Spanish-as-a-second-language program. The following suggestions have been selected from Gladys Lipton's *Practical Handbook to Elementary Foreign Language Programs.** Parents can:

- Help the child see foreign words in newspapers and magazines or on labels on different products
- Purchase books and records on the child's level . . .
- Keep in touch with the child's teacher to learn how they can help
- Assist the teacher by going on trips related to the foreign language work

*Gladys C. Lipton, *Practical Handbook to Elementary Foreign Language Programs* (Lincolnwood, IL: National Textbook Company, 1988), pp. 33–34.

- ► Talk to the class about their experiences in the foreign culture
- ► Speak to the class in the foreign language
- ► Speak to the class about their work in the foreign culture and opportunities for careers with foreign language backgrounds
- ► Encourage but not force the child to speak the foreign language at home
- ► Make sure that they let the child know that they are happy about the child's progress
- ► Serve on an Advisory Board for the school
- ► Try to give the child opportunities for participating in some aspect of the foreign culture at museums, on trips, on television programs, etc.

Parent involvement in the program may extend throughout the school year in conjunction with events and activities that enrich the language-learning experience. To take advantage of the special skills and unique talents of your students' parents, you may wish to have them complete a resource questionnaire, such as the one on the following page.

* Resource Questionnaire *

Name(s) ________________________________

Address: ________________________________

Phone: Day ________________ Evening ________________

I (We) are willing to help in the following way(s):

Please check one or more.

_______ Field trip chaperone

Days available: M TU W TH F

_______ Classroom aide for special units

Day(s) and hour(s) available: ________________

_______ Provide (or demonstrate how to prepare) food for a "Tasting"

Dish and country: ________________

_______ Demonstrate a craft related to Hispanic cultures

Craft and country: ________________

_______ Speak about a career in which Spanish is used

Career: ________________

_______ Speak about a trip to a Spanish-speaking country

Country: ________________

_______ Share a special area of knowledge related to Hispanic cultures

Area: ________________

_______ Share a special skill in promoting or organizing events

_____ Publicity

_____ Community resources

_____ Other: ________________

_______ Other ideas or suggestions: ________________

____

Increasing Community Awareness and Involvement

Periodic events, both large and small, not only serve to enhance the language-learning experience but also provide the opportunity for community members to become aware of and participate in your Spanish-as-a-second-language program. Many other programs in the schools receive public support and acclaim because they are highly visible and frequently publicized. Just as music programs hold concerts, athletic programs hold games and meets, and science programs hold competitions and fairs, your Spanish language program can hold events to which the public is invited and in which community members can become involved. Even without knowledge of the language and cultures, parents and members of the community can share a memorable language experience, whether by attending a single event such as an annual ethnic dinner or fair or by participating in a series of events such as a "Foreign Language Week" or periodic field trips.

A special event may involve parents and the community in any or all of the following tasks:

- Publicity
- Printing
- Decorations
- Food
- Cleanup
- Entertainment

People in the community, both professional and nonprofessional, are often willing to participate in different phases of an event just for the asking. By drawing on the resources in your community, you can plan and implement activities that foster community support; bond parents, students, and the public in a shared experience; and provide an old-fashioned sense of community spirit. The following list may help you expand your contacts with the community:

Community Service

- paramedic
- librarian
- police officer
- fire fighter
- postal worker

Recreation

- athlete
- disc jockey
- pilot or copilot
- travel agent
- flight attendant

Health

- exercise instructor
- nurse or nurse's aide
- physician
- dietitian

Science

- chemist
- florist
- conservationist
- zookeeper

Labor

- construction worker
- custodian
- mechanic
- painter
- landscape service

Other

- baker
- banker
- musician
- photographer
- secretary

In each of these fields, you may find willing guest speakers and volunteers for committees, as well as people who use Spanish in their work. Also, each field may have native speakers of Spanish who would be willing to talk to your students about what they do, how they use Spanish on the job, or even about non-work-related topics, such as family life and schools in other countries.

Selecting Events

Depending on the ages and interests of your students, you may select special events for the school year that not only offer varied language and cultural experiences but also involve the community and parents. It is important to select a variety of events that take place at different times of year, as well as at different times of day. In many one- and two-parent homes, the parents work and are unable to attend events that take place during the school day. Scheduling events at varied times can ensure the participation of individuals who otherwise would be willing but unable to attend.

The instructional units in the *¡Viva el español!* textbook series serve as excellent points of departure for selecting events. *Converso mucho* begins with the immediate world of the student at school and spirals outward to the family; *Ya converso más* begins with the home and spirals outward to the community; and *¡Nos comunicamos!*

explores the world at large. Each textbook contains themes that lend themselves to speaking and cultural events, as well as to single and week-long events. The following suggestions have been tried and found successful in fostering community and parent participation.

Ethnic Dinner / Food Fair

An ethnic dinner or food fair may not be a new event, but it is, nevertheless, a tried-and-true event. For one evening, the school cafeteria or gymnasium can be converted into a series of sidewalk cafés or little *restaurantes* that offer dishes from around the Spanish-speaking world. Volunteers may bring typical dishes that are representative of the countries. The recipes may later be written, printed, and bound into a booklet to share with the community. This event may be held in conjunction with a holiday and may include music, dancing, and exhibits.

Foreign Language Week

To build enthusiasm for and awareness of the value of foreign languages, many programs sponsor a "Foreign Language Week." Activities may range from simple to extravagant, depending on your resources. The following suggestions are not exhaustive, but they may serve as starting points in planning activities:

- Label familiar places and items in Spanish (e.g., door, drinking fountain, principal's office, gymnasium, bathrooms, etc.) throughout the school.
- Decorate the halls with travel posters and/or have students make special posters about speaking Spanish (e.g., *¡Me gusta hablar español!*), visiting other countries, or using polite expressions (e.g., *Mi casa es su casa.*).
- Offer entertainment by the students, such as songs and other music, folk dances, and skits.
- Coordinate lunch menus to go with the foreign language theme (e.g., tacos, Spanish rice, etc.) or have a potluck lunch for the Spanish classes.
- Invite guests to show slides or movies or to give demonstrations of crafts (e.g., paper flowers, piñatas, etc.).
- If money can be obtained from a special school or PTA/PTO fund, a Hispanic entertainer or group could be hired to perform for a school assembly.

- Invite parents, teachers, and other students to visit your Spanish classes during the week.
- Display books and magazines from the Spanish-speaking world, as well as the Big Books students have created themselves.
- Invite speakers from embassies or the consulates in your state to talk about their countries.
- Establish a day when everyone will wear something related to Hispanic cultures or to speaking a foreign language (e.g., hats, sashes, buttons, iron-on decorations, etc.).
- Give all announcements over the public address system in Spanish and English and have all school menus and announcements printed in both languages.

Carnival

Near Pan American Day, students could hold a carnival. Each of the Spanish-speaking countries could be represented by traditional costumes, flags, music, products, or whatever makes each country unique. Students can plan a parade or develop skits or displays. They may also, with the help of their parents, contact community resource people for information or invite them to attend. Each Spanish class could also plan and staff booths for games.

Field Trips

Field trips can provide valuable language and cultural experiences in the real world. They can also give students first-hand experience with cross-cultural communication outside the classroom. A well-planned field trip involves everyone from parents and school administrators to community resource people. The following ideas may help you plan unique, enlightening field trips for your students.

- Television station. If there is a Spanish-language station or a station that features a Spanish-language program in your community, students may benefit from touring the station and meeting the range of workers from announcers to film editors. A film editor or sound engineer may also be able to explain how programs are dubbed in other languages.
- Restaurants. A trip to a Hispanic restaurant may serve as a source of career information as well as a practical chance to use the language and learn about the culture. In conjunction with a unit on foods, students may learn about different spices and

ingredients in many dishes and possibly watch the chef prepare a special dish.

- Bank. Any large bank usually has a person dealing with international currency. Students may learn about exchange rates and actually see foreign currency. In addition, they may explore career opportunities in finance and banking.
- Hospital. Students may meet health-care workers and observe first-hand how knowledge of a second language is important in health-related careers. Doctors, nurses, hospital dietitians, admissions secretaries, and paramedics may explain to students the need for learning a second language and the importance of communicating accurately and clearly.
- University. A university can be a tremendous source of field-trip possibilities. Trips may range from a luncheon with Hispanic graduate students to attending a performance or rehearsal of a visiting dance troupe.
- Bakery or grocery store. A trip to a Hispanic bakery or grocery store may introduce students to the food-service career field and acquaint them with many products whose origins are in Spanish-speaking countries.
- Courthouse. Many courts are open to visits from classes. The courts and lawyers frequently employ interpreters to help with the proceedings when monolingual Spanish speakers are involved in a case. Students may meet interpreters and ask questions about how they learned Spanish, what their work is like, etc.
- Chain store or gift shop. Many specialized chain stores and gift shops import items from other countries. Students may enjoy meeting the store's buyer, learning about the origins of handcrafted items, and hearing first-hand how knowledge of Spanish and Hispanic cultures is part of the everyday job.

Field trips can also be scheduled in conjunction with special community events and visits. Museums hold special traveling exhibits; civic centers often feature performances from foreign dance and musical groups; and city government officials often receive visits from dignitaries and business people from foreign countries. Keeping abreast of the activities in your community can result in rewarding field-trip experiences.

Career Day Parents and others in the community can be a great resource for career-day speakers. Guest speakers and exhibitors can be invited to describe their jobs, talk about advantages and disadvantages, and explain how knowledge of a foreign language is useful and important. A career day may be planned with other teachers in the school or with guidance or career counselors who have many contacts with community resource people and who also may assist in scheduling and coordinating the event.

Planning for Successful Public Awareness

Successful programs almost always have successful public relations. You cannot expect the community to appreciate and rally behind your Spanish-as-a-second-language program if no one is aware of it. Gladys Lipton has underscored the importance of a successful public relations program as follows:

> "There are some people who think that you do not publicize until the program has been running successfully for several years. This author does not agree with that philosophy. If the program has been very carefully planned, with input from many, many people, then the publicity will invite additional input from, perhaps, untouched sources, and that can only be a positive affirmation for the program.
>
> "There are others who feel that 'hype' for a program, to use the vernacular for developing public awareness, is not a professional activity, is unworthy of educational goals. This point of view is not valid in today's world of accountability and taxpayers' sense of economy. Obviously, programs that go unnoticed and unpublicized do not capture the attention of policymakers. The first and foremost premise is that the program *has* to be educationally sound and effective, in terms of what the students are accomplishing. But a sound and effective program need not go unnoticed and unpublicized. As a matter of fact, having students demonstrate their achievements in the foreign language will help the program. It will also communicate to the students that they are, indeed, making great strides in their study of the foreign language."**

**Gladys C. Lipton, *Practical Handbook*, pp. 160–61.

The time and effort expended in developing and implementing an ongoing public relations program can benefit the school, the program, and the students.

Beginning the Public Relations Effort

Beginning a program of public awareness need not be a solo effort; in fact, it is recommended that you enlist the help and cooperation of others. Your public relations committee may include the school principal, interested parents, and teachers in other schools and disciplines, such as the high school journalism teacher.

One of the first steps in organizing your public awareness program is to identify your public. The right hand does not always know what the left hand is doing; thus, your public should include your colleagues in the school, administrators, members of the school board, guidance counselors, as well as students who are not enrolled in your program. Then public awareness may extend to parents, business organizations, educational associations, faculty organizations of colleges and universities, city government officials and workers, and other local and state groups and organizations. People inside and outside the school community need to know about your program, its goals and benefits, and the accomplishments of your students.

Once you have established your committee and identified your public, you will be ready to undertake the following tasks in a successful public relations program, as described by Lipton:

- Designate someone as the contact person
- Establish personal contacts with the media
- Plan for publicity before, during, and after an event
- Be scrupulously accurate with names, dates, places, etc.
- Show appreciation when you get publicity
- Plan to take black-and-white glossy pictures that can be submitted after an event (be sure to get everyone's name). Show children in action!
- Write press releases tersely, one page if possible
- Try to get specific information on deadlines, and work around them
- Be sure to give credit where it is due

- Stick to the facts!
- Have everything and everyone ready when reporters and photographers come to the school
- Don't be disappointed if you're turned down. Perhaps reporters will be able to come next time.†

Carrying Out the Public Awareness Program

Your public awareness program can encompass a range of activities and products, from a brochure about your program to a "media event." Work with your committee to identify specific activities during the school year and then brainstorm the possible ways to publicize them. In all your plans and suggestions, do not overlook the students themselves. Your students can design flyers and posters, distribute leaflets, and enlist the help and cooperation of their parents or older brothers and sisters.

In addition to publicity for scheduled events and activities, be aware of opportunities that arise from unexpected situations and sources. For example, one of your students may use Spanish to perform a public service, such as helping an injured person; students and their families may plan to take or may have taken a trip to an unusual destination; you or your students may receive an award; an exchange student may visit or enroll in your class as a peer tutor. Focusing on human-interest aspects of foreign language study can be a boon to the media who are always looking for positive, upbeat stories to offset the daily news.

Also, be open to invitations to speak to organizations in your community, as well as invitations to hold workshops in other districts. Speaking engagements can be a source of publicity in your community and elsewhere in the state.

Send frequent, well-written press releases. Not every event will be considered newsworthy; nevertheless, press releases serve as reminders that your program is a dynamic one that is worthy of attention. Press releases should never be longer than one page and should address the following questions:

- What is happening? What has happened?
- Who is involved?

---

†Lipton, *op. cit.*, p. 163.

- When will (or did) it take place?
- Where will (or did) it take place?
- How will (or did) it happen?
- Why will (or did) it take place?
- Who is the person to contact for further information?

Press releases should also be timely. That is, be aware of the deadlines for the media. In general, allow two to three weeks before an event to contact the education editor of your local newspaper. Reporters and photographers must have time to schedule their visit or attend the event. At least that much time should be allowed to have your event announced as part of the local television or radio station's public service announcements.

If and when the media respond to your press releases, you should always follow up with a thank-you letter or phone call. A simple act of courtesy can go far in establishing a solid contact person with the media. In fact, someday that person may call you to find out what is happening in your program.

Unit Plans

In this section, you will find many ideas, suggestions, and points of information corresponding to each lesson, unit, and review section in *¡Nos comunicamos!*

Most or all of the following sections are included in the Unit Plans for each lesson and unit in the textbook:

- **Objectives:** a statement of the major linguistic and cultural objectives for the lesson or unit
- **Warm-up / Review Activities:** descriptions of activities that can be used to review previously learned material, as well as to practice the vocabulary or grammar learned in the current unit
- **Lesson Sections or Unit Sections:** informative notes, strategies, ideas, learning activities, and occasionally, exercise answers corresponding to the sections of each unit
- **Informal Assessment Activities:** suggestions for informal, periodic progress checks
- **Extension / Enrichment Activities:** suggestions for additional practice, activities for extending the language and culture skills, and ideas for the classroom.

To coordinate the components of the textbook series with the lessons and units, see the chart "*¡Viva el español!* Sample Unit Plan" on page T-20.

Primera lección (pages 1–7)

The preliminary lessons in *¡Nos comunicamos!* serve to review and practice the vocabulary and structures learned in *Ya converso más* and to limber up the language skills that lay dormant over the summer break.

Setting the Stage

While refreshing students' memories and warming up their language skills, you may also use this time to prepare for activities throughout the school year. The units in *¡Nos comunicamos!* lend themselves to thematic lessons. The book is planned around an imaginary trip as seen from the point of view of an early adolescent. The units allow for practical conversations and the continual, consistent incorporation of culture. Many individual, paired, and small-group activities and projects are possible, depending on the time available and the level of instruction.

During the preliminary lessons, you may have students write to consulates and tourist agencies; find articles in magazines and newspapers; and make, collect, or bring in realia that could be used for role-play and learning activities during the year. For each unit, you may then have the resources on hand to create an atmosphere that allows students to become immersed in the unit's theme.

Beginning the Year

The first few class periods should be devoted to reviewing classroom commands and vocabulary and to other "refresher" activities, such as choosing names in Spanish, practicing numbers, role-playing greetings and farewells, etc. Songs, games, and other activities are also helpful in practicing pronunciation and basic vocabulary and structures in a nonthreatening, "fun" atmosphere.

For your own reimmersion, you may wish to review the following sections of this *Annotated Teacher's Edition:*

1. Methodologies, page T-5
2. General Strategies and Techniques, page T-22
3. The *¡Viva el español!* Testing Program, page T-40

Warm-up / Review Activities

Names. Distribute index cards with students' names printed on them to half the class. At your command—*Busquen a sus compañeros*—students must find their partners for the day's activities. If your class is mixed, try to pair advanced students with students who are having more trouble remembering after the long vacation.

Classroom Vocabulary. Use TPR commands and objects in the classroom to practice classroom vocabulary:

T: Juan, hace calor aquí. Abre la ventana, por favor.

The Home and Family. **A.** Have students prepare personal index cards, answering questions such as the following:

1. ¿Cómo te llamas?
2. ¿Cuál es tu dirección?
3. ¿Cuál es tu número de teléfono?
4. ¿Cuántas personas hay en tu familia? ¿Quiénes son?
5. ¿Cuántos años tienes? ¿Cuál es la fecha de tu cumpleaños?
6. ¿Cuáles son tus deportes y pasatiempos favoritos?
7. ¿Qué te gusta hacer con tus amigos?
8. ¿Por qué te gusta o no te gusta la clase de español?

You may use the information to gear the activities of the units to students' interests and to prepare special in-class activities such as birthday celebrations.

B. Use vocabulary cards from the *Ya converso más Teacher's Resource and Activity Book* to play games, conduct TPR activities, and review vocabulary related to the home, such as rooms and furnishings.

Food. Use pictures from magazines to practice names of food and related vocabulary such as meals, verbs (*querer, tomar, gustar,* etc.), and adjectives.

Lesson Sections

Opening Photograph. Use the photograph on page 1 to ask questions such as the following.

1. ¿Dónde está el muchacho?
2. ¿Qué hace él, cocina o come?
3. ¿Qué usa para preparar el desayuno—el horno o la estufa?
4. ¿Cómo es el muchacho?
5. ¿Qué tiene en la cabeza?
6. ¿De qué color es su camiseta?

A. Una conversación entre amigos, *page 2*. After students are familiar with the conversation, have them scan the written version (or listen to the recorded version again) to answer additional comprehension questions:

1. ¿Cómo se llama el amigo de Carmen?
2. ¿Quién quiere buscar a Beto en la cocina, Carmen o Pepe?
3. Carmen busca a su hermano sobre el refrigerador, ¿verdad?

B. ¿Y tú?, *page 3*. After students have answered the questions orally, you may have them write their answers to questions 1–4 in one paragraph, 5–6 in another, and 7–8 in a third. Encourage students to add to their answers in written form.

CH. ¿Qué nos gusta?, *page 5*. Ask volunteers to present their results to the class.

Extend the activity by naming foods and having the class vote by a show of hands on which ones they like and don't like. Use the results to summarize the class's preferences in sentences (e.g., *Nos gusta el pan tostado. No nos gustan las zanahorias.*).

Informal Assessment Activities

- Use activity D on page 6 for dictation practice.
- Ask students what they want to eat for dinner tonight, or direct pairs of students to ask and answer the question (i.e., *¿Qué quieres comer esta noche?*).
- Observe students in small groups as they play vocabulary identification games, such as "Concentración" (see "Games and Activities").
- Hold informal chats with individuals to elicit basic autobiographical details.

Extension / Enrichment Activities

Individual Work

- Distribute copies of the *Ya converso más* textbook and have students skim the sections related to home and meals (Unidad 1 through Unidad 3, and Unidad 5 through Unidad 7). Assign students to prepare "reminder" reports about culture to share with their classmates.
- Have students keep a log of what they eat for lunch for two or three days. Hold a class discussion of favorite lunch foods, based on the results.

Paired Activity

Have students work in pairs to prepare and present a conversation. Have the partners choose one of the following topics for their conversation:

1. El cuarto favorito
2. La comida favorita
3. Las actividades

Small-Group Activity

If students need additional practice with verbs, have them perform chain activities with assigned verbs. They may begin with verb forms and then progress to questions and answers with the verb forms.

Segunda lección
(pages 8–14)

In the second lesson, students will review how to talk about their daily routines and chores, how to give commands or instructions, and how to talk about sports, games, and pastimes.

Warm-up / Review Activities

Chores. **A.**. Describe a dirty floor, dirty rug, full wastebasket, etc., and have students state what must be done.

T: Juan tiene una escoba. Hay papeles y polvo en el piso. ¿Qué tiene que hacer?

C: Tiene que barrer el piso.

B. Follow up the first review activity by describing a clean room, etc., and have students state what has just been done.

T: Sus dormitorios están limpios. Todas las cosas están en los estantes, en el tocador y en el ropero. ¿Qué acaban de hacer?
C: Acabamos de recoger las cosas.

Sports, Games, and Pastimes.
A. Make and distribute vocabulary cards (Unidad 10, *Ya converso más Teacher's Resource and Activity Book*) to every student. As students stand, one by one, and show their cards, ask them a question:

T: ¿Juegas al baloncesto?
S1: No, no juego al baloncesto.
T: ¿Sabes tocar un instrumento?
S2: Sí, sé tocar un instrumento.

As students recall the vocabulary and related verbs, increase the complexity of the questions (e.g., *Nuestro equipo de béisbol juega en el gimnasio, ¿verdad?*).

B. Call out a month or a season and have students respond with an appropriate sport or leisure activity.

C. Have students break into small groups to do quick chain drills using *jugar.* They may add on to a sentence (e.g., *Mis amigos y yo jugamos al . . .*) or alternate asking and answering questions.

Reflexive Verbs. **A.** Call out a time of day or ask an either-or question and have students respond by naming what they do (e.g., *¿Qué haces por la mañana, vuelves a la casa o te vas de la casa?*).

B. Write the words *primero* and *luego* on the chalkboard. Ask volunteers to call out two activities. Have a student put the two activities in a logical order to form a sentence (e.g., *Primero me lavo la cara, luego me cepillo los dientes.*).

Commands. Have students select a chore or other activity that they wish they could tell someone else to do. Call on students to give examples of their commands.

S1: Estudia la lección.
S2: Saca la basura.
S3: Recoge mis cosas.

Lesson Sections

Opening Photograph. Use the photograph on page 8 to ask questions such as the following:

1. ¿Les gusta estar fuera de la casa?
2. ¿Qué tiene uno de los muchachos, un caballo o una bicicleta?
3. ¿Qué tiempo hace? ¿Hace frío o hace calor?
4. ¿Cómo son los muchachos, son tímidos o son simpáticos?
5. ¿Qué llevan ellos? (*or* ¿Cómo es su ropa?)

A. Una conversación entre familia, *page 9.* Ask volunteers to read the conversation aloud after they have listened to it several times.

Have students skim the page to find answers to the following questions:

1. ¿A Paco le gusta sacar la basura?
2. ¿A Jorge le gusta lavar los platos?
3. ¿Qué puede hacer Paco cuando Jorge tiene que lavar los platos?

Students may enjoy creating their own conversations, using this one as a model. Encourage them to vary the activities and chores.

B. ¿Y tú?, *page 10.* Ask students to choose partners and role-play a conversation between two friends, based on the situation in activity A. One friend must do chores before playing, the other friend has just finished doing the chores. You may wish to provide some model sentences on the chalkboard:

1. No puedo jugar ahora. Tengo que pasar la aspiradora.
2. Yo voy a jugar con el equipo. Acabo de quitar el polvo de los estantes.

C. ¡Pobrecita de Paquita!, *page 11.* Continue by having students think of other things that Paquita should do before her parents come home (e.g., *Lava los platos. Escribe tus tareas.*).

CH. Por la mañana y por la noche, *page 12.* Have advanced students describe a typical morning at home. Encourage them to include details such as what other members of the family do. They may use the exercise as a model.

D. ¿Qué están haciendo?, *page 13.* You may wish to do the activity orally in class before assigning it as individual work.

Informal Assessment Activities

- Use the questions in activity B on page 10 to hold brief, informal conversations with students in pairs or small groups.
- Give a command and have students pantomime the appropriate activity.
- Pantomime an activity, such as brushing your hair, and have students call out what you are doing (e.g., *Usted se peina.*).
- In the middle of an activity, pause to ask a question about what the class is doing at the moment (e.g., *¿Qué estamos haciendo—estamos cantando, estamos bailando o estamos hablando?*).

Extension / Enrichment Activities

Paired / Small-Group Activities

Set up areas of the classroom as activity centers. One center could represent a room or rooms of the house and have items such as brooms, dust rags, wastebaskets, play dishes, etc. Another area could have sports equipment or games.

Students may work in the centers to create conversations, practice directed dialogues, or invent games for their classmates to play.

Individual Work / Class Activity

Distribute blank calendar forms to students ("Games and Activities," *Teacher's Resource and Activity Book*) and have them record their daily activities on the calendar. The completed calendars could be displayed on the bulletin board or used for informal individual assessment questions.

Tercera lección
(pages 15–21)

In the third lesson, students will review and practice vocabulary and structures related to transportation and countries, affirmative and negative words, stem-changing verbs, and people and places in the school.

Warm-up / Review Activities

School Places and People. Take students for a walk through the school and review vocabulary as you go. Combine TPR commands and questions as follows:

T: Jairo, camina a la fuente de agua. ¿Tienes sed? ¿Quieres tomar agua? Alicia, muéstrame la entrada y la salida. Cuando te vas de la escuela, ¿tienes que bajar unas escaleras?
Alonso, camina a la oficina del director. ¿Está la secretaria en la oficina?

Countries and Nationalities. **A.** Give TPR commands to have students point out countries on a wall map of the world (e.g., *Iris, muéstrame la América Central. Hugo, toca Guatemala.*). As students recall the vocabulary with greater speed, increase the complexity of the commands (e.g., *Señala el país donde viven los peruanos.*).

B. Call out a nationality and have students use it in a sentence (e.g., *Los argentinos viven en la Argentina.*). After a student has responded, ask for volunteers to write the sentence on the chalkboard.

C. Combine review of countries with review of modes of transportation. Use vocabulary cards of transportation (Unidad 13 and Unidad 14 of *Ya converso más Teacher's Resource and Activity Book*) to cue sentences such as the following:

1. Puedo ir a Puerto Rico en barco.
2. Quiero ir a España en avión.
3. Voy del Perú a Bolivia en tren.
4. Pienso ir a México en autobús.

Affirmative and Negative Words. **A.** Cut out pictures from old magazines showing empty rooms and rooms with people in them. Display the pictures and ask whether there is anyone in the rooms (e.g., *¿Hay alguien en la sala? No hay nadie en el comedor, ¿verdad?*). Practice *algo* and *nada* by asking about objects in the pictures (e.g., *¿Hay algo sobre la mesa? No hay nada dentro del ropero, ¿verdad?*).

B. Ask questions about things students always or never do. Make some of your questions nonsensical (e.g., *¿Te bañas siempre en el fregadero?*).

Stem-Changing Verbs. **A.** Ask students what they plan to do in their classes and after school today. You may wish to make a chart on the chalkboard, listing students' answers and then use the chart to elicit other singular and plural forms of *pensar* (e.g., *¿Qué piensan hacer Pepe y Ana en la clase de música?*).

B. Have students bring in the television listings for the week and practice asking one another when different programs start, using forms of *comenzar*. They may also ask one another about viewing habits (e.g., *¿Cuándo comienzan tus amigos a mirar la televisión los sábados?*).

C. As a password for entering or leaving the classroom, have students state at what time they always eat lunch (e.g., *Siempre almuerzo a las doce.*). Follow up with questions about what they want to eat for lunch (e.g., *¿Qué quieres comer hoy, una ensalada o un sándwich?*).

Lesson Sections

Opening Photograph. Use the photograph on page 15 to ask questions such as the following:

1. ¿Quiénes son los hombres en la foto?
2. ¿Cuál es delgado?
3. ¿Cuál es grueso?
4. ¿De qué color son los uniformes?
5. ¿Dónde trabajan los policías?
6. ¿Trabajan los policías en nuestra escuela?

A. Una conversación entre amigos, *page 16.* Before playing the conversation for students, have them locate and skim the listing "Countries and Nationalities" in the Appendix on page 354.

You may wish to use a calendar to demonstrate the meanings of *un día* and *algún día*. Help students conclude that both terms refer to some time in the future.

B. ¿Y tú?, *page 17.* Use the questions on the page to elicit information about students' interests in different countries and modes of travel. As students respond, ask follow-up questions such as *¿Conoces a un chileno? ¿Es divertido ir en barco?*

Students may choose partners and alternate asking and answering the questions.

C. ¿Qué hay en la calle? *page 18.* Continue by asking students to look out the window and tell you whom or what they see. You may wish to review or teach the commands *asómate* and *asómense*.

CH. El domingo de Marcos, *page 19.* After students have completed the activity and you have returned their corrected papers, have them write a similar description of what they do on a Sunday. Stipulate beforehand that they must use the verbs *pensar, comenzar, querer,* and *almorzar* in their descriptions.

F. Una carta de un amigo, *page 21.* Before students open their textbooks, read the letter aloud. Ask them to summarize (in English or Spanish) the important points in the letter. Then let them turn to page 21 and find sentences to support their summaries.

Informal Assessment Activities

- Use the outline maps in the *Teacher's Resource and Activity Book* and have students label the countries. Follow up by asking who lives in different countries.
- Use a clock with movable hands to have students show you at what time different activities begin (e.g., *Inés, ¿a qué hora comienza tu clase de piano?*).
- Distribute a floor plan of the school to each student. Ask questions about who works in different places.
- Give students five minutes to write one sentence about what they *plan* to do on the weekend; one about what they *have* to do on the weekend; and one about what they *want* to do on the weekend.
- Use the questions from activities B and D to hold informal chats with students in pairs or small groups.

Extension / Enrichment Activities

Individual Work / Paired Activity

Have students select someone in the school to interview. Give students a list of suggested questions (in English).

Following the interview, ask students to talk about that person and what he or she does, where he or she works, at what time, etc.

Small-Group Activity

Have students work in groups to make a map of a country, labeling the capital and other major cities, and coloring in natural features, such as lakes and mountains.

Class Activity

Have students skim the textbook and sign up to be on bulletin-board committees. Encourage students to find a unit that looks interesting to them and then sign up for the bulletin-board committee for that unit. Committees should meet periodically to plan and prepare their boards.

Unidad 1 (pages 22–45)

Objectives

After completing this unit, students should be able to:

- identify and name travel destinations and the people and activities involved in making plans
- describe actions by using the present tense of regular *-ar, -er,* and *-ir* verbs; irregular verbs *estar, ser,* and *ir;* and *o* to *ue* and *e* to *ie* stem-changing verbs (review)
- identify places and points of interest for travelers in Mexico and Spain.

Warm-up / Review Activities

Transportation. Call out various destinations in the community (and the world). Students respond with an appropriate mode of transportation. To make the activity more challenging, name two destinations and have students respond with one or two appropriate modes of transportation. You may wish to use a wall map of the world to point out the destinations.

T: *(pointing to the map)* Quiero ir de Miami a Caracas.
S1: Usted puede ir en avión o en barco.

Countries. Select a "Warm-up / Review Activity" from the Tercera lección to continue practice of names of countries.

Unit Vocabulary. **A.** Play "El ahorcado" (see "Games and Activities") to practice spelling skills. As students become familiar with the vocabulary, you may wish to play the game with sentences, instead of individual words (e.g., *La viajera viaja al desierto.*).

B. Use vocabulary cards *(Teacher's Resource and Activity Book)* and have students respond to TPR commands and questions.

T: Alfredo, toma la agencia de viajes. Salta a la pizarra. Pon la agencia de viajes en la pizarra. ¿Quién trabaja en la agencia de viajes, el agente de viajes o el viajero?

After two or three vocabulary cards have been lined up along the chalk ledge, have students either make up sentences or complete sentences using the words (e.g., *Voy a la agencia de viajes para comprar un billete.*).

C. Name a natural feature and a location and have students tell you whether or not the feature may be found there.

T: Quiero viajar a las montañas. ¿Hay montañas en Iowa?
C: No, no hay montañas en Iowa.
T: ¿Adónde puedo viajar?
S1: Puede viajar a Colorado. Hay montañas en Colorado.

Unit Grammar. **A.** Call out a verb and have one student use it in a question and another student use it in an answer. You may wish to review *-ar* verbs one day, *-er* verbs the next, and so on.

B. Distribute blank calendar forms ("Games and Activities," *Teacher's Resource and Activity Book*) and have students write a different verb under each day of the week. Call on students to make up a sentence to describe the activity for each day (e.g., *Los lunes estudio en la biblioteca.*). For subsequent practice sessions, have students add another verb under each day to make a new sentence (e.g., *Los lunes siempre estudio y leo mucho.*).

C. Use exercise A on page 35 for review. Vary the questions (e.g., *¡Hola, Felipe! ¿Adónde vas?*).

D. Bring in advertisements from grocery stores to practice *costar* and *pagar.* Display an ad and ask questions about prices (e.g., *¿Cuánto cuestan las manzanas? / Quiero comprar un pavo. ¿Cuánto tengo que pagar?*). For subsequent practice, use newspaper advertisements from travel agencies.

Unit Sections

Panorama de vocabulario

If students tire of TPR exercises, try volume, pace, and grouping variations. Also, combine commands to add variety:

T: Pepe, toma el río. Pon el río en la mesa. Siéntate en el río. Alumnos, ¿quién está en el río?
C: Pepe está en el río.

You may also ask questions about the scenes on pages 24 and 25:

1. ¿Adónde piensa viajar la mujer?
2. ¿Adónde piensa viajar el hombre?
3. ¿Adónde quiere ir el muchacho?
4. ¿Adónde quiere ir su mamá?
5. ¿Qué quiere hacer su mamá en la playa?

You may wish to point out that *viajar, pagar,* and *descansar* are regular *-ar* verbs in the present tense. Have students conclude that *costar* is an *o* to *ue* stem-changing verb by comparing the infinitive to the verb form in the question at the top of page 25.

¡Aprende el vocabulario! ***Exercise A, page 26.*** Repeat the exercise, substituting other verbs (e.g., *¿Dónde vas a pasar las vacaciones? ¿Adónde viajas? ¿Adónde vas para descansar?*).

Exercise B, page 27. After students have completed the exercise orally in class, you may wish to assign it as written homework. It also may be used for dictation practice.

Usando el español

Talking about Actions in the Present. The term *conjugation* is used for the first time with this review of regular verbs. Demonstrate its meaning for the class by reciting the verb forms for a verb and explaining that you have just given the conjugation for that verb. Use the verb charts in the Appendix to have students point to or read the conjugations of the regular *-ar, -er,* and *-ir* verbs.

Using Irregular Verbs. If students need additional practice, you may use exercises from the *Ya converso más* textbook (Unidad 1, *estar;* Unidad 10, *ser*) for practice.

¡Vamos a practicar! ***Exercise B, page 36.*** Ask questions about the illustration to practice *estar* and prepositions:

1. ¿Quién está cerca del cuadro, Gerardo o su tía Anita?
2. ¿Quién está a la izquierda de la lámpara, el tío Francisco o Diego?
3. ¿Quién está lejos de la computadora, Gerardo o su mamá?

Exercise C, page 37. Help students observe that the second sentence in each pair uses *ir a* plus an infinitive.

After students have completed the exercise, follow up by asking questions as follows:

1. ¿Quiénes van a las montañas?
2. ¿Cómo (*or* En qué) van a viajar?

Students may also convert the exercise into brief dialogues.

Using Stem-Changing Verbs. Review the concept of stems by writing several infinitives on the chalkboard and then erasing the infinitive endings. Have students state what the remaining letters are called.

You may wish to point out that *costar* is really only useful in two forms: *cuesta* and *cuestan*. Demonstrate by asking how much various classroom items cost (e.g., *¿Cuánto cuesta un lápiz? ¿Cuánto cuestan dos lápices?*).

¡Vamos a practicar! *Exercise A, page 40.* You may wish to show students the "¡A divertirnos!" illustration in *Converso mucho,* Unidad 8, page 193 to review the saying *El tiempo es oro*. You may also wish to review telling time by using or adapting exercises from that unit.

¡A conversar!

After students are familiar with the conversation, have them scan the text for answers to additional comprehension questions:

1. ¿En qué país hay montañas, valles y muchas playas?
2. ¿Adónde pueden viajar para nadar en el Caribe?
3. ¿Qué país no está muy lejos?
4. ¿Qué tienen que hacer antes de viajar a México?

¡Conversa tú!

Have students work in pairs to ask and answer the questions. After students have completed the questions orally, have them write their answers.

Initiate a class discussion on the advantages of reading about a country or vacation destination before you travel. You may wish to attempt the discussion completely in Spanish.

¡A divertirnos!

Have students bring in items appropriate for travel in different destinations and either model or demonstrate them. Their classmates may guess where they are going.

La cultura y tú

Mexico is a very popular vacation destination. Every year, tourists flock to the beach resorts at Cancún, Mazatlán, Acapulco, Ixtapa, Puerto Vallarta, and many other locations. There they enjoy Mexico's warm climate and thousands of miles of beaches.

Visitors also come to see the Aztec and Mayan ruins of Teotihuacán, Chichén Itzá, Uxmal, and Tulum. Mexico City, the capital, is built on the site of Tenochtitlán, a principal religious center of the Aztec empire. Mexico City itself is a modern, vibrant city with many museums and cultural events to attract countless visitors each year. More accessible to the United States, Tijuana, just over the border from California, is a popular destination for day trips.

You may wish to explain to the class that México, D. F., means *México, Distrito Federal*. Have students note the similarity to Washington, D.C. Help the class observe that the Río Grande is called Río Bravo in Mexico.

Spain has attracted an increasing number of visitors in recent years. Along its Mediterranean and Atlantic coasts, many resort towns receive visitors from early spring to late fall. Since Spain does not have a tropical climate, few of the beach resorts operate year-round.

Visitors to Spain often come to see its historic cities and tour its ancient castles. Madrid, the capital, is a great cultural center, boasting El Prado, one of the world's foremost art museums. Nearby is Toledo, former capital of Spain, which is famous for its fine steel. Another popular destination is the palace of Felipe II at El Escorial. In the south of Spain, tourists visit Granada, Córdoba, and Sevilla, where the Moorish influence is still evident in the architecture.

You may wish to tell the class that *el Golfo de Vizcaya* is also known as *el Mar Cantábrico* in Spain.

You may wish to use this "La cultura y tú" section to reinforce the importance of learning about a country and its people before you travel. You may also help students make a distinction between being a visitor in a country and being a tourist.

Informal Assessment Activities

The following activities form a core of informal assessment suggestions which may be used and adapted for all the units in *¡Nos comunicamos!* You may wish to clip or flag these suggestions for future reference.

Speaking

1. Have volunteers be the leaders to direct the class in TPR activities, using realia or the vocabulary cards for the unit.
2. Ask students to read aloud from the conversation or reading selection or read the sample questions and answers in the "Usando el español" sections. This may be suitable for individuals, pairs, or small groups.
3. Select a question from the unit and have students answer it. For variation, follow up the question with another.
4. As students enter the classroom, ask a personalized question, using vocabulary and grammar from the unit.
5. Play a portion of the Lesson Cassette and have students repeat each word, sentence, or question.
6. Direct students to make up questions to ask their classmates.

Listening

1. Distribute a copy of the "Vocabulary Review" page or pages corresponding to the unit *(Teacher's Resource and Activity Book)*. Call out a vocabulary word and a number and have students write the number on the corresponding picture.
2. State two sentences or questions that incorporate a verb form or part of speech taught in the unit. Have students indicate if the two are the same or different.

3. Prepare a typewritten list of words, sentences, or questions in multiple-choice format. State one of the lines and have students circle the line they hear.
4. Select an exercise from the Exercise Cassette and distribute the corresponding "Tape Exercise" page from the *Teacher's Resource and Activity Book*. Have students listen to and complete the exercise. (For a tapescript of material on the audiocassettes, see the *Teacher's Edition* of the *Workbook*.)
5. Make a statement in Spanish and have students answer or write *sí* if the statement makes sense and *no* if the statement does not make sense.

Reading

1. Write vocabulary words or sentences on index cards. Have students take turns reading them aloud.
2. As students' skills increase, create matching activities on the chalkboard, with a list of vocabulary words or phrases on one side and their definitions or synonyms on the other (e.g., *la persona que vende billetes de avión* on the right and *el agente de viajes* on the left).
3. Write several statements on the chalkboard and ask yes/no or either-or questions based on the statements. To make the activity more challenging, have students make up questions to ask one another.
4. Individually or in pairs, have students read aloud from the "¡A conversar!" or "Vamos a leer" section of the unit.

Writing

1. Use familiar sentences from the exercises or presentations in the unit and dictate them to the class.
2. Create fill-in-the-blank sentences for students to complete with the appropriate word or phrase.
3. Select a photograph in the unit and have students write a sentence to describe it. Vary the activity by having students write an appropriate question or exclamation about the photograph.
4. Assign the composition section in the *Workbook*. Have students exchange papers to correct each other's writing.

Extension / Enrichment Activities

Individual Work / Paired Activities

- Have students make travel posters that highlight the natural features of a country. You may wish to distribute a list of possible slogans for them to adapt or use for their posters (e.g., *Cuando piensas viajar, piensa en ——. ¡Viaje a ——!* or *Siempre hace buen tiempo en ——.*).

- Assign countries to pairs of students. Have them visit a travel agency to find out the following information:

  1. How can you travel to that country? (By plane? boat?)
  2. How much does a ticket cost?
  3. What documents do you need to visit that country? (optional)

  Students should prepare their information to share with the class. (You may wish to contact one or more travel agencies in advance to secure permission and prepare them for students' visits.)

Small-Group Activity

Prepare lists of specific names of different natural features and have students work in small groups to find out where they are located. A list may look like the following:

1. Cordillera de los Andes
2. Río de la Plata
3. Desierto de Atacama

Suggestions for the Classroom

Surprise your students. The night before you begin the unit, transform your classroom into a mock travel agency. Make a nameplate for your desk and add a telephone (real or toy) and other paraphernalia to turn it into a business-type desk. Hang travel posters around the room; display travel itineraries and brochures, and make signs (e.g., *Ocho días, siete noches en Guadalajara—sólo $500*).

Unidad 2 (pages 46–69)

Objectives

After completing this unit, students should be able to:

- identify and name people, places, and activities related to air travel
- talk about doing or making things by using the present tense of *hacer*
- talk about what people say by using the present tense of *decir*
- refer to something that receives the action of a verb by using direct object pronouns
- read a simulated airline ticket and boarding pass
- read about and discuss the 24-hour clock.

Warm-up / Review Activities

Verbs. **A.** Have students role-play a travel agent and travelers. The activities may be short, as in the example:

S1: Quiero ir al desierto.
S2: Hay un desierto en México.
S1: ¿Cuánto cuesta un billete de avión?
S2: Cuesta doscientos dólares.

Follow up by combining commands and questions for the other students (e.g., *Andrés, pon la mano en el hombro del agente de viajes. María, señala al viajero. Alumnos, ¿adónde quiere ir el viajero?* etc.).

B. Have students finish the sentence *Algún día pienso viajar a* ——. Record some of the answers on the chalkboard to use for eliciting responses with plural forms.

C. Ask the question *¿Cómo descansas los fines de semana?* Have volunteers write their classmates' responses on the chalkboard (e.g., *Leo novelas.*).

Unit Vocabulary. **A.** Set up chairs at the front of the classroom to be the "airplane," including seats for the pilots. Make name tags such as *Pasajero No. 2, Piloto No. 1.* Ask volunteers to play the parts of people on an airplane. Students at their seats will direct questions to the players:

S1: Piloto número uno, ¿a qué hora sale el avión?
S2: Sale a las tres en punto.
S3: Pasajera número 2, ¿es cómodo su asiento?
S4: ¡No! Mi asiento es muy incómodo.

B. Write several flight numbers, cities, and times on the chalkboard. Have students answer questions about arrival or departure times. For subsequent practice, state a time that is the same or different from one on your schedule and have students note whether the flight is early, on time, or late. (If students take the bus to school, vary the activity by asking about real-life arrival times: *¿Siempre llega a tiempo el autobús?*)

Unit Grammar. **A.** Set up a mock ticket window or check-in counter and ask volunteers to be customers or travelers. Begin by asking the players *¿Por qué haces fila?* (or *¿Qué haces? / Hago fila.*) Continue by asking students at their seats other questions such as *¿Por qué hacen fila Luis y Rita?*

B. Play a form of "Gossip" by telling the first student in each row a sentence. The second student must ask what you said. The first student replies with your sentence. The third student asks what you said, and the chain continues to the end of the row. Vary the activity by handing students index cards with statements made by different people. Ask students to read what the people said.

T: Juan, ¿qué dice el piloto?
S1: El piloto dice que vamos a aterrizar.

C. Use TPR commands, questions, and classroom or travel-related objects to practice direct object pronouns.

T: Adela, pon la maleta sobre la computadora. ¿Dónde la pones?

Unit Sections

Panorama de vocabulario

In this unit, *el equipaje* is used to mean "luggage" or "group of suitcases." An individual suitcase is *la maleta.*

Set up a corner of the classroom to represent a check-in counter at an airport. Use old suitcases, airline tickets, etc. to practice the vocabulary. Another area of the classroom may be set up as an airplane in which students may role-play various situations to practice the vocabulary.

¡Aprende el vocabulario! *Exercise A, page 50.* To help students with the conjugation of *ver,* tell them to use *leer* as a model.

Usando el español

Talking about Things You Do. Students should have little or no trouble with *hacer,* since its forms have been used as passive vocabulary throughout *Converso mucho* and *Ya converso más.* The only forms that are completely new are *hago* and *hacemos.*

¡Vamos a practicar! *Exercise C, page 58.* Explain that students do not necessarily have to use *hacer* in their responses; they should give answers that are true for them. Ask volunteers to tape-record some of the responses; then you may use the recording to ask questions. You may also wish to videotape students as they interview one another.

Talking about Talking! To practice the forms of *decir,* you may wish to simulate the televised movie reviews in which the reviewers either agree or disagree with one another.

To practice the *que* clauses that follow *decir,* you may wish to write several examples on the chalkboard and have students identify the clauses:

1. El director dice que mañana es día de fiesta.
2. El reportero dice que va a llover por la tarde.
3. Los pasajeros dicen que no les gusta el avión viejo.

¡Vamos a practicar! *Exercise C, page 62.* To supplement the questions, you may wish to have students brainstorm a list of issues that are important to them and then take a vote.

Talking about People and Things. Copy the sentences on page 64 on the chalkboard and have students draw arrows from each verb to the direct object pronoun.

¡Vamos a practicar! *Exercise A, page 65.* Have students choose partners and act out the situation in the exercise. If you have travel-related items in the classroom, use them to model the exercise.

Vamos a leer

Bring in other real-life items related to travel, such as bus tickets, train tickets, etc., and have students practice gleaning as much information as they can from them. Encourage them to use the classroom dictionary only after they have tried to guess the meaning of a word or phrase.

La cultura y tú

In the Spanish-speaking world and throughout Europe, the 24-hour clock is commonly used for schedules and timetables. In everyday life, however, people use the 12-hour clock.

Have students turn to page 46 and read the schedules on the arrival board in the photograph. On the computerized arrival board, the colon is used in the hour; however, in most written examples of time in Spanish, a period is used instead of a colon.

Obtain television schedules from Spanish-language newspapers and have students practice reading the times aloud.

Informal Assessment Activities

In addition to the basic assessment suggestions in Unidad 1 on page T-77, you may wish to do the following:

- Name students and people in the school or community and ask students if they know them. Students should reply with the appropriate direct object pronouns.
- Distribute index cards with communication situations described on them. Have students act out the situations, which may include boarding a plane, giving a ticket to the flight attendant, finding the correct seat, and then telling the flight attendant that the seat is uncomfortable; or going to the airport to meet a friend and asking various people if the flight will arrive on time.

Extension / Enrichment Activities

Individual Work

Have students bring in items related to air travel, such as old airline tickets. They should write or prepare to say as much as they can about their items.

Paired / Small-Group Activities

Obtain pictures of people in an airport, sitting in an airplane, waiting in line, etc. (Check advertisements for airlines and car rental agencies for possible pictures.) Give each pair or group a picture and conduct one of the following activities:

1. Supply a list of questions about the picture, which students discuss and answer in Spanish.
2. Ask students to describe the people and the scene.
3. Ask students to create a brief story about the picture. Include details such as where the people are going, what they are doing or saying, etc.

Class Activity

Take the class on a field trip to an airport. If possible, arrange for an employee of an airline to talk about his or her job and how speaking Spanish or a second language comes in handy in helping passengers with their questions and problems.

Suggestions for the Classroom

Convert the classroom into a mock airport. Draw a flight arrival and departure board on butcher's paper or posterboard. Bring in old suitcases, toy airplanes, etc. Label the doorway *Puerta No. 9H*. Make your desk into an airline counter.

Bulletin-Board Ideas. Obtain pictures of different kinds of workers associated with an airport. These may be obtained from magazines or career awareness kits. Under each picture, write a label with the Spanish word for the job. Title the board *Trabajamos en el aeropuerto.*

Obtain brochures of different airlines whose bases are in Spanish-speaking countries. Arrange the brochures around a world map and connect each brochure to its country with a piece of yarn or colored string. Title the board *¡A viajar!*

Unidad 3 (pages 70–89)

Objectives

After completing this unit, students should be able to:

- ▶ identify and name things related to hotels and hotel rooms
- ▶ talk about actions by using the present tense of *e* to *i* and *u* to *ue* stem-changing verbs and regular, irregular, and stem-changing reflexive verbs (review)
- ▶ read and discuss a story about a family in Argentina
- ▶ read about and discuss tourism in South America.

Warm-up / Review Activities

Reflexive Verbs. Use vocabulary cards and "Panorama de vocabulario" pages from Unidad 8, *Ya converso más Teacher's Resource and Activity Book* to review reflexive verbs through TPR commands and questions, and identification games.

Irregular Verbs. **A.** Type and distribute lines from a poem, proverbs, or song lyrics. Ask individuals, pairs, or small groups to read a line or phrase aloud. Then ask the class to tell you what they are saying.

T: Elena, lee el proverbio en voz alta.
S1: El tiempo es oro.
T: Alumnos, ¿qué dice Elena?
C: Dice que el tiempo es oro.

B. Appoint a leader each day to take a vote on the closing activity. Follow up by asking *¿Cuántos dicen que sí? ¿Cuántos dicen que no?*

C. Use a wall map to practice forms of *hacer un viaje.* Point to a country and have students tell you where they are taking a trip.

T: Beto, tus amigos y tú hacen un viaje a este país. ¿Adónde van?
S: Hacemos un viaje a Venezuela.

Direct Object Pronouns. Begin by using classroom objects and continue by using the unit vocabulary for subsequent review. Ask questions such as the following:

1. ¿Dónde pones tu cuaderno, dentro del pupitre o sobre el pupitre?
2. En una habitación, ¿dónde pones las toallas, en el cuarto de baño o en el ropero?

Students must respond using the appropriate direct object pronoun.

Unit Vocabulary. **A.** Distribute vocabulary cards (*Teacher's Resource and Activity Book*) and ask questions (e.g., *¿Quién tiene la llave? Luisa, ¿qué tienes?*).

B. Obtain brochures from various hotels and have students describe pictures of the rooms.

C. Have students list everything they would need or expect to find in a hotel room, including items of review vocabulary (e.g., *un tocador, una lámpara, un televisor,* etc.). For subsequent practice, turn the activity into a race by rows to see which row can name the most items in a given time.

Unit Grammar. **A.** Write several locations as column headings on the chalkboard (e.g., *la agencia de viajes, el avión, el hotel*). Ask questions using forms of *pedir* and have students name items or services appropriate for each place.

B. See "Warm-up / Review Activities" for the Segunda lección for practice with reflexive verbs.

C. As a password for entering or leaving the classroom, have students answer questions with forms of *dormirse.*

1. ¿A qué hora te duermes cada noche?
2. ¿Se duermen tus papás cuando miran los programas de televisión?
3. ¿Te duermes a veces en las clases?

D. Use vocabulary cards from Unidad 10, *Ya converso más Teacher's Resource and Activity Book* to practice forms of *jugar.*

1. ¿A qué juegan ustedes en la clase de educación física?
2. ¿Cuándo juegan al fútbol americano, en el verano o en el otoño?
3. ¿Dónde juegan al tenis, dentro de la casa o fuera de la casa?
4. ¿Juegas con un equipo o juegas con tus amigos?

Unit Sections

Panorama de vocabulario

You may wish to supplement the vocabulary with words for people who work in a hotel: *el criado, la criada* (maid); *el* or *la recepcionista* (receptionist); *el* or *la gerente del hotel* (hotel manager); *el botones* (bellboy).

Try to bring in as many real items (e.g., keys, towels, soap) as possible to use for presentation and practice of the vocabulary.

¡Aprende el vocabulario! *Exercise A, page 74.* Point out that *necesitar* is a regular *-ar* verb. Demonstrate its meaning with classroom objects before presenting the exercise.

T: Quiero escribir en la pizarra. ¿Qué necesito para escribir? ¿Necesito un bolígrafo? No. ¿Necesito un lápiz? No. Necesito la tiza para escribir en la pizarra.

Exercise B, page 75. Have students role-play a tourist complaining to a hotel manager about items in the room or about other people in the hotel.

Exercise D, page 77. You may wish to bring in blank postcards for students to complete this exercise. The postcards may be displayed on a bulletin board or used for reading practice in subsequent classes.

Usando el español

Using Stem-Changing Verbs. You may wish to have volunteers write verb charts of *servir* and *seguir* on the chalkboard. Remind students that *seguir* has an irregular form (i.e., *yo sigo*).

If any of your students have ever stayed in a hotel, ask them to state what you can ask for in your hotel room and what the hotel will serve you in your room. To practice *jugar,* you may have them describe facilities in a hotel for playing games or exercising.

Using Reflexive Verbs. You may wish to make the distinction between the verb *dormir* and *dormirse* (i.e., to sleep and to fall asleep). Use pantomiming techniques to convey the meaning of *dormirse,* combined with additional comprehensible input:

T: Me gusta mirar la televisión. A veces me duermo durante los programas. Mis hijos nunca se duermen durante sus programas favoritos.

¡A divertirnos!

After students have read the cartoons silently, have them answer questions:

1. ¿Qué tiene la mamá?
2. ¿Qué hace el muchacho?
3. ¿Qué dice la mamá?
4. ¿Qué dice el muchacho?

You may also have volunteers role-play the situation. Instruct students to find the direct object pronoun in the punchline (*los*).

Vamos a leer

Have students scan the reading for the definition of *una pensión* (i.e., *un hotel pequeño con pocas habitaciones*).

Encourage students to use direct object pronouns to answer questions about the reading:

1. ¿Dónde pone Sonia las toallas limpias? [Las pone en las habitaciones.]
2. ¿Cuándo sirve ella el desayuno? [Lo sirve los domingos por la mañana.]

La cultura y tú

Machu Picchu means "Lost City of the Incas." Discovered in 1911 by Dr. Hiram Bingham, the ruins of the ancient Incan civilization stand at an elevation of 6,750 feet (2,045 m) in the Andes mountains and cover about five square miles. Because of its altitude, tourists often find that they feel light-headed and have trouble breathing in the thin atmosphere.

Iguazú Falls are located at the point where Argentina, Brazil, and Paraguay meet. The Pampas, in central Argentina, are a vast, flat plain. The *gauchos* are Argentine cowboys noted for their superb horsemanship.

Have students prepare brief written reports on these and other attractions in South America. The reports may be gathered and bound in a notebook for reference material.

Informal Assessment Activities

See page T-77 for possible assessment activities. You may also describe communication situations, such as the following, and have students prepare short conversations:

1. One of the tourists at your hotel can't hear well. Help out by explaining to him or her what the bellboy is saying about the hotel.
2. Your family has just checked into a modern hotel. There are no towels, soap, or pillows in the room. Call the front desk and ask for what you need.

Extension / Enrichment Activities

Individual Work / Paired Activity

Explain to students that many of the large hotel chains in the United States also have hotels in Spanish-speaking countries. In addition to large hotels, there are smaller establishments called *pensiones* or *posadas*. In Spain, visitors may stay in *paradores,* which are often old castles and convents that have been modernized and converted into hotels.

Have students select one of the kinds of hotels you described and find examples of them in travel books. Students may use the information they gather to do one of the following activities:

1. Present a brief report in Spanish, describing the hotel or inn.
2. Prepare an illustrated poster or brochure for a hotel, inn, or *parador*.
3. Draw a map and use symbols to indicate all the locations of a hotel chain in a given country. Include labels for special features of one or more of the hotels.

Small-Group Activity

Small groups of students may elect to do one of the following:

1. Prepare a humorous skit about staying in a hotel.
2. Write a mystery story about tourists and other characters in a hotel.
3. Adapt the game "¿Quién tiene la culpa?" (see "Games and Activities") to a hotel setting.

Primer repaso (pages 90–95)

The review sections combine vocabulary and grammar from the preceding three units. The activities in the section should help students realize that, little by little, they can express and elicit more information about the world around them.

Select activities according to the abilities and learning needs of your students.

A. Una conversación entre familia, *page 90.* Help students guess the meanings of *el precio* and *razonable* from textual context and from their similarities to the words in English. Have students use the illustration to guess the meanings of *la luna* and *los astronautas*.

B. Haciendo planes, *page 91.* Use the questions in this activity for informal assessment and review. Encourage students to elaborate on their answers, rather than give one-sentence answers. You may wish to record a conversation between yourself and a native speaker, using the questions in the activity.

Help students guess the meaning of *esperar* from the contexts of the caption and the photograph. If necessary, they may look it up in the glossary or the classroom dictionary.

CH. ¿Verdad o mentira?, *pages 92–93.* Have students find the answers at the bottom of page 93 and add up their scores.

Students may enjoy creating similar quizzes based on reports they have given in Spanish or on reading selections in the textbook.

D. Haciendo descripciones, *page 93.* Remind students of vocabulary such as weather expressions, *tener* expressions, and verbs for activities.

If students need help, you may write sample sentences on the chalkboard for them to use as models.

F. En el buzón, *pages 94–95.* You may wish to assess comprehension by asking the following questions:

1. ¿A quién visita Alejandro?
2. ¿Dónde está Cali?
3. ¿Cuándo mira las montañas?
4. ¿Qué piensan hacer Alejandro y sus primos?
5. ¿Qué es un aerotaxi?
6. ¿A qué hora comienza la fiesta?
7. ¿A qué hora piensan llegar los primos?
8. ¿Qué dice Alejandro de sus primos?

Extension / Enrichment Activities

Individual Work / Paired Activities

With the aid of your school librarian, have students research films, filmstrips, videotapes, or recordings that interest them. You may wish to set aside a class period as a "media day" to view movies, listen to records, or watch appropriate Spanish-language television programs related to travel in other countries.

Small-Group Activity

Have students prepare mini-dramas centered on a topic from Unidad 1 through Unidad 3. Encourage them to use costumes, props, etc., for their presentations.

Class Activity

Explain to the class that you will set aside one day for them to be the teachers. Have them form committees to plan and present activities for the warm-up, review, culture, learning games, and closing sections of the class period.

Unidad 4 (pages 96–117)

Objectives

After completing this unit, students should be able to:

- identify and name people and items related to going to a bank and a restaurant
- refer to people and things by using indirect object pronouns
- talk about giving by using the present tense of *dar* and use idiomatic meanings of *dar* appropriately
- identify differences in amounts of money in a Spanish-speaking country
- read a chart of monetary units of various Spanish-speaking countries.

Warm-up / Review Activities

Direct Object Pronouns. Ask five to eight volunteers to come to the front of the class and put their hands behind their backs. Show the class an object and walk behind the group, handing the object discreetly to one of the volunteers. Ask the class to guess which person has the object (e.g., *¿Quién tiene la pluma? ¿Quién la tiene?*). Students must use direct object pronouns in their guesses, or the guess does not count (e.g., *La tiene María.*).

Unit Vocabulary. **A.** Make name tags for bank (or restaurant) personnel and ask volunteers to be employees and customers. Have students at their seats identify people, items, and activities in response to TPR commands and questions.

B. Use photographs or pictures from magazines that show things that are open or closed. Have students identify whether the place or object *está abierto* or *está cerrado*. Follow up by asking questions about places in your community (e.g., *¿Están los bancos abiertos o cerrados a las diez de la noche?*).

Unit Grammar. **A.** Ask a series of questions, such as the following, and have students respond with indirect object pronouns:

1. En el banco, ¿a quién pides dinero?
2. En un avión, ¿a quién pides una manta?
3. En el pasillo, tu amigo te saluda. ¿Qué le dices?

B. Use *gustar* and *doler* to practice the indirect object pronouns. Questions may include the following:

1. ¿A quién le gusta jugar al fútbol americano?
2. Si juegas mucho al fútbol, ¿qué te duele?

C. Use play money and TPR commands to practice forms of *dar* (e.g., *Luis, dale dos billetes a Rita. Alumnos, ¿qué hace Luis?*). To vary the activity, have students role-play a restaurant scene with the waiter giving play food to the customers.

Unit Sections

Panorama de vocabulario

You may wish to review vocabulary for food from Unidad 6 and Unidad 7 in *Ya converso más*. Students may make or bring in play money, plastic or toy food items, and other realia to practice the unit vocabulary.

Present the vocabulary in context by making transparencies of the "Panorama de vocabulario" pages in the *Teacher's Resource and Activity Book*. As you project a page, create little stories about the people in the pictures.

¡Aprende el vocabulario! *Exercises A and B, pages 100–101.* After students have completed the exercises, you may wish to use the sentences for dictation practice. Students may also write questions about the "story problems" to ask their classmates in small-group practice sessions.

Exercise C, page 102. Use the number vocabulary cards (*Teacher's Resource and Activity Book*) to review or practice the numbers from one to a thousand.

Usando el español

Referring to Yourself and Others. You may wish to point out that indirect object pronouns answer the questions "to whom?" or "for whom?" after the verb. Direct object pronouns answer the questions "whom?" or "what?" after the verb.

Talking about Giving. Have students notice the indirect object pronouns in the sentences on page 110. Then have them identify the direct objects in the sentences.

Use TPR commands to practice the idiomatic meanings of *dar*. You may explain that in Spanish-speaking countries, adult friends and acquaintances shake hands to say hello and also to say good-by. Also, when strangers are first introduced to one another, they shake hands upon meeting and shake hands again when one of them leaves.

¡A conversar!

Have students use the conversation as a model for creating their own conversations.

La cultura y tú

Invite a guest speaker from a local bank to talk to the class about exchange rates, foreign currencies, and other bank-related topics.

Many of the currencies listed on page 117 are named for national symbols or for historical figures. Have students research the names of currencies from various Spanish-speaking countries and report their findings to the class.

Many currencies are named *el peso.* The name most probably derives from the weight, or *peso,* of gold coins centuries ago. Students may be interested in knowing that in Puerto Rico, the United States dollar is the official currency; however, the people often refer to it as *el peso.*

Informal Assessment Activities

In addition to the assessment activities listed on page T-77, you may wish to include the following:

Have students make cards to exchange in class. They may be friendship cards, holiday cards, or just funny cards. As students exchange cards, ask each one to state to whom they are giving a card (e.g., *Le doy una tarjeta a Diego.*).

Extension / Enrichment Activities

Individual Work

Have students find articles about exchange rates in the newspaper (usually in the travel or financial section). Students should round off the exchange-rate figures and make charts showing the number of *pesos,* etc., it takes to make one U.S. dollar, five dollars, and ten dollars.

Paired Activity

Have students prepare mini-dramas based on communication situations, such as the following.

1. One person is the customer; one person is the waiter or waitress. The customer finishes lunch and discovers that he or she has no money to pay the bill—not even any coins for the tip.
2. One person is the bank teller; one person is the customer. The customer does not receive the correct amount of money from the teller (cashing a check or changing dollars for other currency).
3. Two close friends. One friend has just received $100.00 from a relative. The other friend helps him or her decide on how to spend (or save) the money.

Small-Group Activity

Usually the picture of a national hero or leader is printed on the currency of a country. Have students choose a country and research the people that appear on different denominations of money. The group should report to the class on the people and why they think those individuals were chosen to be on the currency. If possible, have students obtain examples of different currency to show the class.

Class Activity

Plan a field trip to a restaurant with students and their parents. Have students order for their parents. If a field trip is not possible, invite a restaurant owner, waiter/waitress, or cook to talk to the class.

Unidad 5 (pages 118–141)

Objectives

After completing this unit, students should be able to:

- identify and name places in a city
- talk about people and places by employing the different uses of *estar*
- use direct or indirect object pronouns with infinitives
- read simulated encyclopedia articles about cities
- discuss the importance of plazas in Hispanic cities and towns
- describe the significance of Simón Bolívar in South America.

Warm-up / Review Activities

Indirect Object Pronouns. Bring two large beach balls or small, soft foam-rubber balls to class. Toss one ball to a student while stating what you are doing (e.g., *Le tiro la pelota a Rita.*). Have students continue accordingly. Vary the activity by tossing balls to two students (e.g., *Les tiro las pelotas a José y a Enrique.*).

Dar. Instruct students to hand vocabulary cards or classroom objects to one another and then describe their actions as they perform them.

S1: Le doy una tarjeta a Anita.
S2: Le doy las gracias a Luis.

Unit Vocabulary. **A.** Make enlarged photocopies on 11″ × 17″ paper of the "Panorama de vocabulario" pages for Unidad 5 (*Teacher's Resource and Activity Book*). Display the copies and use them for TPR activities and questions.

B. Play a guessing game by describing a location and having students guess what you have described.

T: Me gusta ir a este lugar. Hay cuadros y retratos antiguos. También hay esculturas modernas.

As students gain confidence, ask volunteers to be the leaders.

Unit Grammar. **A.** Use the enlarged photocopies of the "Panorama de vocabulario" pages to practice *estar* (e.g., *¿Dónde está el zoológico? ¿Está a la derecha, a la izquierda, o en el centro de la página?*).

B. As you instruct students to do various TPR activities, ask the class to describe what they are doing, using the present progressive.

T: ¿Qué hacen María y Carlos?
C: Están dibujando un supermercado.

Vary the activity by having students ask the ones responding to the command what they are doing. Occasionally, have students tell you what they are doing.

C. Use pictures from old magazines combined with pantomiming techniques to practice *estar* and adjectives (e.g., *¿Cómo está el hombre? ¿Está contento o está cansado?*). Vary the questions by asking students how they are feeling. After the class has become familiar with the adjectives on page 132, have volunteers lead the activity.

D. Scatter classroom objects around the room and have students put them away, using the following model:

T: Catalina, tienes que poner los libros en el estante.
S1: Voy a (*or* Acabo de) ponerlos en el estante.

Unit Sections

Panorama de vocabulario

You may wish to teach *la banca,* bench, in conjunction with the plaza illustration.

Explain that *el colegio* is a false cognate, meaning "high school" rather than "college." Students may be interested in the following information about schools:

1. *escuela primaria* (elementary school, through the sixth grade)
2. a. *colegio* (high school for students who plan to go on to the university)
   b. *escuela normal* (high school that prepares students to become teachers)
   c. *escuela técnica* (high school for technical careers in offices)
   d. *liceo* (often a combination of junior high or middle school and high school, run by the government)
3. *universidad*

Generally, boys and girls go to separate schools until they reach university level. As a result, city plazas and parks become popular places for young people to meet one another, usually within the safety of a group of friends.

¡Aprende el vocabulario! *Exercise B, page 123.* After students have completed the exercise, ask volunteers to read the story problem aloud. You may wish to use this exercise for dictation practice.

Exercise C, page 124. For younger students, you may wish to list places in your community on the chalkboard.

Exercise D, page 125. Use the questions as the basis of conversations, including follow-up questions. You may wish to record a model conversation between yourself and another teacher or a native speaker.

Usando el español

Talking about People and Places. Basically this section constitutes a review; however, students have not formally discussed the uses of *estar* to this point.

In connection with using *estar* to express temporary conditions, you may wish to teach the phrases *de buen humor* (in a good mood) and *de mal humor* (in a bad mood), in addition to the adjectives on page 132.

¡Vamos a practicar! *Exercise C, page 132.* Write summaries of the results of the exercise on the chalkboard to practice plural forms (e.g., *Rodrigo, Olga y Mateo están nerviosos.*). You may wish to review noun-adjective agreement by contrasting the captioned pictures with the sentences in the *Modelo.*

Referring to People and Things. Point out to students that native speakers use the direct and indirect object pronouns in both positions—preceding the verb phrase and connected to the infinitive—interchangeably. Neither is a preferred method.

T: Quiero conocer a Margarita Pacheco. La quiero conocer. Quiero conocerla.

Stress extensive oral practice of this section to accustom students to hearing the object pronouns used in both positions. You may wish to play the conversations on the Lesson Cassette each day for students to hear other models of the construction in communication contexts.

¡Vamos a practicar! *Exercise B, page 137.* You may wish to review prepositions in conjunction with this exercise.

Answers:

1. a. Voy a ponerlos en el estante.
   b. Los voy a poner en el estante.
2. a. Voy a ponerlo sobre la mesita.
   b. Lo voy a poner sobre la mesita.
3. a. Voy a ponerlas en el ropero.
   b. Las voy a poner en el ropero.
4. a. Voy a ponerlo sobre el estante.
   b. Lo voy a poner sobre el estante.
5. a. Voy a ponerla en la mesita.
   b. La voy a poner en la mesita.
6. a. Voy a ponerlos en la pared.
   b. Los voy a poner en la pared.

After students have written their answers, ask the questions and instruct students to respond with their *a* answers. Repeat the procedure and have students respond with their *b* answers.

Vamos a leer

This reading is based on actual Spanish-language encyclopedia articles. Encourage students to read for general meaning first, and then for specific information in response to comprehension questions, such as the following:

1. ¿Dónde está Ciudad Juárez?
2. ¿Cómo se llama una persona que vive en una ciudad?
3. ¿Cómo se llama la capital del estado Bolívar?
4. ¿Qué quiere decir (*or* ¿Qué significa) la palabra ciudadanía?

Students may be able to guess the meanings of some of the italicized abbreviations: *f., femenino; adj., adjetivo; s., sustantivo* (noun).

La cultura y tú

Have students guess the meaning of *mayor*. In Spain, *la plaza mayor* is always the principal square or plaza in a city.

In Spanish-speaking countries, the main square of a city or town has traditionally been the commercial and social center. It is in the main square that open markets were originally set up on market days. Now, the open markets are usually held in areas away from the main plaza. Historically, the focal point of the plaza is the church or cathedral (*la catedral*) and people congregated in the plaza after services to socialize. Now, people gather in the plazas in the evenings and on weekends to relax and visit with neighbors.

Simón Bolívar is known as *el Libertador*. Born in Caracas in 1783, he completed his studies in Madrid and returned to Venezuela to work toward the country's independence from Spain. He succeeded in freeing Colombia from Spanish rule in 1819, Venezuela in 1821, and Ecuador in 1822. Bolivia was liberated by Bolívar's faithful lieutenant Antonio José de Sucre, for whom one of Bolivia's capitals is named.

Informal Assessment Activities

See page T-77 for basic assessment suggestions. You may wish to use the questions from the following exercises to hold informal interviews with students in pairs or small groups: C, page 124; D, page 125; and D, page 138.

Extension / Enrichment Activities

Individual Work

Have students find words in a Spanish-language encyclopedia or reference book and summarize the general meanings of the articles (in English or Spanish). Remind students to read the articles quickly first, then more slowly to understand the general meaning, and again to identify words or expressions that present barriers to their understanding. Encourage them to use context to guess the meaning of an unfamiliar word before they resort to a dictionary.

Have students write to national tourist agencies for maps of Spanish or Latin American towns. Have students find the main plazas on the maps and note their central locations.

Small-Group Activity

Have students work together to choose a city that interests them and then find out about places in the city of particular interest. Each person in the group should prepare a presentation on one point of interest.

Have students look up other heroes, such as Benito Juárez and José de San Martín, and find places named for them in Mexico and Argentina, respectively.

Suggestions for the Classroom

Convert the classroom into a mock city, possibly moving desks to create a plaza in the middle of the classroom. Enlist students' help in finding or drawing pictures or making model buildings out of construction paper or posterboard. The displays and arrangements may be left up for learning activities in Unidad 6.

Unidad 6 (pages 142–161)

Objectives

After completing this unit, students should be able to:

- identify, name, and describe ways of getting around in a city

- give instructions or commands by using regular affirmative familiar commands (review)
- give instructions or commands by using regular negative familiar commands
- discuss the metric system used in Spanish-speaking countries.

Warm-up / Review Activities

***Object Pronouns* / Estar.** Read short descriptions of actions and then act them out. Have students answer questions about the descriptions using *estar* and indirect and direct object pronouns appropriately.

1. Elisa está caminando. Está muy contenta. Ella va a visitar a su abuela. Va a darle una tarjeta de cumpleaños.
2. Juan está dibujando un edificio. Va a pintarlo de muchos colores. Piensa darle el cuadro a su papá.
3. Julia no conoce bien a Raúl. Está un poco nerviosa. Raúl está nervioso también. Quiere invitarla a una fiesta.

Unit Vocabulary. **A.** Post signs for the cardinal directions around the classroom and give TPR commands (e.g., *Corre al norte. Anda al sur.*).

B. On the chalkboard (or on a large sheet of posterboard) draw a map of the area around your school and use it to ask questions.

T: Rosa, muéstrame el supermercado. Cuenta las cuadras entre la escuela y el mercado. ¿A cuántas cuadras queda el supermercado?
S: Queda a tres cuadras.

Follow up by asking the class if the place is north, south, east, or west of the school.

C. Have students face one another and take turns asking and answering questions about what is in front of or behind them.

S1: ¿Qué me queda atrás?
S2: La pared te queda atrás. ¿Qué me queda atrás?
S1: El escritorio de la maestra te queda atrás.

Unit Grammar. **A.** Write one or more mock assignments on the chalkboard (e.g., *Leer todo el libro.*) and have students tell one another the assignment for the day. This may be presented as a chain drill or with pairs of volunteers.

B. As students enter the classroom, give each one an affirmative or negative command; then follow up with the opposite command.

Unit Sections

Panorama de vocabulario

If students are interested, you may wish to teach the other cardinal directions: *noreste, sureste, suroeste,* and *noroeste.*

You may also wish to teach the prepositions *delante de* and *detrás de* if students try to express that something is in front or in back of them:

1. Los pupitres me quedan adelante. Los pupitres están delante de mí.
2. La pizarra me queda atrás. La pizarra está detrás de mí.

See the annotations on pages 144–45 for additional presentation suggestions.

Usando el español

Giving Instructions or Commands.

Affirmative familiar commands were first presented in Unidad 12 of *Ya converso más*. The only variations presented here are for the reflexive verbs. You may wish to prepare and distribute a list of reflexive verbs with regular affirmative commands. Help students establish the association of the stressed syllable in the spoken word with the accented syllable in the written word.

Giving Negative Commands. Until students learn the present tense of the subjunctive mood, the present tense indicative *tú* forms serve as adequate models for forming regular negative familiar commands.

Extensive practice with TPR commands is recommended to accustom students to the negative familiar command forms. You may wish to contrast affirmative and negative commands by issuing a command and then pretending to change your mind (e.g., *Camina a la pizarra. ¡No, no! ¡No camines a la pizarra! Camina a la puerta.*).

¡A conversar!

Students may use the conversation as a model to create their own conversations.

La cultura y tú

Students may be interested in learning about the history of the metric system. The metric system was first established as a result of the French Revolution. For over a century, scientists had discussed the creation of a system of measurement. In 1799, the metric system was legally adopted in France. Its use gradually spread throughout the world. The United States and Great Britain are virtually the only countries in the world that do not use the metric system.

In October 1960, the old metric system was replaced by the new International System of Units. Under the new system, the names remain the same, but the definitions of the units were changed to respond to the needs of rapidly advancing science and technology.

Informal Assessment Activities

See page T-77 for suggestions for informal assessment activities. In addition, you may wish to do the following:

1. Take students to the gymnasium or another open, uncluttered area, and have them practice giving commands to one another, alternating between affirmative and negative familiar commands.

2. Ask students to draw a map and then write directions from their homes to their favorite restaurants, museums, parks, or movie theaters.

Extension / Enrichment Activities

Individual Work / Paired Activities

- Have students choose a country and prepare a map, similar to the one on page 146, labeling cities and the distances between them in miles or kilometers.
- Students may research lists of weights and measures in several Spanish-English dictionaries and prepare a large chart of the measures in Spanish for display in the classroom.

Small-Group Activities

Have students draw one map of their community and then label their homes. Each person in the group should give directions for going from one person's house to another's.

Suggestions for the Classroom

In addition to the decorations for Unidad 5, you may wish to make signs with names of cities and the distances between them and post the signs around the classroom. The signs may be used to practice commands with follow-up questions.

Segundo repaso
(pages 162–167)

A. Una conversación entre amigos, *page 162*. Before students read the conversation, have them listen to it on the Lesson Cassette. Have students scan the conversation for examples of commands.

Ask students if anyone has ever given them a surprise party. If so, elicit descriptions of how they felt, if they were truly surprised, etc. Then have students form pairs or small groups to prepare their own conversations.

B. ¿Qué haces?, *page 163*. Review with the class the question of friendship in Hispanic cultures. Friends are the most important people outside a person's family. How do students think a Venezuelan or Mexican student might respond to the situations in the activity?

C. ¿Quién está perdido?, *page 164*. Before students attempt to answer the questions, you may need to practice giving directions, using locations on the map not mentioned in the questions.

Answers will vary. The following are possible responses:

1. Camina al oeste por dos cuadras.
2. Cruza la plaza y camina al norte por una cuadra.
3. Primero, camina al norte por una cuadra. Luego, dobla a la izquierda. (La plaza te queda adelante.) Dobla a la derecha y camina al norte por dos cuadras. Por último, dobla a la izquierda y camina derecho una cuadra.
4. Camina derecho al norte por dos cuadras. (Un restaurante te va a quedar adelante.) Dobla a la derecha y camina al este por una cuadra. (Un edificio de apartamentos va a estar a la

izquierda.) Dobla a la izquierda y camina derecho una cuadra. (Mi casa está en la esquina a la derecha.)

5. Camina tres cuadras al norte. Mi casa está a la derecha en una esquina.

You may wish to point out that people in Spanish-speaking countries often use "landmarks" in giving directions, rather than the cardinal directions (e.g., *Camina una cuadra y dobla a la derecha en la casa rosada. Luego, sigue derecho dos cuadras.)*.

D. Aun más frustraciones, *page 165.* Extend the activity by having students restate their answers by placing the direct object pronoun in front of the phrase (e.g., *Las acabo de comprar.*).

E. ¿Qué falta en las oraciones?, *page 166.* After students have completed the activity, you may wish to use it as dictation practice. Help students guess the different meaning of *llevar* in the paragraph ("to take").

G. ¿Eres práctico o eres romántico?, *page 167.* Have students make up quizzes for their classmates, based on different traits (e.g., *¿Eres paciente o impaciente? ¿Eres tímido o eres valiente?*).

Extension / Enrichment Activities

Individual Work

Have students interview their families to find out where family members want to go over the weekend. Then have them draw a map from their house to their destinations and write directions.

Paired / Small-Group Activity

Have students create conversations based on a situation in which one person knows he or she has to do something and another person either acts as a good influence or a bad influence. You may wish to give students a list of possibilities:

1. Tienes que estudiar, pero tu amigo te invita al cine.
2. Tienes que limpiar la casa, pero quieres jugar al tenis con tu amiga.
3. Tienes que lavarte el pelo, pero quieres ver tu programa de televisión favorito.
4. Tienes que ir al supermercado para comprar comida para la cena. Tus amigos te invitan a comer helados en el parque.

Students may wish to dress up as "angels" and "devils" in the roles of advice-givers. Encourage students to have fun with the activity.

Unidad 7 (pages 168–187)

Objectives

After completing this unit, students should be able to:

- ▶ identify and name places, people, and items related to shopping and buying gifts
- ▶ talk about actions in the past by using the preterite tense of regular *-ar* verbs and *-ar* verbs with spelling changes in the preterite
- ▶ read about and discuss shopping in open-air markets and the custom of bargaining
- ▶ describe special handmade items from a Central American country.

Warm-up / Review Activities

Object Pronouns. **A.** Write a list of questions on the chalkboard. Ask volunteers to read a question aloud and then answer it, using an indirect or direct object pronoun. Questions may include:

1. ¿Quieres conocer a (*name of popular singer*)?
2. ¿A quién le das las gracias por tu ropa?
3. Cuando llegas a casa, ¿dónde vas a poner tus libros?
4. ¿A quién le vas a pedir ayuda si no comprendes tus tareas esta noche?

B. Have students write the names of five people they would like to meet. Each student will make a statement and follow it with a question directed to a classmate:

S: Algún día quiero conocer al presidente de los Estados Unidos. Enrique, ¿quieres conocerlo también?

The classmate named should answer the question, then choose a name from his list to make a statement, followed by a question to a different classmate. The lists may be saved for paired or small-group activities on subsequent days.

Commands. Make a transparency of a map that students prepared for Unidad 6 and use it to practice affirmative and negative commands. Use an erasable marker for students to trace their route from one place to another, according to your commands. To vary the activity, have one student be the "driver" and another, the "navigator." If the person giving directions hesitates, encourage the driver to ask questions (e.g., *¿Qué hago? ¿Doblo a la derecha o a la izquierda?*).

Unit Vocabulary. **A.** Distribute vocabulary cards (*Teacher's Resource and Activity Book*) to students. Use the following model, explaining that each item is a gift for someone else:

T: ¿Quién tiene las sandalias?
S1: Yo tengo las sandalias. *or* Yo las tengo.
T: ¿A quién le vas a dar las sandalias?
S1: Voy a darle las sandalias a mi hermana.

B. Write the words for the stores on the chalkboard. Have students call out items or people you could find in each store. On subsequent days, have students write the words under the corresponding stores.

Unit Grammar. **A.** Point to the preceding day's date on the calendar. Ask questions such as the following:

1. ¿Hablaste con tus amigos ayer?
2. ¿Compraste algo ayer?
3. ¿Adónde caminaste ayer?
4. ¿Qué estudiaste ayer?
5. ¿Tomaste el desayuno ayer?

After students gain confidence, have them elaborate on their answers (e.g., *Sí, hablé con Juan y María ayer. Hablamos una hora.*).

B. Issue different TPR commands (using regular *-ar* verbs) to two students. Follow up by issuing commands or asking questions:

T: Olga, camina a la ventana. Alberto, salta a mi escritorio. (*Students perform appropriate actions.*) Susana, señala a la persona que saltó. Luis, señala a la persona que caminó.

On subsequent days, issue the same command to two students in order to practice the plural forms.

C. Play "El ahorcado" (see "Games and Activities") to practice *-ar* verbs with spelling changes in the preterite.

Unit Sections

Panorama de vocabulario

Have students brainstorm a list of things a customer might say and a list of things a salesclerk might say. After the lists are complete, students may copy them in notebooks for reference in preparing role-play activities.

You may wish to teach the following constructions and words in conjunction with this unit: *¿A cómo es (son) el disco (los zapatos)?* (How much is [are] the record [the shoes]?), *¡Es una ganga!* (It's a bargain!), *estar de venta* (to be on sale), *un descuento de——por ciento* (a——percent discount), *precio(s) rebajado(s)* (reduced price[s]).

Cultural Note: People who live in cities and towns in Spanish-speaking countries are especially fashion conscious. Much attention is paid to being well groomed and having the right accessories. Ready-to-wear clothing is increasingly available; however, people still search for fashion magazines and take pictures of the styles they want to *modistas* (seamstresses) and *sastres* (tailors) to have their clothes made. A dress or suit and the accessories must be *a la última moda* (in the latest style).

¡Aprende el vocabulario! *Exercise A, page 172.* After students have completed the activity, have them role-play the situation, using vocabulary cards or real items. Encourage students to use direct object pronouns whenever possible.

Exercise C, page 173. Review the verb *costar* and have one student be a salesclerk and another, a customer. They may act out the parts, using the following model:

S1: ¿Cuánto cuesta el disco?
S2: El disco cuesta diez dólares.
S1: ¡Diez dólares! ¡Es muy caro!

Encourage students to make up other items and prices.

Los sonidos del idioma

Help students to note the number of syllables in the examples and to relate the natural stress to the number of syllables.

You may wish to write the following rules on the chalkboard:

1. If a word ends in a vowel, *n*, or *s*, you stress the second-to-the-last syllable.
2. If the word ends in a consonant (not *n* or *s*), you stress the last syllable.

Usando el español

Talking about Actions in the Past. You may wish to precede the grammar presentation by teaching words such as *ayer, ayer por la mañana, ayer por la tarde, anoche,* and *la semana pasada.*

Explain that all the verbs students have learned to this point are in the present tense. Now they will learn the verb forms (endings) for the past tense called the *preterite*.

Supplement the illustrations and sentences on page 176 with real-life examples. (You may wish to display a large classroom calendar on the wall during this and subsequent units.)

¡Vamos a practicar! *Exercise B, page 178.* After students have completed the exercise, have them ask you the same questions to practice the *usted* form. You may also follow up the exercise by asking what Óscar did (e.g., *¿Ayer tomó el desayuno Óscar?*).

Exercise C, page 179. Before you ask students to talk about their own activities of the preceding weekend, you may wish to write a list of regular *-ar* verbs on the chalkboard.

Talking about Other Actions in the Past. You may remind students of the verb *colgar* from *Ya converso más.* Have them write the conjugation for the verb *colgar* on the chalkboard.

You may wish to explain that many of the spelling changes in Spanish result from rules of pronunciation.

¡Vamos a practicar! *Exercise A, page 183.* After students have completed the exercise, have them ask one another about what Julio did while he was grounded (e.g., *¿A qué jugó Julio todas las tardes?*).

Exercise B, page 184. After students have completed the exercise orally, you may wish to use the story sentences for dictation practice. Have students exchange papers to correct spelling, paying close attention to the verb forms.

¡A conversar!

Have students make up conversations based on the model. You may have advanced students make up a conversation between Elisa and the vendor as she tries to return the blouse.

La cultura y tú

Open-air markets are very common in Spanish-speaking countries. Usually, each town has a market that takes place one day a week. Larger cities have several markets in different locations and on different days of the week. Occasionally, the markets will specialize in one kind of merchandise, such as produce or handmade crafts.

Bartering is so ingrained in Spanish-speaking cultures that people are amazed at (and sometimes disdainful of) tourists who pay full price. Sometimes bartering does not always result in a reduced price. Often, the customer will talk the vendor into including another item for free (e.g., *¿No me regalas un par de aretes?*).

The girls in the photographs on page 187 are traditional weavers from Guatemala. Using the traditional technique of backstrap weaving (with a loom called *el telar de palitos*), they produce colorful, elaborate patterns. The backstrap loom is attached at one end to a tree or post; the other end is attached to a strap that passes around the back or hips of the weaver.

The *huipiles* worn by the girls in the photos are embroidered in traditional village patterns. Each village has its own patterns and, within the patterns, various symbols have special meanings. Fellow Guatemalans can look at the clothing of a person and tell where he or she lives by the combination of colors, symbols, patterns, etc.

The livelihood of a village sometimes depends solely on the crafts it sells in local or tourist markets, in addition to what it sells to buyers for gift stores and chains in the United States and elsewhere.

In a crafts store or library, you may be able to find traditional Guatemalan embroidery or weaving patterns. Students might enjoy coloring in photocopies of the patterns to represent their own "village."

Informal Assessment Activities

In addition to the suggestions listed on page T-77, you may wish to hold informal discussions with individuals about their activities on the preceding day. Have them write down their answers or describe their activities after they have talked to you.

Extension / Enrichment Activities

Individual Work

Have students write a paragraph about gifts they received for their birthdays or a holiday. Give them the verb *regalar* and a model to work with, and remind them to consult the charts in the textbook if they do not remember a verb form.

Modelo: Para mi cumpleaños, mis padres me regalaron un disco compacto.

Paired / Small-Group Activities

- Students may prepare conversations or skits centered on shopping activities. Encourage them to bring in real items, make signs, and dress up for their roles.
- Have students choose a country and research the crafts that are unique to that country. Students may include information about the origins of the crafts and special skills needed in making the items.

Class Activity

Take a field trip to a local flea market. Encourage students to practice bartering. Follow up the field trip with how they felt about the experience—was it fun, embarrassing, too time-consuming? Discuss what it might be like to live in a rural area of a Spanish-speaking country and have to barter for everything you buy, from rice to clothing.

Unidad 8 (pages 188–211)

Objectives

After completing this unit, students should be able to:

- name activities and items related to the beach and water sports
- talk about past actions, using the preterite tense of *-er* and *-ir* verbs
- talk about specific items and people by using demonstrative adjectives
- talk about what things are for by using the preposition *para*
- read a simulated magazine article about the discovery of the sunken ship *Nuestra Señora de Atocha*
- read about and discuss the land and attractions of Baja California.

Warm-up / Review Activities

Verbs. **A.** Issue TPR commands to students and follow up with questions about what they did:

T: Juan, dibuja una joya en la pizarra. (Student draws.) ¿Qué dibujaste?
S: Dibujé una joya.
T: Alumnos, ¿qué dibujó Juan?
C: Dibujó una joya.

B. By rows, have students make one statement about an activity they did yesterday. Stipulate that each student in a row must use a different *-ar* verb. This activity may be converted into a game, with points awarded to rows.

Unit Vocabulary. **A.** Write two questions on the chalkboard (e.g., *¿Qué puedes ver en la playa?* and *¿Qué puedes hacer en la playa?*) and have students either call out or write appropriate vocabulary words.

B. Play a guessing game by describing an item or an activity and having students guess what it is:

1. Me los pongo cuando hace mucho sol.
2. Esta actividad es como patinar sobre el agua. Necesitas una lancha que va muy rápido.
3. Si no usas la crema de broncear, puedes estar en esta condición.

Unit Grammar. **A.** Call out a statement in the present tense and have students respond with a statement in the preterite tense. You may wish to practice *-er* verbs on one day and *-ir* verbs on the next.

T: Hoy ustedes no corren.
C: Ayer sí corrimos.

B. Use TPR commands followed by questions:

T: Rolando, camina al pasillo, por favor. *(Student leaves.)* ¿Quién salió del salón de clase?
C: Rolando salió.

As students respond more readily, have volunteers ask the questions after you have given a command.

C. Read a series of sentences and ask students comprehension questions.

1. Juana sale de la casa a las ocho. Corre a la parada de autobús. No quiere caminar porque vive muy lejos de la escuela.

Preguntas

1. ¿A qué hora salió Juana de la casa?
2. ¿Adónde corrió ella?
3. ¿Por qué caminó?

D. Display objects around the classroom and have students describe them, using demonstrative adjectives and the preposition *para*. Items may include three posters, three tubes of suntan lotion, three shells, three pairs of shoes, etc.

Unit Sections

Panorama de vocabulario

Make transparencies of the "Panorama de vocabulario" pages for Unidad 8 in the *Teacher's Resource and Activity Book*. Following the initial presentation and practice of vocabulary with TPR commands, project the pictures and have students make up sentences about them.

You may review uses of *estar* with the vocabulary:

1. *Estar quemado* or *bronceado* are examples of temporary conditions.
2. *La mujer está tomando el sol.* This is an example of *estar* and a gerund used to talk about what is happening now.
3. *Las personas están en la playa. Estar* is used to show location in this example.

¡Aprende el vocabulario! *Exercise D, page 195.* After students have completed the exercise, instruct them to read the sentences out loud. This exercise may be used for dictation practice on subsequent days.

Usando el español

Expressing Other Actions in the Past. Have students practice using the preterite *-er* and *-ir* verb endings by conjugating verbs not mentioned on pages 198–99 (e.g., *comer, comprender, abrir, recibir*).

Encourage all students to try all the exercises on pages 200–201. You may wish to divide the class into mixed-ability groups to work on exercise C.

Talking about People and Things. Use classroom items to demonstrate the meanings of the demonstrative adjectives. You may also go for a walk with students and talk about the houses on the street or the parked cars, etc., using the demonstrative adjectives (e.g., *Esta casa está muy cerca de nosotros. Esa casa está más lejos de nosotros. Aquella casa blanca está muy lejos de nosotros.*).

¡Vamos a practicar! *Exercise C, page 205.* Model the exercise with an advanced student. You may need to explain to students that the size of each item relates to its distance from the speakers (i.e., the smallest items are the farthest away).

Talking about What Things Are For. You may wish to practice and reinforce each use of *para* separately by giving numerous examples and having volunteers answer questions based on your examples.

Write some of the examples on the chalkboard and have students describe how *para* is used in each example.

¡Vamos a practicar! *Exercise B, page 208.*

Answers:

1. P: ¿Para qué usas la plancha?
   R: La uso para planchar la ropa.
2. P: ¿Para qué usas las llaves?
   R: Las uso para abrir la puerta.
3. P: ¿Para qué usas el bolígrafo?
   R: Lo uso para escribir.
4. P: ¿Para qué usas el horno?
   R: Lo uso para cocinar.
5. P: ¿Para qué usas el televisor?
   R: Lo uso para mirar mis programas favoritos.
6. P: ¿Para qué usas las sandalias?
   R: Las uso para caminar.

Vamos a leer

Before reading the simulated magazine article in class, you may wish to teach or review how to state years in Spanish.

To assess students' understanding of the reading, ask comprehension questions, such as the following:

1. ¿Qué es *Nuestra Señora de Atocha*—un barco, una iglesia o un museo?
2. ¿Quiénes encontraron oro y plata en la América Central y la América del Sur?
3. ¿Sí o no? Todos los barcos volvieron a España.
4. ¿Quién encontró al *Atocha*?
5. ¿Qué encontraron los buceadores dentro del antiguo barco?
6. ¿Qué aprendemos de los barcos?

Students may be interested in learning of the history behind the *Atocha* story. The Spanish explorers did not go to the New World to seek religious freedom or to establish colonies. Their main interest centered on taking back to Spain all the riches they could find. The *Atocha* was just one of many treasure ships that never returned to home port.

The wreckage of *Nuestra Señora de Atocha* was first discovered in 1973 by Mel Fisher after a great deal of archival detective work and careful searching off the Florida Keys. Although its discovery revealed millions of dollars worth of treasure, the real treasure is the glimpse of life during the seventeenth century gained through studying the artifacts.

La cultura y tú

In recent years, Baja California has become a popular vacation spot for tourists from the United States. For many years, it has been a popular vacation destination for Mexican tourists. The attraction of the desert, the sea, and the gray whales has drawn people to this peninsula in increasing numbers.

You may wish to have students read some of the early accounts of the peninsula and its surrounding waters in the books by Erle Stanley Gardner, the creator of "Perry Mason," and John Steinbeck, who wrote an account of a nature expedition into the Sea of Cortez.

Informal Assessment Activities

In addition to the activities suggested on page T-77, you may wish to distribute blank calendar pages and have students write their activities for one week. Use the calendars to conduct informal interviews or assign a writing project.

Extension / Enrichment Activities

Individual Work

Students may research the Spanish explorers and the early Spanish settlements in the New World, including the United States. Among the explorers, students may choose from the following list:

1. Christopher Columbus (Cristóbal Colón)
2. Vasco Núñez de Balboa
3. Hernán Cortés
4. Francisco Pizarro
5. Juan Ponce de León

Paired / Small-Group Activities

- Students may reread the "La cultura y tú" section for Unidad 1 (pages 44–45) and select a beach area or town to research. Have them describe the sports that are popular at the different beaches and towns. Students should be able to present their reports entirely in Spanish.

- Have students prepare posters with the theme of good health and good habits. Encourage them to use the *Se prohibe. . .* construction to word their main message.

Unidad 9 (pages 212–231)

Objectives

After completing this unit, students should be able to:

- identify and name places and items associated with the country
- talk about past actions by using the preterite tense of the irregular verbs *ir, ser,* and *dar*
- talk about activities by using the preposition *por*
- read a simulated excerpt from a history text about Angel Falls
- read about and discuss a national park in Costa Rica.

Warm-up / Review Activities

Demonstrative Adjectives. Place various stacks of cards at different distances from you. Use TPR commands to practice.

T: Jorge, ven acá. Toma aquellas tarjetas. Dale las tarjetas a Susana.
Tomás, ven acá. Toma estas tarjetas y pásales las tarjetas a las personas en la primera fila.

On subsequent days, vary the items you use for the activity.

Verbs. **A.** Have volunteers pantomime various activities. Students at their seats must guess the activities by asking questions and using verbs in the preterite tense. It does not count if a student guesses correctly but has used the present tense.

B. Distribute action pictures from magazines to pairs of students. Give them three minutes to write down all the questions they can, using verbs in the preterite tense. You may suggest that they write questions they would like to ask of the people in the pictures. On other occasions, you may repeat the activity, but have students write descriptive statements, instead of questions.

Para. Bring to class little trinkets or inexpensive items and make gift tags with students' names. Select students to be gift-givers as their classmates come to the front of the class to receive their gifts. Each student must point to a gift and ask *¿Para quién es el regalo?* The gift-giver must read the tag and respond.

Unit Vocabulary. **A.** Have students draw scenes in response to your TPR commands (e.g., *Rosita, dibuja un salto de agua.*).

B. Write two categories on the chalkboard: *Me gusta* and *No me gusta.* Have students name things they like and don't like about the countryside and then write the names under the corresponding category.

Unit Grammar. **A.** Give students commands and have them respond to questions about what they did (e.g., *¿Adónde fuiste? ¿Qué le diste a la bibliotecaria?*).

B. During this unit, choose an assistant for each day. On subsequent days, ask the class to name who your assistant was (e.g., *¿Quién fue mi asistente el lunes? ¿Quién fue mi asistente ayer?*).

C. Use vocabulary cards from the unit (*Teacher's Resource and Activity Book*). (Be sure there are at least two of every card distributed to students.) Each student should receive two cards that are not the same. The object of the activity is to gain two of the same cards by exchanging cards with other students (and using the preposition *por*).

D. Have students help you plan a class period by stating what activities they would like to do and for how long.

T: ¿Por cuánto tiempo podemos cantar el viernes?

S: Podemos cantar por cinco minutos.

As students call out activities and times, have your assistant write them on the chalkboard.

Unit Sections

Panorama de vocabulario

You may wish to rent or obtain a videotape on tropical life in a Spanish-speaking country (such as a videotaped television nature program). Turn the sound off and ask questions about what is appearing on the screen.

You may also bring in items suitable for backpacking and picnics to use for role-play activities. Students may be able to contribute toy animals or toy farms, or make models as extra-credit projects.

Usando el español

Using Irregular Verbs to Talk about Past Actions. If students need additional practice with the irregular verb forms in the preterite, you may wish to use exercises from units in which the verbs were first reviewed or taught and have students change the sentences and questions from the present to the preterite tense.

As often as possible, reinforce the direct and indirect object pronouns with the preterite of *dar.*

¡Vamos a practicar! *Exercise A, page 222.* Divide the class into small groups and have them practice interviewing one another about past vacations or trips.

Using* por *to Talk about Actions. You may point out to students that native speakers of Spanish often drop the word *por* when they talk about how long something lasted (e.g., *Estuvimos en el autobús [por] dos horas.*). The word *por,* however, is understood.

¡Vamos a practicar! ***Exercise A, page 226.*** Personalize the exercise by having students answer questions such as the following:

1. ¿Qué estudiaste por la mañana?
2. ¿Dónde estuviste ayer por la mañana?
3. ¿Qué estudió tu mejor amigo por la tarde?
4. ¿Estudiaste por la noche?

Exercise C, page 227. After students complete the exercise orally, have them write their answers.

Answers:

1. P: ¿Cuánto pagaste por los discos?
   R: Pagué diez y siete dólares.
2. P: ¿Cuánto pagaste por el collar?
   R: Pagué veinte y cinco dólares.
3. P: ¿Cuánto pagaste por la camisa?
   R: Pagué ocho dólares.
4. P: ¿Cuánto pagaste por las bolsas?
   R: Pagué once dólares.
5. P: ¿Cuánto pagaste por el llavero?
   R: Pagué un dólar.
6. P: ¿Cuánto pagaste por los casetes?
   R: Pagué diez y seis dólares.

Exercise D, page 227. You may wish to write a list of possible jobs on the chalkboard:

1. cortar el pasto (*mow the lawn*)
2. cuidar a los niños (*babysitting*)
3. lavar el auto (*wash the car*)
4. hacer las compras (*do the shopping*)
5. repartir los periódicos (*deliver newspapers*)

¡A divertirnos!

Unlike the idyllic scene in the illustration on page 228, it is thought that the expression originated centuries ago from the practice of meat vendors of substituting cat for rabbit or hare. Equivalents in English might be "Don't take any wooden nickels" or a "wolf in sheep's clothing."

Vamos a leer

You may have students state the main idea in each paragraph. The following questions may be used to assess comprehension:

1. ¿Adónde fue Jimmy Angel en 1937?
2. ¿Por qué voló muy cerca del salto de agua?
3. Su avión aterrizó sin problema, ¿no?
4. ¿Por cuánto tiempo caminó por la selva?
5. ¿Adónde lo llevaron los indios?
6. ¿Dónde está el avión hoy en día?

La cultura y tú

In the late 1960s, Costa Rica established a system of national parks that has become one of the most extensive in Latin America. Eight percent of the country's land is part of the national park system. The parks protect a variety of plants and animals that live in the many climatic zones. Among them are 205 species of mammals, 150 amphibians, 210 reptiles, about 700 butterflies, and 850 species of birds. These are only the species that have been studied and classified! A major reason for protecting the land is also to protect the suspected countless species that have never been studied or sighted before.

Students may have seen nature programs about sea turtles. Tortuguero Park on Costa Rica's Caribbean coast and Santa Rosa Park on the Pacific coast are the sites of large sea turtle nesting areas.

Informal Assessment Activities

See page T-77 for assessment activity suggestions. You may also wish to do the following:

1. Have students tell you about a trip in the country, a walk in the woods, a picnic at a park, etc. Hold the discussion in a small group, approximating the kind of conversation people might have at a social gathering. Encourage students to ask one another follow-up questions.
2. Ask students about something they did the night before. Follow up with questions about how long they did it, with or for whom they did it, etc.

Extension / Enrichment Activities

Individual Work / Paired Activity

Have students choose one of the vocabulary pictures on pages 214 and 215. Instruct them to write a little story about the picture they chose. The stories may be humorous, serious, or exciting.

Class Activity

Invite a zookeeper, conservationist, or farmer to talk to the class. If the talk is given in English, have students write summaries of the talk in Spanish or list in Spanish as much information as they can remember. Collect the summaries and use them to compile a master summary for distribution to the class. The master summary could be used as the basis of role-play activities or dictation practice.

Tercer repaso

(pages 232–237)

A. Una conversación entre amigos, *page 232.* Have students work in pairs to create a conversation based on the model on this page. If students are interested in saying that they become as red as a lobster, you may wish to teach another meaning of *ponerse*, to become (e.g., *Me puse tan rojo como una langosta.*). (The preterite tense of *poner* will be taught in Unidad 13.)

B. ¿Y tú?, *page 233.* After students have completed the activity orally, have them write their answers.

If you do the extension activity on page 233, you may try to tape-record or make a videotape of the presentations.

C. Una excursión a las tiendas, *page 234.* For practice, have students read the story problem, using appropriate intonation and inflection.

You may wish to have advanced students make up a story exercise for their classmates to complete.

D. Una entrevista parcial, *page 235.* Have students choose partners and role-play the interviewer and the photographer.

E. ¿Qué les preguntas a los fotógrafos?, *page 235.* Encourage students to use the present tense in some questions and the preterite tense in others. For additional practice, have students make up questions about the photographs on pages 168–69, 188–89, and 212–13.

H. En el buzón, *page 237.* Students may find pictures in old magazines and write brief paragraphs describing them to a friend. Have students paste the pictures on a blank index card and write the description on the back of the card, including their name. Students may exchange pictures, or you may set up a classroom mailbox for students to "receive mail."

Extension / Enrichment Activities

In addition to the activities listed on the textbook pages, you may wish to do the following:

1. Have students work in pairs or small groups to make up a board game based on a shopping spree, a trip through the jungle, or a day at the beach. You may wish to have some of the better games laminated for durability.
2. Students may make maps that highlight different features of the Spanish-speaking world. For example, one student may make a map that features rain forests in Latin America; another may make a map showing areas where different handcrafted items are made. Maps may be displayed in the classroom or you may wish to have color photocopies made of them to be put in a binder or large book.
3. If students were interested in the early explorers, you may suggest that they research the Indian cultures that the explorers encountered or find information on the early missionaries to the New World.

Unidad 10 (pages 238–257)

Objectives

After completing this unit, students should be able to:

- name different sports and the people who participate in them
- make comparisons by using the irregular forms of *bueno* and *malo (mejor, peor)*
- describe something emphatically by adding the absolute superlative endings *(-ísimo, -ísima)* to adjectives
- read about and discuss the popularity of soccer in Spanish-speaking countries and the importance of the World Cup tournament.

Warm-up / Review Activities

Verbs. **A.** Write statements on index cards and distribute one card to each student. Give students one or two minutes to think of a question that the statement would answer. Call on individuals to say their question and then read the statement on the card. Statements should elicit forms of regular and irregular verbs in the preterite tense.

B. Have volunteers take turns giving TPR commands and then asking their classmates what the individuals did. Encourage students to use *por favor* after their commands.

S: Ana, escribe la palabra *caimán* en la pizarra, por favor. *(Student writes the word.)* Lidia, ¿qué escribió Ana? Raúl, ¿adónde fue Ana para escribir la palabra? Ana, ¿por cuánto tiempo estuviste cerca de la pizarra?

Unit Vocabulary. **A.** Each day, award medals for asking the best question, giving the funniest answer, etc. On the following days, have students tell you who was the *campeón* or *campeona* for the preceding day.

B. Write several fill-in-the-blank sentences high up on the chalkboard. Distribute vocabulary cards *(Teacher's Resource and Activity Book)*. If students have a card that they think will fit in a blank, they should stand under the blank in front of the chalkboard. Ask volunteers to read the "completed" sentences.

Unit Grammar. **A.** Name several famous athletes in the same sport. Have students vote on which athlete is the best one or the worst one.

B. Make a statement that includes the word *muy* (e.g., *Esta palabra es muy difícil.*). Have students restate the sentence using the absolute superlative.

Unit Sections

Panorama de vocabulario

Enlist students' help in bringing in items related to various sports. You may also wish to review vocabulary for sports from Unidad 10 of *Ya converso más*.

Bring in sports sections from Spanish-language newspapers and have students identify words they know in the articles. If possible, show examples of Spanish-language television broadcasts of soccer games, wrestling, and other sports events.

See the annotations on page 240 for a story that uses the vocabulary in context.

¡Aprende el vocabulario! *Exercise A, page 243.* For writing practice, have students change their answers from the present to the preterite tense (e.g., *¿Qué fueron a ver?* / *Fueron a ver el salto de altura.*).

Exercise C, page 244. Students' answers may vary. Accept reasonable responses.

Answers:

1. El campeón recibe una medalla de oro.
2. Necesitas una bicicleta para practicar el ciclismo.
3. Sí.
4. Sí.
5. Los alpinistas practican su deporte en las montañas.
6. Si sabes nadar, puedes participar en la natación.
7. Sí.
8. Si eres boxeador, practicas en un gimnasio.
9. Los espectadores siempre gritan.
10. Tienes que ganar todas las carreras para ser campeón.

Exercise D, page 245. Extend the exercise by changing some of the questions to ask about the preceding year (e.g., *¿Practicaste un deporte el verano pasado? ¿Fuiste espectador o participaste en los deportes?*).

Usando el español

Making Comparisons. You may wish to extend the presentation to include the adverbs *bien* and *mal.*

1. Samuel corrió bien, pero Paco corrió mejor que él.
2. Adela nadó mal ayer, pero Luisa nadó peor que ella.
3. Salí bien en la carrera, pero ellos salieron mejor que yo.

You may point out to students that similar comparisons in English use irregular forms also (i.e., good, better, best; bad, worse, worst).

Emphasizing the Nature of Things. Exaggerate the words ending in *-ísimo* to convey the feeling, as well as the meaning, of the absolute superlative.

Use real-life examples of school assembly programs, athletic events, television programs, etc., to practice the absolute superlative, as well as to review noun-adjective agreement in number and gender.

¡A conversar!

Students may create their own conversations around the theme of *la locura por ganar.* Encourage them to continue the conversation between Lupe and Rudy. For example, what would happen if Lupe finally won a gold medal or trophy?

¡Conversa tú!

Continue the activity by having students complete the following sentences:

1. En los deportes, es más importante . . .
2. En todas las actividades, es mejor . . .

Discuss the answers in class.

La cultura y tú

Soccer is at least as popular in the Spanish-speaking world as football is in the United States. Each local and national team has its ardent fans *(aficionados, fanáticos, entusiastas)* who regularly attend the games, watch them on television, or listen to them on the radio.

The World Cup soccer tournament is held every four years and is one of the most watched events in the world. The Spanish-speaking world is generally well represented among the countries whose teams qualify for the tournament. In 1978 and 1986, the

World Cup was won by the team from Argentina. The first *Copa Mundial,* held in 1930, was won by Uruguay.

Informal Assessment Activities

See page T-77 for suggested assessment activities. In addition, you may wish to do the following:

- Have students compare teams, sports, schools, extracurricular activities, or school classes.
- Ask each student to write a sentence for each of the following:
  1. Name something in which you think you're the best or, at least, very good.
  2. Name something in which you think you're the worst or, at least, not very good.
  3. Name a sport, athlete, or activity about which you feel very enthusiastic.
  4. Name a sport, athlete, or activity about which you feel very negative.

Use the statements to hold individual conversations.

Extension / Enrichment Activities

Individual Work / Paired Activity

Students may choose a sport or an athletic event that interests them (including uncommon activities such as mountain climbing, hang gliding, parachuting, etc.). Have them use Spanish-language newspapers, magazines, and reference books to find special vocabulary related to that activity (e.g., what the playing field is called, what participants are called, words for special equipment or uniforms, the names of positions, etc.). They may share their findings with the class in oral presentations or by preparing their own "Panorama de vocabulario" pages with diagrams or illustrations and labels.

Small-Group Activities

- Students may work in groups to create a commercial for their favorite food, sport, or class, or an activity about which they feel strongly. Encourage them to use props and costumes for their presentations. If facilities are available, you may wish to videotape students' presentations after school and then show them periodically in class for "commercial breaks."
- Students may choose a game or activity they have played often in class and prepare a mock "play-by-play" broadcast of the activity.

Class Activity

Hold a class discussion of *el fútbol* and *el fútbol americano.* As questions come up during the discussion, write them on the chalkboard. Give students a day or two to research the answers and then hold a follow-up discussion.

Unidad 11 (pages 258–279)

Objectives

After completing this unit, students should be able to:

- name people and activities associated with the performing arts
- use irregular verbs to give affirmative and negative familiar commands or instructions
- talk about past actions using the preterite tense of the irregular verbs *decir* and *traer*
- read about and discuss a musical instrument from Venezuela and a folk dance from Mexico.

Warm-up / Review Activities

Irregular Comparisons. Display pictures of athletes or performers around the classroom. As you point to a picture, ask what that person is the best or worst at.

Demonstrative Adjectives. Use three different balls for different sports or three different pictures of sports to elicit statements using the demonstrative adjectives (e.g., *Usamos esa pelota para jugar al baloncesto y aquella pelota para jugar al béisbol. Este deporte es más interesante que ese deporte.*).

Unit Vocabulary. **A.** Have students pantomime various activities. Students at their seats should call out the name of the performer as well as the activity.

C: Julio es actor. Hace un papel. Rita es música. Toca el clarinete.

After a few rounds, ask questions such as *¿Quién fue actor? ¿Quién fue músico?*

B. Describe a performance or activity and have students respond with the appropriate vocabulary word.

1. Estoy muy triste. ¿Qué voy a hacer?
2. Pepe es muy cómico. A él le gusta hacer esto. ¿Qué le gusta hacer?
3. Después de un programa, tenemos que hacer algo. ¿Qué tenemos que hacer?

Unit Grammar. **A.** Describe situations and have students respond with commands that would be appropriate to give.

1. No sabes la tarea. ¿Qué le dices a tu compañera de clase?
2. Acabas de estudiar con tu amigo. Tu amigo va a salir, pero tú quieres jugar con él. ¿Qué le dices?
3. No quieres saber un secreto. Tu amigo quiere decirte el secreto. ¿Qué le dices?

B. Enlist students' help in rearranging the classroom. Give affirmative and negative commands (e.g., *Pon los dibujos en la pared. Ten cuidado con el globo.*).

C. As students enter the classroom, ask them what they brought to class.

D. Each day, teach a proverb or idiomatic expression. On the following day, ask students to tell you what you said.

Unit Sections

Panorama de vocabulario

Enlist students' help in acquiring publications in English and in Spanish that focus on celebrities and other performers. Clear an area of the classroom to make a stage and bring in props such as toy microphones, musical instruments, etc.

If students participate in any of the performing arts, encourage them to look up vocabulary related to their particular interests and teach the vocabulary to the class.

Note: Use the verb *reírse* in its infinitive form during the unit. The verb is used for practice in identifying tenses and verb forms in activities R and S of Unidad 14 (pages 342–43).

Usando el español

Giving Commands and Instructions. You may wish to review the formation of regular affirmative and negative familiar commands before presenting this lesson.

You have probably used many of the irregular commands for TPR activities. Read the lists aloud (page 268) and have students raise their hands if they recognize a word. You may wish to have them guess the infinitive form of the commands before they see the chart in their textbooks.

¡Vamos a practicar! *Exercise B, page 270.* Have students think of commands they will probably never hear from parents or teachers (e.g., *Sal de la clase sin permiso. No hagas la tarea. No vengas a tiempo. Dime una mentira.*).

Talking about Your Actions. You may wish to review clauses that begin with *que* (see Unidad 2, pages 59–60).

¡Vamos a practicar! *Exercise C, page 275.* Choose an advanced student to model the activity for the class.

¡A conversar!

Students may use the conversation as a model for their own conversations, adapting it by changing the person being imitated to a teacher, coach, doctor, etc.

¡Conversa tú!

Continue the personalized questions by asking students what they did the year before (e.g., *¿Asististe al teatro el año pasado? ¿Tocaste un instrumento el año pasado?*).

La cultura y tú

The guitar is thought to have originated in Spain in the sixteenth century. Over the centuries, people in Spanish-speaking countries adapted the guitar by varying its size and shape, the number of strings, and the materials used for the strings. Among the guitars that are unique to various countries are the *cuatro* in Venezuela, the *tiple* in Colombia and the *jarana* in Mexico.

Guitars are popular for folk music and modern music; however, musicians such as Francisco Tárrega and Andrés

Segovia brought it into the concert halls and displayed its versatility in classical music as well.

Folk dances and ballroom dances are popular forms of entertainment in Spanish-speaking countries. Young people, however, are strongly influenced by the increased proliferation of music videos and popular rock stars and tend to be as impatient with "old" dances as young people are in the United States.

Informal Assessment Activities

In addition to the activities suggested on page T-77, you may wish to have students participate in numerous role-play activities that approximate real-life conversations and situations.

Extension / Enrichment Activities

Paired / Small-Group Activities

- Have students do a take-off on the television movie review programs to give their own reviews of books, songs, dances, etc. Encourage them to include advice to the "viewers."
- Students may choose a musical instrument (such as *maracas* or *castañuelas*) and research its origins and popularity in Spanish-speaking countries.
- Students may learn a dance, such as the cha-cha, the rumba, or the merengue, and teach it to the class.

Class Activity

Have the class prepare a talent show. The students may vote on whether to hold the show only for themselves or to invite parents, friends, and other classes to attend. You may wish to show videotapes of variety shows in class to help students "pick out" words and expressions that would be useful in announcing the acts in their show.

Unidad 12 (pages 280–301)

Objectives

After completing this unit, students should be able to:

- name things associated with emergencies and ask for help in an emergency
- talk about past actions using the preterite tense of the irregular verbs *tener, estar, andar,* and *hacer*
- describe actions by using adverbs that end in *-mente*
- read a humorous short story
- read about and discuss medical services in rural areas of Peru and a special group of doctors from the United States.

Warm-up / Review Activities

Verbs. **A.** Ask three volunteers to make statements about something they enjoy. After they have made their statements, ask the other students to tell you what they said.

B. Distribute various items at random to five or six students. Issue commands for them to bring the items to the front of the class, put them on a table, and then return to their seats. After all the students have responded, ask the class to tell you who brought each item to the front.

C. Use exercise D on page 271 to have students practice affirmative and negative commands. You may pretend you are reading letters from people who are seeking advice.

D. One by one, have students alternate giving affirmative and negative commands that they hear regularly:

S1: Pon el libro debajo del asiento.
S2: No me digas la respuesta.
S3: Ven a la pizarra.
S4: No vayas al gimnasio ahora.

Unit Vocabulary. **A.** Make three columns on the chalkboard with the following headings: *la policía, los médicos, los bomberos*. Make statements and have students tell you whom to call.

1. Veo un robo.
2. Hay un choque en la esquina.
3. Mi hijo tiene fiebre.
4. Hay un incendio en la cocina.

Vary the activity by asking questions (e.g., *¿Qué puedes usar para llamar a los bomberos? ¿Qué gritas cuando ves un robo? ¿A quién detiene el policía?*).

B. Play "El ahorcado" (see "Games and Activities") to practice spelling the vocabulary for the unit.

Unit Grammar. **A.** Hand a student an item such as a toy ambulance, and issue a command for the student to give it to someone else. Follow up by asking questions (e.g., *Alumnos, ¿qué tuvo Fernando? Fernando, ¿qué tuviste?*).

B. As students enter the classroom, ask them which class they just came from and where they walked (e.g., *¿En qué clase estuviste? ¿Por dónde anduviste?*)

C. Have students tell you where they stood in line that day (e.g., *Hicimos fila en el comedor. Hice fila para subir al autobús.*).

D. Ask questions that elicit answers with adverbs that end in *-mente*. Begin by asking either-or questions:

1. ¿Puedes ganar una carrera fácilmente o difícilmente?
2. ¿Hicieron la tarea para hoy rápidamente o lentamente?
3. ¿Cómo pasaste la mañana, felizmente o tristemente?
4. ¿Qué haces después de las clases?
5. ¿Qué hacen ustedes durante la clase de ciencias?

Unit Sections

Panorama de vocabulario

This unit lends itself to numerous role-play activities and situations, as well as to review of many vocabulary words and constructions. You may wish to divide the presentations into three sections, each one focusing on new and review vocabulary.

Students may practice describing symptoms, describing a person for the police, placing phone calls, or giving autobiographical information that a police officer, doctor or fire fighter might ask for.

Usando el español

Talking about the Past. In conjunction with this section, you may wish to review some of the *tener* expressions and the uses of *estar*. In connection with *andar,* you may wish to review distances (e.g., *Anduvieron tres kilómetros. Anduve dos cuadras y luego doblé a la derecha.*).

Students may be interested in the use of *andar* to express how a clock works (e.g., *El reloj anda bien. El reloj anda rápido.*). They may contrast this usage with the English equivalent of "run."

Talking about What You Have Done. Point out the spelling change in the *él/ella* form and have students deduce the reason for the change by pronouncing the form as it might have been spelled with the *c* instead of the *z*. Remind students of the spelling changes in *-gar, -car,* and *-zar* verbs that are based on pronunciation.

Describing Actions. This section focuses primarily on the usage of adverbs that end in *-mente*. You may wish to supplement the exercises with your own to give students practice in forming the adverbs.

You may give examples of the adverbs for additional context and then have students answer questions, as follows:

T: Si pides ayuda a los policías, ellos vienen rápidamente. ¿Cómo vienen los policías?

Vamos a leer

Have students bring their English or language arts textbooks to class and give examples of how direct dialogue is punctuated in English (in quotation marks). Have them compare the punctuation in English with the punctuation in the story on page 300.

Ask students to summarize the story (in Spanish or English).

La cultura y tú

In the large cities of Latin America, there are modern, well-equipped hospitals, and medical care is available to the inhabitants of the area. In the rural and less accessible regions, medical care and facilities are not readily available. Many medical problems are treated by *curanderos* with herbal and folk remedies. People in these regions must rely on traveling medical workers and nurses, like the *sanitarios* described in this section. The training and equipment of these workers vary from region to region.

Organizations, such as *Proyecto Perú,* are working to alleviate the problem and take better medical care and health education services to remote areas of Latin America. Their progress is slow. Lack of resources, poor education, and the geographical remoteness of some villages frequently act as barriers. As awareness of the problem increases, however, private and government organizations are devoting their resources to finding a solution.

Informal Assessment Activities

You may wish to supplement the suggestions on page T-77 by assigning paired conversations and role-play activities.

Extension / Enrichment Activities

Paired / Small-Group Activities

- ▶ Tell students to imagine they are writers for a television show—for example, a police show, a show about doctors, or a show about a family that has lots of problems—and prepare an episode in which the characters must deal with an illness, a robbery, or a fire.
- ▶ Have students prepare a conversation about emergencies in which each person tries to outdo the next by having the worst problems. The conversation could take place among people at a party, among passengers on an airplane, or among patients in a hospital ward.

Class Activity

Invite a health-care worker, fire fighter, or police officer to talk to the class. If none are available, you may wish to acquire books that specialize in teaching Spanish to people in public service professions. Distribute lists of high-frequency questions and expressions and have students role-play a public servant and a victim or someone making a complaint.

Unidad 13 (pages 302–321)

Objectives

After completing this unit, students should be able to:

- ▶ name people, places, and activities related to the post office
- ▶ talk about past actions using the preterite tense of the irregular verbs *poder, poner,* and *saber*
- ▶ use knowledge of verb conjugations to select and use the present-tense and preterite-tense forms of the verb *oír*
- ▶ read about and discuss an alternative means of communicating between countries by shortwave radio.

Warm-up / Review Activities

Adverbs. Give various TPR commands and include adverbs that end in *-mente* (e.g., *Anda lentamente a la puerta y tócala tres veces rápidamente.*). Follow up each response by asking the other students to describe what their classmate did.

Verbs. **A.** Ask students what they had to do the night before or over the weekend (e.g., *¿Tuvieron que estudiar mucho anoche? ¿Tuviste que lavar los platos?*). Write several responses on the chalkboard and have volunteers describe what their classmates had to do.

B. Write several times on the chalkboard (e.g., 10:15 A.M., 3:30 P.M., 7:45 P.M., 11:30 P.M.). Ask volunteers to role-play a detective questioning a witness or suspect about his or her whereabouts at those times (e.g., *¿Dónde estuviste el diez de marzo a las diez y cuarto de la mañana?*).

C. Have students call out several destinations and then make up sentences using the preterite tense of *andar* (e.g., *Anduvimos una milla al supermercado.*).

Unit Vocabulary. **A.** Have students make lists of their classmates' addresses for a class address book. Vary the activity by setting up a table with two or three volunteers who will ask classmates to write their addresses in a notebook.

B. Play a guessing game by describing people, places, things, and activities and having students guess what you're describing.

1. El hombre o la mujer que nos trae el correo.
2. La persona que vende estampillas.
3. Tienes que hacer esto antes de mandar un paquete.
4. Tu primo vive muy lejos. En dos días, cumple quince años. ¿Cómo puedes mandarle una tarjeta de cumpleaños?

Unit Grammar. **A.** After students are seated, ask them where they put their things (e.g., *¿Dónde pusiste tu lápiz? ¿Dónde pusieron tus libros de español?*).

B. Each day, ask students if they had learned about a recent local or school event (e.g., *¿Supieron que nuestro director fue a California?*). After a few days, have students ask questions.

C. Have students brainstorm a list of activities and then ask one another if they managed to do one of the activities (e.g., *¿Pudiste leer todo el libro anoche?*).

Unit Sections

Panorama de vocabulario

Set up one end of the classroom as a post office. At the other end of the room, set up mailboxes the students have made from old shoe boxes, oatmeal containers, etc. Use these areas for role-play activities.

Have students brainstorm a list of questions a person might ask at a post office. The following are suggestions:

1. ¿Cómo puedo mandar un paquete a España?
2. ¿Cuánto cuestan las estampillas de correo aéreo?
3. ¿Dónde puedo comprar sobres?

In conjunction with the unit, you may wish to teach the following: *repartir* (to deliver); *pesar* (to weigh); *una caja de cartón,* (cardboard box).

¡Aprende el vocabulario! *Exercise B, page 307.* Answers and wording may vary. Accept reasonable responses.

Answers:

1. Sí, tienes que poner las estampillas en el sobre.
2. No, no puedes enviar tu perro por correo aéreo.
3. No, la carta va dentro del sobre.
4. No, el cartero no vende sobres. El agente de correo vende sobres.
5. Sí, tienes que envolverlo.
6. Claro que tienes que escribir una dirección en el sobre.

Usando el español

Using More Irregular Verbs. In addition to the change of meaning of *saber* in the preterite, you may wish to explain that *poder* also changes meaning slightly in the preterite. In the preterite it is used to express "to manage to" instead of "to be able to."

If students begin to feel overwhelmed at the number of verbs with irregular forms in the preterite tense, remind them of the verb charts in the Appendix section.

¡Vamos a practicar! *Exercise A, page 312.* After students have completed the exercise orally in class, have them write the questions and answers as a homework assignment.

Answers:

1. P: Ricardo, ¿por qué no pudiste asistir al teatro?
   R: No pude porque tuve que escribir un reporte.
2. P: Manolo y Raquel, ¿por qué no pudieron ir a la fiesta?
   R: No pudimos ir porque tuvimos que limpiar el garaje.
3. P: Sra. Enríquez, ¿por qué no pudo usted leer mi historia?
   R: No pude leerla porque tuve que ayudar al director de la escuela.
4. P: Patricia, ¿por qué no pudiste ir al almacén?
   R: No pude ir porque tuve que mandar un paquete por correo.

Talking about What You Hear. This section attempts to have students apply all they have learned about verbs and verb forms by having them first deduce the meaning of *oír* from context and then use a typical reference-book listing of conjugations to select the appropriate verb form for their communication needs.

¡A conversar!

Have students scan the conversation for words and expressions that are unfamiliar to them. Write their guesses on the chalkboard and ask them to explain how they arrived at their definitions. Finally, have them look up the words in the glossary or in a Spanish-English dictionary.

La cultura y tú

Many countries have government-sponsored or national shortwave radio stations that broadcast internationally.

The United States has the Voice of America (*la Voz de América*) and Spain has *Radio Exterior de España*. Some stations conduct broadcasts in several languages.

Technology has advanced to the point that communication from one country to another is accomplished easily. You may wish to have students investigate means of communication by telephone, facsimile machines, air courier services, satellite dishes, etc.

Informal Assessment Activities

In addition to the suggestions on page T-77, you may wish to have students look up an unfamiliar verb in a Spanish-English dictionary and use the verb in a question and a statement.

Extension / Enrichment Activities

Individual Work / Paired Activity

Have students write a fan letter to a famous person. They may send the letter through the classroom "postal service." Students may then select a letter from the classroom mailbox and use it as the basis of a role-play activity.

Class Activity

If there is a ham radio club in your area, invite one of the members to talk to the class about the people in different countries he or she has listened to or talked with. If the person has taped any Spanish-language broadcasts, invite him or her to play the tapes for the class.

Unidad 14 (pages 322—343)

Unidad 14 contains many activities for review and practice of vocabulary and grammar learned during the school year. Specifically, activities A through G practice the vocabulary and grammar from Unidad 10 through Unidad 13. The remaining activities recombine and reintroduce vocabulary and structures from all the units.

B. ¿Qué opinas?, *page 325.* Use the questions to spark a class discussion. Students may also choose a question and then form small groups to discuss it. You may ask a representative from each group to report on the discussion to the class.

Students may also choose a question to try their hand at writing an essay in Spanish. You may put the final corrected essays in a notebook for other students to read. (See "Suggestions for Teaching Writing Skills" on pages T-31 to T-33.)

H. Lee un folleto, *pages 330–31.* Students may work in pairs or small groups to write a travel brochure about your community. Have them vote on features they think might be of interest to people who live in Mexico, Spain, or South America.

LL. Haciendo preparaciones, *page 335.* Have students write questions that Sra. Ruiz might ask to be sure that members of her family managed to complete their tasks. Use the questions for additional role-play activities:

S1: ¿Pudiste sacar la basura de la cocina?
S2: Sí, acabo de sacarla.

O. Hay que saber los datos, *page 340.* Students may consult the Appendix section for the "Countries and Nationalities" chart that includes the definite article with the names of the countries.

Answers:
1. Colombia está en la América del Sur. Está al oeste de Venezuela.
2. Guatemala está en la América Central. Está al sur de México.
3. España está en Europa. Está al sur de Francia.
4. El Ecuador está en la América del Sur. Está al oeste del Brasil.
5. Puerto Rico está en el mar Caribe. Está al este de la República Dominicana.
6. Panamá está en la América Central. Está al sur de Cuba.

P. ¿Qué hizo la periodista?, *pages 340–41.* Encourage students to use appropriate adverbs with their answers (e.g., *Generalmente me desperté a las cinco y media de la mañana.*).

Answers:
1. Me bañé a las seis menos cuarto.
2. Sí, siempre tomé té y un pan dulce.
3. Trabajé ocho horas al día.
4. Viajé en autobús y en el metro en las ciudades.
5. Almorcé a la una en punto cada día.
6. A veces comí una merienda a las cinco y media.
7. Escribí seis horas al día.
8. Me acosté a las once y media cada noche.

Games and Activities

In this resource section, you will find complete instructions for preparing and playing games and conducting activities that correspond to the instructional units in *¡Nos comunicamos!*. The games and activities are listed alphabetically and contain the following information:

- Materials. A complete list of materials needed for the game or activity, including the corresponding black-line masters of the *Teacher's Resource and Activity Book.*
- Players. The number of students who can participate: specifically, the entire class, large groups (8–10 players), medium-size groups (5–8 players), small groups (3–5 players), and pairs.
- Preparation. Instructions for preparing materials in advance, as well as additional vocabulary, demonstrations, or explanations that may be needed before students play the game.
- Procedure. A step-by-step description of how to play the game or conduct the activity.

The games and activities described here are merely suggestions. You should supplement and alter them to suit your teaching situation. It is recommended, however, that you incorporate as many different games and activities as possible in your multisection class period to maintain a lively and interesting classroom atmosphere and provide meaningful practice in using Spanish.

For ease of selection, the games and activities are coded with the same symbols used on the annotated textbook pages to designate levels of difficulty:

○ Lowest level of difficulty

◐ Average level of difficulty

● Highest level of difficulty

The following games and activities are included in this resource section:

1. Adivina el precio
2. El ahorcado
3. Antónimos
4. Busco la fortuna
5. La carta
6. Cinco
7. Completa la categoría
8. Concentración
9. Conquista el mundo
10. ¿Cuánto cuesta la palabra?
11. Descripciones I
12. Descripciones II
13. Dibujitos
14. ¿Dónde estoy?
15. Escoge tu número
16. El maratón
17. Pasapalabra
18. ¿Quién tiene la culpa?
19. ¿Verdad o mentira?
20. El volcán

Advina el precio

Materials

- ▶ Vocabulary cards of objects *(Teacher's Resource and Activity Book)*
- ▶ Removable, self-adhesive notes (1½″ × 2″ or 3″ × 3″)

Players The entire class or a medium-size to large group.

Preparation Designate two or three students as "pricers," and help them assign a dollar value to each of the various items pictured on the vocabulary cards. Then have them write the prices on the self-adhesive notes and stick them to the backs of the appropriate vocabulary cards.

Procedure The "pricers" announce each item as it comes up for bid. They then choose three "contestants" from the class, each of whom gets just one chance to guess the price of the item as indicated on the back of the card. The contestant who comes closest to the price without going over wins a point. The contestant with the most points after three items have been up for bid wins that round and gets to take the place of one of the "pricers." The game continues until everyone has had a chance to be either a pricer or a contestant.

○ El ahorcado

Materials ► Chalkboard and chalk or pencil and paper

Players The entire class, or students working in pairs or small groups.

Preparation None

Procedure Play "Hangman" in Spanish. One person chooses a Spanish word, such as a verb form, and draws lines for the number of letters. The partner guesses the letters of the alphabet (if possible, in Spanish). For each incorrect guess, a part of a figure is drawn. If the figure is complete before the word is guessed, the person who chose the word wins. If not, the person guessing wins.

For review, you may specify that students use prepositions, verbs, or adjectives for their words.

◐ Antónimos

Materials

- ▶ 3″ × 3″ squares of paper or index cards
- ▶ Paper bag

Players Students playing in pairs.

Preparation Make (or have students make) game cards by folding each of several squares of paper in half and then folding it in half once more. On the inner halves, write antonym pairs (e.g., *llegar—salir, subir—bajar, pagar—recibir, dentro de—fuera de, cerca—lejos*), making sure that one antonym is on one side of the fold and its opposite on the other. Make a set of ten antonym pairs for each pair of students. Then put each set into a colorful paper shopping or gift bag and shake well.

Procedure Have students choose partners and give each pair of players a bag. The first player draws a slip of paper from the bag, opens it up, and reads one of the words. The second player must not only pronounce its antonym correctly but also spell it correctly. If successful, the player keeps the antonym pair. If not, he or she returns it to the bag. The bag is then shaken up before the second player draws a game card. The player who collects the most antonym pairs wins the game.

Busco la fortuna

Materials

- Transparency and overhead projector (or the chalkboard and chalk or a large piece of paper and a marking pen)
- 4″ × 6″ index cards
- Play money

Players The entire class or a medium-size to large group.

Preparation On the transparency, chalkboard, or paper, draw dashed lines to stand for the letters of a familiar expression (e.g., *Estoy muy bien. ¡Buena suerte! Mejor tarde que nunca.*). On the index cards, write large amounts of money (or amounts that correspond to the numbers students have learned); shuffle the cards and place them face down on a table. To make the game more interesting, you may add cards such as "lose a turn" (*pierde un turno*), "free spin" (*turno extra*) or "bankrupt" (*bancarrota*). Either make or purchase play money for the winnings.

Procedure Divide the class into teams. One team chooses an index card. If a money amount is on the card, the team gets to guess a consonant in the expression. If the guess is correct, write the consonant on the dashed line(s) where it appears in the expression. Then give the team the matching amount of play money. The team continues playing until it either turns up a bad card (e.g., *bancarrota*) or does not guess a letter correctly. If a team has enough money, it may buy a vowel for an agreed-upon price (*Quiero comprar una vocal.*).

A team may try to guess the expression after it has completed a correct letter guess. The first team to guess the expression correctly wins the game.

La carta

Materials
- Stationery or notebook paper
- Envelopes

Players — The entire class or a medium-size group.

Preparation — None

Procedure — Give each student a sheet of stationery (or have them use notebook paper) and an envelope. Instruct the students each to write a letter in Spanish to someone in the class but not to sign their names to the letters. Then have them each address an envelope (also in Spanish) to that person. (Try to make sure that everyone is not only writing but also receiving a letter.)

Next, ask one or two volunteers to be the mail carriers (i.e., *el cartero* or *la cartera*) and deliver the letters. Afterward, have students read their letters aloud and try to guess who wrote them.

Cinco

Materials

- Blank "Cinco" pages (Master 116), one for each player
- Beans or small squares of colored paper for markers, 20 to 25 for each player

Players

The entire class or small to medium-size groups.

Preparation

Copy and distribute "Cinco" pages made from Master 116 (in the *Teacher's Resource and Activity Book*).

Procedure

Distribute the "Cinco" pages and tell players to write a number in each square. (The range of numbers depends on what you are teaching or practicing at a given time.) You may have players choose a square to be a "free" square by coloring it or drawing a symbol.

Call out a number, and each player with that number will put a marker on the square. When a player has covered five down, five across, or five diagonally, he or she must call out *¡Cinco!* in order to win.

Variation

Players may also write the target vocabulary words or verb forms in blank squares. If you provide a list of words from which students may choose, be sure there are more words than squares on the "Cinco" game page.

◐ Completa la categoría

Materials
- Paper and pencil for each player

Players
The entire class or medium-size to large groups.

Preparation
None

Procedure
Write a category on the chalkboard, such as one of the following:

1. Preguntas que le haces a un agente de viajes
2. Mandatos que hace un maestro
3. Cosas que dice un campeón
4. Preguntas que les hace un médico

Set a time limit. At the count of three, students write all the questions, commands, or expressions they can think of for the category. At the end of the time limit, students count the number of entries. The student with the highest number reads his or her list first. If a question, command, or expression is not appropriate or if the student has repeated an entry, it must be crossed off the list. If the student still has more than the next highest student, he or she wins. If not, the student with the next highest number reads aloud. The procedure continues until a tie is called or a winner is declared.

○ Concentración

Materials
- "Concentración" game board with pockets or bulletin board and envelopes
- Vocabulary cards of the target vocabulary, two sets; or one set of teacher-prepared word cards and one set of the corresponding vocabulary cards

Players The entire class or a medium-size group, a small group, or pairs of students.

Preparation If the game is played with a large or medium-size group, you may wish to make a "Concentración" game board from poster board or tag board. Attach 12 to 16 pockets (four across and three or four down), making sure that each pocket allows easy access to the vocabulary or word card inside. Then number the pockets in order. (You may tack envelopes to a bulletin board for the game board, as well.)

If the game is played with a small group or in pairs, you may simply place the vocabulary cards face down on a table.

Either make the game cards from the target vocabulary card black-line masters in the *Teacher's Resource and Activity Book* or make one set of vocabulary cards and one set of index cards on which you have printed the vocabulary words. Either way, you could include a free card (*libre*) to make the game more interesting.

Procedure **The entire class or a medium-size group.** Divide the group into two teams. The first person on a team goes up to the board and pulls out a card from a pocket, saying or reading the word or phrase corresponding to that card. Then he or she pulls out another card from another pocket, saying or reading the appropriate word or phrase. If the cards match, the team gets a point, the cards are set aside, and the next team member comes up. If the cards do not match, the player returns the cards to their pockets and the other team gets a chance. When all the pockets are empty, the team with the most matched cards wins the game.

Small groups or pairs. Two sets of vocabulary cards or word cards may be mixed together and laid face down on a table. Students may take turns choosing cards and trying to make a match. Each time a card is turned face up, the player must say or read the appropriate word or phrase. If two cards match, the player may continue. If they do not match, the next player tries. At the end, the player with the most matched cards wins.

◐ Conquista el mundo

Materials

- Map of North and South America
- Self-adhesive, removable notes in two colors (one color for each team)
- Teacher-prepared question cards

Players

The entire class or a medium-size group.

Preparation

On a set of index cards, write a question (in Spanish) that can be answered with a vocabulary word, verb conjugation, or preposition. The questions may range from simple to complex, depending on what you want to practice:

Uses of *Estar*

1. Tienes sueño. No duermes bien por la noche. ¿Cómo estás?
2. Ven muchos animales en sus jaulas. ¿Dónde están?

Verbs

1. Tienes sueño. Te acuestas. ¿Qué haces? (dormirse)
2. Comiste el almuerzo. El camarero te dio la cuenta. Luego, ¿qué pasó? (pagar)

Object Pronouns

1. Es tu cumpleaños. Tu amigo tiene un regalo. Tu amigo —— da el regalo. (indirect object pronoun)
2. Tienes que escribir un reporte para mañana. ¿Qué vas a hacer esta noche? (direct object pronoun)

Procedure Divide the class or group into two teams. The first player on the starting team draws a question card. If the player responds correctly, he or she chooses a country, says its name in Spanish, and then "conquers" that country for his or her team by placing a colored self-adhesive note on the map. If the player responds incorrectly, the opposing team gets one chance to answer the same question. If their answer is correct, they may "conquer" a country; if it is incorrect, neither team gets on the map that round. The opposing team then has its chance to draw a card and "conquer" a country.

The teams continue to alternate turns until all the cards have been drawn. The team that has "conquered" the most countries at the end of the game is the winner.

○ ¿Cuánto cuesta la palabra?

Materials

- "¿Cuánto cuesta la palabra?" letter sheet (Master 117), one for each student

Players The entire class, medium-size groups, or small groups.

Preparation Make copies of Master 117 (from the *Teacher's Resource and Activity Book*) and distribute them to students.

Procedure Divide the class or group into teams. One team will say or spell a word in Spanish, and the other team will add up the values for each letter in the word and then state an amount. The letter values are printed on the letter sheet.

S1: ¿Cuánto cuesta la palabra *prima?*

S2: Cuesta sesenta y seis pesos.

Point out to students that vowels with accent marks have higher values than those without. Either award a set point value for each round won or use the values of the words as the scores. Students may add up the totals at the end of the game.

Variation To make the game more challenging, you may set letter limits for each round. Round 1 may require students to say a two-letter word; round 2, a three-letter word; and so on.

● Descripciones I

Materials

- Pictures that illustrate the target vocabulary
- Paper and pencil, one for each group

Players

Small groups or pairs of students.

Preparation

From old magazines or newspapers, compile an assortment of colorful pictures that suggest or illustrate the target vocabulary. You may wish to mount the pictures on heavy-gauge paper and laminate them for durability.

Procedure

Give a picture, a sheet of paper, and a pencil to each group. At a given signal, instruct each group to write, in Spanish, all the words or phrases they can think of to describe their picture. You may set a time limit of, perhaps, three minutes. At the end of the time limit, collect the lists of descriptions. The group that comes up with the longest list of correctly written words and phrases wins the competition.

◐ Descripciones II

Materials

- 3″ × 5″ index cards

Players

The entire class in small groups.

Preparation

Make, or have students make, 20 or more pairs of cards. On one card of each pair, write the name of a person (e.g., a famous athlete, actor, or president; a person well known in the school, such as the principal; or a person in the classroom, such as an aide). On its matching card, write four or five Spanish words or phrases that describe that person's appearance, personality, or job. Make certain that each description is distinctive and will not suit more than one person card in a set. Collect and sort the cards by pairs into sets. Then shuffle each set of cards.

Procedure — Divide the class into small groups and give each group a set of cards. Each group tries to match their name cards with the appropriate word cards. Score two points for each correct match. The winner is the group that scores the most points at the end of a time limit, such as three minutes.

○ Dibujitos

Materials
- ► Drawing paper and pencils
- ► 3″ × 5″ index cards
- ► Digital watch or clock with a second hand (or a one-minute timer)

Players — Medium-size to small groups in two teams.

Preparation — Make (or have students make) a set of game cards by writing a vocabulary word on one side of an index card. Then shuffle all the cards, and place them face down in a pile.

Procedure — Divide the group into two teams. The first player on a team takes the top card from the pile and silently reads the vocabulary word. Then, when you say *Empieza*, the player begins drawing a picture to illustrate the word on the chalkboard or a piece of drawing paper. (No letters or numbers allowed. Players may respond to their teams with hand motions and gestures but not with words.) If the player's team guesses the word before one minute is up, the team scores one point. Then a member of the other team takes a card from the pile.

After four cards have been taken (two by each team), call a *carrera* (or race) round. During this round, one player from each team reads the vocabulary word on the next card. When you say *Empiecen*, both players begin drawing pictures to illustrate the same word. The first team to guess the word correctly wins the *carrera* round and scores five points.

At the end of the time period (eight to ten minutes), the team with the higher score wins the game.

◐ ¿Dónde estoy?

Materials

- Pictures of different locations (from old magazines or newspapers) or vocabulary cards of places *(Teacher's Resource and Activity Book)*
- Manila folders cut in half
- Self-adhesive, removable notes (3″ × 3″ or larger), optional

Players

Small groups or students playing in pairs.

Preparation

Cut manila folders in half along the fold to make large, sturdy, opaque playing cards. On one side of a playing card, paste a picture of a location (e.g., a bank, an airport, a desert, a beach, etc.). On the other side, write a word, phrase, or sentence related to that place. (You may wish to write on self-adhesive removable notes instead, in order to reuse the cards later to practice other verb tenses, expressions, etc.)

Procedure

Place all the cards in a pile so that the pictures are face down. Each player, in turn, reads the word, phrase, or sentence on the top card, tries to guess where he or she would be likely to carry out the activity, and then completes the sentence: *Estoy en* (name of place). Afterward, the player turns over the card to see if he or she is correct. If correct, the player receives another turn; if not, the next player takes a turn. The player who collects the most cards wins the game.

Variation

The game may be played with larger groups in teams. A player picks up a card, without looking at it, and shows it to team members. Team members must call out items, people, or activities associated with that place. The player holding up the card has one chance to guess the location (e.g., *Estoy en el banco.*).

◐ Escoge tu número

Materials

- ► Vocabulary cards or teacher-prepared word cards of the target vocabulary, teacher-prepared question cards
- ► Game board (optional)

Players The entire class, medium-size groups, or small groups.

Preparation This game may be played at the chalkboard, or you may make an "Escoge tu número" game board out of poster board. Write as many categories as you wish to review across the board. Then write a column of numbers under each category to represent point values. To add interest, you may use question marks to indicate a mystery category.

La rutina	La playa	¿?
100	100	100
200	200	200
300	300	300
400	400	400
500	500	500

Select vocabulary cards (*Teacher's Resource and Activity Book*) for the unit vocabulary you wish to review or write the vocabulary words on index cards to practice reading. If you want to make the game more challenging, write questions on the index cards (e.g., *Primero, Juan se lava la cara. Luego, Juan —— la cara. ¿Qué hace Juan?* or *Usas la crema de broncear. ¿Qué vas a hacer?*).

Procedure

Divide the class into two or more teams and select one player from each team to keep score. Teams alternate having a player choose a category and a point value and then identify the illustration (or read the word or answer the question) corresponding to that value. If the player responds correctly, the team receives the point value selected. If the player responds incorrectly, the other team has a chance to give the answer, as well as continue with their turn. The team that accumulates the most points wins the game.

The game may be played as time permits during a class period, or it may be extended over several class periods until a team has reached a specified number of points.

El maratón

Materials
- None

Players The entire class or small groups.

Preparation None

Procedure

Ask for two volunteers to be the players. Name another player as the scorekeeper and have the remaining players be judges.

Player A begins the game by asking a question. Player B answers the question and asks another question. Player A answers that question and asks another question. Play continues until one player cannot ask or answer a question or until one player is successfully challenged by a judge.

As the players proceed, the scorekeeper marks one point for every *pregunta* and *respuesta* made by each player. Students at their seats may challenge a player if they think the question or the answer is incorrect. If the player is unable to correct the error by the count of ten, the challenger must correct it and then take his or her place. The player who is eliminated receives his or her score from the scorekeeper. At the end of the game, the player who has the most points is the winner.

◐ Pasapalabra

Materials ► Index cards (or slips of paper)

Players The entire class or a medium-size to large group.

Preparation Make duplicate sets of game cards by writing each of the target vocabulary words on two separate index cards.

Procedure Divide the class into two teams. Call two players from each team to the front of the room. Give one partner from each team a game card containing the same Spanish word. Ask one team to start the game. The player with the card gives a one-word clue (in Spanish) to his or her partner, who then tries to guess the word on the card. If the partner guesses correctly, the team scores ten points. If not, play passes to the other team. The player with the word card gives a different one-word clue (in Spanish) to his or her partner. If the partner guesses correctly, that team scores nine points; if not, play reverts to the first team for another one-word clue, this time worth eight points. Continue play until a specified point count is reached (e.g., five or zero). Then begin a new round with another vocabulary word.

◐ ¿Quién tiene la culpa?

Materials

- Three large envelopes, one for each word category
- Vocabulary cards (black-line masters) or teacher-prepared word cards (index cards with hand-printed vocabulary words)

Players The entire class or medium-size to large groups.

Preparation Label each of three large envelopes with word categories such as *las personas, los lugares,* and *las cosas.* Fill each envelope with the appropriate vocabulary cards *(Teacher's Resource and Activity Book)* or word cards.

Procedure Select a "crime," such as breaking a window. Then call three volunteers to the front of the room. Each volunteer selects a card from a different envelope and either holds it up or walks around the room for all the students to see. The players at their seats try to solve the crime by stating who is committing it, where it takes place, and how it is done (e.g., *El piloto rompe la ventana del avión con una maleta.* or *La camarera rompe la ventana de la agencia de viajes con unas monedas.*). The first player to piece the crime together correctly wins that round.

The game may be played as review for several rounds, or one round may be played each day for a week or so.

¿Verdad o mentira?

Materials ▸ Pencil and paper for each student

Players Small groups.

Preparation Have each player write three statements at the top of a sheet of paper. Tell players to write two statements that are sensible and might be true and one statement that is absurd and obviously a lie. After each statement, they should write *verdad* or *mentira.*

1. Mi papá es piloto. (mentira)

2. Tengo cincuenta casetes en casa. (verdad)

3. Tengo un salvavidas en la bañera. (mentira)

Procedure Each player in turn reads his or her statements aloud. The other players write the person's name and number their papers from 1 to 3. As they hear each statement, they write *lo creo* if they think it is true or *no lo creo* if they think it is false. The player with the highest number of correct guesses, after everyone has had a turn, wins the game.

Variation To make the game more challenging, require students to write sentences based on geography, distances, etc., or require them to write sentences about past activities.

El volcán

Materials

- Game board (Master 118)
- Number spinner (Master 119)
- Paper fastener
- Overhead projector (optional)
- Game pieces (different colored beans, plastic disks, or other markers), one for each team
- Vocabulary cards (black-line masters) or teacher-prepared word cards (index cards with hand-printed words, phrases, or sentences)

Players

The entire class or a medium-size to large group in teams; two to four players.

Preparation

Use Master 118 (*Teacher's Resource and Activity Book*) to make a transparency of the game board. Color in the blank squares and drawings. Project the transparency of the game board onto a smooth, flat surface and use different colored self-adhesive removable notes as game pieces on the projected surface (or use beans, plastic disks, etc. and place them on top of the transparency on the overhead projector).

If the game is to be played by pairs or small groups, paste a copy of Master 118 on heavy stock or cardboard and color in the blank squares and drawings. Laminate the board for durability.

Use Master 119 to make a number spinner. Cut out the number circle and arrow and paste them on cardboard or heavy stock that has been cut in the same shapes. Punch a hole in the middle of the number circle and the arrow. Insert the paper fastener through the holes in the arrow and circle and then bend the ends loosely on the back.

Procedure Divide the class into two to four teams and give each team a game piece. The object of the game is to escape the erupting volcano and go through the jungle to safety on the other side of the mountains. The first team to arrive wins.

The players on each team take turns spinning for a number. In order to advance the specified number of spaces, the player must draw a vocabulary or word card and either identify or read it correctly. (To make the game more challenging, you may write short sentences for the players to read or make one set of noun/pronoun cards and one set of infinitive cards for students to say the verb form that corresponds to the noun or pronoun.)

Note: The game may be played as a review or closing activity of each class period for a week or more until one team wins.

El salto de agua. One of the spaces on the number spinner is the waterfall. When a player spins the waterfall, the game piece is moved to the nearest waterfall and glides down to the adjoining space below. The only way a team can take a short-cut down the waterfall is to spin it.

La abeja. Some of the spaces on the board are marked with a bee. When a player lands on *una abeja,* the game piece may be moved ahead two spaces if the player can identify or read two cards correctly.

La serpiente. Some of the spaces on the board are marked with a snake. When a player lands on *una serpiente,* the game piece is moved back two squares.

Variation If time is short, cover up some of the "pitfall" *(la serpiente)* squares on the board.

The ACTFL Proficiency Guidelines

In recent years, one of the key forces in foreign-language education has been the proficiency-oriented curriculum and classroom. Through grants from the U.S. Department of Education, the American Council on the Teaching of Foreign Language (ACTFL) has developed and revised generic guidelines for assessing language proficiency in speaking, listening, reading, and writing. These guidelines describe a range of abilities: beginning at the Novice level, progressing through the Intermediate and Advanced levels, and culminating in the Superior to Distinguished levels. The descriptions are intended to be representative of the ranges of ability, not exhaustive and all-encompassing, and to apply to stages of proficiency, rather than achievement within a specific curriculum.

In this section, you will find the descriptions of proficiency in the four skill areas that relate to the students of *¡Viva el español!*—speaking, listening, reading, and writing—at the Novice through Intermediate levels.

Generic Descriptions—Speaking

Novice	The Novice level is characterized by an ability to communicate minimally with learned material.
Novice-Low	Oral production consists of isolated words and perhaps a few high-frequency phrases. Essentially no functional communicative ability.

Novice-Low	Understanding is limited to occasional isolated words, such as cognates, borrowed words, and high-frequency social conventions. Essentially no ability to comprehend even short utterances.
Novice-Mid	Able to understand some short, learned utterances, particularly where context strongly supports understanding and speech is clearly audible. Comprehends some words and phrases from simple questions, statements, high-frequency commands, and courtesy formulae about topics that refer to basic personal information or the immediate physical setting. The listener requires long pauses for assimilation and periodically requests repetition and/or a slower rate of speech.
Novice-High	Able to understand short, learned utterances and some sentence-length utterances, particularly where context strongly supports understanding and speech is clearly audible. Comprehends words and phrases from simple questions, statements, high-frequency commands, and courtesy formulae. May require repetition, rephrasing, and/or a slowed rate of speech for comprehension.
Intermediate	The Intermediate level is characterized by an ability to understand main ideas and some facts from interactive exchanges and simple connected aural texts.
Intermediate-Low	Able to understand sentence-length utterances which consist of recombinations of learned elements in a limited number of content areas, particularly if strongly supported by the situational context. Content refers to basic personal background and needs, social conventions, and routine tasks, such as getting meals and receiving simple instructions and directions. Listening tasks pertain primarily to spontaneous face-to-face conversations. Understanding is often uneven; repetition and rewording may be necessary. Misunderstandings in both main ideas and details arise frequently.
Intermediate-Mid	Able to understand sentence-length utterances which consist of recombinations of learned utterances on a variety of topics. Content

continues to refer primarily to basic personal background and needs, social conventions, and somewhat more complex tasks, such as lodging, transportation, and shopping. Additional content areas include some personal interests and activities, and a greater diversity of instructions and directions. Listening tasks not only pertain to spontaneous face-to-face conversations but also to short routine telephone conversations and some deliberate speech, such as simple announcements and reports over the media. Understanding continues to be uneven.

Intermediate-High

Able to sustain understanding over longer stretches of connected discourse on a number of topics pertaining to different times and places; however, understanding is inconsistent due to failure to grasp main ideas and/or details. Thus, while topics do not differ significantly from those of an Advanced-level listener, comprehension is less in quantity and poorer in quality.

Generic Descriptions—Reading

These guidelines assume all reading texts to be authentic and legible.

Novice

The Novice level is characterized by an ability to
—identify isolated words and phrases when strongly supported by context; and
—identify learned material.

Novice-Low

Able occasionally to identify isolated words and/or major phrases when strongly supported by context.

Novice-Mid

Able to recognize the symbols of an alphabetic and/or syllabic writing system and/or a limited number of characters in a system that uses characters. The reader can identify an increasing number of highly contextualized words and/or phrases including cognates and borrowed words, where appropriate. Material understood rarely exceeds a single phrase at a time, and rereading may be required.

Novice-High Has sufficient control of the writing system to interpret written language in areas of practical need. Where vocabulary has been learned, can read for instructional and directional purposes standardized messages, phrases, or expressions, such as some items on menus, schedules, timetables, maps, and signs. At times, but not on a consistent basis, the Novice-High-level reader may be able to derive meaning from material at a slightly higher level where context and/or extralinguistic background knowledge are supportive.

Intermediate The Intermediate level is characterized by an ability to understand main ideas and some facts from simple connected texts.

Intermediate-Low Able to understand main ideas and/or some facts from the simplest connected texts dealing with basic personal and social needs. Such texts are linguistically noncomplex and have a clear underlying internal structure, for example, chronological sequencing. They impart basic information about which the reader has to make only minimal suppositions or to which the reader brings personal interest and/or knowledge. Examples include messages with social purposes or information for the widest possible audience, such as public announcements and short, straightforward instructions dealing with public life. Some misunderstandings will occur.

Intermediate-Mid Able to read consistently with increased understanding simple connected texts dealing with a variety of basic and social needs. Such texts are still linguistically noncomplex and have a clear underlying internal structure. They impart basic information about which the reader has to make minimal suppositions and to which the reader brings personal interest and/or knowledge. Examples may include short, straightforward descriptions of persons, places, and things written for a wide audience.

Intermediate-High Able to read consistently with full understanding simple connected texts dealing with basic personal and social needs about which the reader has personal interest and/or knowledge. Can get some main ideas and information from texts at the next higher level featuring description and narration. Structural complexity may interfere with comprehension; for example, basic grammatical relations may be misinterpreted and temporal references may rely primarily on lexical items. Has some difficulty with the cohesive factors in discourse, such as matching pronouns with referents. While texts do not differ significantly from those at the Advanced level, comprehension is less consistent. May have to read material several times for understanding.

Generic Descriptions—Writing

Novice The Novice level is characterized by an ability to produce isolated words and phrases.

Novice-Low Able to form some letters in an alphabetic system. In languages whose writing systems use syllabaries or characters, writer is able to both copy and produce the basic strokes. Can produce romanization of isolated characters, where applicable.

Novice-Mid Able to copy or transcribe familiar words or phrases and reproduce some from memory. No practical communicative writing skills.

Novice-High Able to write simple fixed expressions and limited memorized material and some recombinations thereof. Can supply information on simple forms and documents. Can write names, numbers, dates, own nationality, and other simple autobiographical information, as well as some short phrases and simple lists. Can write all the symbols in an alphabetic or syllabic system or 50–100 characters or compounds in a character writing system. Spelling and representation of symbols (letters, syllables, characters) may be partially correct.

Intermediate The Intermediate level is characterized by an ability to meet practical writing needs by communicating simple facts and ideas in a loose collection of sentences.

Novice-Mid

Oral production continues to consist of isolated words and learned phrases within very predictable areas of need, although quantity is increased. Vocabulary is sufficient only for handling simple, elementary needs and expressing basic courtesies. Utterances rarely consist of more than two or three words and show frequent long pauses and repetition of interlocutor's words. Speaker may have some difficulty producing even the simplest utterances. Some Novice-Mid speakers will be understood only with great difficulty.

Novice-High

Able to satisfy partially the requirements of basic communicative exchanges by relying heavily on learned utterances but occasionally expanding these through simple recombinations of their elements. Can ask questions or make statements involving learned material. Shows signs of spontaneity, although this falls short of real autonomy of expression. Speech continues to consist of learned utterances rather than of personalized, situationally adapted ones. Vocabulary centers on areas such as basic objects, places, and most common kinship terms. Pronunciation may still be strongly influenced by first language. Errors are frequent and, in spite of repetition, some Novice-High speakers will have difficulty being understood even by sympathetic interlocutors.

Intermediate

The intermediate level is characterized by an ability to

—create with the language by combining and recombining learned elements, though primarily in a reactive mode;

—initiate, minimally sustain, and close in a simple way basic communicative tasks; and

—ask and answer questions.

Intermediate-Low

Able to handle successfully a limited number of interactive, task-oriented and social situations. Can ask and answer questions, initiate and respond to simple statements, and maintain face-to-face conversation, although in a highly restricted manner and with much linguistic inaccuracy. Within these limitations, can perform such tasks as introducing self, ordering a meal, asking directions, and making purchases. Vocabulary is adequate to express only the most elementary needs. Strong interference from native language may occur. Misunderstandings frequently arise, but with repetition, the

Intermediate-Low speaker can generally be understood by sympathetic interlocutors.

Intermediate-Mid Able to handle successfully a variety of uncomplicated, basic and communicative tasks and social situations. Can talk simply about self and family members. Can ask and answer questions and participate in simple conversations on topics beyond the most immediate needs; e.g., personal history and leisure-time activities. Utterance length increases slightly, but speech may continue to be characterized by frequent long pauses, since the smooth incorporation of even basic conversational strategies is often hindered as the speaker struggles to create appropriate language forms. Pronunciation may continue to be strongly influenced by first language and fluency may still be strained. Although misunderstandings still arise, the Intermediate-Mid speaker can generally be understood by sympathetic interlocutors.

Intermediate-High Able to handle successfully most uncomplicated communicative tasks and social situations. Can initiate, sustain, and close a general conversation with a number of strategies appropriate to a range of circumstances and topics, but errors are evident. Limited vocabulary still necessitates hesitation and may bring about slightly unexpected circumlocution. There is emerging evidence of connected discourse, particularly for simple narrative and/or description. The Intermediate-High speaker can generally be understood even by interlocutors not accustomed to dealing with speaking at this level, but repetition may still be required.

Generic Descriptions—Listening

These guidelines assume that all listening tasks take place in an authentic environment at a normal rate of speech using standard or near-standard norms.

Novice The Novice level is characterized by an ability to recognize learned material and isolated words and phrases when strongly supported by context.

Intermediate-Low	Able to meet limited practical writing needs. Can write short messages, postcards, and take down simple notes, such as telephone messages. Can create statements or questions within the scope of limited language experience. Material produced consists of recombinations of learned vocabulary and structures into simple sentences on very familiar topics. Language is inadequate to express in writing anything but elementary needs. Frequent errors in grammar, vocabulary, punctuation, spelling, and in formation of nonalphabetic symbols, but writing can be understood by natives used to the writing of nonnatives.
Intermediate-Mid	Able to meet a number of practical writing needs. Can write short, simple letters. Content involves personal preferences, daily routine, everyday events, and other topics grounded in personal experience. Can express present time or at least one other time frame or aspect consistently, e.g., nonpast, habitual, imperfective. Evidence of control of the syntax of noncomplex sentences and basic inflectional morphology, such as declensions and conjugation. Writing tends to be a loose collection of sentences or sentence fragments on a given topic and provides little evidence of conscious organization. Can be understood by natives used to the writing of nonnatives.
Intermediate-High	Able to meet most practical writing needs and limited social demands. Can take notes in some detail on familiar topics and respond in writing to personal questions. Can write simple letters, brief synopses and paraphrases, summaries of biographical data, work and school experience. In those languages relying primarily on content words and time expressions to express time, tense, or aspect, some precision is displayed; where tense and/or aspect is expressed through verbal inflection, forms are produced rather consistently, but not always accurately. An ability to describe and narrate in paragraphs is emerging. Rarely uses basic cohesive elements, such as pronominal substitutions or synonyms in written discourse. Writing, though faulty, is generally comprehensible to natives used to the writing of nonnatives.

Scope and Sequence

Lesson / Unit	Active Vocabulary
Primera lección	Review and practice of vocabulary learned in *Ya converso más* Household vocabulary Household furnishings Food Prepositions: *dentro de, fuera de, debajo de, sobre,* and *con* Adverbs: *siempre, a veces,* and *nunca*
Segunda lección	Review and practice of vocabulary learned in *Ya converso más* Household chores Sports Hobbies Expressions of time Prepositions: *antes de* and *después de*

Grammar / Usage	Language / Culture
Review and practice of concepts learned in *Ya converso más* Verbs: review and practice of present tense forms of *estar* Verbs: review and practice of present tense forms of regular *-ar, -er,* and *-ir* verbs Verbs: review and practice of *poner* and *traer* Verbs: review and practice of *gustar* Prepositions: review and practice of prepositions of location Interrogatives: review and practice of question words Adverbs: review and practice of *siempre, a veces,* and *nunca* Verbs: review and practice of *e* to *i* stem-changing verbs	**Language Skills** Listens to and reads a simple conversation; responds to related comprehension questions Responds to personalized questions on living quarters Selects appropriate sentence completions and writes complete sentences Surveys classmates about food preferences and writes their responses Writes complete sentences based on rebuses Responds to personalized questions about household routines by writing complete sentences using *siempre, a veces,* or *nunca*
Review and practice of concepts learned in *Ya converso más* Verbs: review and practice of *jugar a* Verbs: review and practice of familiar affirmative commands Verbs: review and practice of reflexive verbs Verbs: review and practice of *estar* + gerund Verbs: review and practice of *tener que* and *acabar de* constructions	**Language Skills** Listens to and reads a simple conversation; responds to related comprehension questions Responds to personalized questions about chores and leisure Writes sentences using affirmative commands based on visual cues Selects appropriate sentence completions and writes complete sentences

Lesson / Unit	Active Vocabulary
Segunda lección (Continued)	
Tercera lección	Review and practice of vocabulary learned in *Ya converso más* Transportation Daily routines School workers and places Work in the community Descriptive adjectives Adjectives expressing nationality Nouns expressing nationality Prepositions: *en* Countries of the world City places and transportation

Grammar / Usage	Language / Culture
Verbs: review and practice of *saber* + infinitive	Writes sentences about what people are doing based on visual cues, using *estar* + gerund Reads a friendly letter about sports Answers questions contained in the letter
Review and practice of concepts learned in *Ya converso más* Verbs: review and practice of *querer* + infinitive Verbs: review and practice of *hay* Verbs: review and practice of present tense forms of stem-changing verbs Verbs: review and practice of present tense forms of *conocer* and the personal *a*	**Language Skills** Listens to and reads a simple conversation; responds to related comprehension questions Responds to personalized questions about traveling Answers questions based on visual cues Writes complete sentences using appropriate forms of stem-changing verbs Responds to simple personalized questions about school personnel Writes a short descriptive paragraph on a person in the school Reads a friendly letter Answers questions contained in the letter

Lesson / Unit	Active Vocabulary
Unidad 1	

Panorama de vocabulario

Travel

Pensamos viajar

la viajera
el viajero
la selva
el río
las montañas
el valle
el volcán
el desierto
el lago
la playa
el agente de viajes
la agente de viajes
la agencia de viajes
descansar

¿Cuánto cuesta el viaje?

costar
pagar
el billete

Usando el español

visitar
correr
recibir
ir
poder
pensar
estar
ser

Grammar / Usage	Language / Culture

Verbs: singular and plural present tense forms of regular *-ar, -er,* and *-ir* verbs

Verbs: singular and plural present tense forms of *ser, estar,* and *ir*

Verbs: singular and plural present tense forms of regular *o* to *ue* and *e* to *ie* stem-changing verbs

Language Skills

Writes questions based on verbal cues; writes answers based on visual cues

Selects appropriate sentence completions and writes complete sentences

Reads statements about what people would like to do on vacation; writes suggestions in the form of questions

Surveys classmates about vacation preferences and writes their responses

Listens to, pronounces, and discriminates between the vowel sounds of *ae, ea, ao,* and *oa*

Describes actions by using the present tense of regular *-ar, -er,* and *-ir* verbs; irregular verbs *estar, ser,* and *ir*; and *o* to *ue* and *e* to *ie* stem-changing verbs

Identifies and names travel destinations and the people and activities involved in making plans

Forms complete sentences from sentence fragments

Writes a short paragraph about an ideal vacation

Answers questions using appropriate forms of *estar*

States questions and answers from verbal and visual cues using appropriate forms of *ser*

Writes paired sentences using appropriate forms of *ir* and *ir a* + infinitive

Responds to questions about daily activities

Lesson / Unit	Active Vocabulary
Unidad 1 *(Continued)*	
Unidad 2	**Panorama de vocabulario**

Air Travel

En el aeropuerto

el equipaje
la línea aérea
el horario
a tiempo
hacer fila

la maleta
el vuelo
temprano
tarde

el piloto
el aeromozo
el pasajero
los asientos

la piloto
la aeromoza
la pasajera

Grammar / Usage	Language / Culture
	Answers questions using appropriate forms of *poder* Writes questions to ask of a favorite singer Listens to and reads a simple conversation; responds to related comprehension questions Answers personalized questions **Culture** Reads a few short paragraphs on places and points of interest in Mexico and Spain
Verbs: singular and plural present tense forms of *hacer* and *decir* Pronouns: singular and plural direct-object pronouns	**Language Skills** Identifies and names people, places, and activities related to air travel using visual cues Writes sentences about airplane arrivals and departures based on a simulated schedule board Constructs conversations on airline travel with a partner Listens to, pronounces, and discriminates between the vowel sounds of *eo* and *oe* Talks about doing or making things by using the present tense of *hacer* Surveys classmates about what they like to do or make in their spare time and writes their responses Talks about what people say by using the present tense of *decir*

Lesson / Unit	Active Vocabulary	
Unidad 2 (Continued)	**Hacemos un viaje**	
	despegar	volar
	aterrizar	
	llegada	salida
	cómodo	incómodo
	vuelo	
	Usando el español	
	hacer	decir
	me	nos
	te	lo
	los	la
	las	
Unidad 3	**Panorama de vocabulario**	
	Hotel Accommodations	
	Llegamos a un hotel	
	el turista	la turista
	el ascensor	las habitaciones
	la llave	el arte moderno
	¿Qué tenemos en la habitación?	
	la sábana	la manta
	el arte antiguo	las tarjetas postales

Grammar / Usage	Language / Culture
	Surveys classmates to find out how they would vote on various issues and writes their responses Answers questions, substituting direct object pronouns for nouns and proper nouns Writes sentences about personal possessions Uses familiar vocabulary and deductive skills to identify meanings of words on an airline ticket and a boarding pass **Culture** Reads about and discusses the 24-hour clock Uses vocabulary and visual context to answer questions about a simple airline timetable
Verbs: singular and plural present tense forms of regular *e* to *i* and *u* to *ue* stem-changing verbs Verbs: singular and plural present tense forms of regular, irregular, and stem-changing reflexive verbs	**Language Skills** Identifies and names things related to hotels and hotel rooms Completes sentences about satisfactory and unsatisfactory hotel accommodations using descriptive adjectives Writes a postcard to a friend about an imaginary trip abroad Listens to, pronounces, and discriminates between the vowel sounds of *ai, ia, au,* and *ua*

Lesson / Unit	Active Vocabulary	
Unidad 3 *(Continued)*	el jabón la bañera blando frío	las toallas la ducha duro caliente
	Usando el español	
	pedir bañarse dormirse	jugar ponerse
Primer repaso	Review and practice of vocabulary learned in Unidad 1 through Unidad 3	

Grammar / Usage	Language / Culture
	Talks about actions by using the present tense of *e* to *i* and *o* to *ue* stem-changing verbs and regular, irregular, and stem-changing reflexive verbs Writes sentences about the order of daily activities using *primero* and *luego* Completes sentences in a story exercise using infinitive cues Writes sentences about an ideal vacation day **Culture** Reads and discusses a story about a family in Argentina Reads about and discusses tourism in South America
Review and practice of concepts learned in Unidad 1 through Unidad 3	**Language Skills** Listens to and reads a simple conversation; responds to related comprehension questions Reads and answers questions about an imaginary trip; writes answers in paragraph form Answers simple questions using appropriate forms of direct object pronouns Identifies correct and incorrect statements based on common knowledge using appropriate forms of *decir*

Lesson / Unit	Active Vocabulary
Primer repaso *(Continued)*	
Unidad **4**	**Panorama de vocabulario** Banks and Money **Vamos al banco** el banco — la ventanilla el cajero — la cajera la moneda — los billetes abierto — cerrado Restaurants and Food **Tenemos hambre** el restaurante — el menú el camarero — la camarera la cuenta — la propina **Usando el español** me — nos te — le les — dar

Grammar / Usage	Language / Culture
	Writes descriptive sentences based on a photograph Writes sentences based on verbal cues Reads a friendly letter Answers questions contained in the letter
Pronouns: indirect object pronouns Verbs: present tense forms of *dar*	**Language Skills** Identifies and names people and items related to going to a bank and a restaurant Completes story sentences Writes sentences about sensible purchases using *gastar* and *ahorrar* Listens to, pronounces, and discriminates between the vowel sounds of *ei, ie, eu,* and *ue* Refers to people and things by using indirect object pronouns Completes a paragraph about a best friend, using indirect object pronouns Writes a paragraph about a best friend Talks about giving by using the present tense of *dar,* and uses idiomatic meanings of *dar* appropriately Listens to and reads a simple conversation; responds to related comprehension questions Responds to personalized questions

Lesson / Unit	Active Vocabulary
Unidad 4 (Continued)	
Unidad 5	**Panorama de vocabulario** Buildings and City Locations **Vamos a conocer la ciudad** la iglesia, el museo la alcaldía, la plaza la fuente, la escultura el monumento el colegio, la sinagoga el supermercado, el edificio de apartamentos el metro, el zoológico el estadio, el mercado al aire libre **Usando el español** estar + *gerund* me, nos te, lo los, la las

Grammar / Usage	Language / Culture
	Culture Uses familiar vocabulary and visual cues to read and understand a short paragraph on money in Colombia Identifies differences in values of money in a Spanish-speaking country Reads a chart of monetary units and symbols of various Spanish-speaking countries
Verbs: uses of *estar* to talk about location and to describe feelings or temporary conditions Verbs: present progressive voice of *-ar, -er,* and *-ir* verbs Pronouns: direct and indirect object pronouns with infinitives	**Language Skills** Identifies and names places in a city Selects appropriate sentence completions and writes complete sentences Answers personalized questions about features and activities in own city Listens to, pronounces, and discriminates between the vowel sounds of *oi, io,* and *uo* Talks about where people and things are located, how people are feeling, and what people are doing by employing the different uses of *estar* Responds to questions about people's locations based on visual cues Surveys classmates about their feelings and writes their responses Answers personalized questions about feelings based on verbal cues Writes a paragraph about a trip or activity based on a model

Lesson / Unit	Active Vocabulary	
Unidad **5** *(Continued)*	me te les	nos le
Unidad 6	**Panorama de vocabulario** Getting and Giving Directions **¿Adónde vamos?** una cuadra el farol norte oeste la manzana rápido perderse quedar adelante	 el paso de peatones la esquina sur este despacio encontrarse quedar atrás

Grammar / Usage	Language / Culture
	Talks about recipients of actions by using direct or indirect object pronouns with infinitives Writes sentences using appropriate word-order position of direct and indirect object pronouns based on verbal cues Reads simulated encyclopedia articles about cities **Culture** Discusses the importance of plazas in Hispanic cities and towns Describes the significance of Simón Bolívar in South America
Verbs: affirmative and negative familiar commands of regular and reflexive *-ar, -er,* and *-ir* verbs	**Language Skills** Identifies, names, and describes ways of getting around in a city Talks about distances using *estar a* (distance) *de* Identifies relative locations of and distances between various Spanish cities based on a map and verbal cues Selects appropriate sentence completions and writes complete sentences Answers personalized questions about distances and directions in the United States Listens to, pronounces, and discriminates between the vowel sounds of *ui* and *iu*

Lesson / Unit	Active Vocabulary	
Unidad 6 *(Continued)*	**Usando el español** mirar abrir	 correr
Segundo repaso	Review and practice of vocabulary learned in Unidad 4 through Unidad 6	

Grammar / Usage	Language / Culture
	Gives instructions or commands by using regular affirmative and negative familiar commands Transforms sentences with *tener que* into affirmative familiar commands Writes sentences using appropriate negative familiar commands based on verbal cues Listens to and reads a simple conversation; responds to related comprehension questions Answers personalized questions on using maps and getting around a city **Culture** Reads and discusses a passage on the metric system used in Spanish-speaking countries
Review and practice of concepts learned in Unidad 4 through Unidad 6	**Language Skills** Listens to and reads a simple conversation; responds to related comprehension questions Answers personalized questions about possible actions in various common situations Gives directions between city locations based on a generalized city map Transforms affirmative familiar commands into negative and vice-versa Transforms sentences with *tener que* into sentences using *acabar de* and direct object pronouns

Lesson / Unit	Active Vocabulary
Segundo repaso *(Continued)*	

Unidad	
7	**Panorama de vocabulario**

Panorama de vocabulario

Shopping

Compramos regalos

la joyería	las joyas
el joyero	la joyera
el regalo	el brazalete
el collar	el llavero
la zapatería	los zapatos
el zapatero	las sandalias
las bolsas	el cinturón
la tienda de discos	el disco
el disco compacto	el casete

Usando el español

ayer	
la semana pasada	ayer por la mañana
comprar	pagar
llegar	sacar
pensar	almorzar
jugar	

Grammar / Usage	Language / Culture
	Selects appropriate sentence completions and writes complete sentences in paragraph form Writes a paragraph on a preferred activity with a friend, based on a model Reads a simulated personality quiz and selects responses that describe self best
Verbs: preterite tense forms of regular and stem-changing *-ar* verbs and *-ar* verbs with spelling changes (*-gar, -car, -zar*)	**Language Skills** Identifies and names places, people, and items related to shopping and buying gifts Writes sentences about where to go and to whom to talk to buy various items Identifies expensive and inexpensive items using *caro* and *barato,* based on a price list Makes a visual survey of classmates' clothing and writes the results in sentence form Listens to and pronounces two-, three-, and four-syllable words Talks about actions in the past by using the preterite tense Completes sentences using the preterite tense Asks and answers questions based on cues Responds to questions about scheduled activities based on a weekly schedule Writes a schedule and a paragraph on personal activities for the past week Responds to questions about past activities based on cues

Lesson / Unit	Active Vocabulary
Unidad 7 (Continued)	
Unidad 8	**Panorama de vocabulario**

Unidad 8

Panorama de vocabulario

The Beach and Water Sports

Vamos a la playa

el salvavidas
tomar el sol
bronceado
los anteojos
el esquí acuático
las olas
flotar
la sombrilla
la crema de broncear
quemado
el barco de vela
la lancha
bucear

Grammar / Usage	Language / Culture
	Selects appropriate story-sentence completions and writes complete sentences Responds to questions on imaginary activities last Saturday Listens to and reads a simple conversation; responds to related comprehension questions Responds to personalized questions **Culture** Reads about and discusses shopping in open-air markets and the custom of bartering Describes special handmade items from a Central American country
Verbs: preterite tense forms of regular and stem-changing *-er* and *-ir* verbs Adjectives: forms of the demonstrative adjectives *este, ese,* and *aquel* Prepositions: usage of *para*	**Language Skills** Names activities and items related to the beach and water sports Responds to questions about items and activities on a beach based on visual cues Completes story-sentences; writes the completed story Writes a letter to a friend about beach activities Listens to, pronounces, and discriminates between words that differ in syllables accented Talks about past actions by using the preterite tense of *-er* and *-ir* verbs

Lesson / Unit	Active Vocabulary	
Unidad 8 (Continued)	el mar	los caracoles
	las conchas	la arena
	¡Se prohibe nadar!	¡Peligro!
	Usando el español	
	correr	volver
	salir	
	este	esta
	estos	estas
	ese	esa
	esos	esas
	aquel	aquella
	aquellos	aquellas
	para	
Unidad 	**Panorama de vocabulario**	
	Outings	
	Vamos de excursión	
	la selva tropical	el sendero
	la serpiente	el puma
	el caimán	las abejas
	el salto de agua	

Grammar / Usage	Language / Culture
	Answers questions about a past summer based on verbal cues Writes questions to ask other people about their past activities Talks about specific items and people by using demonstrative adjectives Speaks with a partner about near, far, and mid-distance objects based on verbal cues and a model Talks about what things are used for, when something needs to be done, and who is to receive something by using the preposition *para* **Culture** Reads a simulated magazine article about the discovery of the sunken treasure ship *Nuestra Señora de Atocha* Reads about and discusses the land and attractions of Baja California
Verbs: preterite tense forms of *ir, ser,* and *dar* Prepositions: usage of *por*	**Language Skills** Identifies and names places and items associated with the country Selects appropriate sentence completions and writes complete sentences Interviews a classmate about a camping or weekend trip Listens to and pronounces words with written accents

Lesson / Unit	Active Vocabulary	
Unidad 9 *(Continued)*	los árboles	el campo
	la comida enlatada	la merienda
	la mochila	las hormigas
	la granja	
	la vaca	el toro
	el cerdo	los becerros
	el gallo	la gallina
	los pollitos	los gansos
	Usando el español	
	por	dar
	ir	ser
Tercer repaso	Review and practice of vocabulary learned in Unidad 7 through Unidad 9	

Grammar / Usage	Language / Culture
	Talks about past actions by using the preterite tense of the irregular verbs *ir, ser,* and *dar* Writes questions and answers about past actions based on verbal cues Talks about when events happened, how long an event lasted, and the exchange of one thing for another by using the preposition *por* **Culture** Reads a simulated excerpt from a history text about the discovery of Angel Falls in Venezuela Reads about and discusses a national park in Costa Rica
Review and practice of concepts learned in Unidad 7 through Unidad 9	**Language Skills** Listens to and reads a simple conversation; responds to related comprehension questions Responds to personalized questions about past summer activities Selects appropriate sentence completions and writes complete sentences Interviews a classmate about a recent shopping trip and writes responses Writes questions based on responses Writes questions about photographs to ask the photographer

Lesson / Unit	Active Vocabulary
Tercer repaso *(Continued)*	
Unidad **10**	**Panorama de vocabulario** Spectator Sports **Vamos a ver los deportes** perder · ganar la pista · la carrera los espectadores · el salto de altura gritar la gimnasia · la lucha libre el campeón · la medalla de bronce la medalla de plata · la medalla de oro los boxeadores · el boxeo los ciclistas · el ciclismo los alpinistas · el alpinismo el boliche · la natación el trofeo

Grammar / Usage	Language / Culture
	Selects *por* or *para* to complete sentences appropriately Conducts a conversation with a classmate about personal preferences Uses observation skills and learned vocabulary to answer questions based on photographs and text
Adjectives: comparative and superlative forms of *bueno* and *malo* Adjectives: forms and usage of absolute superlatives	**Language Skills** Names different sports and the people who participate in them Answers personalized questions about watching and participating in sports Writes sentences on sports based on verbal cues Listens to and pronounces the consonant sound of *tr* Makes comparisons by using the irregular forms of *bueno* and *malo* (*mejor, peor*) Transforms sentences with *bueno* or *malo* into sentences containing comparative or superlative forms Answers personalized questions using superlative forms of *bueno* and *malo* Describes something emphatically by adding the absolute superlative endings -*ísimo* and -*ísima* to adjectives Writes sentences about personal preferences using absolute superlatives appropriately

Lesson / Unit	Active Vocabulary	
Unidad **10** *(Continued)*	**Usando el español**	
	bueno (-a)	mejor . . . que
	el (la) mejor	
	malo (-a)	peor . . . que
	el (la) peor	
Unidad 11	**Panorama de vocabulario**	
	Theater and Entertainment	
	Vamos al teatro	
	la orquesta	los músicos
	el clarinete	el piano
	la guitarra	el violín
	el tambor	el director
	la obra de teatro	hacer un papel
	el actor	la actriz
	el locutor	la cantante
	el bailarín	la bailarina
	asistir al teatro	reírse
	aplaudir	llorar
	Usando el español	
	poner	tener
	venir	decir

Grammar / Usage	Language / Culture
	Listens to and reads a simple conversation; responds to related comprehension questions Responds to personalized questions **Culture** Reads about and discusses the popularity of soccer in Spanish-speaking countries and the importance of the World Cup tournament
Verbs: affirmative and negative familiar commands of irregular verbs Verbs: preterite tense forms of *decir* and *traer*	**Language Skills** Names people and activities associated with the performing arts Selects appropriate sentence completions and writes complete sentences Writes a short paragraph reviewing a play, concert, or television program Listens to and pronounces the sound of *x* Uses irregular verbs to give affirmative and negative familiar commands and instructions Writes negative familiar commands in response to verbal cues Transforms positive familiar commands into negative Reads statements and gives advice using appropriate command forms Talks about past actions by using the preterite tense of the irregular verbs *decir* and *traer*

Lesson / Unit	Active Vocabulary	
Unidad **11** *(Continued)*	hacer salir traer	ir dar
Unidad **12**	**Panorama de vocabulario** Emergencies **Necesitamos ayuda** estar enfermo tener tos la inyección un choque los primeros auxilios ¡Socorro! el extintor un incendio la alarma de incendios	 las medicinas tener fiebre la camilla la ambulancia ¡Auxilio! un ladrón un robo detener

Grammar / Usage	Language / Culture
	Writes questions and answers about an imaginary class picnic Interviews a classmate about classroom needs and writes his or her responses Describes responses to requests to participate in school activities Listens to and reads a simple conversation; responds to related comprehension questions Responds to personalized questions **Culture** Reads about and discusses a musical instrument from Venezuela and a folk dance from Mexico
Verbs: preterite tense forms of *tener, estar, andar,* and *hacer* Adverbs: formation and usage of adverbs ending in *-mente*	**Language Skills** Names things associated with emergencies and asks for help in an emergency Completes sentences based on an illustration Selects appropriate vocabulary to complete sentences Writes and presents, with a small group, a conversation about an emergency Listens to and distinguishes sounds and words linked together in speech Talks about past actions by using the preterite tense of the irregular verbs *tener, estar, andar,* and *hacer*

Lesson / Unit	Active Vocabulary	
Unidad 12 (Continued)	**Usando el español**	
	rapidamente	lentamente
	fácilmente	difícilmente
	tristemente	felizmente
	frecuentemente	usualmente
	generalmente	correctamente
	tener	estar
	andar	hacer
Unidad 13	**Panorama de vocabulario**	
	The Post Office	
	Vamos al correo	
	la carta	la dirección
	el sobre	las estampillas
	el paquete	envolver
	ir al correo	echar el correo
	el cartero	la cartera
	el agente de correo	la agente de correo
	mandar por correo	el correo aéreo

Grammar / Usage	Language / Culture
	Answers personalized questions about last night's activities Surveys classmates about recent illnesses and writes their responses Writes questions for given responses Asks questions about what people did based on verbal cues Answers questions in preterite tense about standing in line Describes actions by using adverbs that end in *-mente* Writes sentences describing how friends act Reads a humorous short story **Culture** Reads about and discusses medical services in rural areas of Peru and a special group of doctors from the United States
Verbs: preterite tense forms of *poder, poner,* and *saber* Verbs: present and preterite tenses of *oír*	**Language Skills** Names people, places, and activities related to the post office Answers questions about mailing letters and packages Asks and answers questions about mailing items in a paired activity Listens to, pronounces, and discriminates between the intonations for questions, statements, and exclamations

Lesson / Unit	Active Vocabulary	
Unidad **13** *(Continued)*	**Usando el español**	
	oír	saber
	poder	poner

Grammar / Usage	Language / Culture
	Talks about past actions by using the preterite tense of the irregular verbs *poder, poner,* and *saber*

Talks about past actions by using the preterite tense of the irregular verbs *poder, poner,* and *saber*

Writes questions and answers based on verbal cues and a model

Selects appropriate sentence completions and writes complete sentences

Prepares and presents, in pairs or a small group, a conversation about excuses for not doing homework

Uses knowledge of verb conjugations to select and use the present and preterite tense forms of the verb *oír*

Writes questions and answers about hearing noises based on verbal cues and models

Listens to and reads a simple conversation; responds to related comprehension questions

Answers personalized questions about past activities

Culture

Reads about and discusses alternative means of communicating between countries by radio programming, shortwave radio, and television

Lesson / Unit	Active Vocabulary
Unidad **14**	Cumulative review and practice of vocabulary learned in Unidad 1 through Unidad 13

Grammar / Usage	Language / Culture
Cumulative review and practice of concepts learned in Unidad 1 through Unidad 13	**Language Skills** Listens to and reads a simple conversation; responds to related comprehension questions Responds to opinions on sports activities and winning Selects appropriate sentence completions and writes complete sentences Transforms infinitive phrases into affirmative and negative familiar commands Transforms sentences in present tense into preterite tense Writes a report on a field trip or a class visitor Writes appropriate forms of irregular verbs to complete sentences based on verbal or visual cues Uses learned vocabulary and visual context to read and understand a simulated travel brochure about Cancún Writes a conversation between a travel agent and a customer about a proposed trip Answers personalized questions about an imagined trip Answers questions using appropriate adverbs ending in *-mente* Answers questions using appropriate preterite tense forms and direct object pronouns

Lesson / Unit	Active Vocabulary
Unidad 14 *(Continued)*	

Grammar / Usage	Language / Culture
	Writes sentences using *hay que* based on verbal cues and a model Sequences sentences about past events in a logical order Listens to and reads a simple conversation; responds to related comprehension questions Writes questions as a newspaper reporter based on visual cues Answers questions about relative locations of various Spanish-speaking countries Answers personalized questions about daily routines Uses knowledge of verb conjugations, tenses, and forms to select forms of ***reírse*** to complete sentences Surveys classmates about what makes them laugh and writes their responses

¡Viva el Español!

¡NOS COMUNICAMOS!

Ava Belisle-Chatterjee, M.A.
Chicago School District 6
Chicago, Illinois

Marcia Fernández
Chicago School District 6
Chicago, Illinois

Abraham Martínez-Cruz, M.A.
Chicago School District 6
Chicago, Illinois

Linda West Tibensky, M.A.
Oak Park School District 200
Oak Park, Illinois

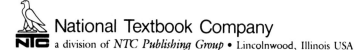

National Textbook Company
a division of *NTC Publishing Group* • Lincolnwood, Illinois USA

Acknowledgments

The publisher would like to thank the following photographers, organizations, and individuals for permission to reprint their photographs.

The following abbreviations are used to indicate the locations of photographs on pages where more than one photograph appears: T (top), B (bottom), L (left), R (right), and C (center).

Cover photos:
Stuart Cohen (BL), David Corona (BR), D. Donne Bryant (T, CR), Kenji Kerins (maracas), National Tourist Office of Spain (C)

Aerolíneas Argentinas, courtesy of Maritz Travel Company: 89CR, 89BL, 224, 274; **American Egg Board:** 5R; **Amigos de las Américas:** 323BR; **Braniff International Airlines: 188BR; California Office of Tourism: 93C (courtesy of Bureau of Reclamation), 188–89; City of Chicago, Department of Aviation:** 54, 91; **Stuart Cohen:** 58L, 8, 13BR, 17, 23TR, 23BR, 29R, 46TL, 46–47, 47TR, 70TL, 70–71, 71TL, 88R, 96TL, 96BL, 97TR, 103L, 103R, 138, 139T, 141, 143BR, 147, 149, 163, 169BR, 175L, 175R, 189TR, 197L, 229L, 235CL, 238BL, 239TR, 258BL, 259BL, 264, 280TL, 302–303, 303TL, 303BR, 308, 320B, 322TL, 331TL, 338CR, 339TR, 339CR, 339BR; **Consulate of Costa Rica:** 79, 161T; **The Cousteau Society, Inc.,** a member-supported non-profit environmental organization: 211BR; **Teresa Cullen:** 258TL; **Gene Dekovic:** 125, 167, 322–23, 339CL; D. **Donne Bryant:** 18T, 18BL, 57, 88L, 187TR, 187BL, 238TL, 239BR, 257BL, 258TR, 323TR; **Fairfax County Council of the Arts: 320T; Manuel Figueroa:** 97BR, 188BL, 195, 237CR, 279, 330, 330 (inset), 331BL, 331BR; **Robert Fried:** 3, 13TR, 15, 18BR, 22BL, 46BL, 70BL, 71BL, 89TL, 93R, 96TR, 96–97, 118TR, 118–19, 139B, 140TR, 142TL, 142–43, 168BL, 169TR, 188TL, 212BL, 212–13, 213BL, 220L, 230, 231L, 231R, 235L, 235CR, 239BL, 246, 257TL, 257TR, 281TR, 338BR, 339TL, 339BL; **Erika Hugo:** 159, 291; **IUPUI Publications:** 256; **Kohler Co.:** 71TR; **James Maharg:** 333; **Sally G. Miller:** 278; **National Broiler Council:** 5TC; **National Tourist Office of Spain:** 106, 118BL, 186, 189BR, 233, 254; **Antonio Obaid:** 220R; **Chip and Rosa María de la Cueva Peterson:** 1, 10, 13CL, 22TL, 22–23, 29L, 47BR, 78, 88C, 101, 115, 116, 118TL, 119TR, 119BR, 140BL, 142BL, 143TR, 150, 161B, 168TL, 168TR, 168–69, 235R, 238–39, 258–59, 259TL, 259TR, 280–81, 281BR, 287, 294, 302TL, 302BL, 303TR, 309T, 311, 325, 338CL, 338BL; **Rice Council for Market Development:** 5R; **James Schmelzer:** 212BR, 219, 237BL, 285; **Marcia Seidletz:** 196, 211TL, 211TR, 212TL, 213TL, 237TL, 341; **Sunkist Growers, Inc.:** 5TL; **Tourism Division, Texas Department of Commerce:** 266; **Dr. Miguel Vasquez:** 13CR, 280BL, 301L, 301R, 309B; **James Vesely:** 197R; **Marina Vine:** 13TL, 93L, 126, 229R, 338T; **Youth for Understanding International Exchange:** 13BL, 322BL.

Project Director: Michael Ross
Project Editor: Marcia Seidletz
Design: David Corona Design
Design Assistant: Kim Meriwether
Content Editor: Minerva Figueroa
Production Editor: Mary Greeley
Artists: James Buckley, Fred Womack
Contributing Artists: Lisa Ansted, Tim Basaldua, Tony Colonna
Contributing Writers: Marcia Gotler, James Maharg, Elizabeth Millán, Catherine Shapiro, Marina Vine
Production Services: Carlisle Communications Ltd.

a division of NTC Publishing Group
4255 West Touhy Avenue
Lincolnwood (Chicago), Illinois 60646-1975 U.S.A.

Printed in the United States of America.
9 0 KP 9 8 7 6 5 4 3 2 1

Contents

Unidad 2 — 46

Unidad 3 — 70

Primera lección

A. Una conversación entre amigos

PEPE: ¡Carmen! ¿Dónde estás?

CARMEN: Estoy dentro de la casa, Pepe. Mi hermana y yo buscamos a Beto.

PEPE: ¿A Beto? A lo mejor está en la escuela o en la casa de un amigo. ¿Está en tu dormitorio?

CARMEN: No. No está debajo de mi cama. Tampoco está dentro de mi ropero.

PEPE: Quizá está en la cocina.

CARMEN: ¡Buena idea! Le gusta la cocina.

PEPE: Bueno, estamos en la cocina. Pero, ¿dónde está Beto?

CARMEN: A lo mejor está sobre el refrigerador.

PEPE: ¿Ustedes buscan a su hermano sobre el refrigerador? ¡Qué extraño!

BETO: ¡Miaou!

CARMEN: ¡Aquí estás, Beto!

Have students listen to the conversation several times before they open their textbooks. Ask them to state (in English or Spanish) what the conversation is about. Then have them read the conversation as they listen to the audiocassette. Finally, ask volunteers to read the conversation aloud.

Preguntas

1. ¿Dónde está Carmen?
2. ¿Qué hacen Carmen y su hermana?
3. ¿Está Beto debajo de la cama? ¿Está dentro del ropero?
4. ¿Dónde está Beto? ¿Está debajo de la mesa?
5. ¿Quién es Beto?

1. Carmen está dentro de la casa.
2. Ellas buscan a Beto.
3. No, no está debajo de la cama. No, no está dentro del ropero.
4. No, no está debajo de la mesa. Está sobre el refrigerador.
5. Beto es un gato.

B. ¿Y tú?

Amalia Rodríguez is a new student in school. She wants to know more about you. Answer her questions. Students may work in pairs to ask and answer the questions.

Primero, lee las preguntas. Luego, contesta en tus palabras.

1. ¿Viven tu familia y tú en una casa o en un apartamento?
2. ¿Les gusta su casa o su apartamento?
3. ¿Vives cerca de la escuela?
4. ¿Cuántos dormitorios tienen ustedes?
5. ¿Hay un comedor?
6. ¿Comen tu familia y tú en la cocina o en el comedor?
7. ¿Hay un teléfono en tu dormitorio?
8. ¿Hay un teléfono en el dormitorio de tus papás?

Extension: With you as the interviewer, have students expand their answers. Ask follow-up questions with each answer they give (e.g., **1. ¿Dónde está tu casa (tu apartamento)? 2. ¿Por qué? 3. ¿Vives cerca de la biblioteca? 4. ¿Cómo son los dormitorios? 5. ¿Es grande o pequeño el comedor? 6. ¿A veces comen ustedes en la sala? 7. ¿Qué tienes en tu dormitorio? 8. ¿Cuántos teléfonos hay en tu casa?**).

¿Es una casa o es un edificio de apartamentos? ¿Hay muchos balcones?

Extension: Have students write two more questions about the picture (e.g., **¿De qué color es el edificio? ¿Es un edificio viejo?**).

C. La casa nueva de Arturo

Arturo's family moved into a new house over the summer. He is writing a report about moving day. He needs your help to get all the words right.

Primero, lee la oración. Luego, lee las palabras entre paréntesis. Por último, completa la oración con la forma apropiada de **poner** o **traer.** Sigue el modelo.

Modelo: Papá y Alonso —— el sillón en la sala. (poner)
Respuesta: **Papá y Alonso ponen el sillón en la sala.**

1. El camión —— todas nuestras cosas. (traer)
2. Mamá y yo —— las lámparas del camión. (traer)
3. Nosotros —— las lámparas en la sala. (poner)
4. Mi hermana —— sus carteles en su dormitorio. (poner)
5. Papá y mi tío Ernesto —— nuestro sofá del camión. (traer)
6. El sofá es muy grande y la puerta es muy pequeña. Por fin, ellos —— el sofá en la sala. (poner)
7. Yo solo —— mi silla grande. (traer) ¡Soy muy fuerte!
8. —— la silla en mi dormitorio. (poner)

Before you present the activity in class, write the subject pronouns on the chalkboard and ask volunteers to complete the conjugations of **poner** and **traer.** You may wish to present some of the exercises from Unidad 5 of *Ya converso más* if students need additional review of these verbs.

Extension: Follow up by asking questions (e.g., **¿Qué trae todas las cosas de la familia de Arturo? ¿Quiénes traen las lámparas del camión? ¿Dónde ponen ellos las lámparas?**).

Review note-taking techniques by using the model or giving an example yourself. Students may invent a shorthand for taking notes (e.g., **Alicia, no/arroz.**).

CH. ¿Qué nos gusta?

What do you and your classmates like to eat? What don't you like to eat? Take a survey and find out.

Before students begin the exercise, identify the food in the photographs. The soup, for example, is **sopa de pollo y legumbres.**

Primero, escoge a cinco compañeros. Ellos tienen que mirar las fotos. Tú tienes que hacer dos preguntas: **¿Qué te gusta comer? ¿Qué no te gusta comer?** Luego, escribe las respuestas. Sigue el modelo.

Modelo: TÚ: María, ¿qué te gusta comer?

MARÍA: Me gustan los limones.

TÚ: ¿Qué no te gusta comer?

MARÍA: No me gusta la sopa.

Respuesta: **A María y a Juan les gustan los limones. A María no le gusta la sopa.** (Etcétera.)

D. La cena de Luisa

You may wish to use exercises from Unidad 12 of *Ya converso más* to review the **e** to **i** stem-changing verbs.

Last night, Luisa and her brother Andrés cooked and served dinner for their parents. Luisa has written some rebus sentences about it.

Primero, lee las palabras y mira los dibujos. Luego, forma una oración. Por último, escribe la oración. Sigue el modelo.

Modelo: Andrés / servir / 

Respuesta: **Andrés sirve las zanahorias.**

1. Primero, yo / servir / 
2. Mamá / pedir / 
3. Andrés / servir /  con 
4. Después, yo / servir /  y 
5. Papá y mamá / pedir /  y 
6. Mamá / pedir / más 

¡Nuestra comida es muy deliciosa!

1. Primero, yo sirvo la ensalada.
2. Mamá pide pan.
3. Andrés sirve pan con margarina.
4. Después, yo sirvo la carne y las legumbres.
5. Papá y mamá piden la sal y la pimienta.
6. Mamá pide más carne.

Extension: Have students make up their own rebus story, using forms of **servir** and **pedir.**

E. Un cuestionario

The Entrevista Company is handing out questionnaires to all the young people at the shopping mall. They want to know about young people and what they do at home. How do you answer their questions?

Primero, lee la oración. Luego, escoge **siempre, a veces** o **nunca.** Por último, escribe una oración completa. Sigue el modelo. Students may work in pairs to role-play the interviewer and interviewee.

Modelo: Caminas a la escuela con tus hermanos.
Siempre A veces Nunca

Respuesta: **Nunca camino a la escuela con mis hermanos.**

Ask volunteers to share their answers with the class.

1. Tu familia y tú comen la cena en la cocina.
Siempre A veces Nunca

2. Escribes cartas a tus abuelos.
Siempre A veces Nunca

3. Tus hermanos y tú corren en la casa.
Siempre A veces Nunca

4. Tus primos van a tu casa.
Siempre A veces Nunca

5. Tú cocinas el desayuno.
Siempre A veces Nunca

Extension: After students have completed the activity, have them change the statements in the exercise into questions (e.g., **1. ¿Cuántas veces caminas a la escuela con tus hermanos?**).

6. Tu familia y tú abren las ventanas en el invierno.
Siempre A veces Nunca

7. Tu mamá bate huevos con la batidora eléctrica.
Siempre A veces Nunca

8. Aprendes mucho cuando miras la televisión.
Siempre A veces Nunca

Segunda lección

A. Una conversación entre familia

JORGE: ¡Mamá! ¡Mamá!

MAMÁ: Sí, hijo. ¿Qué pasa?

JORGE: Diana y todos mis amigos juegan al fútbol hoy. Quiero jugar con ellos.

MAMÁ: Bien. Primero, saca la basura y recoge las cosas en tu dormitorio.

JORGE: Pero, mamá, ellos están jugando ahora.

MAMÁ: Bueno, primero, recoge las cosas en tu dormitorio. Luego, puedes jugar al fútbol con tus amigos. Paco puede sacar la basura.

PACO: ¡Ay, mamá!

JORGE: ¡Muchas gracias, mamá!

MAMÁ: Pero esta noche, Jorge, tú tienes que lavar los platos. Paco puede mirar la televisión.

JORGE: ¡Ay, mamá!

PACO: ¡Muchas gracias, mamá!

After students have listened to the conversation several times, ask them to state what the conversation is about (in English or Spanish). Have students open their textbooks and skim the conversation to confirm their summaries.

Preguntas

1. ¿Qué juegan los amigos de Jorge?
2. ¿Puede jugar Jorge?
3. Primero, ¿qué tiene que hacer Jorge?
4. ¿Qué tiene que hacer Paco?
5. ¿Qué va a hacer Jorge esta noche?

Wording may vary.
1. Todos sus amigos juegan al fútbol.
2. Sí, puede jugar. (*or* No, no puede jugar ahora.)
3. Jorge tiene que sacar las basura y recoger las cosas en su dormitorio.
4. Paco tiene que sacar la basura.
5. Jorge va a lavar los platos esta noche.

B. ¿Y tú?

Before assigning this activity, write a list of chores on the chalkboard to review vocabulary from Unidad 4 of *Ya converso más*.

Elena Caratriste thinks she is the only one in the world who has to do chores before she can spend time with her friends. How do you answer her questions?

Briefly review the conjugation of **jugar** and the construction **tener que** + infinitive.

Primero, lee las preguntas. Luego, contesta en tus palabras.

1. ¿Juegan al fútbol tus amigos y tú?
2. ¿Cuántas veces a la semana juegas con tus amigos?
3. ¿Qué deportes te gustan?
4. ¿Juegas con un equipo?
5. ¿Tienes que recoger tus cosas antes de jugar con tus amigos?
6. ¿Tienes que sacar la basura? ¿Cuándo sacas la basura?
7. ¿Sabes planchar la ropa? ¿Planchas tu ropa?
8. ¿Qué tienes que hacer esta noche?

Ask volunteers to share their answers with the class.

Extension: Continue by asking other questions: **¿Lava los platos en el lavaplatos o en el fregadero? ¿Hay muchos platos o pocos platos? A la mujer, ¿le gusta lavar platos?**

¿Qué hace la mujer? En tu casa, ¿quién lava los platos?

C. ¡Pobrecita de Paquita!

The house is a mess because little Paquita didn't do her chores. Her parents are going to come home any minute! It's up to you to tell Paquita what to do.

Primero, mira el dibujo. Luego, forma una oración. Por último, escribe la oración. Sigue el modelo.

Modelo:

Have students find other examples of commands in activity A. Quickly review familiar affirmative commands of regular **-ar**, **-er**, and **-ir** verbs.

1. ¡Plancha la ropa!
2. ¡Barre el piso!
3. ¡Recoge las cosas!
4. ¡Saca la basura!

Respuesta: ¡Lava la ropa!

1.

3.

2.

4.

CH. Por la mañana y por la noche

Nina is writing a report on what she and her family do in the mornings and at night. Help her finish her sentences.

Primero, lee la oración. Luego, lee la lista de palabras. Por último, escoge la palabra apropiada y completa la oración. Sigue el modelo.

You may wish to use exercises from Unidad 8 of *Ya converso más* to review reflexive verbs.

despertarse	ponerse	quitarse
cepillarse	peinarse	bañarse
lavarse	irse	acostarse

Modelo: Mi papá —— a las seis y media de la mañana.
Respuesta: **Mi papá se despierta a las seis y media de la mañana.**

1. Mi hermanita y yo —— a las siete.
2. Yo —— los dientes y —— la ropa antes del desayuno.
3. Mi hermanita —— la cara y —— . Tiene el pelo largo y bonito.
4. Después del desayuno, nosotras —— de la casa. Es la hora de la escuela.
5. A las nueve de la noche, yo —— en el cuarto de baño.
6. Mi hermanita —— en su cama a las nueve y media. Yo —— a las diez.

Answers may vary. Accept reasonable responses.
1. nos despertamos
2. me cepillo / me pongo
3. se lava / se peina
4. nos vamos
5. me baño
6. se acuesta / me acuesto

Extension: Continue by asking questions: **¿A qué hora se despiertan Nina y su hermanita? ¿Qué hace Nina antes del desayuno? ¿Quién tiene el pelo largo y bonito? ¿Qué hace ella? ¿Cuándo se van las muchachas de la casa? ¿Qué hace Nina a las nueve de la noche? ¿A qué hora se acuestan las muchachas?**

D. ¿Qué están haciendo?

As you look around, you see a lot of busy people. What is everyone doing right now? You may wish to copy on the chalkboard the chart on page 281 of *Ya converso más* to review how the present progressive is formed.

Primero, mira las fotos. Luego, escribe por lo menos una oración sobre cada foto. Si necesitas ayuda, lee la lista de palabras. Sigue el modelo.

Modelo: **6.** Los muchachos están aprendiendo.
La maestra está hablando con la clase.

Ask volunteers to share their sentences with the class.

1. 

4. 

Extension: Have students convert their sentences into present-tense forms and then discuss how the meaning changes [the present progressive means at this moment; the present means in the present].

2. 

5. 

3. 

6. 

hablar	trabajar	poner
aprender	vender	estudiar
bailar	jugar	preguntar
escribir	comprar	contestar

E. Una carta de un amigo

Your friend Tomás loves sports and all kinds of activities. In his letter, he tells you about his busy life.

Lee la carta y contesta las preguntas.

21 de septiembre

¡Hola!

Acabo de jugar al béisbol con mis amigos. Me gusta mucho el béisbol. ¿Juegas tú al béisbol con tus amigos? ¿Sabes jugar muy bien?

Mañana voy a hacer muchas cosas. Voy a tocar mi trompeta en la orquesta de la escuela. Yo no toco muy bien, pero me gusta mucho. ¿Sabes tú tocar un instrumento? Mis amigos tocan muy bien. ¿Saben tus amigos tocar un instrumento?

Mañana voy a montar a caballo también. No sé montar a caballo, pero voy a aprender. También voy a sacar fotos. En mi escuela hay un club de fotografía. Mis amigos del club y yo sacamos muchas fotos. ¿Saben sacar fotos tus amigos y tú?

Bueno, ahora me voy. Tengo que jugar al volibol.

¡Hasta luego!

Tomás

Have students scan the letter for unfamiliar vocabulary (e.g., **trompeta, la orquesta, el club**). Help students recognize that these words are cognates and have the same meaning in Spanish and English, although they are pronounced differently.

Students may either number and write the questions before answering them or attempt to answer them in a letter to Tomás.

Tercera lección

A. Una conversación entre amigos

Before presenting the conversation, have students scan the table of contents to find charts that might help them review the words for countries and nationalities.

PILAR: ¿Adónde quieres ir?

JOSÉ: Quiero ir a España.

PILAR: ¡A España! Pero . . .

JOSÉ: Sí, quiero ir a España en avión. Quiero conocer a los españoles. También quiero ir a Puerto Rico.

PILAR: Pues, ¿por qué?

JOSÉ: Porque los puertorriqueños son muy simpáticos. Además, puedo ir a Puerto Rico en barco.

PILAR: ¡Qué interesante! Ahora, ¿adónde . . .

JOSÉ: También pienso ir al Canadá un día. Y tú, Pilar, ¿adónde quieres ir algún día?

PILAR: No sé. Pero ahora quiero ir al cine. Quiero ver *Los tigres de la India.* Podemos ir en autobús. ¿Quieres?

JOSÉ: ¡Buena idea! ¡Vamos al cine!

Extension: Ask students to scan the conversation and write two more questions (e.g., **¿Cómo puede ir a Puerto Rico? ¿Qué quiere ver Pilar en el cine?**)

Preguntas

1. ¿Cómo quiere ir a España José?
2. ¿Por qué quiere ir a Puerto Rico?
3. ¿Adónde piensa ir un día?
4. ¿Adónde quiere ir Pilar?
5. ¿Cómo pueden ir Pilar y José al cine?

Ask students to explain the misunderstanding between José and Pilar. Write a list of synonyms on the chalkboard: **hoy, en este momento, en el futuro.** Have volunteers write the words **ahora, un día,** and **algún día** with the appropriate synonyms (**un día** and **algún día** would both correspond to **en el futuro**).

Answers may vary. Accept reasonable responses.
1. Quiere ir a España en avión.
2. Quiere ir a Puerto Rico porque los puertorriqueños son muy simpáticos.
3. Un día piensa ir al Canadá.
4. Pilar quiere ir al cine.
5. Pueden ir al cine en autobús.

B. ¿Y tú?

The Azteca Travel Agency wants to know how young people feel about traveling. How do you answer their questions?

Lee la pregunta y contesta en tus palabras.

Present the questions in class to be sure students understand them completely.

1. ¿Adónde quieres ir algún día? ¿Por qué?

2. ¿Cómo quieres ir? ¿en avión? ¿en tren? ¿en barco?

Ask volunteers to role-play a travel agent and a customer.

3. ¿Adónde piensas ir este fin de semana?

4. ¿Cómo piensas ir? ¿a pie? ¿en coche? ¿en autobús?

5. ¿Te gustan más los aviones o los trenes?

6. ¿Conoces a alguien de la América Latina?

7. ¿De dónde eres tú? ¿Eres del Paraguay?

8. ¿De dónde son tus amigos? ¿Son mexicanos? ¿Son puertorriqueños?

Extension: Review adjectives by having students answer questions about the boy in the picture: **¿Cómo es el pelo del muchacho? ¿Es largo o corto? ¿Es liso o rizado el pelo? ¿De qué color es el pelo? ¿De qué color son los ojos? ¿Cómo es la chaqueta del muchacho? ¿De qué color es su camisa?** Continue by asking questions about **los policías** on page 15.

Este chico es mexicano. ¿Eres tú mexicano o estadounidense?

C. ¿Qué hay en la calle?

Use items in the classroom to review affirmative and negative words.

Little Paquito is waiting for his friends to arrive. He's not tall enough to see out the window, so he asks you to tell him what you see.

Primero, mira la foto. Luego, lee y contesta cada pregunta con una oración completa. Sigue el modelo.

Modelo:

¿Hay alguien en la calle?

Respuesta: Sí, hay alguien en la calle.

Ask other questions about the **modelo** picture: **No hay nada en el estacionamiento, ¿verdad? ¿Qué son los automóviles?**

1.

a. ¿Hay algo en la calle?
b. ¿Qué es?
c. No hay nadie, ¿verdad?

1. a. Sí, hay algo en la calle.
   b. Es un autobús.
   c. Verdad. No hay nadie en el autobús.

2.

a. ¿Hay alguien en la plaza?
b. ¿Hay algo en los balcones?
c. ¿Hay alguien dentro de los edificios?

2. a. No hay nadie en la plaza.
   b. No, no hay nada en los balcones.
   c. Sí, hay alguien dentro de los edificios.

CH. El domingo de Marcos

Marcos has written about his Sunday, but he has made some mistakes with verbs. Help him correct his sentences.

Primero, lee la oración. Luego, cambia la palabra en letras negras a una palabra correcta. Por último, escribe la oración correcta. Sigue el modelo.

Be sure students understand that the verb choice is correct, but the form of the verb is incorrect.

Modelo: Hoy, yo **piensa** ir a la casa de María.

Respuesta: **Hoy, yo pienso ir a la casa de María.**

Mi domingo

1. Me levanto a las nueve y tengo hambre. Yo **comenzamos** a preparar el desayuno.
2. Mi papá se levanta y también **quiero** comer. Preparamos el desayuno juntos.
3. Me voy de la casa y **cierran** la puerta.
4. Voy a la casa de María. Ella **pienso** ir al centro.
5. Nosotros no **pueden** ir en autobús porque no hay autobuses los domingos.
6. Cuando volvemos del centro, tenemos hambre. **Almuerza** en la casa de María.
7. Yo **piensa** comer sopa y un sándwich.
8. Los hermanos de María están en casa. Ellos **queremos** un almuerzo muy extraño.
9. Ellos **pienso** comer espaguetis con gelatina.
10. Yo **probamos** los espaguetis con gelatina. ¡Qué horror!

1. comienzo
2. quiere
3. cierro
4. piensa
5. podemos
6. Almorzamos
7. pienso
8. quieren
9. piensan
10. pruebo

Ask volunteers to read the "story" aloud, substituting the corrected forms of the verbs. If students need help, have them turn to the charts of stem-changing verbs in the back of the book.

D. Un cuestionario

Whom do you know in your school? Claudia Curiosa, the school counselor, has handed out a questionnaire to find out.

Primero, lee la pregunta. Luego, contesta la pregunta con una oración completa. Sigue el modelo.

Modelo: ¿Conoces al director o a la directora?

Respuesta: **Sí, conozco a la directora.**

Extension: Have students write two or three questions they could ask Claudia Curiosa about people in the school.

1. ¿Conoces a los conserjes? ¿Cómo se llaman?
2. ¿Conoces a la enfermera? ¿Hay un enfermero en la escuela? ¿Vas mucho a la enfermería?
3. ¿Conocen tus papás a tus maestros?
4. ¿Conocen tus compañeros y tú a la secretaria? ¿Cómo se llama? ¿Dónde trabaja?
5. De tus maestros, ¿quién es el más alto? ¿Quién es el más cómico?
6. De tus maestras, ¿quién es la más simpática? ¿Quién es la más impaciente?

You may wish to use exercises from Unidad 11 in *Ya converso más* to review **conocer** and the personal **a**, and exercises from Unidad 9 to review comparative and superlative constructions.

E. Una descripción

Choose someone in the school to describe. See if your classmates can guess who it is.

Escoge a una persona de la escuela. Escribe cuatro oraciones sobre la persona. Comparte tu descripción con tus compañeros.

You may wish to review the descriptions before students read them to the class.

You may convert this activity into a game for warm-up activities over the course of a week or you may display a selection of descriptions on the bulletin board with a blank sheet next to each one for students to write down their guesses.

F. Una carta de un amigo

Jerónimo Cárdenas has just moved out of town and wants to exchange letters with a pen pal from his old school.

Primero, lee la carta. Luego, contesta las preguntas.

Have students scan the letter for unfamiliar vocabulary; then read the letter for general meaning. Finally, have them read the letter carefully before they answer Jerónimo's questions.

15 de octubre

Hola amigo o amiga,

Yo vivo en Santa Bárbara y voy a la escuela Martín. Muchas personas de mi familia todavía viven en tu comunidad. Conozco a muchas personas allá. ¿Conoces tú a muchas personas de tu comunidad?

Mi tía es conserje en la escuela secundaria. ¿Conoces a los conserjes en tu escuela? Mi abuelo es médico. Trabaja en el hospital y examina a muchos pacientes. ¿Conoces tú a unos médicos? Mi primo es conductor de autobús. Somos todos muy altos en mi familia, pero él es el más alto. ¿Son altos en tu familia? ¿Quién es el más alto o la más alta? Mi tío es policía. Algún día quiero ser policía, como mi tío. ¿Qué quieres ser algún día?

Ahora tengo que ayudar a mi mamá. Por favor, escríbeme pronto. No conozco a nadie en Santa Bárbara.

Hasta pronto,

Jerónimo

You may wish to ask comprehension questions such as the following:

1. ¿Dónde vive Jerónimo?
2. ¿Quiénes viven en nuestra comunidad?
3. ¿En qué trabaja su tía?
4. ¿Quién es médico? ¿Qué hace él?
5. ¿Quién es el más alto de la familia de Jerónimo?
6. ¿Qué quiere ser Jerónimo algún día?

Unidad 1

After completing this unit, students should be able to:

- identify and name travel destinations and the people and activities involved in making plans
- describe actions by using the present tense of regular **-ar, -er,** and **-ir** verbs; irregular verbs **estar, ser,** and **ir;** and **o** to **ue** and **e** to **ie** stem-changing verbs (review)
- identify places and points of interest for travelers in Mexico and Spain.

The photographs may be used for informal assessment and review by combining commands and questions:

- ► Señala una agencia de viajes.
- ► Muéstrame a una agente de viajes. ¿Cómo es ella?
- ► ¿Hay playas en este lago? ¿Cómo es el lago?
- ► ¿Dónde están los muchachos? ¿Descansan ellos?

Panorama de vocabulario

Pensamos viajar

la agencia de viajes

la selva

la viajera

el río

las montañas

el volcán

el viajero

el valle

el agente de viajes

Students may already know another synonym for **la montaña: la sierra. El monte** may refer to one mountain (e.g., mount) or to a patch of land covered by trees and shrubs.

¿Cuánto cuesta el viaje?

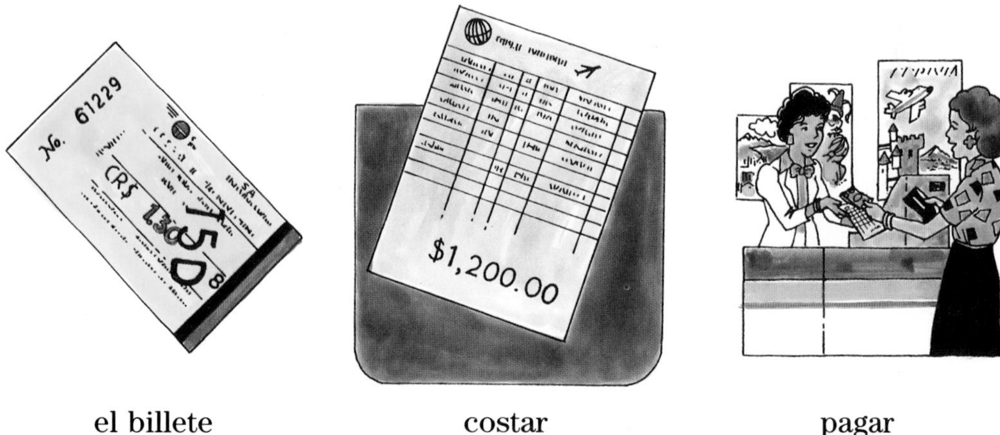

el billete | costar | pagar

El boleto is also used throughout much of Latin America to mean ticket.

¡Aprende el vocabulario!

A. María's friends are all going to different places on vacation. Help her find out where her friends are going.

Primero, lee el nombre y haz una pregunta. Luego, mira el dibujo y contesta la pregunta. Sigue el modelo.

Modelo:

Marta

Have students role-play the exercise with a partner. Have them repeat the exercise, pretending to ask about the person's family (e.g., **¿Adónde van ustedes, Isabel? Vamos al lago.**).

Respuesta: **P: ¿Adónde vas, Marta?**

R: Voy a la playa.

1. Isabel

1. P: ¿Adónde vas, Isabel?
R: Voy al lago.

2. Eduardo

2. P: ¿Adónde vas, Eduardo?
R: Voy a las montañas.

3. José

3. P: ¿Adónde vas, José?
R: Voy a la selva.

4. Ana

4. P: ¿Adónde vas, Ana?
R: Voy al desierto.

5. Beatriz

5. P: ¿Adónde vas, Beatriz?
R: Voy al volcán.

6. Humberto

6. P: ¿Adónde vas, Humberto?
R: Voy al río.

B. The Hernández family can't decide where to go on vacation. Luckily, they have agreed to ask someone for help.

Primero, lee la oración. Luego, escoge una palabra o una frase para completar la oración. Sigue el modelo.

Modelo: La familia Hernández va a una ——.

a. selva b. agencia de viajes

Respuesta: **La familia Hernández va a una agencia de viajes.**

Students may enjoy playing the roles of mother, father, and travel agent.

1. Los papás hablan con la ——.

   a. agente de viajes b. viajera

2. EL PAPÁ: Trabajo mucho todos los días. Yo quiero ——.

   a. descansar b. pagar

3. LA MAMÁ: Nuestros hijos quieren nadar. Ellos quieren ir a ——.

   a. un volcán b. un lago

4. LA AGENTE: ¿Piensan —— muy lejos?

   a. pagar b. viajar

5. EL PAPÁ: Sí. ¿Cuánto va a —— un viaje largo?

   a. costar b. pagar

6. LA AGENTE: ¿Cuántos —— van a ir?

   a. valles b. viajeros

7. LA MAMÁ: Hay nueve personas en la familia. Tenemos que comprar nueve ——.

   a. agencias b. billetes

8. LA AGENTE: Un viaje largo para nueve personas cuesta diez mil dólares. Aquí está ——.

   a. la cuenta b. el cartel

Extension: Advanced students may try to make up their own scenes between a travel agent and a customer.

C. Imagine that your friends are asking you for advice on where they can go on vacation. What advice do you give them?

Primero, lee las oraciones. Luego, forma una pregunta. Lee la lista de palabras. Sigue el modelo.

el lago	las montañas	el desierto
la playa	la selva	el valle

Modelo: Alicia: Quiero descansar. También quiero nadar. ¿Adónde puedo ir?

Respuesta: **¿Por qué no vas a la playa?**

Extension: Continue the activity by having some volunteers state what activities they enjoy and others suggest places they should visit.

1. Edilberto: Quiero ver un volcán y un valle. ¿Adónde puedo ir?
2. Juanito: Quiero ir a un lugar donde hace mucho calor. También me gusta mucho el sol. ¿Adónde puedo ir?
3. Mariela: Me gustan mucho las plantas. Quiero sacar fotos de plantas y animales. ¿Adónde puedo ir?
4. Esteban: Me gusta mucho nadar y me gustan las playas pequeñas. No me gusta el océano. ¿Adónde puedo ir?

1. ¿Por qué no vas a las montañas?
2. ¿Por qué no vas al desierto?
3. ¿Por qué no vas a la selva?
4. ¿Por qué no vas al lago?

D. Take a survey of your classmates to find out where they want to spend their vacations.

Pregunta a diez compañeros de clase **¿Dónde quieres pasar las vacaciones?** Escribe las respuestas. Primero, lee el modelo.

Answers will vary. You may want to review note-taking techniques with the class before beginning this activity.

Modelo: TÚ: ¿Dónde quieres pasar las vacaciones?

ANA: Quiero pasar las vacaciones en la playa.

Respuesta: **1. Ana quiere pasar las vacaciones en la playa.**

Extension: Have students present their results to the class. Combine the results of the surveys to make a chart of the class vacation preferences.

Los sonidos del idioma

Las vocales: **ae, ea; ao, oa**

Escucha y repite. Compara los sonidos de las vocales.

ae	ea	ao	oa
aeropuerto	idea	bacalao	toalla
caer	tarea	ahora	barbacoa
maestro	impermeable	caos	boa

You may explain to students that the vowel combinations on this page represent two vowels with two sounds. Later, they will practice two-vowel combinations that have only one sound.

1. El maestro trae su impermeable al aeropuerto.
2. Ahora el bacalao está en una toalla cerca de la barbacoa.
3. Una boa en el salón resulta en el caos.

Este lago está en las montañas de Venezuela. ¿Quieres ir a Venezuela?

Para comprar un billete de avión, tienes que ir a la agencia de viajes.

Extension: Ask students questions about the pictures (e.g., **¿Qué tiempo hace en las montañas? ¿Hace sol? ¿Cómo es la agencia? ¿Cuántos agentes hay en esta agencia?**).

Usando el español

Talking about Actions in the Present

Rule: To show which person does an action in the present, first drop the infinitive ending (**-ar**, **-er**, or **-ir**) of a regular verb. Then add the correct ending to the stem—the main part of the verb.

You already know many regular **-ar, -er,** and **-ir** verbs. You have used them to talk about the things you do. So far, you have talked about actions in the present.

When you use verb forms to talk about the present, you say the verb is in the present tense. Look at the charts of some regular **-ar, -er,** and **-ir** verbs.

Singular

	visitar	**correr**	**recibir**
yo	visit**o**	corr**o**	recib**o**
tú	visit**as**	corr**es**	recib**es**
él / ella / usted	visit**a**	corr**e**	recib**e**

Have students locate the charts of regular **-ar, -er,** and **-ir** verbs in the Appendix.

Plural

	visitar	**correr**	**recibir**
nosotros (-as)	visit**amos**	corr**emos**	recib**imos**
vosotros (-as)	visit**áis**	corr**éis**	recib**ís**
ellos / ellas / ustedes	visit**an**	corr**en**	recib**en**

The charts on the preceding page show you the conjugations of three regular **-ar, -er,** and **-ir** verbs in the present tense.

Have volunteers read the questions and answers aloud.

Practice reading the following questions and answers:

Pregunta: ¿Cuándo visitas a tu abuela?
Respuesta: Visito a mi abuela todos los sábados.

Pregunta: ¿Cuánto pagan ustedes por los billetes?
Respuesta: Pagamos cien dólares.

Pregunta: Tus papás corren todos los días, ¿verdad?
Respuesta: Sí, siempre corren antes del desayuno.

Pregunta: ¿Qué van a comer esta tarde?
Respuesta: Siempre comemos sándwiches por la tarde.

Pregunta: ¿Recibes cartas de tus primos?
Respuesta: No, nunca recibo cartas de ellos.

Pregunta: ¿Dónde viven los López?
Respuesta: Viven en la calle Juárez.

How observant are you?

Which verb forms in the questions and answers come from **-ar** verbs?

Which verb forms come from **-er** verbs?

Which verb forms come from **-ir** verbs?

[**Visitas**, **visito**, **pagan**, and **pagamos** come from **-ar** verbs.
Corren, **comer**, and **comemos** come from **-er** verbs.
Recibes, **recibo**, and **viven** come from **-ir** verbs.]

¡Vamos a practicar!

A. Before the Uribe family can leave on vacation this afternoon, they have many things to do.

Primero, lee la frase. Luego, forma una oración. Sigue el modelo.

Extension: Have students repeat the exercise, stating which family member performs each task (e.g., **Mi papá seca la ropa.**).

Modelo: lavar la ropa

Respuesta: **Lavamos la ropa por la mañana.**

1. secar la ropa
2. barrer el piso
3. abrir todas las cartas
4. leer todas las cartas
5. sacar la basura
6. recibir los billetes

1. Secamos la ropa por la mañana.
2. Barremos el piso por la mañana.
3. Abrimos todas las cartas por la mañana.
4. Leemos todas las cartas por la mañana.
5. Sacamos la basura por la mañana.
6. Recibimos los billetes por la mañana.

B. You're curious about what Elisa Uribe and her family always do on their vacations.

Primero, lee la pregunta y la frase entre paréntesis. Luego, forma una oración. Sigue el modelo.

Modelo: Elisa, ¿qué haces en las vacaciones? (descansar mucho)

Respuesta: **Siempre descanso mucho.**

1. ¿Qué hace tu papá? (sacar fotos)
2. ¿Qué hacen tus hermanos? (subir la montaña)
3. ¿Qué hace tu mamá? (leer novelas en la playa)

1. Mi papá siempre saca fotos.
2. Mis hermanos siempre suben la montaña.
3. Mi mamá siempre lee novelas en la playa.

Extension: Continue the activity by asking students what they and members of their families do on vacation.

4. ¿Qué hacen tus abuelos? (nadar en el lago)
5. ¿Qué hace tu hermana? (correr en el valle)

4. Mis abuelos siempre nadan en el lago.
5. Mi hermana siempre corre en el valle.

C. Imagine that you have won a trip to the vacation spot of your choice. Now that you are there, what do you and your family do every day?

Primero, lee la lista de actividades. Luego, escribe cinco oraciones. Lee el modelo.

Answers will vary. This activity can be assigned as homework, after completing several examples orally in class.

subir la montaña	descansar en la playa
sacar fotos	caminar por la selva
nadar mucho	comer mucho
leer novelas	escribir cartas
montar a caballo	correr

Modelo: **1.** Nado mucho todos los días.
2. Saco fotos todos los días.
3. Mis papás escriben cartas todos los días.
4. Mi hermana lee novelas todos los días.
5. Nosotros comemos mucho todos los días.

Extension: You might wish to have students write five sentences telling what members of their family never do or sometimes do on their vacations.

Enrichment: Students may work in pairs or small groups to prepare a vacation activity "Big Book" based on this exercise.

Using Irregular Verbs

Rule: The irregular verbs **estar, ser,** and **ir** have different forms you must learn because their endings do not follow the pattern of regular and stem-changing verbs.

You have also talked about yourself and others and the things you do by using three important irregular verbs: **estar, ser,** and **ir.**

Singular

	estar	**ser**	**ir**
yo	estoy	soy	voy
tú	estás	eres	vas
él / ella / usted	está	es	va

Help students to observe the differences between these verbs and regular **-ar, -er,** and **-ir** verbs.

Plural

	estar	**ser**	**ir**
nosotros (-as)	estamos	somos	vamos
vosotros (-as)	estáis	sois	vais
ellos / ellas / ustedes	están	son	van

Have students find charts of **estar, ser,** and **ir** in the Appendix.

How observant are you?

Do you use the verbs in the chart to talk about the past or the present?

What tense is the conjugation of **estar**? of **ser**? of **ir**?

[You use the verbs in the chart to talk about the present. The tense of all three conjugations is the present.]

¡Vamos a practicar!

A. All your friends have gone away for the weekend. They promised to call you, though.

Primero, lee la pregunta. Luego, forma una oración con las palabras entre paréntesis. Sigue el modelo.

Modelo: ¡Hola, Carlos! ¿Dónde estás?
(cerca de un volcán)

Respuesta: **Estoy cerca de un volcán.**

This activity can be assigned as homework after you have presented it orally in class.

1. ¡Hola, Ana y Marta! ¿Dónde están?
(en una selva)
2. ¡Hola, Eduardo! ¿Dónde estás?
(en la playa)
3. ¡Hola, Susana! ¿Dónde estás?
(cerca de una montaña)
4. ¡Hola, Luis y Ricardo! ¿Dónde están?
(en el desierto)
5. ¡Hola, Enrique! ¿Dónde está tu hermana Ema?
(en el lago)
6. ¡Hola, Carlota! ¿Dónde están tus hermanos Jorge y David?
(cerca del río)

1. Estamos en una selva.
2. Estoy en la playa.
3. Estoy cerca de una montaña.
4. Estamos en el desierto.
5. Está en el lago.
6. Están cerca del río.

Extension: Have students expand the conversations as a paired role-play activity.

◐ B. Gerardo just returned from his family reunion. You want to know if his family is still the same.

Primero, mira el dibujo. Luego, lee las palabras. Por último, forma una pregunta y una respuesta. Sigue el modelo.

Modelo: tía Anita / bonita

Respuesta: **P: ¿Todavía es bonita tu tía Anita?**

R: Sí, es bonita.

Before beginning the activity, help students identify the people in the illustration. Have students work in pairs to ask and answer the questions.

1. tu primo Diego / delgado
2. tus bisabuelos / gruesos
3. tus primas / cómicas
4. tu tío Francisco / inteligente
5. tu abuela / tímida
6. tu abuelo / alto

1. P: ¿Todavía es delgado tu primo Diego?
   R: Sí, es delgado.
2. P: ¿Todavía son gruesos tus bisabuelos?
   R: Sí, son gruesos.
3. P: ¿Todavía son cómicas tus primas?
   R: Sí, son cómicas.
4. P: ¿Todavía es inteligente tu tío Francisco?
   R: Sí, es inteligente.
5. P: ¿Todavía es tímida tu abuela?
   R: Sí, es tímida.
6. P: ¿Todavía es alto tu abuelo?
   R: Sí, es alto.

Extension: Ask students to describe members of their families to the class. You may wish to have students brainstorm for possible adjectives they could use to describe people. Volunteers may write the lists on the chalkboard.

C. Where are your friends going? How are they going? What are they going to do?

Primero, lee la frase **a** y escribe una oración. Luego, lee la frase **b** y escribe otra oración. Sigue el modelo.

Modelo: a. Samuel / al desierto / autobús
b. sacar fotos

Respuesta: a. **Samuel va al desierto en autobús.**
b. **Va a sacar fotos.**

1. a. Eva y Beto / a las montañas / avión
b. viajar muy lejos

2. a. el Sr. Gutiérrez / al lago / coche
b. nadar y descansar

3. a. la Srta. Alonso / a la selva / autobús
b. montar a caballo

4. a. Carmen / al río / barco
b. ir de pesca

5. a. Ignacio y Rita / al desierto / a pie
b. estudiar los animales y las plantas

1. a. Eva y Beto van a las montañas en avión.
   b. Van a viajar muy lejos.
2. a. El Sr. Gutiérrez va al lago en coche.
   b. Va a nadar y descansar.
3. a. La Srta. Alonso va a la selva en autobús.
   b. Va a montar a caballo.
4. a. Carmen va al río en barco.
   b. Va a ir de pesca.
5. a. Ignacio y Rita van al desierto a pie.
   b. Van a estudiar los animales y las plantas.

Using Stem-Changing Verbs

Rule: Some verbs with **o** in their stems change the **o** to **ue** in all forms of the present tense, except **nosotros** (and **vosotros**). Similarly, some verbs with **e** in their stems change the **e** to **ie** in all forms, except **nosotros** (and **vosotros**).

So far in this unit, you have reviewed the regular **-ar, -er,** and **-ir** verbs and three irregular verbs. Now look at the following chart of a stem-changing verb in the present tense.

Ask students where they might find more charts of stem-changing verbs in the book. Have them look up stem-changing verbs they know in the classroom dictionary and note whether the verbs have a special listing indicating the stem change.

o to ue: poder

Singular		Plural	
yo	**puedo**	nosotros (-as)	podemos
tú	**puedes**	vosotros (-as)	podéis
él / ella / usted	**puede**	ellos / ellas / ustedes	**pueden**

[You would use the same endings as for regular **-ar** verbs to conjugate **almorzar, probar,** and **costar.**]

Recall some other **o** to **ue** stem-changing verbs you have learned: **almorzar, probar,** and now **costar.** These verbs change their stems, but they do not end in **-er.** What verb endings would you use to conjugate **almorzar** and **probar**?

Volver is an **o** to **ue** stem-changing verb, too. What endings would you use for **volver**? [You would use the same endings as for regular **-er** verbs to conjugate **volver.**]

Now look at the following chart of another stem-changing verb.

e to ie: pensar

Singular		Plural	
yo	**pienso**	nosotros (-as)	**pensamos**
tú	**piensas**	vosotros (-as)	**pensáis**
él, ella, usted	**piensa**	ellos, ellas, ustedes	**piensan**

Recall some other **e** to **ie** verbs you have learned: **comenzar** and **cerrar.**

How observant are you?

What forms do not change for stem-changing verbs?

What tense are the verbs in the chart? [The **nosotros** and **vosotros** forms do not change. The verbs in the chart are in the present tense.]

Have volunteers read the sample questions and answers aloud.

Practice reading the following questions and answers:

Pregunta: ¿Puedes ir al cine mañana?

Respuesta: No, no puedo. Mañana comienzan mis clases de baile moderno.

Pregunta: ¿Dónde piensan pasar las vacaciones?

Respuesta: Pensamos ir a las montañas del Perú. Podemos caminar mucho en las montañas.

¡Vamos a practicar!

A. This is a fast-paced world! As they say in Spanish: **El tiempo es oro.** How precious is your time?

Primero, lee la hora. Luego, contesta la pregunta. Sigue el modelo.

Modelo:  ¿A qué hora comienzan tus clases?

Respuesta: **Mis clases comienzan a las ocho de la mañana.**

You may wish to assign this activity as homework after presenting it orally in class.

1.  ¿A qué hora almuerzan tus amigos y tú?

1. Almorzamos a las once y cuarto.

2.  ¿A qué hora piensas ir a la biblioteca?

2. Pienso ir a la biblioteca a las dos y media.

3.  ¿A qué hora comienzas a estudiar?

3. Comienzo a estudiar a las seis y media.

4.  ¿A qué hora cierras tus libros?

4. Cierro mis libros a las ocho menos cinco.

5.  ¿A qué hora comienza tu programa favorito?

5. Mi programa favorito comienza a las ocho.

6.  ¿A qué hora puedes ir a tu dormitorio?

6. Puedo ir a mi dormitorio a las diez y cuarto.

B. What is a typical day like for you?

Primero, lee la pregunta. Luego, contesta en tus palabras. Sigue el modelo.

Modelo: ¿Puedes visitar a tus amigos todos los días?

Respuesta: **No, no puedo.**

Answers will vary. Accept reasonable responses that include the correct verb forms.

1. ¿Pueden tus amigos mirar la televisión cada noche?
2. ¿Pueden tus amigos y tú hablar una hora por teléfono?
3. ¿Almuerzan tus compañeros y tú en casa o en la escuela?
4. ¿Cuánto cuesta el almuerzo en la escuela?
5. ¿Pruebas comida diferente en la escuela?
6. ¿Prueban tu familia y tú comida interesante en casa?
7. ¿Cuántas horas al día puedes mirar la televisión?
8. ¿Puedes ver programas a las once de la noche?

1. pueden
2. podemos
3. almorzamos
4. cuesta
5. pruebo
6. probamos
7. puedo
8. puedo

C. Imagine that you can interview your favorite singer. What questions will you ask?

Escribe ocho preguntas a tu cantante favorito. Primero, lee unos ejemplos.

Modelo:
1. ¿Cuánto cuesta su instrumento musical?
2. ¿Puede viajar mucho?
3. ¿Adónde piensa viajar este año?
4. ¿Con quién almuerza usted todos los días?

Etcétera.

Extension: Have students work in pairs to create dialogues between a reporter and a famous singer. Have volunteers role-play their dialogues for the class.

¡A conversar!

¿Adónde vamos?

After students are familiar with the conversation, have them role-play it for the class.

MAMÁ: Hijos, su papá y yo pensamos hacer un viaje fuera de los Estados Unidos.

PAPÁ: Sí. ¿Adónde quieren pasar las vacaciones?

EVA: Bueno, podemos ir al Ecuador. En el Ecuador hay montañas, valles y muchas playas. Podemos ver el Océano Pacífico.

HUGO: Podemos ir a la República Dominicana. Probamos frutas tropicales. También vamos a nadar en el Mar Caribe. Papá, tú puedes descansar en la playa.

PAPÁ: Es cierto. Pero prefiero ir a otro lugar. Cuesta mucho pasar las vacaciones en una isla.

MAMÁ: Podemos ir a México. México no está muy lejos. Hay playas bonitas, montañas, selvas . . . Pues, hay de todo.

EVA: ¡Buena idea!

MAMÁ: ¿Cuánto cuestan cuatro billetes de avión?

PAPÁ: No sé. Mañana voy a hablar con el agente de viajes.

HUGO: Tenemos que leer muchos libros sobre México.

EVA: ¡Estos estudios sí me gustan!

Preguntas

Accept shortened or complete responses, as shown for question 1.

1. ¿Qué piensan hacer los papás?
2. ¿Adónde quiere ir Eva? ¿Por qué?
3. ¿Adónde quiere ir Hugo? ¿Por qué?
4. ¿Por qué el papá no quiere ir a una isla?
5. ¿Qué hay en México?

1. Un viaje fuera de los Estados Unidos. / Piensan hacer un viaje fuera de los Estados Unidos. / Los papás piensan hacer un viaje fuera de los Estados Unidos.
2. Eva quiere ir al Ecuador. Quiere ver las montañas, los valles, las playas y el Océano Pacífico.
3. Hugo quiere ir a la República Dominicana. Quiere probar frutas tropicales y nadar en el Mar Caribe.
4. El papá no quiere ir a una isla porque cuesta mucho.
5. En México hay playas bonitas, montañas, selvas y de todo.

¡Conversa tú!

1. ¿Dónde vives tú?
2. ¿Hay montañas y valles en tu estado?
3. ¿Hay lagos y playas en tu estado?
4. ¿Piensas viajar en el futuro?
5. ¿Adónde quieres ir?
6. ¿Puedes visitar a tu familia en otro país?
7. ¿Conoces a un agente de viajes?
8. ¿Hay una agencia de viajes cerca de tu casa?

Have students make up their own conversations between themselves and a travel agent.

¡A divertirnos!

¿Adónde van?

This illustration can be used to review clothing vocabulary. Ask students what they would wear or take if they were going to the jungle, the desert, the beach, or the mountains.

Mira a las personas. ¿Adónde piensa viajar cada persona?

La cultura y tú

See Unit Plans, Unidad 1, for additional background information.

¿Dónde quieres pasar las vacaciones?

A muchas personas de los Estados Unidos les gusta pasar las vacaciones en países de habla española. Mira los mapas de México y España y lee las descripciones. ¿Piensas tú pasar las vacaciones en España o en México algún día?

Have students scan the passages for unfamiliar words and phrases and look them up in the Spanish-English Glossary.

En México, puedes hacer muchas cosas. Puedes nadar en el Océano Pacífico o en el Golfo de México. Puedes caminar en el desierto de Baja California. También, puedes visitar las ruinas mayas y aztecas. De las ruinas puedes aprender algo sobre la historia del país. Además, México es muy conveniente para los estadounidenses. Está muy cerca de los Estados Unidos. Tampoco cuesta mucho ir a México. Puedes ir en avión, en tren o en tu propio automóvil.

Have students find Mexico and Spain on a world map or a globe.

España está más lejos que México. Es un país de Europa. En España puedes nadar en el Océano Atlántico o en el Mar Mediterráneo. Si quieres, puedes ver las montañas de la Sierra Guadarrama o los Montes Pirineos. También, puedes conocer muchas ciudades muy interesantes, como Granada, Madrid y Barcelona.

España es un país muy viejo y tiene una historia larga y emocionante. Puedes ver palacios y castillos muy viejos. También puedes probar las famosas naranjas de Valencia. Puedes viajar a España en avión o en barco.

Ask comprehension questions about the readings (e.g., **¿Cuál está más cerca de los Estados Unidos, México o España? ¿Dónde puedes nadar en México?**).

Some students may have traveled to Mexico or Spain. Ask these students to talk about their experiences.

Enrichment: Have pairs or small groups of students choose a location on one of the maps and research the location. The groups may present their reports to the class.

Unidad

After completing this unit, students should be able to:

- identify and name people, places, and activities related to air travel
- talk about doing or making things by using the present tense of **hacer**
- talk about what people say by using the present tense of **decir**
- refer to something that receives the action of a verb by using direct object pronouns
- read a simulated airline ticket and boarding pass
- read about and discuss the 24-hour clock.

The photographs may be used for informal assessment and review by combining commands and questions:

- ► Toca el equipaje. ¿Está el equipaje dentro o fuera del avión?
- ► Muéstrame a una aeromoza. ¿Es bonita?
- ► Mira el horario. ¿A qué hora llega el vuelo 802 de Acapulco? ¿Va a llegar temprano, tarde o a tiempo?
- ► ¿Cómo se llama la aerolínea? ¿Suben o bajan los pasajeros?

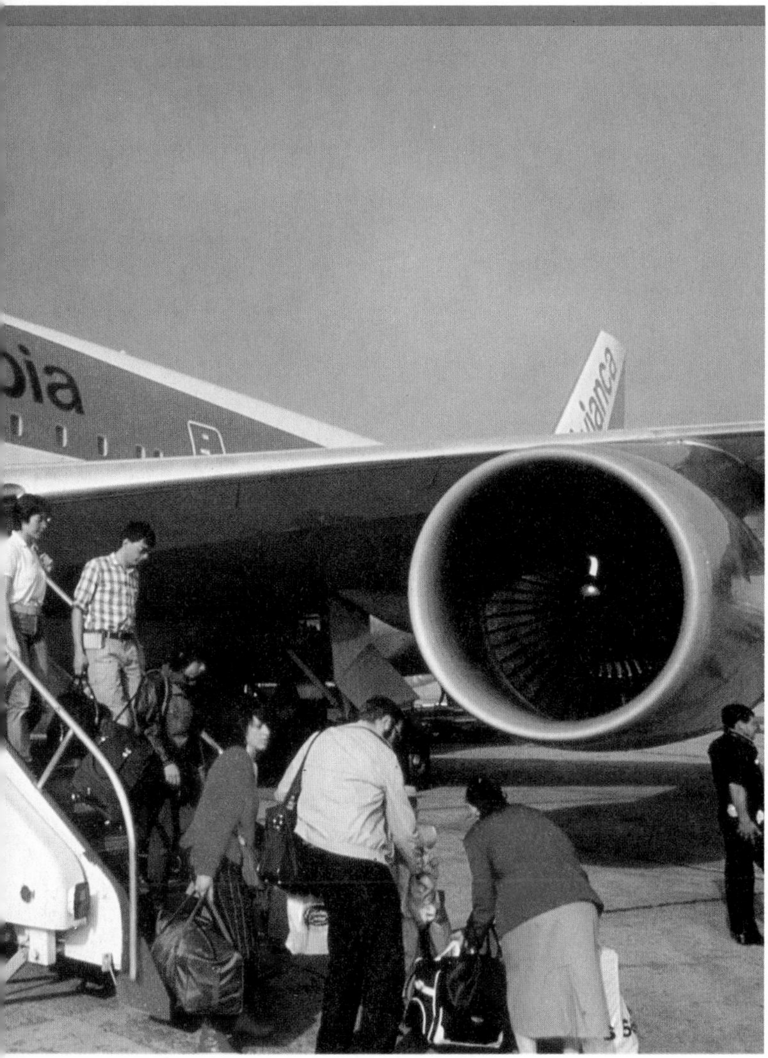

Panorama de vocabulario

En el aeropuerto

In some countries, **hacer cola** is used to refer to waiting in line.

Help students observe that **piloto** is the same in the masculine and the feminine. Only the definite article identifies the gender.

Las aeromozas are also known as **las azafatas,** although this word has no equivalent in the masculine form. Another term for flight attendant is **el** or **la asistente de vuelo.**

Hacemos un viaje

Have students compare the sentence **(El avión vuela)** with the infinitive **volar.** Help them form the conclusion that **volar** is an **o** to **ue** stem-changing verb.

El avión despega.
(despegar)

El avión vuela.
(volar)

El avión aterriza.
(aterrizar)

El asiento es cómodo.

El asiento es incómodo.

Note: The word **sala** is also used to refer to a gate or waiting area at an airport.

Llegadas

Vuelos	Horas	Puertas
516 Madrid	1:45	F6
101 Paris	3:15	
265 Frankfurt	3:50	

Salidas

Vuelos	Horas	Puertas
753 Buenos Aires	2:15	G10
611 Dallas	2:35	G14
302 Miami	3:25	

El vuelo número cinco diez y seis llega a las dos menos quince.

El vuelo número seis once sale a las tres menos veinte y cinco.

To help students practice the verbs **llegar** and **salir,** ask questions based on the schedule (e.g., **¿A qué hora llega el vuelo 265? ¿Cuándo sale el vuelo 611 para Dallas? ¿Dónde están los pasajeros que salen para Buenos Aires? ¿A qué puerta llegan los pasajeros de Madrid?**).

¡Aprende el vocabulario!

A. Enrique and his family are at the airport. While they wait for Enrique's uncle to arrive, they have the chance to look around. What do they see?

Primero, mira el dibujo. Luego, contesta la pregunta **¿Qué ven?** Sigue el modelo.

Modelo:

If students have trouble guessing the meaning of **ven**, help them deduce the infinitive form of the verb **(ver)** and have them look it up in the Spanish-English Glossary.

You may use this activity to review the personal **a.**

Respuesta: Ven a un piloto.

1.

2.

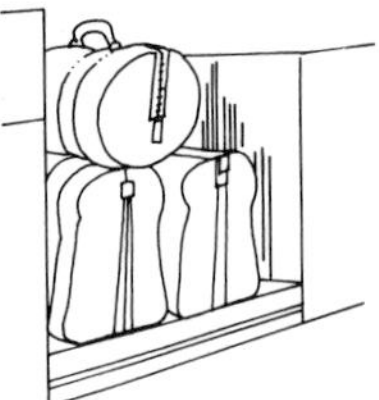

3.

4.

5.

6.

7.

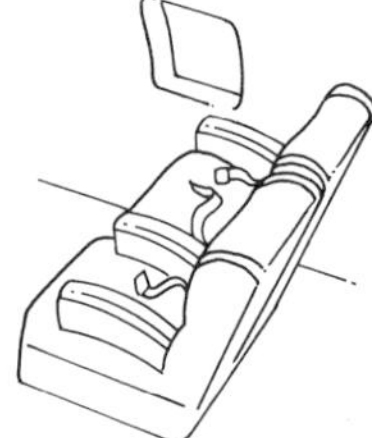

8.

9.

1. Ven el horario.
2. Ven el equipaje.
3. Ven a una aeromoza.
4. Ven a un pasajero.
5. Ven a una piloto.
6. Ven una maleta.
7. Ven unos asientos.
8. Ven a un aeromozo.
9. Ven a una pasajera.

B. You have been asked to meet this year's exchange students at the airport. Check to see if their flights are arriving early, on time, or late.

Primero, lee la hora y el número del vuelo. Luego, busca el vuelo en el horario. Por último, escribe si el avión llega **temprano, a tiempo** o **tarde.** Sigue los modelos.

Modelo: 8:15 Vuelo 258
Respuesta: **El vuelo 258 llega temprano.**

Modelo: 11:45 Vuelo 232
Respuesta: **El vuelo 232 llega a tiempo.**

Modelo: 12:30 Vuelo 113
Respuesta: **El vuelo 113 llega tarde.**

Before assigning the exercise, make sure students understand that the schedule shows the time each flight is supposed to arrive; the time in the exercise is its actual arrival.

Llegadas					
Vuelo	267	8:00	Vuelo	30	11:10
Vuelo	258	8:30	Vuelo	124	11:30
Vuelo	57	9:20	Vuelo	89	11:40
Vuelo	302	9:45	Vuelo	232	11:45
Vuelo	172	10:10	Vuelo	113	12:10
Vuelo	220	10:45			

1. 9:45 Vuelo 302
2. 11:30 Vuelo 89
3. 11:45 Vuelo 124
4. 10:10 Vuelo 172
5. 10:00 Vuelo 57
6. 8:00 Vuelo 267
7. 10:40 Vuelo 220
8. 11:30 Vuelo 30

1. El vuelo 302 llega a tiempo.
2. El vuelo 89 llega temprano.
3. El vuelo 124 llega tarde.
4. El vuelo 172 llega a tiempo.
5. El vuelo 57 llega tarde.
6. El vuelo 267 llega a tiempo.
7. El vuelo 220 llega temprano.
8. El vuelo 30 llega tarde.

Extension: Have students use the schedule to ask one another questions about arrival times.

◐ C. Poor Luisa must have jet lag! She is trying to write a report about her first plane trip, but she doesn't get all the words right. Help her straighten out her report.

Primero, lee la oración. Luego, cambia la palabra que está en letras negras. Por último, escoge la palabra apropiada y escribe la oración correcta. Sigue el modelo.

aeromozos	línea	vuela
despega	pilotos	maleta
horario	asiento	fila

Modelo: En el aeropuerto, voy a la **piña** aérea Mexicana.

Respuesta: **En el aeropuerto, voy a la línea aérea Mexicana.**

1. Primero tengo que hacer **lista** porque hay muchas personas.
2. Busco el número del vuelo en el **gimnasio.**
3. Tengo que buscar un **equipaje** cómodo en el avión.
4. Pongo mi **manzana** pequeña debajo del asiento.
5. Los **vuelos** ayudan a los pasajeros.
6. Hay dos **pizarras** en el avión. Ellos saben volar.
7. Muy pronto, el avión **despierta.**
8. ¡Estamos en las nubes! El avión **vuelve** muy alto.

1. fila
2. horario
3. asiento
4. maleta
5. aeromozos
6. pilotos
7. despega
8. vuela

Make sure students understand that each word in heavy black letters must be replaced by a word in the list. Do this activity orally in class before assigning it as homework.

Extension: Have students make up two more sentences with one inappropriate word. They may then write these on the chalkboard for their classmates to solve.

D. With a partner, prepare a conversation between two people at an airport.

Primero, escoge a un compañero de clase. Luego, escoge un lugar y un par de personas de la lista. Por último, conversa con tu compañero. Lee los ejemplos de preguntas.

Answers will vary. If students have trouble getting started, choose a role and model a brief conversation with a volunteer.

Lugares

1. Viajes Aéreos (una agencia de viajes)
2. Aeropuerto Internacional de Bucaramanga
3. La oficina de Aerotímido (una línea aérea)
4. Dentro de un avión viejo

Ask volunteers to read their questions and answers. Encourage students to role-play their conversations in front of the class.

Personas

1. Srta. Victoria Vuelomucho (una piloto)
2. Don Diego Descansa (un pasajero)
3. Sr. Pepe Pereza (un aeromozo)
4. Sra. Adela Activa (una agente de viajes)
5. Miguelito Jovencito (un pasajero)
6. Srta. Mónica Bonita (una aeromoza)
7. Doña Catalina Quejas (una pasajera)
8. Sr. Gregorio Guapo (un piloto)

Students may bring props and costumes to dramatize their conversations. To give students a clue to the different characters, have them look up the surnames of the characters in a dictionary (e.g., **pereza** = laziness; **quejas** = complaints; **guapo** = handsome; etc.).

¿Adónde vas con ocho maletas?

¿Cuál es el número del vuelo?

¿Va a salir a tiempo (tarde, temprano)?

¿Estamos aterrizando (despegando, volando) ahora?

¿A qué hora vamos a llegar (salir)?

¿Qué piensa hacer en México (España, Chile, etc.)?

Los sonidos del idioma

Las vocales: **eo, oe**

Escucha y repite. Compara los sonidos de las vocales.

eo	oe
empleo	roedor
museo	corroer
correo	coherente

Help students observe that the vowels **e** and **o** are strong sounds and are pronounced separately in the words. The letter **h** in **coherente** is silent, so the **o** and **e** are pronounced the same as in the other examples.

1. No veo el museo desde esta calle, pero sí veo el correo.
2. Los ratones son roedores.
3. Leonor tiene deseos de leer un cuento coherente.

El avión despega. Sale para Costa Rica.

Help students sharpen their skills of observation by answering questions such as the following: **¿Es grande o pequeño el aeropuerto? ¿Cuántas ventanas tiene el avión? ¿Es nuevo o viejo el avión?**

Usando el español

Talking about Things You Do

Rule: **Hacer** is irregular in the **yo** form. To form its other endings, you drop the **-er** and add regular **-er** verb endings to the stem **(hac-)**.

Study the following scene and read the paragraph that describes it.

Have volunteers read the passage aloud.

Hace mal tiempo hoy. Los otros pasajeros y yo **hacemos** fila para subir al avión. **Hago** un viaje para visitar a mis tíos. Ellos viven en California. Mis tíos siempre **hacen** muchos planes. Pensamos **hacer** un viajecito a Disneylandia. ¡Qué emoción!

Students may need to look up **emoción** in the Spanish-English Glossary.

The words in heavy black letters come from the infinitive **hacer.** Which sentence in the paragraph uses the infinitive? Which forms of **hacer** use the stem of the infinitive and regular **-er** endings? Which verb form in the paragraph is different?

Is **hacer** a regular, stem-changing, or irregular verb?

[The sixth sentence uses the infinitive. The following forms use the stem of the infinitive and regular **-er** endings: **hace, hacemos,** and **hacen.** The **yo** form **(hago)** is different.]

[**Hacer** is an irregular verb.]

Now look at the chart of the verb **hacer.**

Have students locate another chart of **hacer** in the appendix.

Hacer

Singular		Plural	
yo	hago	nosotros (-as)	hacemos
tú	haces	vosotros (-as)	hacéis
él, ella, usted	hace	ellos, ellas, ustedes	hacen

The verb **hacer** has many different meanings. You already know some of them. Read the following questions and answers to see if you can guess some of the meanings of **hacer:**

Pregunta: ¿Qué **hacen** ustedes aquí?
Respuesta: **Hacemos** fila para entrar al cine.

Pregunta: ¡Hola, Paquito! ¿Qué **haces** con el papel?
Respuesta: **Hago** un avioncito del papel. Este avión puede volar en la casa.

Pregunta: ¿Qué tiempo **hace** hoy?
Respuesta: **Hace** muy buen tiempo. **Hace** sol y **hace** calor.

Pregunta: ¿Adónde van los Morales?
Respuesta: Ellos **hacen** un viaje a Guatemala. Van a visitar a sus amigos.

Ask pairs of students to practice reading the sample questions and answers aloud. Help students identify the various meanings of **hacer.**

¡Vamos a practicar!

A. It looks like the whole neighborhood is going to the movies. Who is standing in line? Present this activity in class before assigning it as homework.

Primero, lee los nombres. Luego, contesta la pregunta **¿Quién hace fila?** o **¿Quiénes hacen fila?** Sigue el modelo.

Modelo: Víctor y Manuela
Respuesta: **Víctor y Manuela hacen fila.**

Extension: Have students ask the questions **¿Quién hace fila?** or **¿Quiénes hacen fila?**, according to the number of people in the answers.

1. el Sr. Serna
2. tú
3. Gloria y Luis
4. yo
5. Evaristo
6. Rosa, Anita e Iris

1. El Sr. Serna hace fila.
2. Tú haces fila.
3. Gloria y Luis hacen fila.
4. Yo hago fila.
5. Evaristo hace fila.
6. Rosa, Anita e Iris hacen fila.

¿Cuántas personas hacen fila?

Note: In Spanish-speaking countries, waiting in line is often either chaotic or nonexistent. To observers who are used to neat, orderly lines, this can often be disturbing.

B. Your classmates and teachers are very talented. Walk around the arts and crafts fair to find out what people are making.

Primero, lee el nombre o los nombres. Luego, forma una pregunta. Por último, contesta la pregunta con la frase entre paréntesis. Sigue el modelo.

Modelo: Alberto (un pájaro de papel)

Respuesta: **P: Alberto, ¿qué haces?**

R: Hago un pájaro de papel.

1. la Sra. Ruiz (un suéter rojo)
2. Emilia y Juanita (unas tazas y unos platillos)
3. Rodrigo y Mario (un mapa de Europa)
4. Humberto (un coche de plástico)
5. el Sr. Tamayo (un avión de papel)

You may wish to have students work in pairs to ask and answer the questions.

1. P: Sra. Ruiz, ¿qué hace?
   R: Hago un suéter rojo.
2. P: Emilia y Juanita, ¿qué hacen?
   R: Hacemos unas tazas y unos platillos.
3. P: Rodrigo y Mario, ¿qué hacen?
   R: Hacemos un mapa de Europa.
4. P: Humberto, ¿qué haces?
   R: Hago un coche de plástico.
5. P: Sr. Tamayo, ¿qué hace?
   R: Hago un avión de papel.

C. What do your classmates like to do or make in their spare time?

Primero, escoge a cinco compañeros. Luego, haz la pregunta **¿Qué haces en tu tiempo libre?** Por último, escribe las respuestas en una lista. Lee el modelo.

Modelo: TÚ: Julio, ¿qué haces en tu tiempo libre?

JULIO: Hago trenes de plástico.

Respuesta: **1. Julio hace trenes de plástico.**

Encourage students to explain why they chose the activities on their lists. They may either write their reasons or explain them orally to the class.

Talking about Talking!

Rule: **Decir** is an irregular verb. The **yo** form ends in **-go.** The **e** in the stem changes to **i** in all the forms except **nosotros** (and **vosotros**).

Study the pictures and read the sentences below them.

Siempre **digo** la verdad. No me gustan las galletas.

Nunca **decimos** mentiras. No nos gusta la película.

¿Qué **dice** la aeromoza?
Dice que vamos a despegar muy pronto.

¿Qué **dicen** los muchachos?
Dicen que somos bonitas y simpáticas.

The verb forms in heavy black letters all come from the infinitive **decir.** Which form of **decir** is different? Would you say that **decir** is a regular or an irregular verb? [The **yo** form is different. **Decir** is an irregular verb.]

Extension: Based on the examples on this page, have students make up a verb chart of the forms of **decir.** Then have them turn the page and confirm their guesses.

Now study the chart of **decir.**

Ask students where they might find another chart of **decir** in the book. Have students look up **decir** in the classroom dictionary and note any special listing indicating the verb's irregular forms.

Decir

Singular		Plural	
yo	digo	nosotros (-as)	decimos
tú	dices	vosotros (-as)	decís
él		ellos	
ella	dice	ellas	dicen
usted		ustedes	

Have students read the sample questions and answers aloud.

Practice reading the following questions and answers:

Pregunta: ¿Qué dice la maestra?
Respuesta: Dice **que tenemos un examen mañana.**

Pregunta: ¿Quién es la persona más honesta que conoces?
Respuesta: Eduardo es el más honesto. Siempre dice la verdad.

Pregunta: ¿Qué dicen ustedes a las muchachas?
Respuesta: Sólo decimos **que son muy simpáticas.**

How observant are you?

What word follows a form of **decir** in two of the answers? What follows that word in the two answers? Is it like a complete sentence? Why?

The words in heavy black letters are a clause. A clause is almost like a complete sentence, except that it is preceded by a word like **que.**

[The word **que** follows a form of **decir** in two of the answers. A verb follows **que** in the two answers. It is like a complete sentence because it has a subject and a verb.]

¡Vamos a practicar!

A. Imagine that today is **el Día de los Inocentes,** which is like April Fool's Day in Spanish-speaking countries. Is everybody telling the truth? Or are some telling a lie?

Primero, completa la oración con una forma de **decir.** Luego, mira el dibujo. Por último, decide si las personas dicen la verdad o una mentira. Sigue el modelo.

Modelo: Horacio —— que hace sol.

Respuesta: **Horacio dice que hace sol.**
Él dice una mentira.

Students might want to know that **el Día de los Inocentes** is celebrated on December 28.

1. dice / Ella dice la verdad.
2. decimos / Ustedes dicen una mentira.
3. dices / Tú dices una mentira.
4. dicen / Ellos dicen la verdad.

1. Elisa —— que su asiento es incómodo.

2. Nosotros —— que está nevando hoy.

3. Tú —— que el avión vuela muy alto.

4. Ellos —— que hay un tigre en el pasillo.

Extension: Have students make up true and false statements to see if they can stump the class.

◐ B. The members of the Spanish Club are voting on whether or not they will go to Spain this summer. How do the members vote?

Primero, lee las palabras. Luego, forma una oración con la palabra entre paréntesis. Sigue los modelos.

Modelo: Patricia y Diana (no)
Respuesta: **Ellas dicen que no.**

Modelo: Jaime (sí)
Respuesta: **Él dice que sí.**

You may wish to assign this activity as homework before going over it in class.

Note: Students may notice that in these sentences, **que** does not introduce a clause. This is a common, idiomatic use of **decir que.**

1. Olga (sí)
2. Benito y Ana (no)
3. tú y yo (sí)
4. Carmen y Fidel (sí)
5. la Srta. Burgos (sí)
6. el Sr. Zuluaga (no)

1. Ella dice que sí.
2. Ellos dicen que no.
3. Nosotros decimos que sí.
4. Ellos dicen que sí.
5. Ella dice que sí.
6. Él dice que no.

● C. How do your classmates vote? Take a survey and find out.

Primero, escoge una pregunta. Luego, haz la pregunta a diez compañeros de clase. Por último, escribe las respuestas.

Extension: Have students tally their results and decide what is most important to the classmates they surveyed. They may then compare their results and decide what is most important to the class.

Preguntas

1. ¿Es importante tener mucho dinero?
2. ¿Es importante comer bien?
3. ¿Es importante cepillarse los dientes tres veces al día?
4. ¿Es importante estudiar mucho?
5. ¿Es importante tener muchos amigos?
6. ¿Es importante viajar a otros países?

Talking about People and Things

Rule: Direct object pronouns take the place of direct object nouns. The direct object pronoun comes before the verb.

Study the following pictures and sentences.

Miro **la televisión.**

La miro cada noche.

Ponemos **el equipaje** aquí.

Lo ponemos en el coche.

¿Haces **tortas** de chocolate?

Sí, **las** hago para tu fiesta de cumpleaños.

¿Pintan **retratos**?

Sí, **los** pintamos para la clase de arte.

Have students read the examples aloud. Help them make the connection between the direct object pronoun and the objects the people are talking about.

In the second sentence of each pair, one word is used to refer to something in the first sentence. What does the word **la** refer to? What does the word **lo** refer to? What does the word **las** refer to? What does the word **los** refer to?

The words **lo, los, la,** and **las** are direct object pronouns.

[**La** refers to **la televisión. Lo** refers to **el equipaje. Las** refers to **las tortas de chocolate. Los** refers to **los retratos.**]

In a sentence, the direct object receives the action of the verb. Read the following sentences. Which word in each sentence is the direct object?

[The direct objects are **el billete, las maletas, los platos**, and **una manzana.**]

1. Compro **el billete.**
2. Ellos traen **las maletas.**
3. Ponemos **los platos** en la mesa.
4. Usted come **una manzana.**

Have students note that the arrows connect the verbs to the direct objects.

[(1) **Lo** is the direct object pronoun. It refers to **el billete.** (2) **Las** is the direct object pronoun. It refers to **las maletas.** (3) **Los** is the direct object pronoun. It refers to **los platos.** (4) **La** is the direct object pronoun. It refers to **una manzana.**]

A pronoun is a word that stands for a noun. A direct object pronoun stands for the noun that is the direct object in the sentence. Now read the following sentences. Which word in the second sentence is the direct object pronoun? What does it refer to in the first sentence?

1. Compro el billete. **Lo** compro en la agencia de viajes.
2. Ellos traen las maletas. **Las** traen al coche.
3. Ponemos los platos en la mesa. **Los** ponemos sobre el mantel.
4. Usted come una manzana. ¿**La** come para el almuerzo?

When you use a direct object pronoun, where does it go? Does it go before the verb or after the verb? [The direct object pronoun goes before the verb.]

¡A divertirnos!

Un trabalenguas chistoso

Once students know the tongue twister well, have volunteers say it three times as fast as they can. Have students find the direct object pronoun.

TONTÍN: Tomás toma el té con un tenedor.

TONTÓN: ¡No, tontito Tontín! ¡Tomás lo toma en taza como tú!

You can also use direct object pronouns to refer to people. Read the following questions and answers.

¿Conoces a Eduardo?

Sí, lo conozco.

¿Conoces a Juanita?

Sí, la conozco.

¿Me buscas?

No, no te busco.

¿Quién te ayuda?

La maestra me ayuda.

Now study the chart of direct object pronouns.

Have students find another chart of direct object pronouns in the back of the book.

Singular	Plural
me	nos
te	os
lo	los
la	las

¡Vamos a practicar!

A. Alma is very forgetful. Help her get ready to go on vacation.

Primero lee la pregunta. Luego, contesta con **sí** o **no.** Usa **lo, los, la** o **las** en tu respuesta. Sigue el modelo.

Modelo: ¿Tienes los billetes? (sí)
Respuesta: **Sí, los tengo.**

1. Sí, lo tengo.
2. Sí, las tengo.
3. No, no la tengo.
4. No, no lo tengo.
5. Sí, los tengo.
6. No, no la tengo.

1. ¿Tienes tu equipaje? (sí)
2. ¿Tienes tus blusas? (sí)
3. ¿Tienes tu maleta? (no)
4. ¿Tienes tu vestido? (no)
5. ¿Tienes tus suéteres? (sí)
6. ¿Tienes una novela? (no)

Extension: Continue by asking students if they brought what they need to class. They should answer using direct object pronouns (e.g., **¿Tienes tu cuaderno? Sí, lo tengo.**).

B. What a coincidence! You have run into an old friend at the airport. How does your friend answer your questions?

Primero, lee la pregunta y mira el dibujo. Luego, contesta la pregunta con **lo, los, la** o **las.** Sigue el modelo.

This activity may be assigned as homework.

Modelo:  ¿Conoces al piloto?

Respuesta: **Sí, lo conozco.**

Extension: Continue the activity by asking about people in your school, class members, etc. (e.g., **¿Conoces al Sr. Herrera?**).

1. ¿Conoces a la aeromoza?

2. ¿Conoces a Juan y Hugo?

3. ¿Conoces a Lidia?

4.  ¿Conoces al aeromozo?

5. ¿Conoces a Elena y María?

6. ¿Conoces al Sr. López?

1. No, no la conozco.
2. Sí, los conozco.
3. Sí, la conozco.
4. Sí, lo conozco.
5. No, no las conozco.
6. No, no lo conozco.

C. Imagine that your best friend is having a party. Who is invited? How does your friend answer your questions?

Primero, lee las palabras. Luego, forma una oración. Sigue el modelo.

Modelo: ¿Invitas a Óscar?

Respuesta: **Sí, lo invito.**

1. Sí, lo invito.
2. Sí, la invito.
3. Sí, los invito.
4. Sí, las invito.
5. Sí, los invito.
6. Sí, te invito (a ti).

1. ¿Invitas al Sr. Gómez?

2. ¿Invitas a Marta?

3. ¿Nos invitas a nosotros?

4. ¿Invitas a Hortensia y Elisa?

5. ¿Invitas a Samuel y Diego?

6. ¿Me invitas a mí?

◐ D. Who does what in your school?

You may wish to assign this activity as homework after presenting it in class.

Primero, lee la pregunta. Luego, contesta la pregunta con las palabras entre paréntesis. Sigue el modelo.

Modelo: ¿Quién hace preguntas? (la maestra)

Respuesta: **La maestra las hace.**

1. El conserje lo limpia.
2. Los alumnos las escriben.
3. Yo las aprendo.
4. El bibliotecario los pone en los estantes.
5. La cocinera la cocina.
6. La directora los conoce (a todos).

1. ¿Quién limpia el pasillo? (el conserje)
2. ¿Quién escribe las respuestas? (los alumnos)
3. ¿Quién aprende las lecciones? (yo)
4. ¿Quién pone los libros en los estantes? (el bibliotecario)
5. ¿Quién cocina la comida? (la cocinera)
6. ¿Quién conoce a todos los alumnos? (la directora)

Extension: Have students work in pairs to ask each other two questions about who does what in school or at home (e.g., **¿Quién limpia tu dormitorio? ¿Quién examina a los enfermos?**).

● E. Where do you keep your things?

Escribe una lista de cinco cosas personales. Luego, para cada cosa, describe dónde la pones. Primero, lee el modelo.

Modelo:

1. Mi ropa. La pongo en el ropero.
2. Mis libros. Los pongo en el estante.
3. Mis camisas. Las pongo en el tocador.
4. Mi radio. Lo pongo sobre mi escritorio.
5. Mi juego electrónico. Lo pongo en la sala.

Lists will vary. Check for agreement between nouns and direct object pronouns.

Extension: Have students exchange lists with a partner. Students may ask each other questions about the lists and about personal items not on the lists (e.g., **¿Dónde pones tus cuadernos? Los pongo en mi escritorio.**).

Vamos a leer

¿Qué necesitas para viajar en avión?

Antes de viajar en avión, tienes que comprar un billete. En el aeropuerto, recibes una tarjeta de embarcación. Si no la tienes, no puedes entrar al avión. Lee los ejemplos de un billete y una tarjeta de embarcación. ¿Cuántas palabras puedes adivinar?

Students should try to deduce the meanings of unfamiliar words from context before looking them up in the Spanish-English Glossary or a dictionary.

Aeroviva

Boleto de pasaje en avión					**Número** 2093190
Agencia de viajes: Viajes Descanso y Placer					
Nombre del pasajero: Rosario Medellín					
De: Nueva York / Kennedy	**Vuelo:**	**Fecha:**	**Salida:**	**Llegada:**	**Reservaciones:**
	329	18 dic.	7.13	12.57	OK
A: San José, Costa Rica	**Tarifa:** $858				

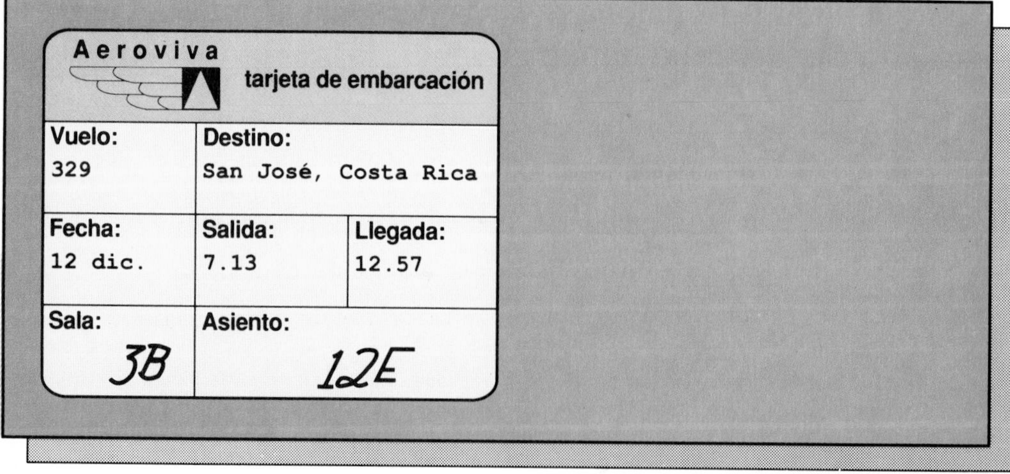

Aeroviva

tarjeta de embarcación

Vuelo: 329	**Destino:** San José, Costa Rica	
Fecha: 12 dic.	**Salida:** 7.13	**Llegada:** 12.57
Sala: 3B	**Asiento:** 12E	

Enrichment: Bring real boarding passes and airline tickets in English and Spanish to class. Have students guess the meanings of the words in the tickets and boarding passes.

La cultura y tú

See Unit Plans, Unidad 2, for additional information and suggestions.

¿Qué hora es?

Todos los días, ves muchos horarios. Hay horarios de clases, horarios de autobuses y horarios de salidas y llegadas en el aeropuerto. En los países hispanos también puedes encontrar muchos horarios, pero son un poco diferentes. Mira este horario de Aeroviva en el aeropuerto de La Paz. ¿Sabes a qué hora es el vuelo a Brasilia?

In order to convert times from the 24-hour clock to the 12-hour clock, subtract 12 from the time. Have students convert the times on the schedule to the 12-hour clock.

AEROVIVA Salidas

Hora	Vuelo	Destino
9.38	112	San José
11.23	609	Caracas
13.02	487	Santiago
16.15	223	Brasilia
19.41	581	Washington, D.C.
20.58	256	México, D.F.
22.30	704	Asunción
00.14	120	Buenos Aires

Ask students how we differentiate morning and afternoon hours in English. [We use A.M. and P.M.] Ask which system seems more practical to them.

Para los horarios oficiales, la gente de los países hispanos cuenta de la medianoche a la medianoche sin interrupción. Es decir que las horas de la medianoche al mediodía son de 0.00 a 12.00 y después del mediodía, las horas son de 13.00 a 24.00. En estos horarios hay veinte y cuatro horas en vez de doce.

Enrichment: Have students convert their class schedules or television schedules to the 24-hour clock. Teachers of students' afternoon classes might be willing to post their class times according to the 24-hour clock for a day.

Unidad 3

After completing this unit, students should be able to:

- identify and name things related to hotels and hotel rooms
- talk about actions by using the present tense of **e** to **i** and **u** to **ue** stem-changing verbs and regular, irregular, and stem-changing reflexive verbs (review)
- read and discuss a story about a family in Argentina
- read about and discuss tourism in South America.

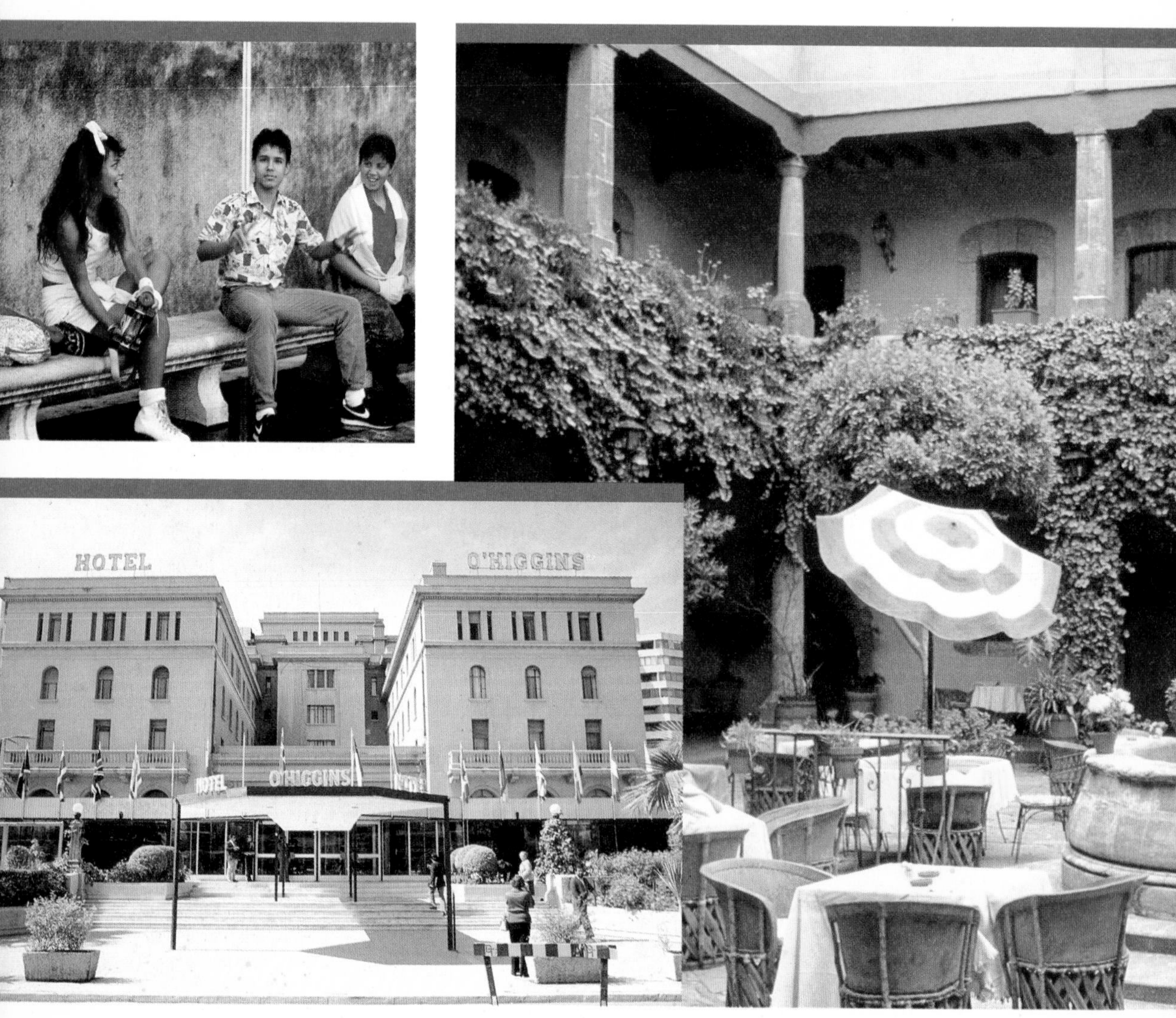

The photographs may be used for informal assessment and review by combining commands and questions:

- ▶ Toca el cuarto de baño. ¿Hay toallas? ¿Hay una bañera?
- ▶ Señala a unos turistas.
- ▶ ¿Qué pide la señora? ¿Pide la llave?
- ▶ ¿Es grande o pequeño el Hotel O'Higgins?
- ▶ ¿Es moderno o antiguo el patio del hotel?

Panorama de vocabulario

Llegamos a un hotel

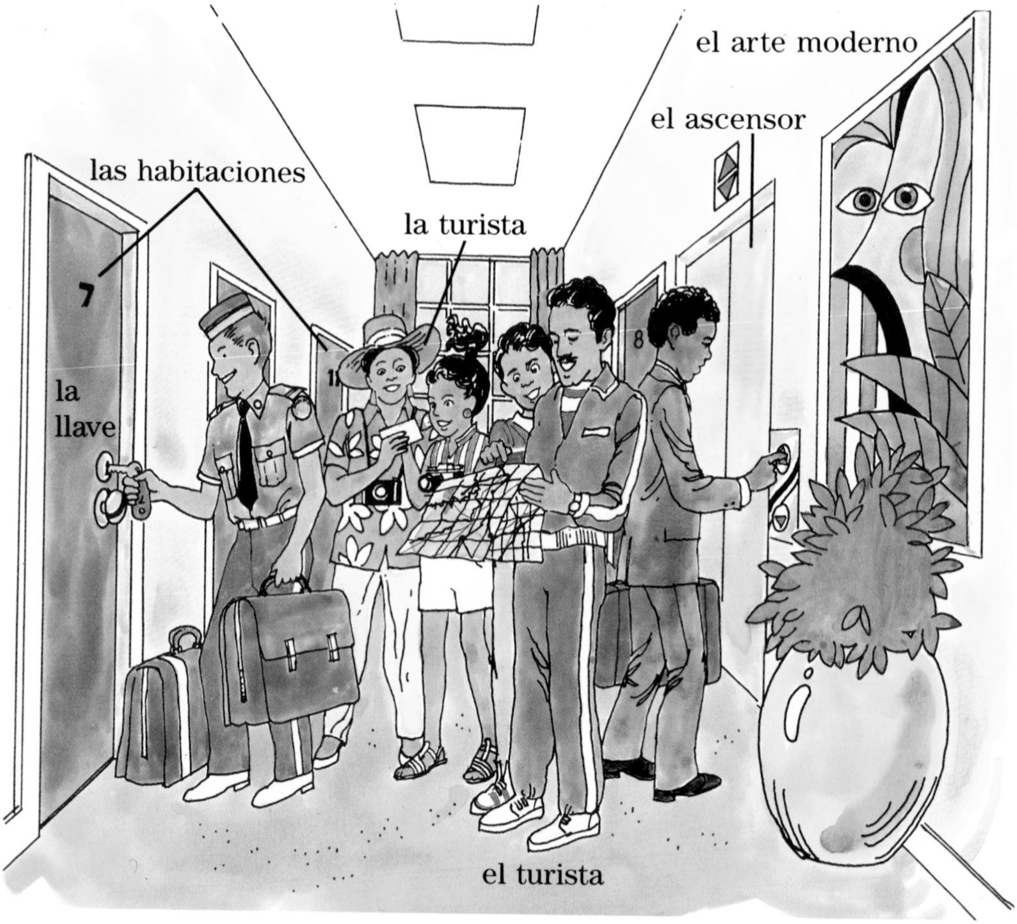

el arte moderno
el ascensor
las habitaciones
la turista
la llave
el turista

Ask students if the word **turista** changes its ending. How do they know if the word refers to a male or a female tourist? [The definite or indefinite article.]

Use photographs from magazines and other sources to contrast the words **moderno** and **antiguo.**

¿Qué tenemos en la habitación?

In Latin America, another word for blanket is **la cobija.** You may wish to teach one of the following words for bedspread: **la colcha, la sobrecama.** Bring a pillow to class and use other objects to give additional context to the adjectives **blando** and **duro.**

Another term for **la bañera** is **la tina.** You may wish to teach **el lavabo** (bathroom sink or washbasin).

¡Aprende el vocabulario!

A. Pedro is very tired when he finally gets to his hotel room. He doesn't notice that many things are missing from the room. Help the hotel clerk find out what Pedro needs.

Primero, mira el dibujo. Luego, contesta la pregunta **¿Qué necesita usted?** Sigue el modelo.

Modelo: 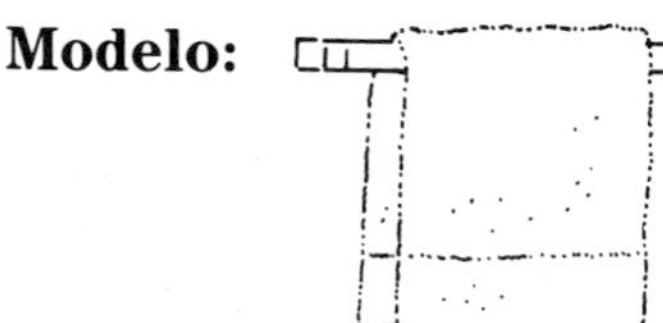

Respuesta: Necesito una toalla.

1. 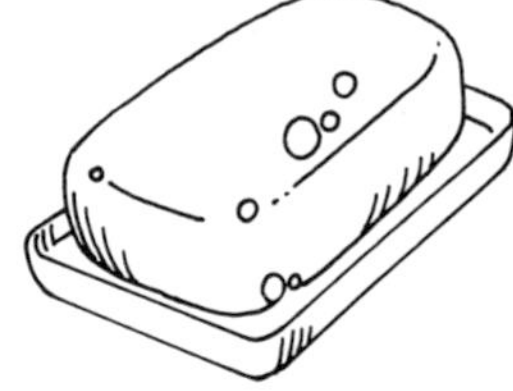

3. 

5. 

2. 

4. 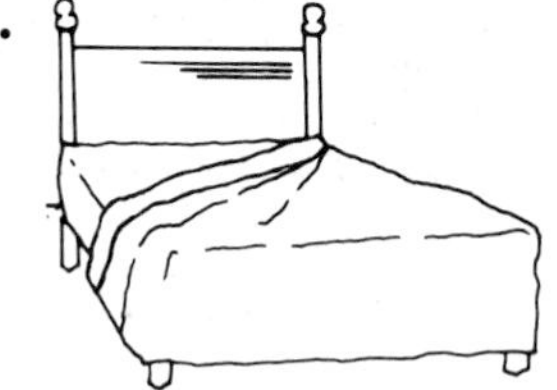

6. 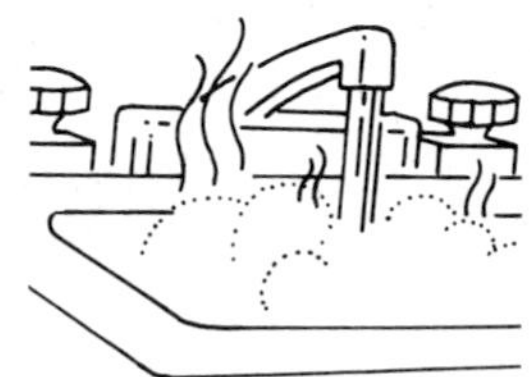

1. Necesito jabón.
2. Necesito una manta.
3. Necesito una llave.
4. Necesito una sábana.
5. Necesito unas tarjetas postales.
6. Necesito agua caliente.

Extension: To reinforce the use of direct object pronouns with the present vocabulary, ask students if Pedro has the pictured items (e.g., **¿Tiene Pedro una toalla?**). Students should use direct object pronouns in their answers (e.g., **No, no la tiene.**).

B. Pedro is very picky. Now that he has rested, he has nothing but complaints for the management of the hotel. Figure out what his problems are.

Primero, mira el dibujo. Luego, lee la oración. Por último, completa la oración. Sigue el modelo.

Modelo: —— no tiene agua caliente.

1. La bañera
2. El ascensor
3. dura
4. La turista
5. blando
6. Los turistas

Respuesta: La ducha no tiene agua caliente.

1. —— es muy pequeña.

2. —— sube, pero no baja.

3. La cama es muy ——.

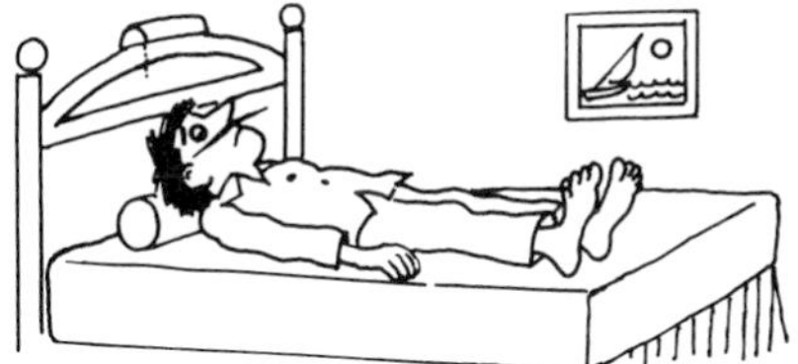

4. ¡—— habla mucho!

5. El sillón es muy ——.

6. —— me despiertan.

◐ C. The Arango sisters are twins, but you'd never guess it. Amalia is sweet and good natured. Aurelia is mean and bad tempered. How would they answer your questions?

Primero, lee la pregunta. Luego, contesta como Amalia o Aurelia. Usa las listas de palabras para formar las respuestas. Lee los modelos.

antiguo	duro	limpio
blando	feo	moderno
bonito	frío	simpático
caliente	impaciente	sucio

Modelo: Amalia, ¿te gusta la habitación?
Respuesta: **Sí, me gusta mucho. Es muy moderna.**

Modelo: Aurelia, ¿cómo es tu cama?
Respuesta: **¡Es horrible! Es muy dura.**

1. Aurelia, ¿está bien el agua en la ducha?
2. Amalia, ¿te gustan los cuadros?
3. Amalia, ¿cómo es tu cama?
4. Aurelia, ¿cómo son los sillones?
5. Aurelia, ¿te gustan las toallas?
6. Amalia, ¿cómo son los turistas?
7. Aurelia, ¿cómo son las sábanas?
8. Amalia, ¿cómo es la manta?
9. Aurelia, ¿por qué no te gusta el hotel?
10. Amalia, ¿por qué te gusta el hotel?

Answers will vary. Possible answers:
1. ¡Es horrible! Es muy fría.
2. Sí, me gustan mucho. Son muy bonitos.
3. Es muy blanda.
4. ¡Son horribles! Son muy duros.
5. No, no me gustan. Son muy sucios.
6. Son muy simpáticos.
7. ¡Son horribles! Son muy feas.
8. Es muy bonita.
9. No me gusta porque es muy antiguo.
10. Me gusta porque es muy moderno.

For answer 1, you may have to explain that **el agua** is a feminine noun. Remind students that they know other irregular masculine and feminine nouns, such as **la mano** and **el día.**

D. Imagine that you're on vacation and are staying at a hotel. What do you write when you send a postcard to your best friend?

Primero, escoge una ciudad o un país. Luego, escribe una tarjeta postal a un amigo. Lee la tarjeta postal de Gregorio.

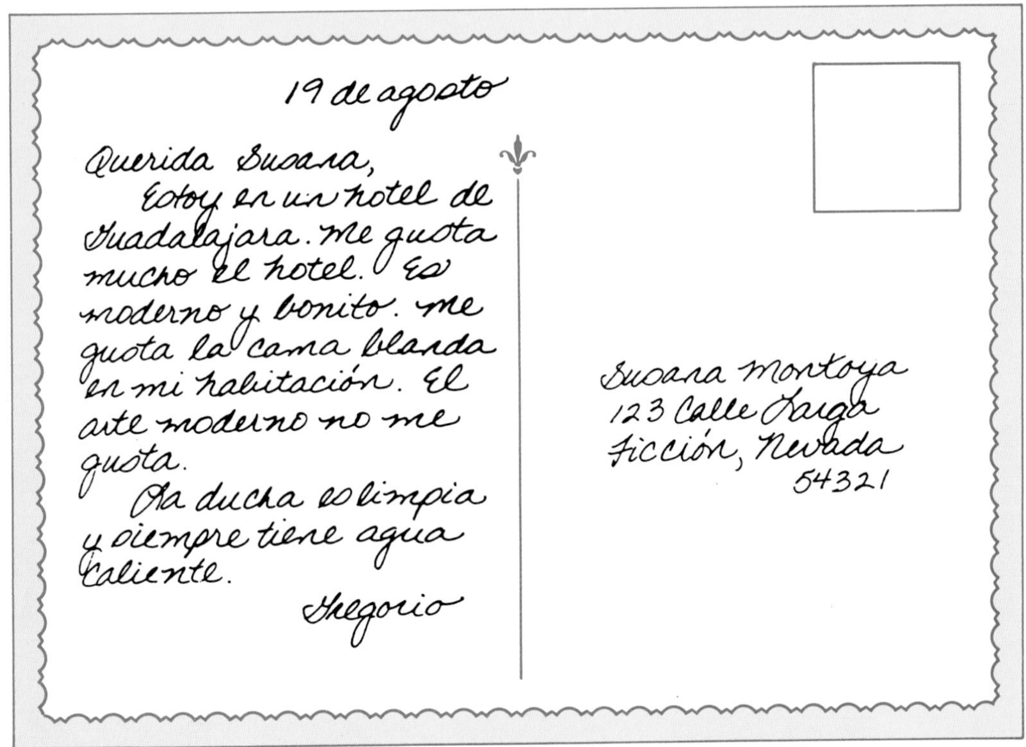
19 de agosto

Querida Susana,

Estoy en un hotel de Guadalajara. Me gusta mucho el hotel. Es moderno y bonito. Me gusta la cama blanda en mi habitación. El arte moderno no me gusta.

La ducha es limpia y siempre tiene agua caliente.

Gregorio

Susana Montoya
123 Calle Larga
Ficción, Nevada
54321

Have students write at least three sentences. Students may wish to address their postcards to a classmate. Have students exchange postcards and ask each other questions about the imaginary hotels they visited.

Enrichment: Have students bring in postcards of places they have visited or that they have received and make a bulletin-board display of the real postcards and the postcards students have written.

Los sonidos del idioma

Las vocales: **ai, ia; au, ua**

Escucha y repite. Compara los sonidos de las vocales.

ai	ia	au	ua
baile	copia	automóvil	cuaderno
traigo	estudia	restaurante	guapo
Haití	gracias	gaucho	agua

Beginning with these diphthongs, students will be practicing two vowels with one sound. You may wish to contrast these vowel combinations with those in Unidad 2 and Unidad 3, in which the two vowels are pronounced separately.

1. El estudiante estudia la historia de Haití.
2. ¿Cuántos vasos de agua bebes cuando tienes sed?
3. El gaucho es muy guapo y baila un baile especial.

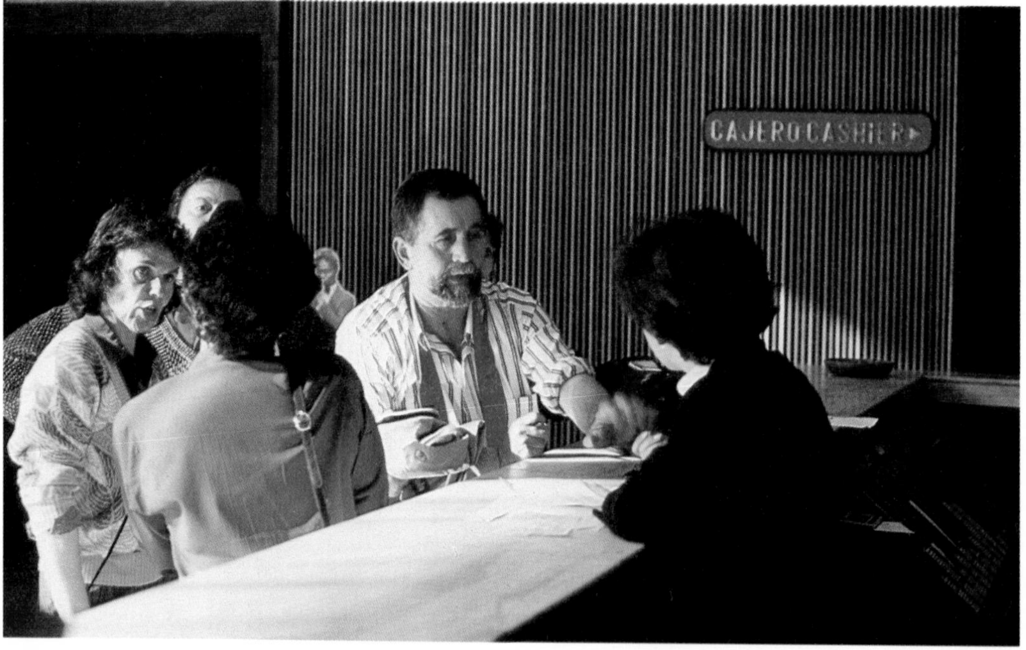

Los turistas comienzan sus vacaciones. Piden una habitación en el hotel.

Have students role-play the situation in the photo. Point out that all transactions usually begin with an exchange of pleasantries, contrasted with the direct question common in the United States.

Usando el español

Using Stem-Changing Verbs

Rule: **Pedir** is a stem-changing verb that changes the **e** to **i** in the stem in all forms of the present tense, except **nosotros** (and **vosotros**).

Many useful verbs are stem-changing verbs. You have reviewed some **e** to **ie** verbs and some **o** to **ue** verbs. Now look at the conjugation of an **e** to **i** stem-changing verb in the present tense.

Have students find another example of an **e** and **i** stem-changing verb in the appendix.

e to i: pedir

Singular		Plural	
yo	pido	nosotros (-as)	pedimos
tú	pides	vosotros (-as)	pedís
él / ella / usted	pide	ellos / ellas / ustedes	piden

Recall that the verbs **servir** and **seguir** are **e** to **i** stem-changing verbs, too.

Which verb forms do not change the stem? In which verb forms does the stem change from **e** to **i**?

[The **nosotros** and **vosotros** forms do not change in the stem. The stem changes from **e** to **i** in the **yo**, **tú**, **él (ella, usted)**, and **ellos (ellas, ustedes)** forms.]

El muchacho pide ayuda al policía. ¿A quién pides ayuda cuando estás en la ciudad?

Now study the chart of a **u** to **ue** stem-changing verb.

u to ue: jugar

Singular		Plural	
yo	**jue**go	nosotros (-as)	jugamos
tú	**jue**gas	vosotros (-as)	jugáis
él, ella, usted	**jue**ga	ellos, ellas, ustedes	**jue**gan

Is the conjugation of **jugar** in the present tense? In which forms of **jugar** does the stem change from **u** to **ue**? [The conjugation of **jugar** is in the present tense. The stem changes from **u** to **ue** in all the forms of **jugar**, except **nosotros** (and **vosotros**).]

Practice reading the following questions and answers:

Pregunta: ¿Por qué **piden** unas toallas?
Respuesta: Las **pedimos** porque no hay toallas en el cuarto de baño.

Pregunta: **¿Juegan** ustedes al volibol?
Respuesta: Sí, lo **jugamos.** El gimnasio del hotel es excelente para jugar al volibol.

Pregunta: **¿Sirven** ustedes el desayuno en las habitaciones?
Respuesta: Sí, lo **servimos** en las habitaciones. Es un servicio especial.

Have volunteers read the sample questions and answers aloud.

¡Vamos a practicar!

A. Imagine that you and your family are spending the weekend in a hotel. When you arrive, though, you don't find what you need. What do you ask for?

Primero, mira el dibujo. Luego, forma una oración. Sigue el modelo.

Modelo:

Note: Point out to students that when referring to "some" of any object, the definite article is omitted.

Extension: Have students substitute direct object pronouns for the nouns in these sentences.

Respuesta: Pedimos la llave.

1. 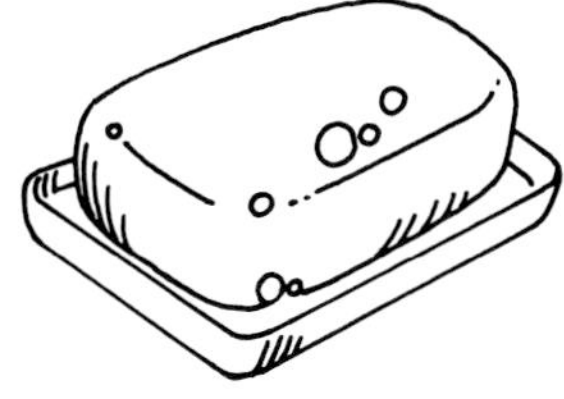

2. 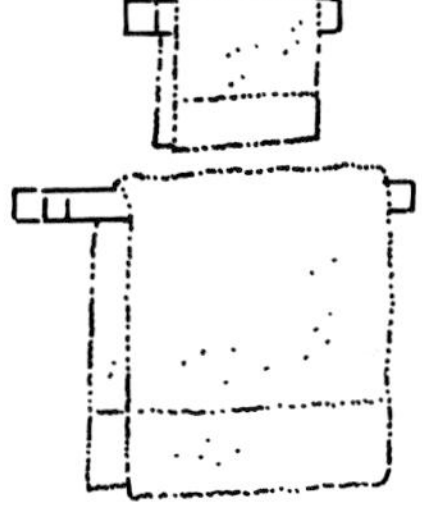

3. 

4. 

5. 

6. 

1. Pedimos jabón.
2. Pedimos toallas.
3. Pedimos almohadas.
4. Pedimos tarjetas postales.
5. Pedimos una manta.
6. Pedimos una sábana.

◐ B. Marcela and her family love to play all kinds of games and sports. She has a lot to say about her family's activities.

Primero, lee las frases. Luego, forma una oración. Sigue el modelo. You may wish to assign this activity as homework.

Modelo: nosotras / tenis
Respuesta: **Nosotras jugamos al tenis.**

1. Yo juego al volibol.
2. Mamá y papá juegan al dominó.
3. Mi hermana juega al fútbol.
4. Mis hermanos juegan al béisbol.
5. Mi prima y yo jugamos al ajedrez.
6. Mi tío juega al baloncesto

1. yo / volibol
2. mamá y papá / dominó
3. mi hermana / fútbol
4. mis hermanos / béisbol
5. mi prima y yo / ajedrez
6. mi tío / baloncesto

● C. Imagine that you and your family get to spend a week in a hotel, being waited on hand and foot. What do you ask for? What do you do for fun?

Escribe tres oraciones con **pedir** y tres oraciones con **jugar.** Primero, lee el modelo.

Modelo:
1. Nosotros pedimos la habitación más bonita del hotel.
2. Mi mamá pide cuatro almohadas muy blandas.
3. Yo pido un almuerzo muy grande.
4. Mi papá y yo jugamos al fútbol americano.
5. Mis hermanas juegan al tenis.
6. Mi mamá no juega a nada. Ella descansa.

Answers will vary. You may wish to assign this activity as homework after presenting the **Modelo** in class.

Extension: Have students form pairs or small groups and make up conversations between people settling into a hotel room and a desk clerk.

Using Reflexive Verbs

Rule: You use reflexive verbs to talk about actions people do on or to themselves. Reflexive verbs can be regular, irregular, or stem-changing.

You have learned many verbs to talk about your daily routine. The verbs you use to talk about what you do for yourself are called reflexive verbs. Look at the chart of some reflexive verbs.

Have students find a chart of a reflexive verb in the appendix.

	bañarse	**ponerse**	**dormirse**
yo	me baño	me pongo	me duermo
tú	te bañas	te pones	te duermes
él / ella / usted	se baña	se pone	se duerme
nosotros (-as)	nos bañamos	nos ponemos	nos dormimos
vosotros (-as)	os bañáis	os ponéis	os dormís
ellos / ellas / ustedes	se bañan	se ponen	se duermen

One verb in the chart is new: **dormirse.** It is a reflexive verb. Is it also a regular **-ir** verb? Is it an irregular verb? Is it a stem-changing verb?

[No, **dormirse** is not a regular **-ir** verb. It is not an irregular verb. It is a stem-changing verb.]

Recall some other reflexive verbs you have learned to talk about your daily routine: **Note:** Remind students that **ir** means to go; **irse** means to leave.

acostarse	irse	peinarse
cepillarse	lavarse	quitarse
despertarse	levantarse	secarse

Which ones are regular verbs?
Which ones are stem-changing verbs?
Which one is an irregular verb?

[**Cepillarse, lavarse, levantarse, peinarse, quitarse,** and **secarse** are regular verbs. **Acostarse** and **despertarse** are stem-changing verbs. **Irse** is an irregular verb.]

Practice reading the following questions and answers. See if you can guess the meaning of **dormirse** from context.

Pregunta: ¿A qué hora **te duermes** cada noche?
Respuesta: Siempre **me acuesto** a las once. Generalmente, **me duermo** a las once y diez.

Pregunta: ¿Qué hace Raúl antes de irse de la casa?
Respuesta: Generalmente, **se baña, se pone** la ropa y toma el desayuno. Luego, **se cepilla** los dientes y **se va** de la casa.

Have volunteers read the sample questions and answers aloud.

¡Vamos a practicar!

A. Mario Muchaprisa is the most organized person in the whole world! He always does things in the right order. How does he answer your questions about his daily routine?

Primero, lee la pregunta. Luego, forma una oración. Sigue el modelo. Extension: Continue the activity by asking questions about the order in which students perform morning and evening tasks.

Modelo: ¿Qué haces primero, te levantas o te despiertas?

Respuesta: **Primero, me despierto. Luego, me levanto.**

1. ¿Qué haces primero, te bañas o te secas? 1. Primero, me baño. Luego, me seco.
2. ¿Qué haces primero, te peinas o te vas de la casa?
3. ¿Qué haces primero, te lavas la cara o te quitas la camisa?
4. ¿Qué haces primero, te cepillas los dientes o te acuestas?
5. ¿Qué haces primero, te duermes o te acuestas?

2. Primero, me peino. Luego, me voy de la casa.
3. Primero, me quito la camisa. Luego, me lavo la cara.
4. Primero, me cepillo los dientes. Luego, me acuesto.
5. Primero, me acuesto. Luego, me duermo.

B. Mario's two sisters are just like him. Ask them the same questions you asked Mario. Have students work in pairs to ask and answer the questions.

Primero, cambia las preguntas del ejercicio A. Luego, contesta las preguntas. Sigue el modelo.

Modelo: ¿Qué hacen primero, se levantan o se despiertan?

Respuesta: **Primero, nos despertamos. Luego, nos levantamos.**

1. P: ¿Qué hacen primero, se bañan o se secan?
   R: Primero, nos bañamos. Luego, nos secamos.
2. P: ¿Qué hacen primero, se peinan o se van de la casa?
   R: Primero, nos peinamos, Luego, nos vamos de la casa.
3. P: ¿Qué hacen primero, se lavan la cara o se quitan las camisas?
   R: Primero, nos quitamos las camisas. Luego, nos lavamos la cara.
4. P: ¿Qué hacen primero, se cepillan los dientes o se acuestan?
   R: Primero, nos cepillamos los dientes. Luego, nos acostamos.
5. P: ¿Qué hacen primero, se duermen o se acuestan?
   R: Primero, nos acostamos. Luego, nos dormimos.

◐ C. Alicia enjoys going on vacation with her father. She doesn't have to hurry or follow a schedule on vacation. Help her describe a typical vacation day.

Primero, lee la oración. Luego, lee la lista de palabras y escoge la palabra apropiada. Por último, completa la oración. Sigue el modelo.

despertarse	secarse	peinarse
cepillarse	levantarse	dormirse
bañarse	quitarse	ponerse
irse	acostarse	lavarse

Modelo: Por las mañanas —— a las nueve y media.

Respuesta: **Por las mañanas me despierto [me levanto] a las nueve y media.**

1. En la bañera, —— con agua bien caliente.
2. Luego, —— con una toalla muy blanda.
3. Me miro en el espejo y —— . Tengo el pelo muy rizado. ¡Qué lata!
4. Después, —— los dientes y —— la ropa.
5. —— de la habitación. Tomo el desayuno en el patio del hotel.
6. Por la noche —— la ropa y —— el pijama.
7. Siempre —— a las once y media de la noche.
8. En mi cama grande y blanda, leo mis novelas favoritas. Generalmente, —— a la medianoche.

1. me baño (or me lavo)
2. me seco
3. me peino
4. me cepillo / me pongo
5. Me voy
6. me quito / me pongo
7. me acuesto
8. me duermo

D. Imagine that you're on vacation and you don't have to stick to a schedule. Write about your ideal day on vacation. Is it like Alicia's in exercise C?

Escribe por lo menos ocho oraciones sobre un día de vacaciones. Usa los verbos del ejercicio C.

Have volunteers read their sample schedules to the class and be prepared to answer questions from the class about the schedules.

Enrichment: Have students write their schedules on pages decorated with pictures of places they would like to visit (cut out of old magazines or travel brochures). These pages can be bound into a class book called **De vacaciones.**

¡A divertirnos!

Un muchacho listo

Have students try to guess the meaning of **listo** from the cartoon.

Vamos a leer

Una familia de la Argentina

Esta es la historia de Sonia. Ella vive con su familia en San Carlos de Bariloche en la Argentina.

Bariloche es un pueblo muy bonito, cerca de un lago muy hermoso en las altas montañas. Cada invierno, muchos turistas vienen a Bariloche para esquiar en las montañas.

La familia de Sonia tiene una pensión. Su pensión es un hotel pequeño con pocas habitaciones. En la pensión, la gente come el desayuno y la cena. A veces las personas almuerzan en la pensión.

Durante la semana, Sonia va al colegio. Los fines de semana, ayuda a sus padres en la pensión. Pone las toallas limpias en las habitaciones y, los domingos por la mañana, sirve el desayuno a los turistas. Su hermano Alberto ayuda a su mamá en la cocina. Algún día, su hermano quiere ser el dueño de la pensión. Pero, algún día, Sonia quiere ser dentista y vivir en Buenos Aires, la capital.

Ask comprehension questions about the reading (e.g., **¿Dónde está Bariloche? ¿Qué hace Sonia durante la semana?**).

La cultura y tú

See Unit Plans, Unidad 3, for additional background information.

El turismo en la América del Sur

Ya sabes que en España y México hay muchas playas bonitas y muchos sitios interesantes. ¿Pero sabes que muchos turistas visitan sitios en la América del Sur también?

First, have students read the passage to understand the gist and guess the meanings of unfamiliar words from context. Then, have students look up the words they do not know in the Spanish-English Glossary and reread the passage.

Los turistas no van solamente a las playas. Cada año, casi quinientos mil turistas de varios países visitan el Perú. Generalmente van para ver Machu Picchu. Allá en las altas montañas de los Andes, ven las ruinas de la civilización de los incas.

Have students find Peru and Argentina on a world map or a globe.

Más de un millón de turistas visitan la Argentina cada año. Muchos de los turistas van para ver las bellezas de la naturaleza. En la frontera de la Argentina con el Brasil, visitan las cataratas de Iguazú.

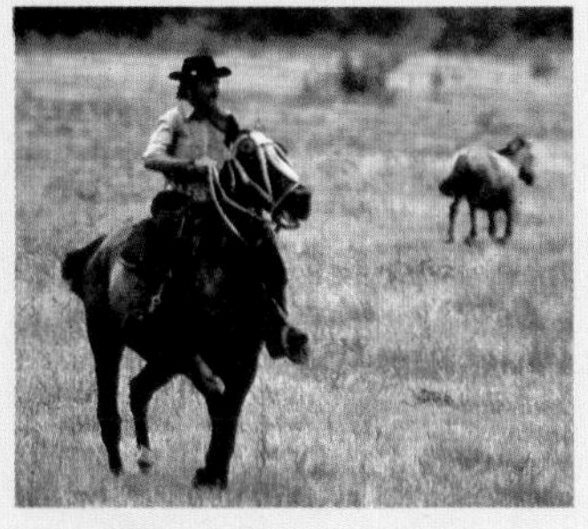

Muchas personas visitan también la Pampa en el centro de la Argentina. Allá, en el llano grande, viven los gauchos. Ellos son muy buenos jinetes.

Enrichment: Have students prepare travel brochures explaining why tourists should visit your community.

Primer repaso

A. Una conversación entre familia

Have volunteers role-play the conversation.

AGENTE: ¿Adónde piensan viajar?

PAPÁ: Pensamos viajar a las montañas.

PEPE: ¡No quiero ir a las montañas!

ALMA: Podemos visitar a nuestros primos en Bolivia.

PEPE: ¡No quiero ir a Bolivia!

AGENTE: Hay un hotel hermoso y moderno en la República Dominicana y . . .

PAPÁ: ¿De veras? ¿Cuesta mucho?

AGENTE: El precio es muy razonable.

PEPE: ¡No quiero ir a un hotel!

ALMA: Pepe, ¿adónde quieres viajar?

PEPE: ¡A la luna! ¡Quiero viajar a la luna como los astronautas!

PAPÁ: ¡Ay de mí!

Extension: Have students skim the conversation and write two more questions to ask their classmates (e.g., **¿Por qué quiere ir Alma a Bolivia? ¿Por qué quiere ir a la luna Pepe?**).

Preguntas

1. ¿Dónde están el papá, Pepe y Alma?
2. ¿Qué piensa hacer el papá?
3. ¿Qué piensa hacer Alma?
4. ¿Qué dice el agente sobre la República Dominicana?
5. ¿Cuesta mucho el hotel?
6. ¿Adónde quiere ir Pepe?

1. Están en una agencia de viajes.
2. El papá piensa viajar a las montañas.
3. Alma piensa ir a Bolivia.
4. La agente de viajes dice que hay un hotel hermoso y moderno en la República Dominicana.
5. No, el hotel no cuesta mucho.
6. Pepe quiere ir a la luna.

B. Haciendo planes

What is your idea of a wonderful trip? Imagine that you can take a trip anywhere in the world. Where will you go? How will you travel? Where will you stay? It's never too soon to start planning.

Lee y contesta las preguntas en tus palabras. Luego, escribe tus respuestas en un párrafo.

1. ¿Adónde piensas viajar?
2. ¿Con quién piensas viajar?
3. ¿Vas a viajar en avión?
4. ¿Adónde vas para comprar los billetes?
5. ¿Tienes maletas o necesitas más equipaje?
6. ¿Quieres estar en un hotel moderno o antiguo?
7. ¿Quieres una habitación grande o pequeña?
8. ¿Cómo te gusta tu cama, blanda o dura?
9. ¿Cuál usas más, la bañera o la ducha?
10. ¿A quiénes vas a escribir las tarjetas postales?

Do this activity orally in class and have volunteers write students' answers on the chalkboard. Students may then write the answers in paragraphs as homework.

Extension: Students may find it interesting to find out where others would like to travel. Have volunteers read their paragraphs aloud. Make a chart of students' vacation preferences.

Estas personas esperan la llegada de sus maletas. Cuando viajas, ¿vas con mucho equipaje? ¿Tienes que esperar mucho cuando viajas con equipaje?

C. La pasajera difícil

Linda Aérea is a flight attendant who is trying to please a very difficult passenger. Every time she brings her something, the passenger doesn't want it. You may wish to assign this activity as homework.

Primero, lee la pregunta de la aeromoza. Luego, responde como la pasajera. Lee el modelo.

Modelo: ¿Quiere usted la almohada?
Respuesta: **No, no la quiero.**

1. ¿Quiere usted un té?
2. ¿Quiere un vaso de agua?
3. ¿Quiere las tarjetas postales?
4. ¿Quiere una manta?
5. ¿Quiere unos libros?
6. ¿Quiere un café?

1. No, no lo quiero.
2. No, no lo quiero.
3. No, no las quiero.
4. No, no la quiero.
5. No, no los quiero.
6. No, no lo quiero.

CH. ¿Verdad o mentira?

Welcome to the game show **¿Verdad o mentira?** Every time you guess correctly whether our panelist is telling you the truth or a lie, you score ten points. How well will you do?

Primero, lee la oración. Luego, escribe si es verdad o mentira. Por último, busca las respuestas en la página 93 y suma tus puntos. Lee el modelo.

Modelo: Luis: El Canadá está en la América del Sur.
Respuesta: **Luis dice una mentira.**

Extension: Ask volunteers to play the roles of the game show panelists and game show contestants.

1. Iris: Los aviones nunca aterrizan a tiempo.
2. Hernán: Los pilotos siempre se duermen durante los vuelos.
3. Marcos: Puedes comprar un billete en una agencia de viajes.

4. Rosa: Los turistas siempre se bañan con agua fría.
5. Hugo: España está muy lejos del Perú.
6. Anita: Chile está muy cerca de Bolivia.
7. Óscar: Primero te duermes y luego te acuestas.
8. Martín: Dos personas no pueden jugar al dominó.
9. Sara: Un pasajero paga por una habitación en un avión.
10. Lidia: Cada año muchos turistas viajan a la Argentina.

Extension: For each **mentira** answer, have students write a correct sentence (e.g., **Los aviones a veces aterrizan a tiempo.**).

D. Haciendo descripciones

Imagine that you're visiting one of the places in the pictures. Describe it to your best friend. Choose a photo and brainstorm a few sample sentences with the class before assigning this activity as homework.

Escoge una foto. Luego, escribe por lo menos cinco oraciones sobre ese lugar.

1.

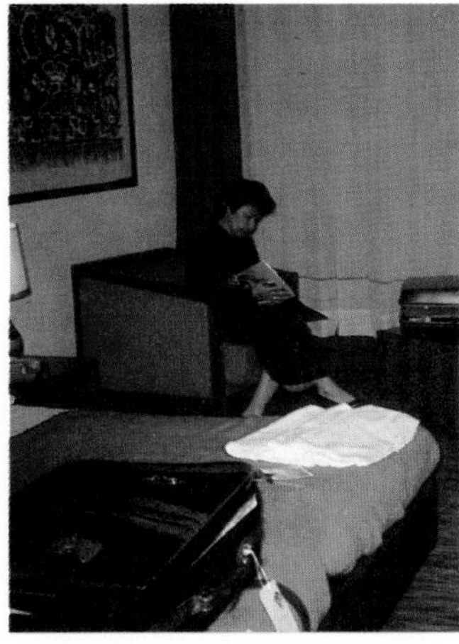

2.

3.

Respuestas a **¿Verdad o mentira?** Recibes 10 puntos por cada respuesta correcta.
1. mentira **3.** verdad **5.** verdad **7.** mentira **9.** mentira
2. mentira **4.** mentira **6.** verdad **8.** mentira **10.** verdad

E. Una encuesta en el hotel

The managers of the hotel La Posada need your help. They want you to take a survey of the guests to find out the first thing they do when they get their rooms. Have students work in pairs to ask and answer the questions.

Primero, lee la descripción de la persona y haz una pregunta. Luego, contesta la pregunta con las palabras entre paréntesis. Sigue el modelo.

Modelo: un hombre grueso (quitarse los zapatos)

Respuesta: **P: Señor, ¿qué hace usted primero?**

R: Primero, me quito los zapatos.

1. P: Señora, ¿qué hace usted primero?
R: Primero, me peino.
2. P: Señor, ¿qué hace usted primero?
R: Primero, pido más toallas y jabón.
3. P: Señora, ¿qué hace usted primero?
R: Primero, me acuesto y me duermo unos minutos.

1. una mujer bonita (peinarse)
2. un abuelo (pedir más toallas y jabón)
3. una abuela (acostarse y dormirse unos minutos)
4. unos alumnos (comenzar a escribir tarjetas postales)
5. un muchacho de 13 años (cerrar las ventanas)
6. una muchacha de 13 años (bañarse y ponerse ropa limpia)

4. P: ¿Qué hacen ustedes primero?
R: Primero, comenzamos a escribir tarjetas postales.
5. P: ¿Qué haces primero?
R: Primero, cierro las ventanas.
6. P: ¿Qué haces primero?
R: Primero, me baño y me pongo ropa limpia.

F. En el buzón

Alejandro is having fun on his trip to Cali, Colombia. What does he tell you in his letter?

Lee la carta y contesta las preguntas.

Have students scan and then read the letter for comprehension before answering the questions.

8 de octubre

¡Hola!

¿Cómo estás? ¿Vas a la escuela todos los días? ¡Qué lástima!

Yo voy a lugares interesantes todos los días. Visito a mis primos en Cali. Cali está en el valle del río Cauca. Desde mi habitación puedo mirar las montañas. Las miro cada mañana, cuando me despierto. ¿Puedes ver montañas desde tu ventana?

La semana que entra, mis primos y yo pensamos hacer un viaje a la selva. Mi tío Pedro trabaja en la selva del Chocó. Él estudia mariposas raras. Tenemos que ir en un avión pequeño. Mis primos dicen que es un aerotaxi. ¿Qué piensas hacer tú la semana que entra? ¿Vas a viajar en aerotaxi o tienes que ir a la escuela? (¡Ja, ja!)

Esta noche vamos a una fiesta. ¡Comienza a las nueve de la noche! Yo digo que tenemos que llegar a las nueve en punto. Pero mis primos dicen que nadie va a llegar a tiempo. Dicen que a lo mejor llegamos a las nueve y media. ¡Bueno! ¡Ellos saben más que yo!

¿Vas a ir a una fiesta? ¿Cuándo comienza? ¿Cuándo vas a llegar?

Saludos a todos,

Alejandro

Extension: Have students write a letter in reply to Alejandro. Display letters on the bulletin board.

Enrichment: Use the letter as the basis of a discussion of **la hora latina.** You may wish to explain that attitudes toward time are more relaxed than they are in the United States. Especially for social functions, punctuality is not necessary. Advanced students may research **la hora latina** and report their findings to the class.

Unidad

After completing this unit, students should be able to:

- ▶ identify and name people and items related to going to a bank and a restaurant
- ▶ refer to people and things by using indirect object pronouns
- ▶ talk about giving by using the present tense of **dar** and use idiomatic meanings of **dar** appropriately
- ▶ identify differences in amounts of money in a Spanish-speaking country
- ▶ read a chart of monetary units of various Spanish-speaking countries.

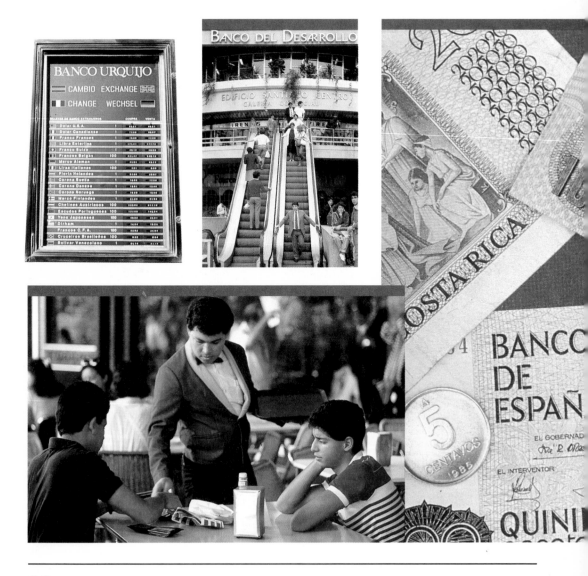

The photographs may be used for informal assessment and review:

- ► Muéstrame una moneda de la Argentina. Muéstrame un billete del Perú.
- ► ¿Está abierta o cerrada la ventanilla del banco? ¿Qué número es la ventanilla?
- ► ¿Qué hace el camarero? ¿A quién sirve?
- ► ¿Cómo es el Banco del Desarrollo? ¿Puedes subir en ascensor o en las escaleras eléctricas?

Panorama de vocabulario

Vamos al banco

el banco
el cajero
los billetes
cerrada
la ventanilla
la cajera
abierta
las monedas

Extension: If students exhibit an interest in learning other terms related to banking, you may wish to teach the following words:

la cuenta de ahorros savings account
depositar to deposit
ingresar en to deposit in
retirar de to withdraw from
con interés de——por ciento at an interest of——percent

Tenemos hambre

Other words used to mean **el menú** are **la carta** and **la lista de platos.** Throughout much of Latin America **el mesero** and **la mesera** are also used for **el camarero** and **la camarera.** In Spain you may also ask for **la nota**, instead of **la cuenta.**

Extension: Students may want to know different ways of paying a bill: **en efectivo** (cash), **con un cheque de viajero** (traveler's cheque), or **con una tarjeta de crédito** (credit card).

¡Aprende el vocabulario!

A. Elena has a new job at the bank. What new words must she learn?

Primero, mira el dibujo. Luego, lee la oración. Por último, completa la oración. Sigue el modelo.

Modelo: Elena trabaja en ——.

Respuesta: **Elena trabaja en el banco.**

1. los billetes
2. las monedas
3. cajera
4. cajero
5. ventanilla
6. cerrado

1. Elena cuenta ——.

2. También cuenta ——.

3. Elena es ——.

4. Hugo también es ——.

5. Su —— está abierta.

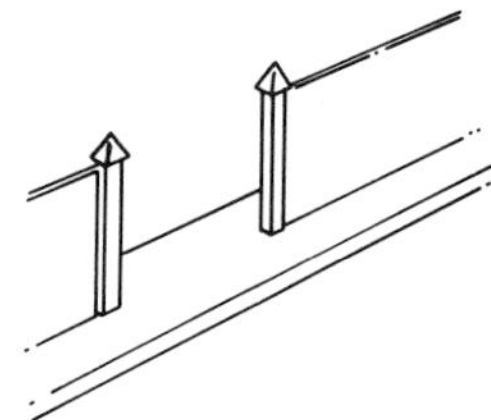

6. Los domingos el banco está ——.

You may wish to review the use of **ser** with professions, dropping the direct article unless an adjective is used (e.g., **Elena es cajera. Elena es la cajera alta.**).

B. What a disaster! Eugenio is running some errands, but he's so hungry he can't think straight. Help him out.

Primero, lee la oración. Luego, completa la oración con una o dos palabras apropiadas. Sigue el modelo.

Modelo: Necesito dinero. Primero, voy ——.

Respuesta: **Primero, voy al banco.**

You may wish to assign this activity as homework after reviewing it in class.

1. En el banco voy a hablar con —— bonita.
2. Voy a pedir veinte dólares en —— y un dólar en ——.
3. ¡Ay! ¡Todas —— están cerradas!
4. ¡Qué bueno! Una está ——.
5. ¡Tengo mucha hambre! Voy —— muy cerca de aquí.
6. Antes de comer, voy a leer ——.
7. —— es muy impaciente. No sé qué comer.
8. Ahora voy a pagar ——, pero no voy a poner —— en la mesa.

1. la cajera
2. billetes / monedas
3. las ventanillas
4. abierta
5. a un restaurante
6. el menú
7. El camarero *or* La camarera
8. la cuenta / una propina

Sharpen students' observation skills by asking questions (e.g., **¿Cuántos dólares va a cambiar el hombre? ¿Cuántos billetes va a recibir el hombre?**).

Esta persona cambia sus dólares por pesos mexicanos. ¿Adónde vas para cambiar dinero?

C. What do you prefer, to spend your money or to save your money? Maybe the following offers will tempt you.

Primero, lee la frase y el precio. Luego, escribe unas oraciones. Sigue los modelos. Answers will vary.

Modelo: Botas negras—$10.00
Respuesta: **Sí, quiero las botas. Prefiero gastar mi dinero.**

Modelo: Un viaje al desierto—$5,000.00
Respuesta: **No quiero el viaje. Prefiero ahorrar mi dinero.**

Have students guess the meaning of **preferir** from its similarity to the English verb. Help students observe that **preferir** is a stem-changing verb like **querer**.

1. Un avión—$100,000.00
2. Una camiseta—$7.00
3. Una novela—$4.69
4. Un viaje a la selva—$1,500.00
5. Un viaje corto en autobús—$39.95
6. Una cena en un restaurante—$21.00
7. Una bicicleta moderna—$654.70.
8. Una semana en un hotel moderno—$893.00
9. Un radio—$19.75
10. Un televisor antiguo—$5.00

Extension: When students answer that they wish to save their money, have them state what they would prefer to spend the money on (e.g., **No quiero un avión. Prefiero gastar mi dinero en una casa bonita.**).

Enrichment: Have students research current exchange rates and convert all the amounts in the exercise to another currency. Students may consult the chart on page 117 to find the appropriate symbol to write with the amounts.

Los sonidos del idioma

Las vocales: **ei, ie; eu, ue**

Escucha y repite. Compara los sonidos de las vocales.

ei	ie	eu	ue
peine	bien	reunión	abuela
béisbol	invierno	deuda	bueno
reina	pierna	neutral	escuela

1. La reina se peina bien antes de la fiesta.
2. Hay una reunión sobre las deudas de la escuela.
3. No juego al béisbol afuera en el invierno.

Remind students that the two vowels together have only one sound. Be alert to the tendency to pronounce two vowel sounds: **bi-en,** instead of **bien.**

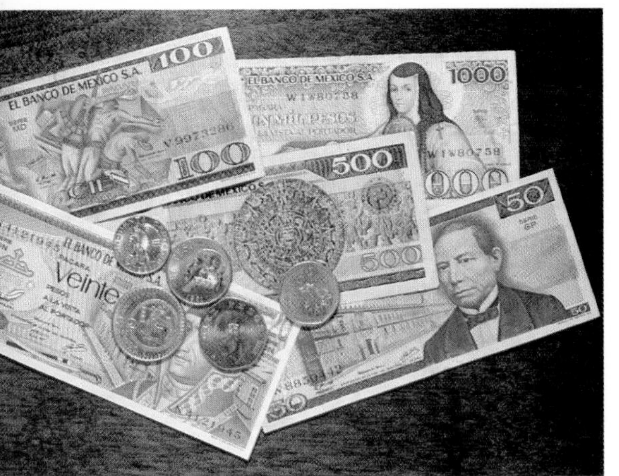

Este dinero es de México. ¿Cuántos billetes hay? ¿Cuántas monedas hay?

El camarero sirve a la gente en el restaurante.

Have students create brief question-and-answer exchanges based on the photographs. You may write some questions on the board to get them started (e.g., **¿Cuántos billetes quiere usted? ¿Qué prefiere usted, monedas o billetes? ¿Está abierto el restaurante? ¿Podemos ver el menú?**).

Usando el español

Referring to Yourself and Others

Rule: Indirect object pronouns tell you to whom or for whom an action is done. Indirect object pronouns replace indirect object nouns.

Study the pictures and read the sentences.

Have volunteers read the examples aloud. Help them observe the connection between the indirect object pronouns and the people in the pictures to whom they refer.

RAÚL: ¿Qué **le** pide Juan al maestro?

OLGA: Juan **le** pide ayuda.

If students need practice distinguishing between direct and indirect objects, you may wish to write some examples on the chalkboard and then label the words accordingly (I.O.; D.O.):
El camarero nos sirve la comida. (**nos** = I.O., **la comida** = D.O.)
La maestra me lee un poema. (**me** = I.O., **un poema** = D.O.)

CAMARERO: ¿Cómo **les** puedo servir a ustedes?

JOSEFINA: A nosotras **nos** puede traer un menú, por favor.

Follow up by asking questions (e.g., **¿Qué sirve el camarero? ¿A quién sirve la comida?**).

CARLOS: Mi abuelo **me** escribe una carta cada semana.

ROSITA: ¡A mí nadie **me** escribe!

The words in heavy black letters are called indirect object pronouns. An indirect object pronoun tells you to whom or for whom something is done.

Study the chart of indirect object pronouns.

Have students locate another chart of indirect object pronouns in the book.

Singular	Plural
me	nos
te	os
le	les

Have volunteers read the sample questions and answers aloud. You may wish to have students role-play the people mentioned in each sentence. As each indirect pronoun is read, point to the person it refers to.

Now read the following questions and answers:

¿Qué te duele a ti?

A mí me duele el brazo.

¿A quién pago la cuenta?

Me paga la cuenta a mí, señor.

¿A quién le canta Diego?

Siempre le canta canciones románticas a Julia.

¿Qué les gusta a ustedes?

A nosotros nos gusta el jamón.

¿Qué les sirve la camarera?

Nos sirve la sopa.

¿Qué le piden ustedes al dueño del hotel?

Le pedimos la cuenta.

How observant are you?

[The pronouns **me, te, le, nos,** and **les** have been used with **gustar** and **doler.**]

You have been using **gustar** and **doler** for a long time. What pronouns have you been using with **gustar** and **doler**?

What words do you use to emphasize to whom or for whom something is done? Do you place the indirect object pronoun before or after the verb?

[To emphasize to whom or for whom something is done, you use **a** plus a noun or pronoun. You place the indirect object pronoun before the verb.]

¡Vamos a practicar!

A. What restaurants do you and your friends like?

Primero, lee la pregunta. Luego, completa la pregunta. Por último, escribe la respuesta con **sí** o **no.** Sigue el modelo.

Modelo: ¿A ti —— gustan los restaurantes mexicanos? (sí)

Respuesta: **P: ¿A ti te gustan los restaurantes mexicanos?**

R: Sí, a mí me gustan mucho.

Have students work in pairs to ask and answer the questions.

1. ¿A Juan —— gustan los restaurantes franceses? (no)
2. ¿A ellos —— gustan los restaurantes chinos? (sí)
3. ¿A Carlota y a Berta —— gustan los restaurantes peruanos? (sí)
4. ¿A ti —— gustan los restaurantes argentinos? (no)
5. ¿A Bárbara —— gustan los restaurantes españoles? (sí)

1. le / No, a Juan no le gustan.
2. les / Sí, a ellos les gustan mucho
3. les / Sí, a ellas les gustan mucho
4. te / No, a mí no me gustan.
5. le / Sí, a ella le gustan mucho.

Extension: Have students answer the questions according to their own preferences.

Review this exercise carefully in class to make certain students have grasped the correct agreement of **gustar** and **doler** as well as agreement of indirect object pronouns.

Este restaurante es muy elegante. ¿Te gusta comer en los restaurantes elegantes?

B. Margarita is feeling sorry for herself. She thinks no one likes her or wants to do things for her. Try to cheer her up.

Primero, completa la pregunta. Luego, escribe la respuesta con las palabras entre paréntesis. Sigue el modelo.

Modelo: ¿Quién —— compra novelas? (a veces / mi papá)

Respuesta: **P:** **¿Quién te compra novelas?**

R: **A veces mi papá me compra novelas.**

Have students work in pairs to ask and answer the questions.

1. ¿Quién —— escribe cartas? (a veces / mi tía)
2. ¿Quién —— prepara el desayuno? (siempre / mi mamá)
3. ¿Quiénes —— traen camisetas cómicas? (a veces / mis primos)
4. ¿Quién —— dice la verdad? (siempre / tú)

1. te / A veces mi tía me escribe cartas.
2. te / Mi mamá siempre me prepara el desayuno.
3. te / A veces mis primos me traen camisetas cómicas.
4. te / Tú siempre me dices la verdad.

C. Poor Pablo! He never has enough money. How much does he ask for?

Primero, lee las frases. Luego, contesta la pregunta **¿Cuánto pide Pablo?** Por último, forma una oración. Sigue el modelo. Do more examples with the class before assigning this activity as homework.

Modelo: a nosotras / seis dólares

Respuesta: **A nosotras nos pide seis dólares.**

1. A mí me pide ocho dólares.
2. A ti te pide cincuenta centavos.
5. A ellas les pide veinte centavos.
6. A él le pide once dólares.

1. a mí / ocho dólares
2. a ti / cincuenta centavos
3. a nosotros / tres dólares
4. a ustedes / cinco dólares
5. a ellas / veinte centavos
6. a él / once dólares
7. a ellos / quince dólares
8. a ella / ochenta centavos

3. A nosotros nos pide tres dólares.
4. A ustedes les pide cinco dólares.
7. A ellos les pide quince dólares.
8. A ella le pide ochenta centavos.

D. Lupita has written an essay about her best friend María. However, she forgot to use indirect object pronouns. Help her out.

Primero, lee todas las oraciones. Luego, completa cada oración. Por último, escribe las oraciones. Sigue el modelo.

Modelo: Siempre —— digo la verdad a María.
Respuesta: **Siempre le digo la verdad a María.**

1. le	**5.** nos
2. me	**6.** le
3. le	**7.** le
4. nos	**8.** nos

Mi mejor amiga

María es mi mejor amiga. (**1**) Yo —— digo mis secretos. (**2**) Y ella —— dice sus secretos. (**3**) A veces —— pido ayuda con mis lecciones. Ella es muy inteligente.

(**4**) A nosotras —— gusta jugar al tenis. (**5**) También —— gusta ir a nuestro restaurante favorito. (**6**) Al camarero, yo —— pido helado de chocolate. (**7**) María —— pide helado de fresas. (**8**) El camarero siempre —— trae unas galletas con los helados. Él es muy simpático.

Extension: Have students make up brief exchanges between the two best friends, based on one of the situations in the paragraph:
S1: ¿Te digo un secreto?
S2: ¿Qué?
S1: A mí me gusta mucho Juan.

E. Now it's your turn. What is your best friend like? What do you do together?

Escribe un párrafo sobre tu mejor amigo o amiga. Si necesitas ayuda, lee y contesta las preguntas.

Students' paragraphs will vary, but should make good use of indirect object pronouns.

1. A ustedes, ¿qué les gusta hacer?
2. ¿Qué le dices a tu amiga o amigo?
3. ¿Qué le pides a tu amigo o amiga?
4. ¿Qué te pide tu amigo a ti?
5. ¿Tu amigo te compra cosas?
6. ¿Le compras cosas a tu amigo?

Enrichment: Include students' essays in a Big Book entitled **Mi mejor amigo o amiga.**

Students might enjoy creating their own illustrations of sayings.

¡A divertirnos!

Ask students to think of everyday situations in which this saying would apply.

Una expresión extraña

Have students try to guess the meaning of the saying from the illustration, then look up the meanings of the words to confirm their guesses. Ask them if they know a similar English expression ("Don't look a gift horse in the mouth.").

A caballo regalado no hay que mirarle el diente.

Talking about Giving

Rule: You use **dar** to talk about giving. **Dar** is irregular in the **yo** form but has regular **-ar** endings in the other forms.

Study the following pictures and read the sentences.

Siempre le **doy** la mano a mi amigo.

A Miguel le **damos** las gracias.

¿Qué nos **da** la cajera?
Sólo nos **da** unas monedas.

¿Qué le **dan** a su mamá?
¡Siempre le **damos** dolor de cabeza!

Have the class study the examples and deduce the different uses of **dar.**

The words in heavy black letters come from the infinitive **dar.** From the examples, would you say that **dar** is a regular or an irregular verb? Which verb form is different? [**Dar** is an irregular verb. The **yo** form is different.]

Dar is used in many expressions. What do you think **dar la mano** means? What do you think **dar las gracias** means?

[**Dar la mano** means to shake hands. **Dar las gracias** means to thank.]

Now study the chart of the verb **dar.**

Ask students to locate another chart of **dar** in the appendix.

Dar

Singular		Plural	
yo	doy	nosotros (-as)	damos
tú	das	vosotros (-as)	dais
él / ella / usted	da	ellos / ellas / ustedes	dan

How observant are you?

What other verb do the forms of **dar** resemble—**estar, ir,** or **ser**?

[The forms of **dar** resemble **ir.**]

Practice reading the following questions and answers:

Pregunta: Srta. Ortega, ¿qué les **da** usted a sus alumnos?
Respuesta: Siempre les **doy** libros y cuadernos a mis alumnos.

Pregunta: ¿Qué le **das** a Rita para su cumpleaños?
Respuesta: Le **doy** una camiseta rosada.

Pregunta: ¿Le **damos** los billetes al aeromozo antes de entrar al avión?
Respuesta: No. Le **damos** los billetes al aeromozo después de entrar al avión.

Have volunteers read the sample questions and answers aloud. Help students observe that indirect object pronouns precede the forms of **dar** in the sentences.

¡Vamos a practicar!

A. The Spanish Club is having a rummage sale to raise money for a trip to Costa Rica. Who is giving items to the rummage sale?

Primero, lee la oración. Luego, completa la oración con la forma apropiada de **dar.** Sigue el modelo.

You may wish to assign this activity as homework.

Modelo: Daniel —— libros viejos.

Respuesta: **Daniel da libros viejos.**

1. Roberto y Sarita —— botas pequeñas.
2. Amalia —— un abrigo de invierno.
3. Estela y yo —— tazas y platillos.
4. También, yo —— cinco carteles bonitos.
5. El Sr. Gómez —— una lámpara.
6. Ustedes —— un televisor de blanco y negro.
7. La Sra. Álvarez —— un juego electrónico.
8. Felipe y Tomás —— coches de plástico.

1. dan
2. da
3. damos
4. doy
5. da
6. dan
7. da
8. dan

B. Courtesy is important when you travel in Spanish-speaking countries.

Primero, lee la oración y la pregunta. Luego, contesta la pregunta. Sigue el modelo. Have students work in pairs to ask and answer the questions.

Modelo: La aeromoza te trae un vaso de agua. ¿Qué haces?

Respuesta: **Le doy las gracias a la aeromoza.**

1. El cajero les da los billetes a ustedes. ¿Qué hacen?
2. La camarera te sirve la cena. ¿Qué haces?
3. El dueño del hotel les trae toallas limpias. ¿Qué hacen?
4. Tú le das una propina al taxista. ¿Qué hace él?

1. Le damos las gracias al cajero.
2. Le doy las gracias a la camarera.
3. Le damos las gracias al dueño del hotel.
4. El taxista me da las gracias.

Extension: Have students think of other situations in which one person thanks another.

C. What do different people give you?

Primero, lee las palabras. Luego, escoge unas palabras de las listas y escribe una oración. Sigue el modelo.

Accept variations in students' answers.

Modelo: un camarero

Respuesta: **Un camarero me da el menú.**

1. los maestros
2. un piloto
3. una cajera
4. los agentes de viaje
5. una médica
6. los taxistas

el menú	billetes de avión
un examen médico	exámenes difíciles
un viaje en avión	billetes y monedas
dolor de cabeza	un viaje en coche

1. Los maestros me dan exámenes difíciles.
2. Un piloto me da un viaje en avión.
3. Una cajera me da billetes y monedas.
4. Los agentes de viajes me dan billetes de avión.
5. Una médica me da un examen médico.
6. Los taxistas me dan un viaje en coche.

Extension: Continue by naming people in the school and community and having students tell you what each individual gives.

¡A conversar!

La hora del almuerzo

Have volunteers role-play the conversation after the class has listened to it and read it several times.

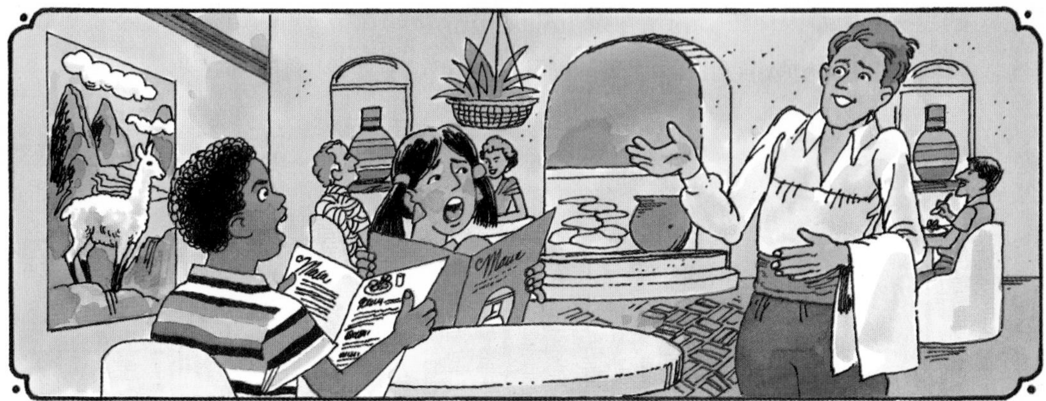

LETICIA: Es la hora del almuerzo. Tengo mucha hambre. Hay un restaurante peruano muy cerca de aquí.

ALONSO: ¡Es cierto! Nuestro amigo Pablo es camarero en el restaurante.

LETICIA: Aquí estamos ... pero hay mucha gente. ¿Hacemos fila?

ALONSO: Mmmm ... ¡mira, Leticia, hay una mesa libre! No tenemos que hacer fila. Ahora llamamos a Pablo.

LETICIA: Sí. Él nos va a servir rápido porque es nuestro amigo.

ALONSO: Y después le damos una propina grande.

LETICIA: ¡Hola, Pablo! Quiero tomar una limonada y unas arepas con queso y tomate, por favor.

ALONSO: Lo mismo para mí, Pablo. ¡Tenemos mucha hambre!

PABLO: Lo siento mucho, amigos. No les puedo servir ahora. Es la hora de mi almuerzo. ¡Yo también tengo mucha hambre!

Preguntas

Encourage students to answer in complete sentences.
1. Van a un restaurante peruano.
2. Su amigo Pablo trabaja en el restaurante.
3. No, no hacen fila. Hay una mesa libre.
4. Le van a dar una propina grande.
5. No, Pablo no les sirve el almuerzo.
6. Pablo va a almorzar. Tiene mucha hambre.

1. ¿Adónde van Alonso y Leticia?
2. ¿Quién trabaja en el restaurante?
3. ¿Hacen fila Leticia y Alonso?
4. ¿Qué le van a dar a Pablo después del almuerzo?
5. ¿Les sirve el almuerzo Pablo?
6. ¿Qué va a hacer Pablo?

¡Conversa tú!

1. ¿Vives cerca de un restaurante?
2. ¿Cuántas veces al mes vas a un restaurante?
3. ¿Te gusta hacer fila?
4. ¿Generalmente, ¿les das propinas grandes a los camareros?
5. ¿Cuándo les das propinas pequeñas a los camareros?

Have students work in pairs to interview each other, using these questions. Students may think of more questions to ask each other about restaurant habits.

¿Te gustan los restaurantes al aire libre?
¿A veces comes afuera?
¿Cuándo?

La cultura y tú

See Unit Plans, Unidad 4, for additional information.

¡Tanto dinero!

¿Sabes algo del dinero de los países de habla española? Cada país en el mundo hispano tiene su unidad monetaria distinta. Si visitas un país y no conoces el dinero, los precios te pueden sorprender.

¿Es mucho dinero $800? ¿Puedes pagar $800 por la ropa? Esta tienda no está en los Estados Unidos. Está en Colombia. Allá, $800 no son ochocientos dólares sino ochocientos pesos. En Colombia, ochocientos pesos es un precio razonable por la ropa.

Bring bills and coins from Spanish-speaking countries to class for students to look at. Some students may have foreign currency that they could bring for "show and tell."

Mira la lista de países y unidades monetarias. ¿Tienen muchos nombres diferentes las unidades monetarias? ¿Cómo son los símbolos?

País	Nombre	Subdivisión	Símbolo
Bolivia	peso	100 centavos	$B
Chile	peso chileno	1000 escudos	$
Costa Rica	colón	100 céntimos	₡; ¢
Ecuador	sucre	100 centavos	S/
España	peseta	100 céntimos	Pta; P
Guatemala	quetzal	100 centavos	Q̸; Q
Honduras	lempira	100 centavos	L
México	peso	100 centavos	$
Nicaragua	córdoba	100 centavos	C$
Panamá	balboa	100 centésimos	B/
Paraguay	guaraní	100 céntimos	₲; G
Perú	sol	100 centavos	S/; $
Venezuela	bolívar	100 céntimos	B; Bs.

Enrichment: Collect the foreign exchange listings in the newspaper every day for a week or more. Bring the clippings to class so that sutdents can observe the fluctuations of currency exchange. You may also wish to assign students to follow the exchange rates of different currencies over a period of time.

Unidad 5

After completing this unit, students should be able to:

- identify and name places in a city
- talk about people and places by employing the different uses of **estar**
- use direct or indirect object pronouns with infinitives
- read simulated encyclopedia articles about cities
- discuss the importance of plazas in Hispanic cities and towns
- describe the significance of Simón Bolívar in South America.

The photographs may be used for informal assessment or review:

- ► Muéstrame un monumento. ¿Es antiguo o moderno el monumento?
- ► ¿Cómo es el estadio?
- ► ¿Cómo es la álcaldía?
- ► ¿Dónde está la señora? ¿Qué compra ella?
- ► ¿Hay muchas personas en el metro?

Panorama de vocabulario

Vamos a conocer la ciudad

The mayor **(el alcalde** or **la alcaldesa)** may work in **la alcaldía** or in **el ayuntamiento.**

la iglesia

el museo

la escultura

la alcaldía

la plaza

la fuente

el monumento

In Spain, **un apartamento** is usually no more than two bedrooms; larger apartments are called **pisos.**

Una escuela is usually a primary school; **un colegio** is a high school; and **un colegio mayor** refers to a university-type residence hall.

el zoológico

El zoológico may be **el parque zoológico,** or simply **el zoo.**

el estadio

el mercado al aire libre

¡Aprende el vocabulario!

○ A. Sr. and Sra. García are two very brave people! They have gone sightseeing with their seven children. Right now, they're having trouble keeping track of everyone.

Primero, lee la pregunta y mira el dibujo. Luego, contesta la pregunta. Sigue el modelo.

1. Rita está cerca de la iglesia.
2. Luisa está cerca de la sinagoga.
3. Iris está cerca del zoológico.
4. Tomás está cerca del estadio.
5. Pepe está cerca de la alcaldía.
6. Juan está cerca del supermercado.

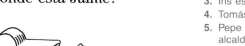

Accept personal pronouns in the place of names.

Extension: Continue the activity by asking other questions (e.g., **¿Quién está cerca del estadio?**).

Modelo: ¿Dónde está Jaime?

Respuesta: Jaime está cerca de la escultura.

1. ¿Dónde está Rita?

2. ¿Dónde está Luisa?

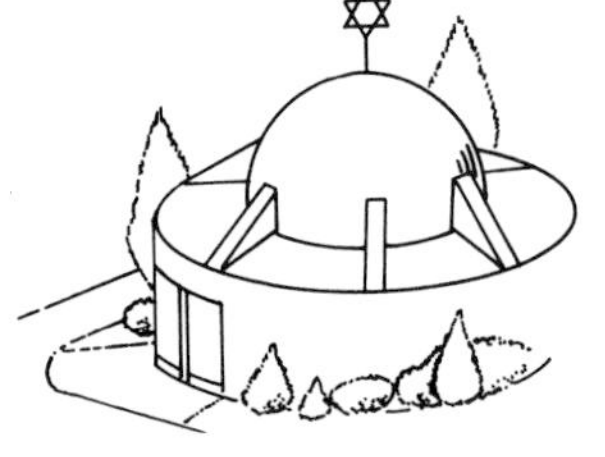

3. ¿Dónde está Iris?

4. ¿Dónde está Tomás?

5. ¿Dónde está Pepe?

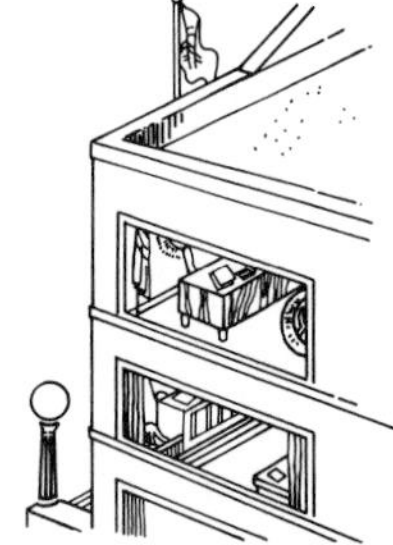

6. ¿Dónde está Juan?

B. Mariano has written a composition about what he is doing on Saturday. Help him complete his sentences.

Primero, lee las oraciones. Luego, lee la lista de palabras. Por último, completa las oraciones. Escribe tus respuestas. Sigue el modelo.

al colegio	una plaza	un apartamento
al estadio	al supermercado	al zoológico
la alcaldía	un monumento	el metro

Modelo: No vivo en una casa. Vivo en ——.

Respuesta: **No vivo en una casa. Vivo en un apartamento.**

Mi sábado

1. Hoy es sábado. No tengo que ir ——.
2. Por la mañana, voy —— con mi papá para comprar carne y zanahorias.
3. A la una voy —— para ver a los Titanes. Es mi equipo favorito de béisbol.
4. Voy a tomar —— porque no me gusta el autobús.
5. La entrada para tomar el tren está en —— grande.
6. Está muy cerca de —— histórico.
7. Después, voy a visitar a mi amigo Emilio. Él vive en —— también.
8. Él y yo siempre vamos —— por la tarde. Nos gusta ver los animales.

1. al colegio
2. al supermercado
3. al estadio
4. el metro
5. una plaza
6. un monumento
7. un apartamento
8. al zoológico

Extension: Have students write three or four sentences about what they like to do on Saturdays.

◐ C. Imagine that a student from Mexico is going to visit you this summer. He has called with all kinds of questions about your community and where you live.

Lee y contesta las preguntas. Escribe las respuestas en oraciones completas. Lee el modelo.

Answers will vary. Have students work in pairs to ask and answer the questions.

Modelo: ¿Hay un zoológico en tu ciudad?

Respuesta: **Sí, hay un zoológico.**

[No, no hay un zoológico.]

1. ¿Hay un mercado al aire libre en tu ciudad?
2. ¿Vives cerca de la alcaldía?
3. ¿Hay una plaza en tu ciudad? ¿Hay una fuente en la plaza?
4. ¿Vives en un edificio de apartamentos?
5. ¿Viajas a veces en el metro?
6. ¿Hay un colegio en tu ciudad? ¿Cómo se llama?
7. ¿Hay un museo en tu ciudad?
8. ¿Cuántas iglesias y sinagogas hay en tu ciudad—muchas o pocas?
9. ¿Vives cerca o lejos de un estadio?
10. ¿Vives cerca o lejos de un supermercado?

Extension: Have students work in pairs to create conversations between a visitor from Mexico and a person in your community. Volunteers may present their conversations to the class.

Enrichment: Students may choose a city or town in a Spanish-speaking country and write at least ten sentences about what may be found there. The major travel books are good sources of information on individual cities; some even include maps with points of interest highlighted.

D. Ana María has never been to your area before. Answer her questions about where to go.

Primero, lee la pregunta. Luego, escribe una respuesta. Sigue el modelo. Answers will vary. Have students answer using names of places in your community (e.g., **Puedes ver un equipo de fútbol en el estadio Clemente.**).

Modelo: ¿Dónde viven muchas personas?

Respuesta: **Viven en un edificio de apartamentos.**

1. ¿Dónde puedo ver un equipo de fútbol?
2. ¿Dónde puedo comprar leche y azúcar?
3. ¿En qué puedo viajar en tu ciudad?
4. ¿Dónde puedo ver tigres y osos?
5. ¿Dónde hay escultura y arte antiguo?
6. ¿Dónde puedo comprar frutas frescas?
7. ¿En qué escuela puedo estudiar?
8. ¿Dónde puedo ver una fuente?

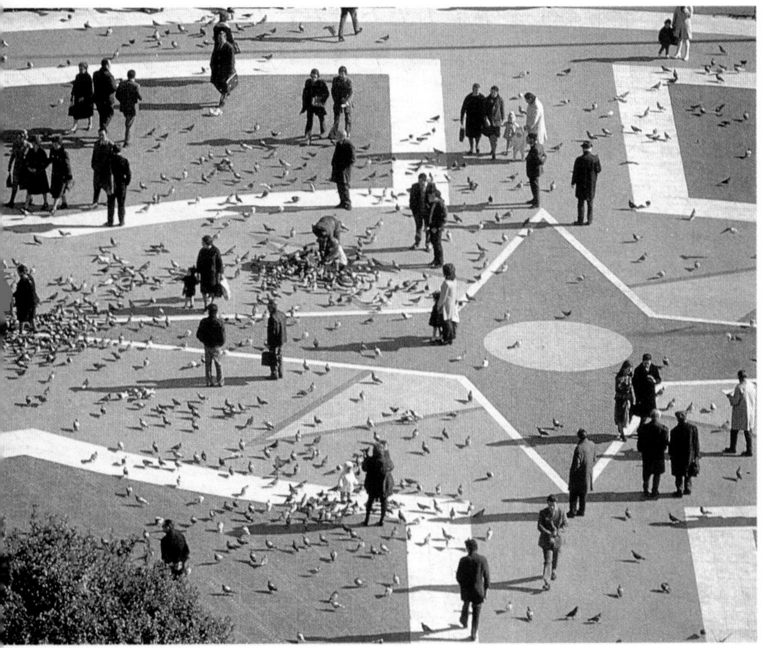

Extension: Have students describe a walk through the Plaza Cataluña. You may wish to teach the word **el pichón** (pigeon).

La Plaza Cataluña está en Barcelona, España. ¿Hay plazas bonitas en tu comunidad?

A possible description: **Hace sol, pero hace frío. Llevo mi abrigo de invierno. Hay muchos pichones en la plaza. Les doy comida a los pichones.**

Los sonidos del idioma

Las vocales: **oi, io; uo**

Escucha y repite. Compara los sonidos de las vocales.

oi	io	uo
oigo	diario	arduo
boina	preciosa	cuota
Loida	camiones	antiguo

The **io** diphthong presents the strongest temptation to pronounce the single vowel sound as two syllables. The word **Mario** in English has three syllables or sounds; whereas in Spanish it only has two.

1. Oigo música preciosa en el colegio antiguo.
2. Vamos con Mario en un arduo viaje en avión.
3. Hay un monstruo rubio en el colegio de Loida.

Students will learn about Simón Bolívar in "La cultura y tú" on page 141. As a prereading activity, you may wish to have them do preliminary research on Simón Bolívar in the school encyclopedia. They may answer questions such as **¿Quién es Simón Bolívar? ¿Es un hombre importante? Generalmente, ¿de quiénes son los monumentos? ¿Son de personas importantes?**

Este monumento está en la plaza Bolívar en Caracas, Venezuela. Es un monumento a Simón Bolívar.

Usando el español

Talking about People and Places

Rule: **Estar** can be used with a gerund to show what is happening now. It can also show where people or things are located or how someone is feeling.

Study the following scene and read the paragraph below it.

Have volunteers read the paragraph aloud.

Have students use the illustration as a clue to guess the meaning of **la jaula.** Demonstrate through pantomime the meanings of **contento** and **triste.**

Esta tarde mis amigos y yo **estamos** visitando el zoológico. Aurelia y yo **estamos** muy contentos, pero Julio **está** triste. No le gusta ver los animales en las jaulas. A nosotros nos gusta ver el oso polar. La jaula del oso polar **está** cerca de una fuente grande. Después de caminar por todo el zoológico, **estamos** muy cansados. Nos duelen los pies. Todavía tenemos que caminar a la parada de autobús. La parada **está** muy lejos del zoológico. ¡Caramba!

In the paragraph, the verb **estar** is used in different ways. Find the sentence that uses **estar** to talk about what the friends are doing now. Find two sentences that use **estar** to talk about where things are located. Find two sentences that use **estar** to talk about how people are feeling at the moment. [The first sentence uses **estar** to talk about what the friends are doing now. The fifth and ninth sentences use **estar** to talk about where things are located. The second and sixth sentences use **estar** to talk about how people are feeling at the moment.]

Recall that you can use **estar** to talk about what you are doing now. Read the following examples:

¿Qué estás haciendo ahora?	Estoy estudiando.
¿Qué hacen tus hermanos?	Están comiendo.
¿Qué está haciendo Iris?	Está abriendo la ventana.

Have students read the sample sentences aloud. You may wish to use some exercises from Unidad 11 of *Ya converso más* to review the present progressive.

Which answer uses **estar** and the gerund (**-ando** form) of a regular **-ar** verb? Which answer uses **estar** and the gerund (**-iendo** form) of a regular **-ir** verb? Which word is the gerund of a regular **-er** verb? From the examples, what two ways can you ask about what people are doing at this moment?

[The first answer uses **estar** and the gerund of an **-ar** verb. The third uses **estar** and the gerund of an **-ir** verb. The second uses **estar** and the gerund of an **-er** verb. You can use **hacer** or **estar** plus the gerund.]

You can also use **estar** to talk about where things or people are located. Read the following examples:

¿Dónde está el colegio?	Está en la Calle Juárez.
¿Dónde están ustedes?	Estamos en el estadio.
¿Dónde está la escultura?	Está en la plaza. Está cerca del museo.

Which examples use **estar** to talk about where things are located? Which example uses **estar** to talk about where people are located?

[The first and third use **estar** to talk about where things are located. The second uses **estar** to talk about where people are located.]

You can also use **estar** to describe feelings or temporary conditions. Read the following examples:

¿Cómo estás, Geraldo?	Estoy mal. Me duele la cabeza.
¿Cómo está la sopa?	¡La sopa está muy caliente!

¿Qué tiempo hace?	Está nublado. Va a llover.
¿Cómo estás hoy, Rita?	Estoy muy contenta. Acabo de recibir una carta de Víctor.

How does Geraldo feel? Will he always feel this way or is his condition likely to change? In fifteen minutes, will the soup still be very hot or will it change? In the other examples, are the conditions likely to change or are they permanent conditions?

[Geraldo feels bad. His condition is likely to change. In fifteen minutes, the temperature of the soup will change. In the other examples, the conditions are likely to change.]

¡A divertirnos!

Una entrevista cómica

Ask students if they already knew this joke in English. Have students work in pairs or small groups to create their own cartoons using forms of **estar.** These may be pasted onto large sheets of newsprint to make a class "comics page."

¡Vamos a practicar!

A. It's a beautiful day in Teresa's neighborhood! Everyone seems busy. What are all her neighbors doing?

Primero, mira el dibujo y lee las preguntas. Luego, lee la lista de palabras. Por último, contesta cada pregunta con una forma de **estar** y una palabra de la lista. Sigue el modelo. Before beginning this activity, help students identify the people in the illustration.

Modelo: ¿Qué está haciendo Tomás?

Respuesta: **Está pintando la casa.**

1. Inés está corriendo.
2. Carlos está abriendo el garaje.
3. La Sra. Luna y Pepe están subiendo las escaleras.
4. Éster y yo estamos jugando.
5. El Sr. Uribe está descansando.
6. Ana y Luis están comiendo.

1. ¿Qué está haciendo Inés?
2. ¿Qué está haciendo Carlos?
3. ¿Qué están haciendo la Sra. Luna y Pepe?
4. ¿Qué hacemos Éster y yo?
5. ¿Qué hace el Sr. Uribe?
6. ¿Qué hacen Ana y Luis?

Extension: Ask students to expand their answers (e.g., **Inés está corriendo en la calle.**).

jugando	comiendo	descansando	corriendo
caminando	abriendo	pintando	subiendo

B. Where are the people and things in the neighborhood?

Primero, mira el dibujo en la página 130. Luego, lee la pregunta y las frases. Por último, contesta la pregunta con la frase apropiada. Sigue el modelo.

You may wish to assign this activity as homework after reviewing it in class.

Modelo: ¿Dónde está el Sr. Uribe?
en el techo en el jardín en el patio

Respuesta: **El Sr. Uribe está en el patio.**

1. ¿Dónde está el radio?
cerca de Ana cerca de Tomás cerca de Pepe
2. ¿Dónde están los pájaros?
en el jardín sobre el techo en el garaje
3. ¿Dónde está Inés?
en el patio en la calle en la casa
4. ¿Dónde está el perro?
cerca de Carlos cerca de Éster cerca de Luis

1. El radio está cerca de Tomás.
2. Los pájaros están en el jardín.
3. Inés está en la calle.
4. El perro está cerca de Luis.

Extension: Continue the activity by asking about other items in the illustration.

C. How are you and your classmates feeling today? Look at the picture for some possibilities.

Primero, mira los dibujos. Luego, haz la pregunta **¿Cómo estás?** a cinco compañeros de clase. Por último, escribe las respuestas. Lee el modelo.

Use pantomime techniques to demonstrate the meanings of the adjectives before assigning the exercise.

contenta

triste

cansado

confundida

enojado

nerviosa

Modelo:
1. Rodrigo está nervioso.
2. Carmen Rosa está cansada.
3. Amalia está triste.
4. Edilberto está contento.
5. Mariela está enojada.

Extension: Have students ask their classmates why they feel the way they do.

D. How do you feel at different times and in different situations?

Primero, lee las oraciones. Luego, describe cómo estás. Escribe una o dos oraciones. Sigue el modelo. Answers will vary.

Modelo: Tus papás te dicen que puedes ir al zoológico.

Respuesta: **Estoy contento. Me gusta ir al zoológico.**

1. Tu mejor amigo está muy mal. Tiene la gripe. No puede ir a tu casa.
2. Tienes un examen muy difícil. Comienza en diez minutos.
3. Contestas todas las preguntas correctamente.
4. Tus papás te dicen que no puedes ir al cine. Tienes que limpiar tu dormitorio.
5. Acabas de correr de la escuela a tu casa.
6. No comprendes la lección. Haces preguntas.

Extension: Have students think of other situations that would make them feel a certain way.

E. Describe a trip or an activity with friends as though you are experiencing it now.

Escribe un párrafo. Si necesitas ayuda, contesta las preguntas. Lee el párrafo en la página 127 como modelo.

1. ¿Dónde estás con tus amigos?
2. ¿Qué están haciendo? ¿Qué están mirando?
3. ¿Cómo están tus amigos? ¿Cómo estás tú?

Students may enjoy writing a conversation with a partner rather than a paragraph. Volunteers may present their conversations to the class.

Referring to People and Things

Rule: Both direct and indirect object pronouns may be connected to the infinitive form of the verb.

Study the pictures and read the questions and answers.

Have students read the sample sentences. Help them note the expressions that use infinitive forms.

P: ¿Tengo que recoger mis **cosas**?
R: Sí, tienes que **recogerlas** ahora mismo.

P: ¿Qué puedo comprar para mi **mamá**?
R: Puedes **comprarle** unas frutas tropicales.

In the first pair of questions and answers, what word is connected to the infinitive **recoger**? What does the word refer to? Is the word a direct or indirect object pronoun? [**Las** is connected to **recoger.** It refers to **cosas.** It is a direct object pronoun.]

In the second pair of questions and answers, what word is connected to the infinitive **comprar**? What does the word refer to? Is the word a direct or indirect object pronoun? [**Le** is connected to **comprar.** It refers to **mamá.** It is an indirect object pronoun.]

Have students turn to page 109 to find an example of an indirect object pronoun connected to an infinitive **[mirarle].**

Read the following examples: Have volunteers read the sample sentences aloud.

Direct

Busco mis libros.
Los voy a buscar en la sala.
Voy a buscar**los** debajo del sofá.

Leo una novela.
La tengo que leer esta noche.
Tengo que leer**la** ahora.

Acabo de llamar a Luisa.
La acabo de llamar.
Acabo de llamar**la** por teléfono.

Indirect

¿Vas a traer mis libros?
¿**Me** vas a traer los libros hoy?
¿Vas a traer**me** los libros ahora?

Tengo que pedir ayuda.
Le voy a pedir ayuda a Juan.
Voy a perdir**le** ayuda esta tarde.

Hago una pregunta a ustedes.
¿**Les** puedo hacer una pregunta?
¿Puedo hacer**les** la pregunta ahora?

If a sentence contains an infinitive, where can you put the direct object pronoun to make one word? [You can connect it to the infinitive.]

If a sentence contains an infinitive, where can you put the indirect object pronoun to make one word? [You can connect it to the infinitive.]

If the infinitive is part of a phrase, like **voy a buscar** or **tengo que leer,** where else can you put the direct object pronoun?

If the infinitive is part of a phrase, like **vas a traer** or **puedo hacer,** where else can you put the indirect object pronoun?

[If the infinitive is part of a phrase, you can put the direct object pronoun before the conjugated verb. / If the infinitive is part of a phrase, you can put the indirect object pronoun before the conjugated verb.]

Ask students if they can think of other expressions that use the infinitive form of a verb.

Here is a chart of both the direct and indirect object pronouns for your reference.

Direct		Indirect	
Singular	Plural	Singular	Plural
me	nos	me	nos
te	os	te	os
lo	los	le	les
la	las	le	les

Exercise A:
1. Voy a buscarla cerca del monumento.
2. Voy a buscarlo detrás de la fuente.
3. Voy a buscarlas en el museo.
4. Voy a buscarlos debajo de la escultura.
5. Voy a buscarlos en la alcaldía.

¡Vamos a practicar!

A. Taking care of a group of six-year-olds can be hair-raising. Every time you turn around, another one has disappeared!

Primero, lee la oración y la frase entre paréntesis. Luego, forma una oración con **lo, los, la** o **las.** Sigue el modelo.

You may wish to assign this activity as homework.

Modelo: Tengo que buscar a Enrique. (en la plaza)

Respuesta: **Voy a buscarlo en la plaza.**

1. Tengo que buscar a Laura. (cerca del monumento)
2. Tengo que buscar a Claudio. (detrás de la fuente)
3. Tengo que buscar a Celia y a Rosa. (en el museo)
4. Tengo que buscar a David y a Miguel. (debajo de la escultura)
5. Tengo que buscar a Rolando y a María. (en la alcaldía)

B. Imagine that an earthquake has turned your bedroom into a disaster area. Where are you going to put your things?

Primero, lee las palabras. Luego, contesta la pregunta **¿Dónde vas a poner . . .?** Por último, escribe dos respuestas. Sigue el modelo. See Unit Plans, Unidad 5, for answers to exercise B.

Modelo: ¿tus calcetines? (el tocador)

Respuesta: **a. Voy a ponerlos dentro del tocador.**

b. Los voy a poner dentro del tocador.

1. ¿tus libros? (el estante)
2. ¿tu radio? (la mesita)
3. ¿tus camisetas? (el ropero)
4. ¿tu teléfono? (el estante)
5. ¿tu lámpara? (la mesita)
6. ¿tus carteles? (la pared)

Extension: Go around the room pointing out familiar objects and asking students where you should put the objects.

C. Susana is going shopping. It seems that everyone she knows has a birthday this month. What can she buy for people?

Primero, lee la oración. Luego, escribe dos oraciones. Sigue el modelo. **Extension:** Have students tell the class what they might buy family members for upcoming birthdays.

Modelo: Puedo comprar una camiseta para Elisa.

Respuesta: **a. Puedo comprarle una camiseta.**

b. Le puedo comprar una camiseta.

1. Puedo comprar unos libros para Francisco.
2. Puedo comprar un cuaderno para Carla.
3. Puedo comprar bolígrafos para Gustavo y Nora.
4. Puedo comprar un reloj para mi abuela.

1. **a.** Puedo comprarle . . .
   b. Le puedo comprar . . .
2. **a.** Puedo comprarle . . .
   b. Le puedo comprar . . .
3. **a.** Puedo comprarles . . .
   b. Les puedo comprar . . .
4. **a.** Puedo comprarle . . .
   b. Le puedo comprar . . .

D. Imagine that you are going to meet five of your favorite celebrities—in person! What are you going to do?

Primero, lee las listas de posibilidades. Luego, escribe el nombre de la persona. Por último, escribe una oración sobre lo que vas a hacer. Lee los ejemplos.

dar un beso	dar tu número de teléfono
hacer una pregunta	cantar una canción
pedir su autógrafo	decir un secreto
pedir ayuda con tus tareas	comprar una camiseta

Modelo: **1.** Plácido Domingo
Voy a pedirle su autógrafo.
2. Bill Cosby
Le voy a dar un beso.
Etcétera.

Enrichment: Have students cut out pictures of their chosen celebrities from old newspapers or magazines and paste them onto a page with their sentences. The pages can be made into a classroom Big Book.

El hombre y el muchacho están comprando película. ¿Qué le das al vendedor o a la vendedora cuando compras algo?

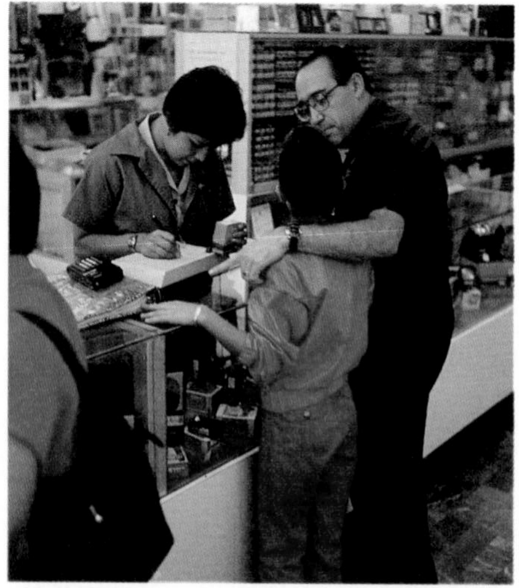

Vamos a leer

Unos artículos de la enciclopedia

Puedes aprender mucho de las enciclopedias. Los artículos te ofrecen mucha información sobre muchos temas. Primero, tienes que leer los artículos rápidamente para buscar la información que quieres. Luego, tienes que leerlos con cuidado.

Vamos a leer unos ejemplos de los artículos que puedes encontrar en una enciclopedia.

Extension: Have students look up a few words in a Spanish-language encyclopedia.

CIUDAD *f.* Una población grande; región o área donde viven muchas personas. // —*Bolívar* Ciudad de Venezuela, capital del estado de Bolívar. // —*Juárez* Ciudad de México, en el estado de Chihuahua, situada a orillas del río Bravo, en la frontera de los EE.UU. // —*Real* Provincia de la región Castilla la Nueva en España, situada cerca del río Guadiana.

CIUDADANÍA *f.* La población de una ciudad.

CIUDADANO NA *adj.* y *s.* Persona que vive en una ciudad o que vive cerca de una ciudad.

CIUDADELA *f.* Una fortaleza en el interior de una ciudad.

Have students scan the articles rapidly for unfamiliar words, then read them more carefully. Help students deduce the function of the dashes in the subentries.

La cultura y tú

See Unit Plans, Unidad 5, for additional information.

Visitamos las plazas

En los países hispanos, hay muchas ciudades antiguas. Estas ciudades casi siempre tienen plazas. Generalmente, hay una plaza grande en el centro de la ciudad. En España se llama la plaza mayor.

Explain to the class that **plazas** are popular meeting places in the Spanish-speaking world. In the evenings and on weekends, people of all ages gather there to socialize or to pass the time. Ask students where they usually go to meet friends.

Mira la foto de la plaza de la Constitución en San Sebastián, España. Es la plaza mayor de San Sebastián. Por todos lados de la plaza hay tiendas y apartamentos.

Esta plaza está en la ciudad de Saltillo, en México. No es una ciudad muy grande, pero tiene una plaza. A las personas les gusta caminar los domingos y en las tardes en la plaza. ¿Hay muchas personas en esta plaza? ¿Hay tiendas?

Esta foto es de la plaza Bolívar de Caracas en Venezuela. En todas las ciudades de Venezuela siempre hay una plaza Bolívar, y en todas las plazas Bolívar siempre hay un monumento o una escultura de Simón Bolívar.

Simón Bolívar es el héroe de cinco países de la América del Sur, de la misma manera que George Washington es un héroe en los Estados Unidos. Para Venezuela, Colombia, Perú, Ecuador y Bolivia, Simón Bolívar es el libertador, el padre de la patria.

En los Estados Unidos hay ciudades y otros lugares con el nombre de George Washington. En muchos países de la América del Sur, también hay ciudades, parques, calles y otros sitios con el nombre de Bolívar. ¿Sabes qué país tiene su nombre? ¿Qué unidad monetaria lleva el nombre de Simón Bolívar? (Mira la página 117.)

Enrichment: Have students research the life of Simón Bolívar. You may also wish to have students study maps of the countries mentioned in this section to find as many places as possible that are named after Bolívar.

Unidad

After completing this unit, students should be able to:

- ▶ identify, name, and describe ways of getting around in a city
- ▶ give instructions or commands by using regular affirmative familiar commands (review)
- ▶ give instructions or commands by using regular negative familiar commands
- ▶ discuss the metric system used in Spanish-speaking countries.

The photographs may be used for informal assessment or review:

- ► Dame instrucciones para ir a Buenos Aires. ¿Adónde vas si vas al oeste por esta carretera?
- ► ¿Qué leen las muchachas?
- ► Muéstrame una manzana en la ciudad.
- ► ¿Por dónde camina esta familia? ¿Están en la calle o están en un paso de peatones?
- ► ¿Dónde puedes pedir información, según el letrero?

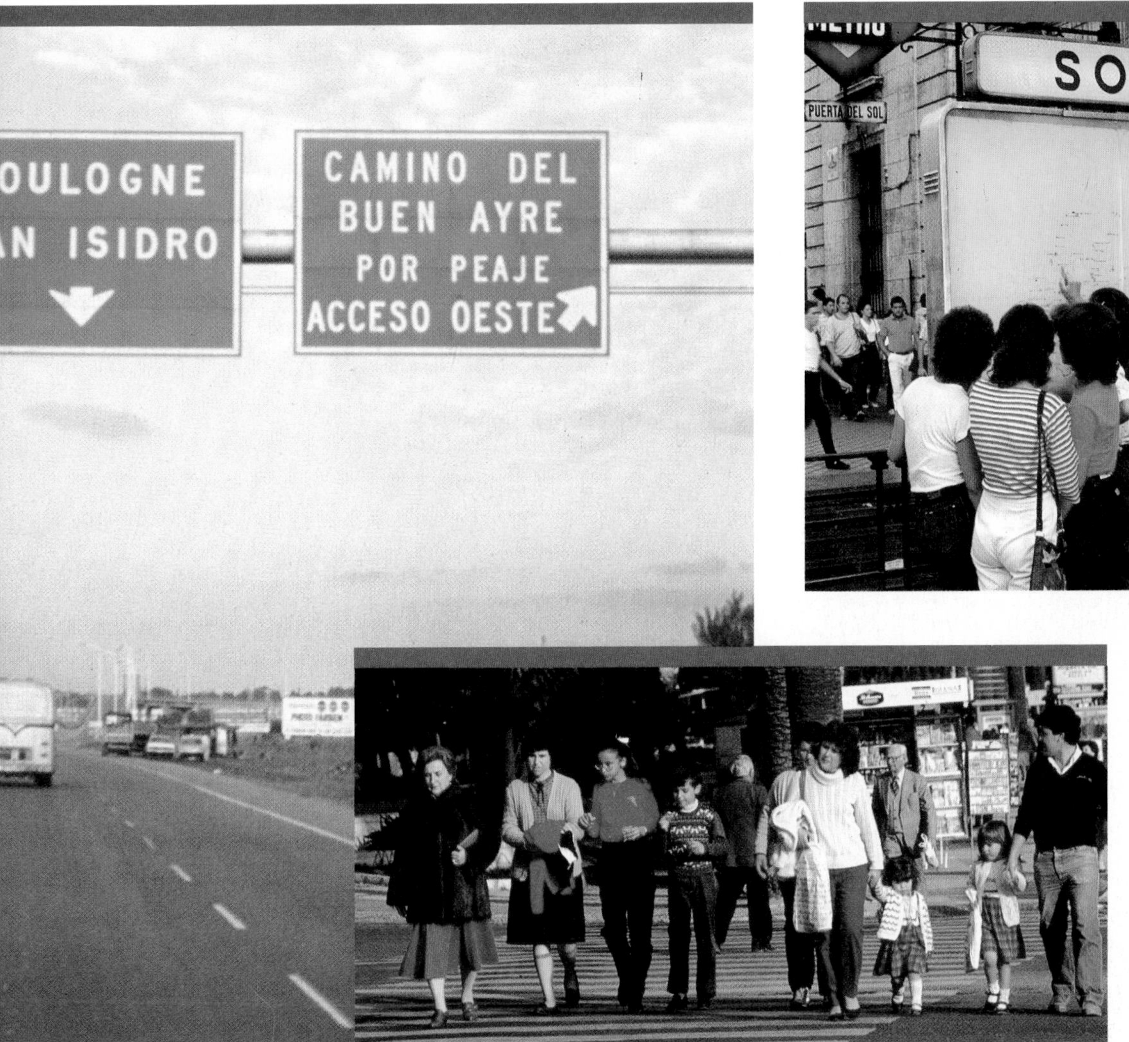

Panorama de vocabulario

¿Adónde vamos?

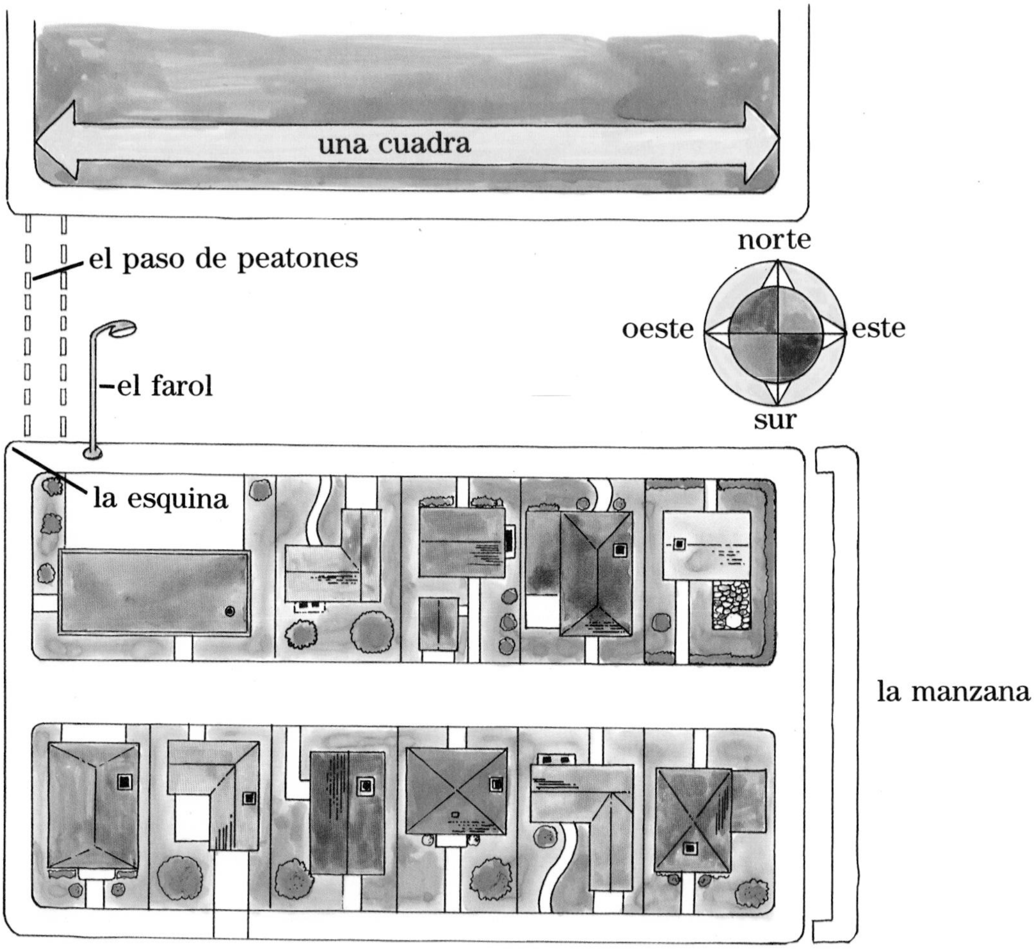

If possible, take students for a walk outside the school to give them real-life contexts for the terms introduced in this unit (e.g., **Sigan derecho una cuadra. Doblen a la izquierda. Crucen la calle por el paso de peatones. El estacionamiento queda adelante. La escuela nos queda atrás. Unas casas están al norte.**).

Be sure students make the distinction between **una cuadra** (a block "long") and **una manzana** (a "square" block). You may wish to introduce other phrases: **dar la vuelta a la manzana,** to go around the block; **caminar hacia el norte (el sur, el este, el oeste),** to walk (toward the) north (south, east, west).

Va rápido.

Va despacio.

Alternative terms for **rápido** and **despacio** are **de prisa** and **lento.**

Queda adelante.

Queda atrás.

perderse

encontrarse

You may wish to provide contextual sentences for the verbs **perderse** and **encontrarse:**

1. La muchacha se pierde en el almacén. No le gusta perderse. Ella lee un mapa.
2. Por fin, ella se encuentra con su papá en el almacén. Está contenta al encontrarse con su papá. Ahora, los dos pueden volver a casa.

Help students observe that both verbs are stem-changing.

¡Aprende el vocabulario!

A. Imagine that you have to prepare a report on Spain for your geography class. You will have to know where certain cities are located.

Primero, estudia el mapa. Luego, lee la oración. Por último, completa la oración. Sigue el modelo.

Extension: Continue by choosing other pairs of cities and having students state their relationship (e.g., **Madrid—Barcelona: Madrid queda al oeste de Barcelona.**).

Modelo: Madrid queda —— de Málaga.
Respuesta: **Madrid queda al norte de Málaga.**

If students are curious, introduce **noroeste, noreste, sureste, and suroeste.**

1. Salamanca queda —— de Segovia.
2. Barcelona queda —— de Valencia.
3. Madrid queda —— de Burgos.
4. Valencia queda —— de Madrid.
5. Málaga queda —— de Cádiz.
6. Toledo queda —— de Madrid.

1. al oeste 2. al norte 3. al sur 4. al este 5. al este 6. al sur

Before assigning this exercise, you may wish to use the number vocabulary cards in the *Teacher's Resource and Activity Book* to practice stating numbers in the hundreds.

B. Your geography teacher liked your report on Spain. Now she wants you to tell her the distances between cities.

Estudia el mapa del ejercicio A. Lee y contesta las preguntas. Sigue el modelo.

Modelo: ¿A cuántos kilómetros está Madrid de Barcelona?
Respuesta: **Madrid está a 621 kilómetros de Barcelona.**

1. ¿A cuántos kilómetros está Barcelona de Valencia?
2. ¿A cuántos kilómetros está Granada de Córdoba?
3. ¿A cuántos kilómetros está León de Madrid?
4. ¿A cuántos kilómetros está San Sebastián de Granada?
5. ¿A cuántos kilómetros está Segovia de Sevilla?
6. ¿A cuántos kilómetros está Valencia de León?

1. Barcelona está a 349 kilómetros de Valencia.
2. Granada está a 166 kilómetros de Córdoba.
3. León está a 333 kilómetros de Madrid.
4. San Sebastián está a 903 kilómetros de Granada.
5. Segovia está a 560 kilómetros de Sevilla.
6. Valencia está a 685 kilómetros de León.

Extension: Find a map of your area that shows distances. Display the map in class and use it to ask questions about the distances between different points. You may have students express distances first in **millas** and then in **kilómetros.**

Estos muchachos están cruzando la calle. ¿Cruzan dentro o fuera del paso de peatones?

C. Imagine that you're on the third floor of an office building. You can see everything that's happening on the street below. What do you see?

Primero, mira el dibujo. Luego, lee la oración. Por último, completa la oración. Sigue el modelo.

You may wish to assign this activity as homework.

Modelo: Hay un parque en ——.

Respuesta: **Hay un parque en una manzana.**

1. El muchacho cruza la calle en ——.
2. El muchacho va al parque. El parque le queda ——.
3. Un autobús dobla ——.
4. Una mujer corre muy ——.
5. Un turista estudia un mapa. No quiere ——.
6. El turista está lejos del parque. El parque le queda ——.
7. Hay un pájaro en cada ——.
8. Una muchacha camina muy ——.

1. el paso de peatones
2. adelante
3. a la derecha
4. rápido
5. perderse
6. atrás
7. farol
8. despacio

Extension: Continue by asking questions (e.g., **¿Quién está cerca del parque? ¿Cuántos faroles hay en el dibujo? ¿Dónde queda el coche?**).

Students may consult a map of the United States to answer some of the questions. Have them work in pairs to ask and answer the questions.

D. Josué Zamora lives in Bolivia. He has never visited your city and state. He wants to know more about where you live.

Escribe diez oraciones sobre el estado y la ciudad donde vives. Lee las preguntas si necesitas ayuda.

Enrichment: Students may work in pairs or small groups to make maps of your community or state, labeling places and indicating distances between them. The maps can be used for a bulletin-board display.

Preguntas

1. Para ir a la capital de los Estados Unidos, ¿en qué dirección tienes que ir?
2. ¿A cuántas millas está tu ciudad de la capital del estado?
3. Para ir al Océano Pacífico, ¿en qué dirección tienes que ir?
4. Para ir al Golfo de México, ¿hacia dónde vas?
5. Para visitar el Canadá, ¿hacia dónde vas?
6. ¿A cuántas millas o cuadras está tu casa de la escuela?
7. ¿Vives al norte, al sur, al oeste o al este de la escuela?
8. ¿A cuántas millas o cuadras está tu casa del supermercado?
9. ¿A cuántas millas o cuadras está tu casa de un aeropuerto?
10. ¿A cuántas millas o cuadras está tu casa de la casa de un amigo?

Esta calle se llama la Gran Vía. Está en Madrid, España. ¿Hay mucho tráfico? ¿Pueden las personas cruzar la calle?

Los sonidos del idioma

Las vocales: **ui, iu**

Escucha y repite. Compara los sonidos de las vocales.

ui	**iu**
cuidar	ciudad
Luisa	triunfo
buitre	viuda

As students listen to the cassette, point out that the diphthongs **ui** and **iu** are pronounced as two vowels with one sound. Be alert to a tendency in students to pronounce the **iu** combination in words as two sounds, instead of one.

1. El juicio en Suiza los va a llevar a la ruina.
2. ¡Qué ruido! Van a destruir toda la ciudad.
3. ¡Cuidado! Hay un buitre en la cocina de la viuda.

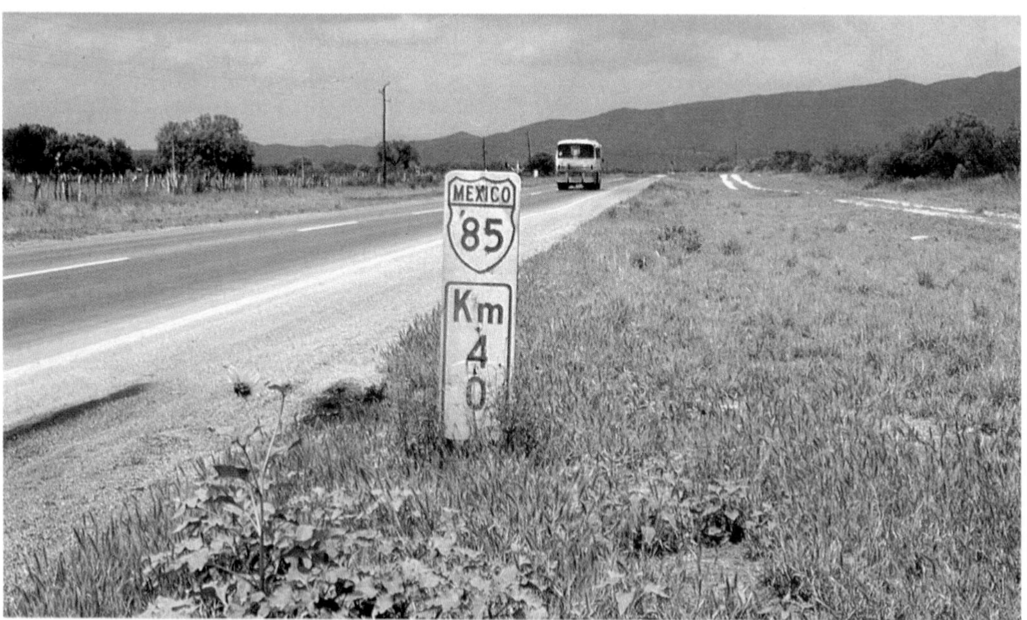

¿A cuántos kilómetros está México?

Ask students other questions about the photo: **¿Cuál es el número de la carretera? ¿Está la carretera cerca o lejos de una ciudad?**

Usando el español

Giving Instructions or Commands

Rule: You use familiar commands when addressing friends, family members, and classmates. The familiar command form is the same as the **él** / **ella** form of the present tense.

Study the following pictures and read the conversations.

PACO: ¡Ay! Estoy cansado.

INÉS: **Camina** un poco más. El parque queda adelante.

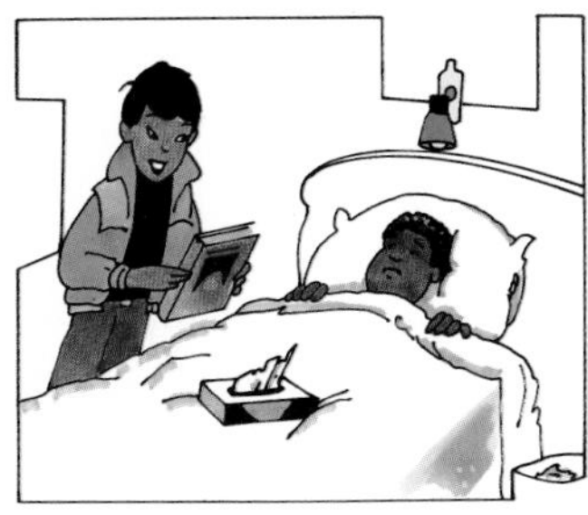

MARIO: ¿Qué tengo que hacer para la clase de inglés?

LUIS: **Lee** la tercera lección y **escribe** un reporte.

In the first conversation, what does Inés tell her little brother? In the second conversation, what does Luis tell his friend to do?

[Inés tells her little brother to walk a little farther. In the second conversation, Luis tells his friend to read and write.]

Recall that the forms in heavy black letters are familiar commands. You use these forms with people you address in the **tú** form, such as friends, members of your family, and classmates.

You may wish to supplement this review of familiar affirmative commands with examples and exercises from Unidad 12 in *Ya converso más.*

Read the following chart of familiar commands.

Ask students where else they can find the familiar command forms of verbs in the book.

	Infinitive	Él / Ella	Familiar Command
-ar verbs	mirar	mira	**¡mira!**
-er verbs	correr	corre	**¡corre!**
-ir verbs	abrir	abre	**¡abre!**

Have volunteers read the sample questions and answers aloud.

Practice reading the following questions and answers:

Pregunta: ¿Cómo voy al museo?

Respuesta: Sigue derecho dos cuadras. Luego, **dobla** a la izquierda y **camina** una cuadra. El museo está en la esquina.

Pregunta: ¿Todavía estás en la cama? ¡**Levántate** ahora mismo!

Respuesta: ¡Ay, mamá! Quiero dormir diez minutos más.

Pregunta: Papá, ¿puedo jugar con Esteban?

Respuesta: ¡**Cepíllate** los dientes y **lávate** la cara! Luego, puedes salir.

Pregunta: ¿Qué te pasa? ¡**Corre** más rápido! Vamos a llegar tarde a la fiesta.

Respuesta: ¡Ay! No me gustan las fiestas.

[**Levántate, cepíllate,** and **lávate** are reflexive verbs. The reflexive pronoun is connected to the verb. A written accent mark has been added.]

How observant are you?

Find three examples of reflexive verbs. Where does the reflexive pronoun go in each command? What has been added to each command?

¡Vamos a practicar!

A. If you ever need a favor, just ask Eugenia. She's always doing things for other people.

Primero, lee la frase. Luego, forma una oración. Sigue el modelo.

This activity may be assigned as homework.

Modelo: traer los libros

Respuesta: **Eugenia, trae los libros, por favor.**

1. Eugenia, abre la puerta, por favor.
2. Eugenia, lava los platos, por favor.
3. Eugenia, plancha la camisa, por favor.
4. Eugenia, escribe esta nota, por favor.
5. Eugenia, barre el piso, por favor.
6. Eugenia, recoge los papeles, por favor.

1. abrir la puerta

2. lavar los platos

3. planchar la camisa

4. escribir esta nota

5. barrer el piso

6. recoger los papeles

Extension: Have students think of other commands to give Eugenia.

B. Imagine that you're babysitting little Paquita. It's her bedtime and she's not tired. You have to tell her everything twice.

Primero, lee la oración. Luego, cambia la oración. Sigue el modelo.

Modelo: Tienes que quitarte los zapatos.

Respuesta: **¡Quítate los zapatos!**

1. ¡Cepíllate los dientes!
2. ¡Báñate en la bañera!
3. ¡Usa jabón y agua caliente!
4. ¡Sécate con una toalla!
5. ¡Péinate!
6. ¡Quita las cosas de la cama!

1. Tienes que cepillarte los dientes.

2. Tienes que bañarte en la bañera.

3. Tienes que usar jabón y agua caliente.

4. Tienes que secarte con la toalla.

5. Tienes que peinarte.

6. Tienes que quitar las cosas de la cama.

Extension: Students might enjoy creating and role-playing a conversation between themselves and Paquita.

C. Have you ever had a day like Roberto is having? He can't do anything right! What do people tell him to do?

Primero, lee las oraciones. Luego, completa las oraciones con las formas apropiadas de las palabras entre paréntesis. Sigue el modelo.

Modelo: ¡Ay, Roberto! Primero, —— los platos. Luego, —— los platos con la toalla. (lavar / secar)

Respuesta: **¡Ay, Roberto! Primero, lava los platos. Luego, seca los platos con la toalla.**

1. ¡Ay, Roberto! Primero, —— la novela. Luego, —— tu reporte. (leer / escribir)
2. ¡Ay, Roberto! Primero, —— tres cuadras. Luego, —— a la derecha. (caminar / doblar)
3. ¡Ay, Roberto! Primero, —— las cosas de la alfombra. Luego, —— la aspiradora. (recoger / pasar)
4. ¡Ay, Roberto! Primero, —— la ciudad en el mapa. Luego, —— la pregunta. (buscar / contestar)

1. lee / escribe
2. camina / dobla
3. recoge / pasa
4. busca / contesta

D. You are writing the advice column for the school newspaper. What advice do you give?

Primero, lee la frase. Luego, escoge una frase apropiada de la lista. Por último, escribe una oración. Sigue el modelo.

You may wish to assign this activity as homework after doing one or two more examples with the class.

Modelo: Si no comprendes la pregunta, . . .

Respuesta: **Si no comprendes la pregunta, pide ayuda.**

1. Si estás cansado, . . .
2. Si tienes hambre, . . .
3. Si estás aburrido con un programa de televisión, . . .
4. Si estás triste, . . .
5. Si tienes una camiseta vieja, . . .
6. Si vas a una fiesta, . . .
7. Si tienes mucho calor, . . .
8. Si tus maestros te dan muchas tareas, . . .

1. descansa un poco.
2. come una manzana.
3. lee un libro.
4. habla con un amigo.
5. compra una nueva.
6. llega a tiempo.
7. abre una ventana.
8. estudia mucho.

Enrichment: Have students write letters to an imaginary advice columnist. Students may then exchange letters and respond with advice.

pedir ayuda	comer una manzana
llegar a tiempo	hablar con un amigo
leer un libro	escribir las instrucciones
comprar una nueva	abrir una ventana
descansar un poco	estudiar mucho

Help students guess the meaning of the expression. Negative familiar commands will be introduced on the following page.

¡A divertirnos!

Once students understand the meaning of the expression ("Don't pull my leg."), help them observe that similar expressions in English and Spanish use different parts of the body.

Giving Negative Commands

Rule: Negative familiar commands are like the **tú** forms of the verbs. Commands of **-ar** verbs are spelled with an **e;** commands of **-er** and **-ir** verbs are spelled with an **a.**

Study the pictures and read the conversations.

Have volunteers role-play the sample conversations. Ask students to guess the meanings of the phrases in heavy black letters.

ROSA: Estoy enojada con Ramón.

LIDIA: Pues, **no hables** con él.

CARLOS: Todavía tengo mucha hambre.

DIEGO: ¡**No comas** mi sándwich!

ANA: José, ¿puedo entrar?

JOSÉ: ¡No! Por favor, ¡**no abras** la puerta!

What verb forms are like the words in heavy black letters—**yo** forms, **tú** forms, or **él / ella** forms? How is **no hables** different from **no hablas**? How is **no comas** different from **no comes**? How is **no abras** different from **no abres**?

[The **tú** form is like the words in heavy black letters. **No hables** is spelled with an **e,** not an **a. No comas** is spelled with an **a,** not an **e. No abras** is spelled with an **a,** not an **e.**]

Study the following chart.

Ask students where else they would find negative command forms of verbs in the book.

	Infinitive	Tú	Negative Familiar Command
-ar verbs	mirar	miras	**¡no mires!**
-er verbs	correr	corres	**¡no corras!**
-ir verbs	abrir	abres	**¡no abras!**

What letter do you change in the **tú** form of a regular **-ar** verb to make the negative familiar command? What letter do you change in the **tú** form of a regular **-er** verb to make the negative familiar command? What letter do you change in the **tú** form of a regular **-ir** verb to make a negative familiar command?

[For regular **-ar** verbs, you change the **a** before the final **s.** For regular **-er** and **-ir** verbs, you change the **e** before the final **s.**]

Practice reading the following questions and answers:

Pregunta: ¿Doblo a la derecha?

Respuesta: No, **no dobles** a la derecha. Dobla a la izquierda.

Pregunta: ¿Puedo escribir en este papel?

Respuesta: No, **no escribas** en mi reporte. Escribe en el papel amarillo.

Pregunta: ¿Puedo leer la carta de tu primo?

Respuesta: No. Por favor, **no leas** la carta. Es personal. Lee la carta de mi abuela.

Have volunteers practice reading the sample questions and answers aloud. Ask students to think of everyday situations in which they would use negative commands (e.g., telling someone not to open the window in the school bus).

¡Vamos a practicar!

○ A. Maricarmen's little sister is trying to help her clean the house.

Primero, lee la oración y la palabra entre paréntesis. Luego, completa la oración. Sigue el modelo.

Modelo: ¡No —— el piso con tu camisa! (limpiar)

Respuesta: **¡No limpies el piso con tu camisa!**

1. ¡No —— el polvo con las manos! (quitar)
2. ¡No —— los platos en agua fría! (lavar)
3. ¡No —— el piso con el trapeador! (barrer)
4. ¡No —— sobre el piso limpio! (correr)
5. ¡No —— la puerta del horno! (abrir)

1. quites
2. laves
3. barras
4. corras
5. abras

Extension: Have students make up an affirmative familiar command to follow each negative command (e.g., **¡Limpia el piso con el trapeador!**).

○ B. As Fernando reads the newspaper, he takes notes on all the good advice. What has he recorded?

Primero, lee las oraciones. Luego, completa la oración con la forma apropiada de la palabra entre paréntesis. Sigue el modelo.

Modelo: Cepíllate los dientes después de comer. No (usar) un cepillo viejo.

Respuesta: **No uses un cepillo viejo.**

1. gastes
2. comas
3. abras
4. hables

1. Ahorra el dinero. No (gastar) mucho en juegos y otras cosas.
2. Come tres veces al día. No (comer) muchos dulces.

3. Si no conoces a la persona, no (abrir) la puerta de la casa.

4. Si estás comiendo, no (hablar) con comida en la boca.

Enrichment: Have students bring in newspaper or magazine articles and use negative and positive familiar commands to tell the class what good advice the articles contain.

◐ C. How well can you state the rules of conduct in public places?

Primero, lee las palabras. Luego, escribe una oración. Sigue el modelo.

Modelo: el zoológico / abrir las jaulas

Respuesta: **En el zoológico, no abras las jaulas.**

1. el cine / hablar durante la película
2. el museo / correr en los pasillos
3. el mercado al aire libre / gastar mucho dinero
4. la escuela / subir las escaleras muy rápido
5. la alcaldía / entrar en las oficinas
6. el parque / escribir en las paredes

1. En el cine, no hables durante la película.
2. En el museo, no corras en los pasillos.
3. En el mercado al aire libre, no gastes mucho dinero.
4. En la escuela, no subas las escaleras muy rápido.
5. En la alcaldía, no entres en las oficinas.
6. En el parque, no escribas en las paredes.

Extension: Ask students to write more rules of good public conduct.

¡No dobles a la izquierda!

Bring in other pictures of traffic signs and have students state the appropriate command for each sign.

¡A conversar!

¡Abre los ojos!

MARCOS: ¿Me ayudas, Jorge? ¡Este mapa no sirve!

JORGE: Sí, cómo no. ¿Qué buscas?

MARCOS: Tengo que ir a la plaza Bolívar.

JORGE: No hay problema. Conozco bien la plaza. Sigue derecho tres cuadras. Luego, dobla a la derecha y camina un kilómetro al norte. ¡No dobles al sur o te vas a perder! Por fin, cruza la calle Pilar y la plaza te queda adelante.

MARCOS: Pero, mira, Jorge. Según este mapa, la plaza queda aquí, en el centro de la ciudad.

JORGE: ¡Ay, Marcos! ¡Abre los ojos! No uses este mapa.

MARCOS: ¿Por qué no?

JORGE: Porque este mapa es de Ciudad Jardín. ¡Estamos en Aguaslimpias!

Have students guess the meaning of **según** from context first; then confirm their guesses by looking it up in the Spanish-English Glossary.

Preguntas

1. ¿Qué busca Marcos?
2. ¿Quién conoce el lugar?
3. ¿Qué le dice Jorge?
4. Según el mapa, ¿dónde está la plaza Bolívar?
5. ¿De qué ciudad es el mapa?

1. Marcos busca la plaza Bolívar.
2. Jorge conoce el lugar. (*or* Jorge lo conoce.)
3. *Answers will vary. Accept appropriate paraphrasing.*
4. Según el mapa, la plaza Bolívar queda aquí (*or* en el centro de la ciudad).
5. El mapa es de Ciudad Jardín.

¡Conversa tú!

1. ¿Cuándo usas un mapa?
2. ¿Sabes leer los mapas?
3. ¿Cuántos kilómetros puedes caminar?
4. Si te pierdes, ¿pides ayuda?
5. ¿Cómo buscas un lugar que no conoces?

After students have answered the questions orally in class, have them adapt their answers in a written paragraph as advice to a friend who is always getting lost.

La cultura y tú

See Unit Plans, Unidad 6, for additional information.

El sistema métrico

You may wish to teach the words for other metric measurements: **el gramo, el miligramo, el metro, el centímetro, el milímetro, el litro.**

¿Es muy rápido 88,5 kilómetros por hora? Pues, en esta carretera en Costa Rica, los coches van a 88,5 kilómetros por hora y aun más rápido. En los Estados Unidos también puedes ir a 88,5 kilómetros por hora en coche porque son 55 millas por hora.

En esta unidad, hablamos un poco de las distancias y de las millas y los kilómetros. A lo mejor, ya sabes algo del sistema métrico. ¿Sabes que las personas de los países de habla española usan el sistema métrico? Cuando viajas en el mundo hispano, tienes que usar kilómetros y kilogramos y no millas y libras.

Si tienes hambre en Toledo, España, puedes comprar frutas en esta tienda. ¡Cuidado! Si pides un kilogramo de manzanas, la vendedora te va a dar 2,2 libras de frutas. ¡Son muchas manzanas!

Enrichment: Have a "metric day" in class. Bring meter sticks or metric rulers and have students measure and label various classroom items. If you use a decimal system for the labels, remember that in Spanish, you use a comma in the place of a decimal point (e.g., **3,2 metros**).

Segundo repaso

Have volunteers role-play the conversation after the class has listened to and read it several times.

A. Una conversación entre amigos

RAÚL: ¡Mari! ¡No camines tan rápido! Estoy cansado y me duelen los pies.

MARI: ¡Ay, Raúl! Siempre te duele algo. ¡Corre! No quiero llegar tarde.

RAÚL: ¿Por qué tienes tanta prisa? Sólo vas a visitar a Celia. La visitas todos los días.

MARI: Sí, pero hoy es un día especial.

RAÚL: ¿Por qué me dices que es especial?

MARI: Seguimos derecho una cuadra. ¡Rápido!

RAÚL: ¡Puf! Contéstame, por favor.

MARI: Bueno, te digo la verdad. Hoy cumplo catorce años.

RAÚL: ¡Felicitaciones!

MARI: Gracias. Celia me da una fiesta de sorpresa. ¡No quiero llegar tarde para mi sorpresa!

1. Raúl está cansado.
2. Mari tiene prisa.

Preguntas

1. ¿Cómo está Raúl?
2. ¿Quién tiene prisa?
3. ¿Por qué tiene prisa?
4. ¿A quién va a visitar?

3. Tiene prisa porque no quiere llegar tarde.
4. Va a visitar a Celia.

5. ¿Qué le dice Mari a Raúl sobre este día?
6. ¿Por qué no quiere llegar tarde?

5. Mari le dice que hoy es su cumpleaños.
6. No quiere llegar tarde porque Celia le da una fiesta de sorpresa.

B. ¿Qué haces?

What would you do in the following situations?

Primero, lee las oraciones. Luego, contesta la pregunta en tus palabras. Lee el modelo.

Modelo: Tu amigo te hace una pregunta personal. ¿Qué haces?

Respuesta: **Le doy una respuesta. [No le doy una respuesta.] [Le contesto. / No le contesto.]**

You may wish to assign this activity as homework after doing one or two more examples with the class.

1. Tu amigo tiene frío. Tú tienes dos abrigos. ¿Qué haces?
2. Tus padres te dan dinero para ir al cine. ¿Qué haces?
3. Estás en la escuela. No tienes un lápiz. Tu amigo tiene muchos lápices. ¿Qué haces?
4. Estás en un restaurante. El camarero no te da buen servicio. ¿Qué haces?
5. Tu amigo quiere comprar algo en el supermercado, pero no tiene dinero. Tú sí tienes dinero. ¿Qué haces?
6. Tus amigos están haciendo sus tareas, pero no saben las respuestas. Tú sí sabes las respuestas. ¿Qué haces?

Extension: Have volunteers read their answers aloud in class. Where there are conflicting answers, have the class discuss the reasons for the answers.

En el banco pides diez dólares, pero la cajera te da veinte dólares. ¿Qué haces?

C. ¿Quién está perdido?

You've invited some friends to your house, but they all seem to be lost! You have to give them directions. See Unit Plans, Segundo repaso, for answers to activity C.

Primero, lee las preguntas y mira el mapa. Luego, dales instrucciones a tus amigos. Lee el modelo.

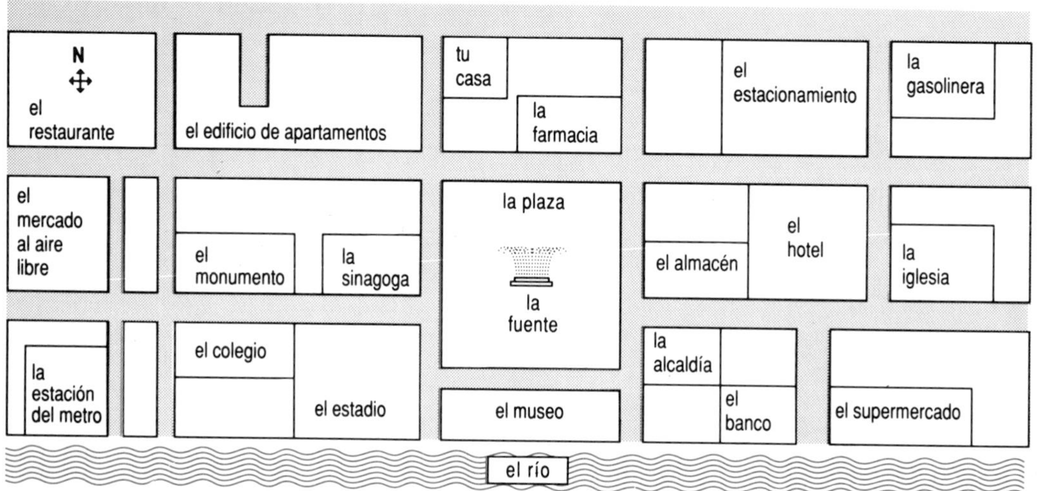

Modelo: Estoy al oeste del colegio. ¿Cómo voy a tu casa?
Respuesta: **Camina al norte por dos cuadras. Luego, dobla a la derecha. Camina una cuadra al este. Mi casa está en la esquina.**

1. Estoy en la gasolinera. ¿Cómo voy a tu casa?
2. Estoy en la plaza, al sur de la fuente. ¿Cómo voy a tu casa?
3. Estoy en una esquina. Puedo ver un banco y un supermercado. ¿Cómo voy a tu casa?
4. Estoy en la estación del metro. ¿Cómo voy a tu casa?
5. Estoy en el estadio. ¿Cómo voy a tu casa?

Extension: Have students give directions to other places on the map.

Enrichment: Bring a map of your community to class and have students give each other directions to various places from your school.

CH. Una tarde frustrante

All afternoon, Samuel's parents have given him conflicting instructions. If his mother tells him to do something, his father tells him not to do it, and vice versa. No wonder Samuel feels dizzy!

Primero, lee la instrucción. Luego, cambia la instrucción. Sigue el modelo. Students may enjoy role-playing Samuel's parents giving the conflicting instructions.

Modelo: ¡Mira la televisión!

Respuesta: **¡No mires la televisión!**

1. ¡No escribas tu reporte!
2. ¡Habla por teléfono!
3. ¡No abras la ventana!
4. ¡No leas tu novela!
5. ¡Barre el piso!
6. ¡Corre en la casa!

1. ¡Escribe tu reporte!

2. ¡No hables por teléfono!

3. ¡Abre la ventana!

4. ¡Lee tu novela!

5. ¡No barras el piso!

6. ¡No corras en la casa!

D. Aun más frustraciones

Now Samuel's parents agree, but they keep telling him to do something after he's already done it! He's really confused now!

Primero, lee la oración. Luego, escribe una respuesta. Sigue el modelo. This activity may be assigned as homework.

Modelo: Tienes que comprar más manzanas.

Respuesta: **Acabo de comprarlas.**

1. Tienes que lavar los platos.

2. Tienes que leer tu novela.

3. Tienes que cerrar la ventana.

4. Tienes que recoger tus cosas.

5. Tienes que quitar el polvo.

6. Tienes que limpiar el garaje.

1. Acabo de lavarlos.
2. Acabo de leerla.
3. Acabo de cerrarla.
4. Acabo de recogerlas.
5. Acabo de quitarlo.
6. Acabo de limpiarlo.

E. ¿Qué falta en las oraciones?

Graciela wrote two paragraphs about her best friend Carmen, but she had some trouble. Help her out.

When students have completed the exercise, have volunteers read the paragraphs aloud.

Primero, lee cada oración. Luego, escoge la palabra que va con la oración. Por último, escribe los párrafos. Sigue el modelo.

Modelo: A Carmen (le, la) gustan las ciudades grandes.

Respuesta: **A Carmen le gustan las ciudades grandes.**

(1) Carmen y yo (somos, estamos) contentas cuando vamos al zoológico. **(2)** A nosotras (me, nos) gusta ver los animales. **(3)** El zoológico (es, está) a tres kilómetros de la casa de Carmen. **(4)** A veces el papá de Carmen (me, nos) lleva al zoológico. **(5)** Yo siempre (le, lo) doy las gracias al Sr. Ortiz. Él es muy generoso. **(6)** A veces (le, la) da dinero a Carmen para comprar helados. **(7)** A mí (me, nos) gustan mucho los helados.

Esta tarde Carmen quiere visitar el museo. **(8)** Yo no (le, lo) quiero visitar. **(9)** Ahora, Carmen (es, está) enojada conmigo. **(10)** ¿Qué (le, la) puedo decir? ¡Así es la vida!

1. estamos
2. nos
3. está
4. nos
5. le
6. le
7. me
8. lo
9. está
10. le

F. ¿Qué haces con tu amigo?

Describe an activity you like to do with a friend.

Escribe un párrafo sobre una actividad que te gusta hacer con tu amigo o tu amiga. Escribe por lo menos ocho oraciones. Usa los párrafos de Graciela como modelo.

Extension: Have volunteers read their paragraphs aloud and answer questions from the class about what they wrote.

Enrichment: Include students' paragraphs in a classroom Big Book.

G. ¿Eres práctico o eres romántico?

What are you like? Are you a doer or a thinker? Are you a practical person or are you a dreamer?

Lee las oraciones y escoge la oración que te describe.

1. a. Me gusta darles tarjetas a mis amigos.
   b. Me gusta escribirles poemas a mis amigos.
2. a. Me gusta ir al museo para ver el arte.
   b. Me gusta ir al estadio para ver los deportes.
3. a. Me gusta viajar en tren porque va despacio.
   b. Me gusta viajar en avión porque va rápido.
4. a. Me gusta ayudar a mis papás.
   b. Me gusta recibir instrucciones de mis papás.
5. a. Me gustan las ciudades grandes.
   b. Me gustan las ciudades pequeñas.
6. a. Me gusta invitar a mis amigos a mi casa.
   b. Me gusta salir a otros lugares con mis amigos.

Este monumento está en la Plaza Mayor de Madrid, España. ¿Está cerca o lejos de tu casa? ¿Están cansadas las personas?

Extension: Have students determine from their answers whether they are practical or romantic. Take a survey of the class and find out how many students are romantics and how many are practical.

Extension: Have students think of more survey questions to determine whether someone is practical or romantic.

Unidad 7

After completing this unit, students should be able to:

- identify and name places, people, and items related to shopping and buying gifts
- talk about actions in the past by using the preterite tense of regular **-ar** verbs and **-ar** verbs with spelling changes in the preterite
- read about and discuss shopping in open-air markets and the custom of bargaining
- describe special handmade items from a Central American country.

The photographs may be used for informal assessment or review:

- ¿Qué compra la mujer? ¿Compra un regalo o compra algo para usar en la cocina?
- ¿Qué necesita el muchacho, un disco o un casete?
- ¿Dónde puedes comprar cinturones? ¿Compraste alguna vez un cinturón como éstos?
- Muéstrame unos regalos para niños. ¿Cómo son los regalos, modernos o antiguos?

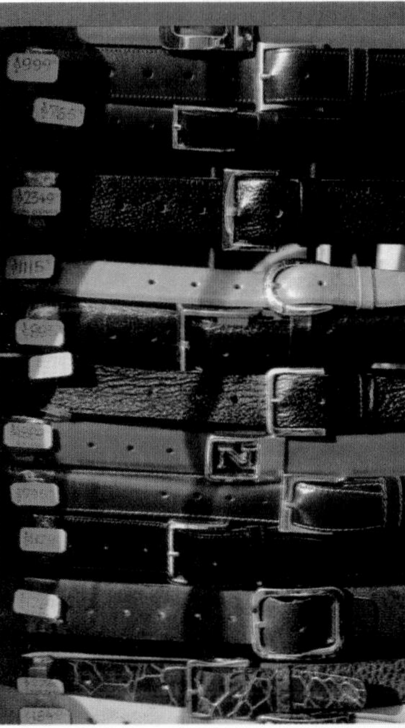

Panorama de vocabulario

Compramos regalos

el joyero
la joyería
la joyera
las joyas
el regalo
el collar
el brazalete
el llavero

Another word for bracelet is **la pulsera.**

Students may be interested in learning other words associated with jewelry or accessories: **el anillo** or **la sortija,** ring; **los aretes,** earrings; **la cadena,** chain; **dorado (-a),** golden; **plateado (-a),** silver.

Enrichment: Have students work in pairs or small groups to make up a short story about one person in one of the pictures on these pages. You may write a list of questions on the chalkboard to get them started:
¿Cómo se llama la persona?
¿Por qué está en la tienda?
¿Qué busca?
¿Está contenta la persona?
¿Va a comprar algo en la tienda?

You may want to mention that a "cheap" or stingy person is called **tacaño (tacaña).**

La bolsa is also known as **el bolso** in Spain, and **la cartera** in many Latin American countries.

la tienda de discos

Students may enjoy learning other terms related to records and cassettes: **estereofónico (-a),** stereophonic; **una grabadora,** tape recorder; **un tocadiscos,** record player; **un estereo,** stereo (a shortened term for stereo record player); **una grabación digital,** digital recording.

Spanish-speaking people in the United States also use **el compact disc** and **el CD** for **el disco compacto.** The Real Academia in Spain has recognized **el casete** as the appropriate spelling; however, students will find many variations in Spanish-language publications.

¡Aprende el vocabulario!

○ A. Juan can't decide what to buy his sister for her birthday. His friends Ernesto and Teresa are trying to help him. What do they tell him to do—buy or don't buy?

Primero, lee la oración y mira el dibujo. Luego, completa la oración. Sigue el modelo.

Modelo: ¡No compres  !

Respuesta: **¡No compres el brazalete!**

1. el collar
2. el llavero
3. la bolsa
4. el casete
5. las sandalias
6. el cinturón
7. el disco compacto
8. el disco

1. ¡No compres  !

2. ¡Compra  !

3. ¡Compra  !

4. ¡No compres  !

5. ¡Compra  !

6. ¡No compres  !

7. ¡Compra  !

8. ¡No compres  !

Extension: Have students answer as Juan would respond (e.g., **No, no voy a comprar el brazalete.**).

◐ B. Rita wants to buy some gifts for her family. She knows what she wants, but she doesn't know where to go or whom to see. What would you tell her?

Primero, lee las palabras. Luego, forma dos oraciones. Usa las palabras de la lista. Sigue el modelo.

Do one or two more examples with the class before assigning this activity as homework.

Modelo: un par de zapatos
Respuesta: **Tienes que ir a la zapatería. Habla con el zapatero.**

1. un collar
2. un disco compacto
3. un brazalete
4. un par de sandalias
5. unas joyas
6. un casete

la tienda de discos	la joyera
la joyería	el zapatero
la zapatería	la vendedora

1. Tienes que ir a la joyería. Habla con la joyera.
2. Tienes que ir a la tienda de discos. Habla con la vendedora.
3. Tienes que ir a la joyería. Habla con la joyera.
4. Tienes que ir a la zapatería. Habla con el zapatero.
5. Tienes que ir a la joyería. Habla con la joyera.
6. Tienes que ir a la tienda de discos. Habla con la vendedora.

C. Imagine that you're shopping with friends. They want you to buy everything, but you look at the price first. Which items are inexpensive? Which ones are expensive?

Primero, lee el precio. Luego, forma una oración con **barato** o **caro.** Sigue los modelos.

Modelo: Sandalias, $15.00
Respuesta: **Las sandalias son baratas.**

Modelo: Joyas, $368.95
Respuesta: **Las joyas son caras.**

Answers will vary. Be sure students understand the meanings of **barato** and **caro** before you assign the exercise.

1. Disco, $10.00
2. Cinturón, $25.00
3. Collar, $40.00
4. Llavero, $2.50
5. Casete, $8.00
6. Bolsa, $37.50

Extension: Depending on whether or not an article is expensive, have students advise each other to buy it or not. Have them use familiar commands.

Enrichment: Have students bring in advertisement pages of newspapers or magazines. The class can decide which items are **barato** and which are **caro.**

D. What is everyone wearing today? Take a look at your classmates and find out.

Primero, lee la pregunta. Luego, mira a tus compañeros de clase y contesta la pregunta. Sigue el modelo. Answers will vary.

Modelo: ¿Cuántas personas llevan zapatos azules?

Respuesta: **Ocho personas llevan zapatos azules.**

1. ¿Cuántas personas llevan sandalias?
2. ¿Cuántas personas llevan brazaletes?
3. ¿Cuántas personas llevan collares?
4. ¿Cuántas personas llevan cinturones?
5. ¿Cuántas personas llevan joyas?

Extension: Continue the activity by asking about other items of apparel.

E. Imagine that you have won two hundred dollars to go on a one-hour shopping spree. What do you want to buy? Where do you have to go to find what you want?

Escribe una lista de las cosas que quieres comprar. También escribe dónde tienes que ir. Lee el ejemplo.

1. Quiero comprar unas sandalias. Tengo que ir a la zapatería.
2. Quiero comprar unos discos compactos. Tengo que ir a la tienda de discos.

Etcétera.

Answers will vary. You may wish to brainstorm more sample sentences with the class before assigning the activity as homework.

Extension: Continue the activity by asking what students would buy for friends and family members.

Los sonidos del idioma

Las palabras en sílabas

Escucha y repite.

Point out that syllables help us determine which part of the word will be stressed when we say the word aloud.

ca-sa	es-**pe**-ra	pri-ma-**ve**-ra
li-bro	co-**me**-mos	a-pren-**de**-mos
an-tes	mer-**ca**-do	ham-bur-**gue**-sa

1. La casa roja queda en esta calle.
2. Espera la llegada de Marcela en el mercado.
3. La primavera es hermosa en la Argentina.

Sometimes the stress is shown with an accent mark (e.g., **México, televisión**); however, most of the time, words in Spanish do not require a written accent.

Estas joyas están en una joyería de Santiago, Chile. ¿Te gustan las joyas?

¿Adónde vas para comprar zapatos y cinturones?

Enrichment: Have students cut out advertisements from "teen" magazines and write questions about them (e.g., **¿Te gustan los casetes? ¿Quieres comprar este cinturón de muchos colores?**).

Usando el español

Talking about Actions in the Past

Rule: You use the preterite tense to talk about actions in the past. To form the preterite of regular **-ar** verbs, add the endings **-é, -aste, -ó, -amos,** and **-aron** to the stem.

Study the pictures and read the sentences below them.

Make certain that students understand that the pictures illustrate events that happened "yesterday" or in the past.

Ayer **compré** un collar.

Ayer **compramos** unos casetes.

¿Elisa **compró** dos regalos?
Sí, **compró** un llavero y un cinturón.

¿**Compraron** muchas cosas?
Sí, **compraron** zapatos, discos y brazaletes.

[The people are talking about buying things in the past. The words are in the past tense.]

In the examples, are the people talking about buying things now or in the past? Would you say that the words in heavy black letters are in the present tense or the past tense?

The verb forms in the examples are in the past tense that is called the preterite tense.

Look at the following chart of an **-ar** verb in the preterite tense.

Have students locate the chart of a regular **-ar** verb in the preterite in the appendixes.

Comprar

Singular		Plural	
yo	compr**é**	nosotros (-as)	compr**amos**
tú	compr**aste**	vosotros (-as)	compr**asteis**
él / ella / usted	compr**ó**	ellos / ellas / ustedes	compr**aron**

What ending do you use to talk about your own actions in the past? What ending do you use to talk about the past action of two or more people? Which ending is the same in the present tense and the preterite tense?

[You use **-é** to talk about your own past actions. You use **-aron** to talk about the past action of two or more people. The **-amos** ending is the same in the present and the past.]

Practice reading some questions and answers that use regular **-ar** verbs in the preterite tense: Have students read the sample questions and answers aloud.

Pregunta: ¿Adónde caminaste **ayer**?
Respuesta: Caminé al parque.

Pregunta: ¿Adónde viajaron los Morales **la semana pasada**?
Respuesta: Viajaron a Puerto Rico. Vuelven mañana.

Pregunta: ¿Con quién habló Ricardo **ayer por la mañana**?
Respuesta: Habló con el director de la escuela.

How observant are you?

What do the words **ayer, la semana pasada,** and **ayer por la mañana** refer to—the present or the past? [These words refer to the past.]

¡Vamos a practicar!

A. Today is Rita's birthday. What did people buy her?

Primero, lee la oración. Luego, completa la oración. Sigue el modelo.

Modelo: José y Jorge le —— un casete.

Respuesta: **José y Jorge le compraron un casete.**

1. Adela y yo le —— una bolsa.
2. Sus papás le —— un collar y un brazalete.
3. Alberto le —— una novela.
4. Su tía le —— un suéter.
5. Enrique y Ramón le —— un disco compacto.

1. compramos
2. compraron
3. compró
4. compró
5. compraron

Extension: Ask students what their family or friends bought them for their last birthday.

B. Óscar was very busy yesterday. How does he answer your questions?

Primero, lee las palabras. Luego, forma una pregunta. Por último, contesta la pregunta con **sí** o **no.** Sigue el modelo.

Following the model, students should use the **tú** and **yo** forms in their questions and answers.

Modelo: visitar a tu abuelo (sí)

Respuesta: **P:** **¿Visitaste a tu abuelo ayer?**

R: **Sí, visité a mi abuelo.**

1. tomar el desayuno (sí)
2. mirar la televisión (no)
3. planchar tus camisas (sí)
4. caminar a la tienda (sí)
5. comprar un regalo (sí)
6. descansar un poco (no)

1. tomaste / tomé
2. miraste / miré
3. planchaste / planché
4. caminaste / caminé
5. compraste / compré
6. descansaste / descansé

C. Carmen and Rafael have such busy schedules that no one can keep track of them. Their father always seems to be a day late. How do they answer his questions?

Primero, mira el calendario y lee las frases. Luego, lee la oración y la pregunta. Por último, contesta la pregunta. Sigue el modelo.

Extension: Have students make up schedules of what they did last weekend. They may exchange schedules and ask each other about their activities.

lunes	martes	miércoles	jueves	viernes
cantar C	estudiar C+R	comprar un regalo C+R	limpiar la casa C+R	bailar C
visitar a abuelita R	caminar una milla C	nadar R		montar a caballo R

Modelo: Hoy es miércoles. ¿Cuándo van a estudiar?

Respuesta: **Estudiamos ayer.**

1. Hoy es miércoles. Carmen, ¿cuándo vas a caminar una milla?
2. Hoy es jueves. Rafael, ¿cuándo vas a nadar?
3. Hoy es martes. Rafael, ¿cuándo vas a visitar a tu abuela?
4. Hoy es viernes. ¿Cuándo van a limpiar la casa?
5. Hoy es sábado. Carmen, ¿cuándo vas a bailar?
6. Hoy es jueves. ¿Cuándo van a comprar un regalo?
7. Hoy es martes. Carmen, ¿cuándo vas a cantar?
8. Hoy es sábado. Rafael, ¿cuándo vas a montar a caballo?

1. Caminé una milla ayer.
2. Nadé ayer.
3. Visité a mi abuela ayer.
4. Limpiamos la casa ayer.
5. Bailé ayer.
6. Compramos un regalo ayer.
7. Canté ayer.
8. Monté a caballo ayer.

D. What was your schedule like last week? Make up a schedule like Carmen and Rafael's. Then describe your activities for the week.

Primero, prepara un calendario de cinco días. Escribe tus actividades de cada día. Luego, escribe un párrafo sobre tus actividades. Si necesitas ayuda, lee las palabras en las listas. Before assigning this activity as homework, you may wish to brainstorm some possible sentences with the class.

estudiar	descansar	lavar	comprar
nadar	visitar	limpiar	mirar
bailar	caminar	planchar	preparar

Extension: After students have written their paragraphs, have them choose partners and interview each other about last week's activities.

You may wish to introduce **tener la culpa** (to be guilty).

¡A divertirnos!

¿Quién es el culpable?

Reinforce other forms of the preterite by asking questions (e.g., **¿Quién tiene la culpa? ¿La persona que nadó?**).

Talking about Other Actions in the Past

Rule: You change the spelling of the **yo** form of **-ar** verbs that end in **-car** and **-gar** to keep the hard consonant sound. Some stem-changing verbs do not change their stem in the preterite; **almorzar,** however, has a spelling change in the **yo** form.

Study the chart of three **-ar** verbs in the preterite tense.

	pagar	**llegar**	**sacar**
yo	**pagué**	**llegué**	**saqué**
tú	pag**aste**	lleg**aste**	sac**aste**
él / ella / usted	pag**ó**	lleg**ó**	sac**ó**
nosotros (-as)	pag**amos**	lleg**amos**	sac**amos**
vosotros (-as)	pag**asteis**	lleg**asteis**	sac**asteis**
ellos / ellas / ustedes	pag**aron**	lleg**aron**	sac**aron**

[**Pagar** and **llegar** end in **-gar. Sacar** ends in **-car.** The **yo** form changes spelling. The other endings are the same.]

Which two verbs end in **-gar**? What verb ends in **-car**? Which verb form changes spelling in the preterite tense—**tú, él,** or **yo**? Are the other endings like the endings for regular **-ar** verbs?

From what you know about pronunciation, how would you pronounce the **yo** forms if the spelling did not change: **pagé, llegé, sacé**? Why do you think the spelling changes for these verbs in the **yo** form? When the spelling changes, do the words sound more like their infinitives?

[**Pagé** and **llegé** would be pronounced with the soft **g** sound; **sacé** would be pronounced with the soft **c** sound. The spelling for these verbs changes to keep the same **g** and **c** sounds as in the other forms of the preterite. When the spelling changes, the words sound more like their infinitives.]

Now study the chart of some stem-changing verbs in the preterite tense.

	pensar (ie)	**almorzar (ue)**	**jugar (ue)**
yo	pens**é**	almor**cé**	jug**ué**
tú	pens**aste**	almorz**aste**	jug**aste**
él / ella / usted	pens**ó**	almorz**ó**	jug**ó**
nosotros (-as)	pens**amos**	almorz**amos**	jug**amos**
vosotros (-as)	pens**asteis**	almorz**asteis**	jug**asteis**
ellos / ellas / ustedes	pens**aron**	almorz**aron**	jug**aron**

Do you change the stem of **pensar (pens-)** when you add the endings of the preterite tense? [No, the stem of **pensar** does not change.]

Do you change the **o** to **ue** in the stem of **almorzar** in the preterite tense? What spelling change occurs in the **yo** form?

Do you change the **u** to **ue** in the stem of **jugar** in the preterite tense? What spelling change occurs in the **yo** form?

[No, you do not change the **o** to **ue** in **almorzar** in the preterite. In the **yo** form, the **z** changes to **c.** / No, you do not change the **u** to **ue** in **jugar** in the preterite. In the **yo** form, there is a **u** before the final **é.**]

Point out to students that this rule applies to other **-ar** stem-changing verbs, such as **cerrar** and **acostarse.** Have them find examples of these two verbs in the sample questions and answers. Students may draw the conclusion that a verb can be stem-changing in one tense and regular in another tense. If they are ever in doubt, they should consult a Spanish-English dictionary or the verb charts in a reference book.

Practice reading the following questions and answers: Have volunteers read the sample questions and answers aloud.

Pregunta: ¿A qué hora **se acostaron** ustedes anoche?
Respuesta: **Nos acostamos** a las once.

Pregunta: Luis **jugó** al fútbol con un equipo, ¿no?
Respuesta: ¡Claro! Él **jugó** con los Leones.

Pregunta: ¿**Cerraron** bien la puerta?
Respuesta: Sí, la **cerramos** con llave.

¡Vamos a practicar!

A. Julio came home late one time too many. Last week he was grounded for the entire week! What did he do while he was grounded?
You may wish to assign this activity as homework after presenting it in class.

Primero, lee la pregunta. Luego, contesta la pregunta con la frase entre paréntesis. Sigue el modelo.

Modelo: ¿A qué hora llegaste cada noche? (a las siete)
Respuesta: **Llegué a las siete.**

1. ¿A qué jugaste todas las tardes? (a los juegos electrónicos)
2. ¿Dónde almorzaste todos los días? (en casa)
3. ¿A qué hora te acostaste cada noche? (a las nueve)
4. ¿En qué pensaste? (en salir con mis amigos)

1. Jugué a los juegos electrónicos.
2. Almorcé en casa.
3. Me acosté a las nueve.
4. Pensé en salir con mis amigos.

Extension: Have students make up other questions to ask Julio, using the preterite of regular **-ar** verbs (e.g., **¿Estudiaste mucho? ¿Limpiaste tu cuarto?**).

B. Yesterday, Julio was finally pardoned! To celebrate, he went out with his friends. How does he describe his first day of freedom?

Primero, lee la oración. Luego, completa la oración con la forma apropiada de la palabra entre paréntesis. Sigue el modelo.

Modelo: Yo —— con mis amigos ayer. (almorzar)

Respuesta: **Yo almorcé con mis amigos ayer.**

1. Para celebrar, yo —— la cuenta. (pagar)
2. El almuerzo —— ocho dólares. (costar)
3. Luego, nosotros —— al fútbol. (jugar)
4. Martín —— fotos del grupo. (sacar)
5. Después, caminamos al cine. La película —— a las cuatro. (comenzar)
6. Por fin, yo —— a casa a las seis y media. (llegar)

1. pagué
2. costó
3. jugamos
4. sacó
5. comenzó
6. llegué

Extension: For each sentence, have students write a follow-up question for Julio (e.g., **¿Dónde almorzaron? ¿A quién pagaste? ¿Costó mucho el almuerzo?**).

C. Imagine that you had been grounded for a week. Last Saturday was the first day you could be with your friends. What did you do?

Lee y contesta las preguntas. Si necesitas ayuda, lee la palabra en letras negras y busca el modelo en las páginas 181 y 182. Accept reasonable answers that include the appropriate verb forms.

1. me desperté
2. busqué
3. almorcé
4. almorzamos
5. jugué
6. jugamos

1. ¿A qué hora te despertaste? (modelo: **pensar**)
2. ¿Buscaste a tus amigos? (modelo: **sacar**)
3. ¿Almorzaste con tus amigos?
4. ¿Dónde almorzaron?
5. ¿Jugaste con tus amigos?
6. ¿A qué jugaron?

¡A conversar!

En el mercado al aire libre

MAMÁ: ¿Qué compraste en el mercado, Elisa?

ELISA: Compré un regalo para abuelita. Le compré una blusa.

MAMÁ: ¡Qué bueno! ¿Cuánto pagaste?

ELISA: Pagué muy poco, mamá. Caminé por todo el mercado y busqué una blusa con un precio barato.

MAMÁ: ¿Examinaste bien la blusa?

ELISA: No, mamá. No la examiné. Sólo miré el precio.

MAMÁ: Pues, mira, ¡no hay botones en la blusa! ¡Por eso pagaste tan poco dinero!

ELISA: ¡Caramba! Vuelvo al mercado ahora mismo.

Have students guess the meaning of **botones** from context.

Preguntas

1. ¿Qué compró Elisa?
2. ¿Cuánto pagó?
3. ¿Qué buscó ella?
4. ¿Examinó bien el regalo?
5. ¿Por qué no pagó mucho por el regalo?

1. Compró una blusa.
2. Pagó muy poco (dinero).
3. Ella buscó un precio barato.
4. No, no lo examinó bien.
5. No pagó mucho porque no hay botones en la blusa.

¡Conversa tú!

1. ¿Dónde compras regalos?
2. ¿Buscas precios caros o baratos?
3. ¿Miras bien los regalos antes de comprarlos?
4. Generalmente, ¿cuánto pagas por un regalo?
5. ¿Por qué es importante examinar bien los regalos antes de comprarlos?

Extension: Have students think of a gift they bought recently and describe their purchase (e.g., **Compré el regalo en el almacén. Busqué un precio barato. Lo miré bien antes de comprarlo. Pagué seis dólares.**).

La cultura y tú

See Unit Plans, Unidad 7, for additional information.

Vamos de compras

Cuando viajas fuera de los Estados Unidos, a veces compras regalos para tu familia o tus amigos. ¿Vas a las tiendas para comprar estos regalos o los compras en el mercado al aire libre?

Ask students to describe any experiences they have had at open-air markets or flea markets.

En los países hispanos hay muchos mercados al aire libre como el mercado en la foto. Este mercado se llama el Rastro y está en Madrid, España. El Rastro está abierto los domingos por la mañana y cubre más de una milla cuadrada. Allí puedes comprar de todo: joyas, zapatos, ropa y hasta arte antiguo.

Enrichment: Students may enjoy setting up an open-air market in the classroom. Groups of students may set up booths to sell real items or pictures of items. Have students bargain for the goods they want to buy.

Puedes encontrar precios muy buenos en los mercados al aire libre, pero muchas veces tienes que regatear. Cuando regateas, el vendedor te dice un precio y luego tú le dices un precio más bajo. Después de hablar un rato del precio, te pones de acuerdo con el vendedor sobre el precio y lo pagas. Casi nunca tienes que regatear en los Estados Unidos, pero en los mercados de los países hispanos es una tradición muy popular.

En los mercados al aire libre de Guatemala, puedes comprar ropa muy bonita. Las mujeres guatemaltecas se especializan en el tejido y el bordado. Hacen ropa, manteles y decoraciones muy lindos y coloridos.

Have students read the passages for the gist and guess the meanings of unfamiliar words from context. Then, have them look up the meanings of words they do not know in the Spanish-English Glossary.

Estas muchachas llevan huipiles, camisas bordadas muy populares en Guatemala. Detrás de ellas, puedes ver manteles bordados con dibujos tradicionales.

Some students may have clothing or other handmade items from Spanish-speaking countries. Have these students bring in the clothing or objects to show to the class.

Esta chica también lleva un huipil. Ella está tejiendo con un telar especial que se llama un telar de palitos. Probablemente fue el telar de su mamá o aun de su abuela. El tejido es una tradición muy antigua en Guatemala.

Unidad

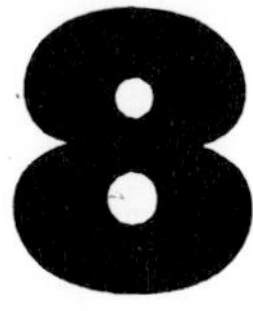

After completing this unit, students should be able to:

- name activities and items related to the beach and water sports
- talk about past actions, using the preterite tense of **-er** and **-ir** verbs
- talk about specific items and people by using demonstrative adjectives
- talk about what things are for by using the preposition **para**
- read a simulated magazine article about the discovery of the sunken ship *Nuestra Señora de Atocha*
- read about and discuss the land and attractions of Baja California.

The photographs may be used for informal assessment or review:

- Muéstrame a un muchacho que prefiere los deportes acuáticos.
- ¿Cómo son las olas del mar? ¿Son fuertes?
- ¿Qué está mirando el buceador?
- ¿Quién está flotando en el agua?
- ¿Hay alguien en la playa? ¿Cómo es la concha? ¿Buscaste conchas el verano pasado?

Panorama de vocabulario

Vamos a la playa

bronceada

la crema de broncear

los anteojos

el salvavidas

la sombrilla

quemado

tomar el sol

Note: There are many alternative words for vocabulary related to the beach: in some regions, **las gafas, los espejuelos,** or **los lentes** may be used instead of **los anteojos (de sol); la crema bronceadora** may be used instead of **la crema de broncear;** and **el parasol** may be used instead of **la sombrilla.**

If students are interested, you may point out that lifeguard can be referred to as **el** or **la salvavidas** or **el** or **la vigilante;** a lifeboat is **un bote salvavidas** or **una lancha de socorro;** a lifejacket is **un chaleco salvavidas.**

Words for other water sports can be used to show how one language borrows from another: surfing is **el surfing;** windsurfing is **el windsurf.** You may point out that if students look for surfing in the dictionary, they may find other, complicated equivalents, such as **el patinaje sobre las olas.** However, in everyday speech, speakers have found it more convenient to borrow the English terms.

Enrichment: Have students look up terms related to the rodeo to discover how English has borrowed words from Spanish.

Enrichment: Have students make up signs using **se prohibe.** You may wish to introduce and use the following phrases: **masticar chicle** (chewing gum), **fumar** (smoking), **correr en el pasillo** (running in the hallway), **comer en la biblioteca** (eating in the library). Signs may be displayed in the classroom and around the school building.

¡Aprende el vocabulario!

A. The Vásquez twins, Juan and Julia, are planning a day at the beach. What things are they bringing to the beach? What things are already there?

Primero, lee la pregunta. Luego, contesta la pregunta con **sí** o **no.** Sigue los modelos.

Modelo: ¿Traen las olas?
Respuesta: **No, no traen las olas.**

Modelo: ¿Traen un salvavidas?
Respuesta: **Sí, traen un salvavidas.**

1. Sí, traen la crema de broncear.
2. No, no traen la arena.
3. Sí, traen sus anteojos.
4. Sí, traen una sombrilla.
5. No, no traen unos caracoles.
6. No, no traen el mar.
7. Sí, traen su barco de vela.
8. No, no traen unas conchas.

1. ¿Traen la crema de broncear?
2. ¿Traen la arena?
3. ¿Traen sus anteojos?
4. ¿Traen una sombrilla?
5. ¿Traen unos caracoles?
6. ¿Traen el mar?
7. ¿Traen su barco de vela?
8. ¿Traen unas conchas?

You may wish to remind students that they can find the verb chart of **traer** in the back of their textbooks.

B. Once the twins get to the beach they can't decide what to do. So they try to do everything!

Primero, mira el dibujo. Luego, lee la oración. Por último, completa la oración. Sigue el modelo.

Modelo: Juan quiere buscar ——.

Respuesta: **Juan quiere buscar conchas.**

1. A Juan le encanta ——.

2. Julia sabe —— muy bien.

3. A Julia le gusta ——.

4. Juan busca ——.

5. Juan y Julia hacen una casa de ——.

6. Julia quiere ——.

1. el esquí acuático
2. bucear
3. flotar
4. caracoles
5. arena
6. tomar el sol

Extension: Ask students what beach activities they enjoy or do not enjoy.

Have students guess the meaning of **encantar** and confirm their guesses by looking it up in the classroom dictionary or the glossary in their textbooks.

C. This is Susana's first time at the beach. She has a lot of questions about the things she sees.

Primero, lee la pregunta. Luego, mira el dibujo y contesta la pregunta. Sigue el modelo.

Modelo: ¿Tiene anteojos el muchacho?

Respuesta: **No, el muchacho no tiene anteojos.**

1. ¿Hay conchas en la arena?
2. ¿Hay un salvavidas en la playa?
3. ¿Bucea el muchacho?
4. ¿El muchacho usó la crema de broncear?
5. ¿Hay una lancha en el mar?
6. ¿Hay olas en el mar?
7. ¿A quién le gusta el esquí acuático?
8. ¿Hay una sombrilla en la playa?

Wording may vary.
1. No, no hay conchas en la arena.
2. Sí, hay un salvavidas en la playa.
3. No, el muchacho no bucea.
4. No, el muchacho no usó la crema de broncear.
5. Sí, hay una lancha en el mar.
6. No, no hay olas en el mar.
7. A la mujer le gusta el esquí acuático.
8. No, no hay una sombrilla en la playa.

Extension: Continue asking questions about the scene (e.g., **¿Está quemado el muchacho? ¿Qu[é] busca la muchacha?**).

Enrichment: Have students cut beach scenes out of old magazines or the travel section of the newspaper. Have them write sentences or a paragraph about their picture and then make a Big Book of all the pictures and sentences.

D. Help Jaime finish his story about a day at the beach.

Primero, lee la oración. Luego, completa la oración con una palabra o una frase de la lista. Por último, escribe la oración completa. Sigue el modelo.

un salvavidas	anteojos	conchas
caracoles	crema de broncear	peligro
sombrilla	tomar el sol	quemado

Modelo: Mi mamá siempre lleva ——. A ella nunca le duelen los ojos.

Respuesta: **Mi mamá siempre lleva anteojos.**

1. A mi hermana Rosita le gusta descansar. Se acuesta en la playa para ——.
2. Mi papá no sabe nadar. Siempre lleva —— en el agua.
3. Hay —— cuando las olas están muy altas y fuertes.
4. Mi abuelita siempre se sienta debajo de su ——.
5. Mi hermanito Pepito colecciona —— y —— en la playa.
6. Yo nunca uso ——. Siempre tengo dolor porque estoy ——.

1. tomar el sol
2. un salvavidas
3. peligro
4. sombrilla
5. caracoles / conchas
6. crema de broncear / quemado

This activity may be assigned as homework after you have presented it in class.

Students may use the context of the photo to guess the meanings of **respira** and **el tubo esnorkel.**

Manuel está flotando en el agua. Respira por un tubo esnorkel. ¿A ti te gusta flotar en el mar?

E. Imagine that you are spending a day at the beach. Write a letter to your best friend about what you are doing.

Escribe una carta a un amigo. Describe un día en la playa. Primero, lee la carta de Francisca.

> Querida Alicia,
>
> Te escribo desde la playa. Estoy debajo de mi sombrilla. Veo a muchas personas bronceadas.
>
> Voy a bucear con mis primos. Ellos me dicen que no hay peligro. Tengo un poco de miedo.
>
> Voy a ponerme mucha crema de broncear. No quiero estar quemada. También me pongo los anteojos. Hace mucho sol hoy.
>
> Tu amiga,
>
> *Francisca*

Ask volunteers to read their letters aloud. Encourage students to include statements about what they are doing and what they are wearing.

Use the photos on pages 196 and 197 to review affirmative and negative words (e.g., **¿Hay alguien en las piedras? ¿Hay alguien cerca de la piscina? ¿Hay alguien en la lancha?**).

No hay nadie en la playa. Hay muchas piedras en la arena y en el mar. ¿Hay peligro?

Los sonidos del idioma

La entonación

Escucha y repite.

After students have listened to the cassette, have them practice saying the pairs of words aloud.

papa	papá	leo	león
esta	está	sabana	sábana
río	rió	saco	sacó

To reinforce the importance of observing accent marks, the students may look up the meanings of the words.

1. ¿Cómo como la papa de papá?
2. El libro sobre el león de la sabana está en la sábana.
3. El árbol cayó en el río y el niño se rió.
4. José sacó los artículos del saco.

As a class, have them discuss how misunderstandings may occur if someone does not pronounce a word with the proper stress.

¿Qué hacen las personas? ¿Están bronceadas?

¿Qué va a hacer el hombre?

Usando el español

Expressing Other Actions in the Past

Rule: To form the preterite of regular **-er** and **-ir** verbs, you add the endings **-í**, **-iste**, **-ió**, **-imos**, and **-ieron** to the stem.

Study the charts of two regular **-er** and **-ir** verbs in the preterite.

Have students look up the charts of regular **-er** and **-ir** verbs in the preterite in the appendix.

Correr

Singular		Plural	
yo	corr**í**	nosotros (-as)	corr**imos**
tú	corr**iste**	vosotros (-as)	corr**isteis**
él / ella / usted	corr**ió**	ellos / ellas / ustedes	corr**ieron**

Salir

Singular		Plural	
yo	sal**í**	nosotros (-as)	sal**imos**
tú	sal**iste**	vosotros (-as)	sal**isteis**
él / ella / usted	sal**ió**	ellos / ellas / ustedes	sal**ieron**

What endings do you add to the stems of regular **-er** and **-ir** verbs to make the preterite tense? Recall that **salir** has an irregular form in the present tense (**yo salgo**). Is **salir** regular or irregular in the preterite tense?

[To make the preterite tense, you add the endings **-í**, **-iste**, **-ió**, **-imos**, and **-ieron** to the stem of regular **-er** and **-ir** verbs. **Salir** is regular in the preterite tense.]

Now study the chart of a stem-changing **-er** verb in the preterite tense.

You may wish to have students look up the present-tense forms of stem-changing verbs in the appendix and compare them to the preterite forms.

Volver (ue)

Singular		Plural	
yo	volv**í**	nosotros (-as)	volv**imos**
tú	volv**iste**	vosotros (-as)	volv**isteis**
él / ella / usted	volv**ió**	ellos / ellas / ustedes	volv**ieron**

Does the stem change when you add the preterite endings?

Other stem-changing verbs you know that do not change in the preterite tense are **doler (ue)** and **perderse (ie).** [No, the stem does not change.]

Have students find the examples of **doler** and **perderse** in the questions and answers.

Practice reading the following questions and answers:

Pregunta: ¿Cuándo **aprendiste** a hablar francés?
Respuesta: Lo **aprendí** en Francia el año pasado.

Pregunta: ¿Cuánto tiempo **vivió** Amalia en México?
Respuesta: Ella **vivió** con una familia mexicana por tres meses.

Pregunta: ¿Cómo pasaste el fin de semana?
Respuesta: Primero, **corrí** dos millas en la lluvia. Luego, me **dolió** la cabeza. Además, **me perdí.** Nunca llegué a la playa. Entonces, **volví** a mi casa y me acosté.

Extension: To practice these verbs in the preterite, ask students questions (e.g., **¿Te dolieron los brazos ayer? ¿Te dolió la pierna ayer? ¿Te perdiste en el pasillo ayer? Juan se perdió en el gimnasio, ¿verdad?**). Have students conclude that they will only use two forms of **doler** in the preterite: **dolió** and **dolieron.**

¡Vamos a practicar!

A. Lucía's friends learned a lot last summer. How do they answer her questions?

Primero, lee la pregunta. Luego, contesta la pregunta con las palabras entre paréntesis. Sigue el modelo.

Modelo: Manuel, ¿qué aprendiste el verano pasado? (montar a caballo)

Respuesta: **Aprendí a montar a caballo.**

1. Susana y Teresa, ¿qué aprendieron el verano pasado? (bucear en el mar) 1. Aprendimos a bucear en el mar.
2. Sr. Corona, ¿qué aprendió el verano pasado? (usar la computadora) 2. Aprendí a usar la computadora.
3. Rogelio, ¿qué aprendiste el verano pasado? (sacar fotos) 3. Aprendí a sacar fotos.
4. Srta. Gutiérrez, ¿qué aprendieron sus alumnos el verano pasado? (hablar francés) 4. Mis alumnos aprendieron a hablar francés.
5. Pepita, ¿qué aprendiste el verano pasado? (jugar al volibol) 5. Aprendí a jugar al volibol.

Extension: Have students ask each other if they, a friend, or a family member learned a specific skill last year.

B. Poor Alejandro! His weekend was a disaster. What happened?

Primero, lee la oración. Luego, completa la oración con la forma apropiada de la palabra entre paréntesis. Sigue el modelo.

After completing the exercise as a class, ask volunteers to read the little "story" aloud.

Modelo: Primero, (salir) de la casa a las ocho.

Respuesta: **Primero, salí de la casa a las ocho.**

1. Busqué la calle Octavia, pero (perderse).
2. (Volver) a la casa de mi amigo Ernesto Solís.
3. Él y yo (comer) unos sándwiches.
4. Después de comer, me (doler) el estómago.
5. Luego, me (doler) los brazos y la cabeza.
6. Mis papás (recibir) una llamada del Sr. Solís.
7. También, mi amigo (correr) a mi casa para traer a mis papás.
8. ¡Yo (aprender) a quedarme en casa los sábados!

1. me perdí
2. Volví
3. comimos
4. dolió
5. dolieron
6. recibieron
7. corrió
8. aprendí

Extension: Ask volunteers to describe a recent "disaster" in their lives.

C. Imagine that you're a reporter for the nightly news. You have to interview people about what they did last weekend. Prepare your questions first!

Primero, lee las listas de palabras. Luego, escribe cinco preguntas. Lee el ejemplo.

comer	abrir	doler
correr	perderse	volver
recibir	aprender	salir

Modelo: 1. ¿A qué hora salieron ustedes?
2. ¿Adónde corrieron ustedes?
3. ¿Cuándo se perdieron?
4. ¿Qué les dolió?
5. ¿Qué aprendieron?

Extension: Have students work with a partner or a small group to answer each other's questions. Students may use props to present their interviews as part of the "nightly news."

Talking about People and Things

Rule: You use demonstrative adjectives to talk about or point out specific people or things. The adjectives agree in number and gender with their nouns.

Study the pictures and read the sentences.

Este chico está bronceado.

Ese chico está un poco quemado.

Aquel chico está muy quemado.

Esta chica sabe nadar bien.

Esa chica sabe flotar.

Aquella chica no sabe ni flotar ni nadar.

Help students make the connection between the demonstrative adjective and the distance of the person in the picture.

Which words in heavy black letters help you talk about this boy or this girl? Which words help you talk about that boy or that girl? Which words help you talk about that boy or that girl over there?

[**Este** and **esta** help you talk about this boy or this girl. **Ese** and **esa** help you talk about that boy or that girl. **Aquel** and **aquella** help you talk about that boy or that girl over there.]

The words **este, ese, aquel, esta, esa,** and **aquella** are called demonstrative adjectives.

Study the chart of demonstrative adjectives.

Singular		Plural	
Masculine	**Feminine**	**Masculine**	**Feminine**
este	esta	estos	estas
ese	esa	esos	esas
aquel	aquella	aquellos	aquellas

Have students role-play the sample conversations.

Practice reading the following conversations:

DIANA: Las conchas son muy bonitas, ¿no?

LUISA: ¿Cuáles? **Estas** conchas no son bonitas.

DIANA: ¡No, chica! **Esas** conchas, a la izquierda, son bonitas.

JORGE: Los barcos de vela van muy rápido.

BETO: ¿**Estos** barcos que están aquí?

JORGE: No, no, no. Los barcos de las velas rosadas.

BETO: ¿**Esos** barcos en el puerto?

JORGE: ¡No, hombre! **Aquellos** barcos que están muy lejos. ¡Van tan rápido que casi no los veo!

How observant are you?

Are demonstrative adjectives like other adjectives? Does the masculine singular form agree with a masculine singular noun? Do the other demonstrative adjectives agree in number and gender with their nouns? Find examples.

[Yes, demonstrative adjectives are like other adjectives. The masculine singular form agrees with a masculine singular noun. Yes, the other demonstrative adjectives agree in number and gender with their nouns. Examples are **estas (esas) conchas; estos (esos, aquellos) barcos.]**

¡Vamos a practicar!

A. Anita and her farsighted aunt are spending a day at the beach. What does Anita point out to her aunt?

Primero, mira el dibujo. Luego, haz una oración. Sigue el modelo.

Modelo:

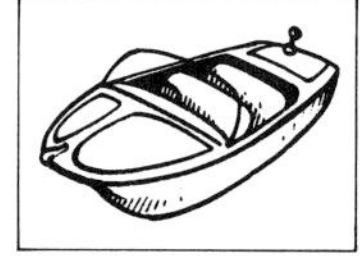

Respuesta: **¡Mira esta lancha!**

1. ¡Mira este barco de vela!
2. ¡Mira estas conchas!
3. ¡Mira estos anteojos!
4. ¡Mira esta sombrilla!

1.

2. 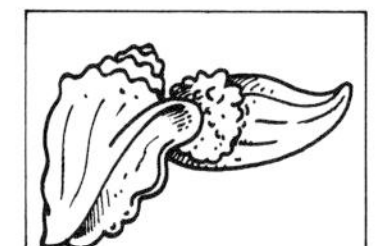

3. 

4. 

B. Anita's aunt needs new glasses. She can only see things that are very far away. She's not sure what Anita is pointing out.

Primero, lee la pregunta. Luego, completa la pregunta. Sigue el modelo.

Modelo: ¿—— lancha?

Respuesta: **¿Aquella lancha?**

1. Aquel
2. Aquellas
3. Aquellos
4. Aquel

Extension: Have students play the roles of Anita and her aunt, this time using objects that are available in the classroom.

1. ¿—— barco de vela?

2. ¿—— conchas?

3. ¿—— anteojos?

4. ¿—— sombrilla?

C. Andrés and Diego are shopping for birthday presents for Emilia. Which items do they want to buy?

Primero, mira el dibujo y lee la conversación. Luego, completa lo que dice Andrés (**A**) y lo que dice Diego (**D**). Sigue el modelo.

Modelo:

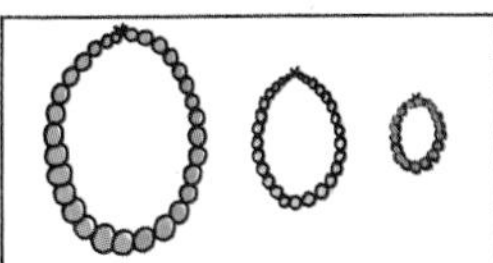

A: ¿Te gusta —— collar rojo?
D: No. Prefiero —— collar amarillo.
A: Voy a comprar —— collar azul.

Respuesta: **A:** **¿Te gusta aquel collar rojo?**
D: **No. Prefiero ese collar amarillo.**
A: **Voy a comprar este collar azul.**

1.

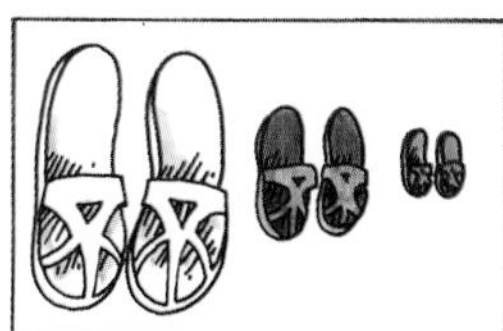

A: ¿Te gustan —— sandalias marrones?
D: No. Prefiero —— sandalias blancas.
A: Voy a comprar —— sandalias verdes.

A: esas / **D:** estas / **A:** aquellas

2.

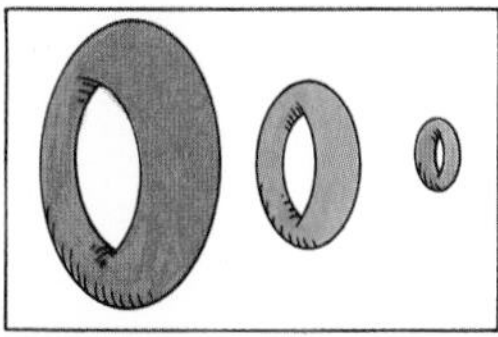

D: ¿Te gusta —— brazalete rosado?
A: No. Prefiero —— brazalete rojo.
D: Voy a comprar —— brazalete azul.

D: aquel / **A:** este / **D:** ese

3.

D: ¿Te gusta —— disco?
A: No. Prefiero —— casetes.
D: Voy a comprar —— disco compacto.

D: este / **A:** esos / **D:** aquel

D. Imagine that you and a friend are also shopping for presents. Choose three items you want to buy and draw three pictures of each item. Then place the pictures at different distances from you on a table. Hold a discussion with a partner, like the discussions between Andrés and Diego.

Primero, escoge tres cosas de las listas. Luego, haz tres dibujos de cada cosa. Pon los tres dibujos en una mesa. Por último, conversa con un compañero sobre las cosas. Sigue los ejemplos del ejercicio C.

una bolsa	unos casetes	un cinturón
una camiseta	unos caracoles	unos anteojos
unos zapatos	un libro	una sombrilla

Extension: Repeat this activity using classroom objects and other vocabulary familiar to students.

¡A divertirnos!

Una adivinanza

Students should use the visual clues as well as the words in the riddle to find the solution **(La a)**.

Flota en el medio del mar;

con las olas siempre está.

Mira en la playa y la vas a encontrar.

La a

Talking about What Things Are For

Rule: **Para** has many uses. You use it to talk about when an action must be completed; whom something is for; or the purpose of a thing or an action.

Study the pictures and read the sentences. Notice the three different uses of the word **para.**

Hoy es jueves. Tengo que lavar el coche **para** el sábado. El sábado nos visita abuelita.

Compré el regalo ayer. Es un traje de baño **para** mi papá.

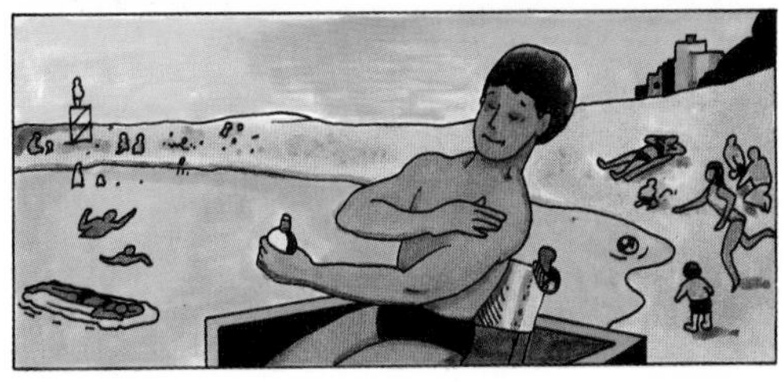

Uso la crema de broncear **para** tomar el sol. No quiero quemarme.

Provide additional examples such as: **Tienen que hacer la tarea para mañana. Mi hijo compró este bolígrafo para mí. Uso el bolígrafo para escribir.**

In each example, the preposition **para** is used in a different way. In which example is **para** used to show what something is used for? In which example is **para** used to indicate when something is supposed to be done? In which example is **para** used to indicate who will receive something?

[The third example uses **para** to show what something is used for. The first example uses **para** to indicate when something is supposed to be done. The second example uses **para** to indicate who will receive something.]

¡Vamos a practicar!

○ A. Carolina has a lot of deadlines to meet this week. By what days does she have to have things done?

Primero, lee las palabras. Luego, usa las palabras para contestar la pregunta **¿Qué tienes que hacer?** Sigue el modelo. You may wish to assign this activity as homework after doing one or two more examples with the class.

Modelo: escribir el reporte / el martes

Respuesta: **Tengo que escribir el reporte para el martes.**

Extension: Ask students to answer questions based on homework or tasks they must perform (e.g., **¿Para cuándo tienes que hacer la tarea?**).

1. planchar el vestido / mañana
2. lavar el coche / el viernes
3. leer la novela / el miércoles
4. pintar un cartel / el lunes
5. aprender el baile / el jueves
6. comprar un regalo / el sábado

1. Tengo que planchar el vestido para mañana.
2. Tengo que lavar el coche para el viernes.
3. Tengo que leer la novela para el miércoles.
4. Tengo que pintar un cartel para el lunes.
5. Tengo que aprender el baile para el jueves.
6. Tengo que comprar un regalo para el sábado.

◐ B. For a four-year-old, Paquito sure asks a lot of questions. How do you answer him?

Primero, lee las palabras. Luego, escribe una pregunta y una respuesta. Sigue el modelo. Have students work in pairs to ask and answer the questions.

Modelo: la crema de broncear

Respuesta: **P:** **¿Para qué usas la crema de broncear?**

R: **La uso para tomar el sol.**

Extension: Have students think of more questions a curious four-year-old would ask.

See Unit Plans, Unidad 8, for answers to exercise B.

1. la plancha
2. las llaves
3. el bolígrafo
4. el horno
5. el televisor
6. las sandalias

C. Sara is having a party for all her friends because she forgot their birthdays. Unfortunately, her little sister has opened all the belated birthday presents!

Primero, lee las palabras y el nombre. Luego, forma una pregunta y una respuesta. Sigue el modelo.

Modelo: la sombrilla (Adela)

Respuesta: **P: ¿Para quién es la sombrilla?**

R: La sombrilla es para Adela.

1. los discos (Manuel)
2. el collar (Dorotea)
3. la camiseta (Ignacio)
4. los carteles (Verónica)
5. los anteojos (Eduardo)
6. el llavero (Carlos)

Have students work in pairs to ask and answer the questions. Students may enjoy role-playing this activity.

D. Plan ahead for your friends' birthdays. By what date do you need to buy a gift? Whom is it for? What is the gift used for?

Primero, escoge a tres amigos. Luego, lee y contesta las preguntas para cada amigo.

Preguntas

1. ¿Para cuándo necesitas un regalo?
2. ¿Qué vas a comprar?
3. ¿Para quién es el regalo?
4. ¿Para qué va a usar el regalo tu amigo?

Exercise C:

1. **P:** ¿Para quién son los discos?
   R: Los discos son para Manuel.
2. **P:** ¿Para quién es el collar?
   R: El collar es para Dorotea.
3. **P:** ¿Para quién es la camiseta?
   R: La camiseta es para Ignacio.
4. **P:** ¿Para quién son los carteles?
   R: Los carteles son para Verónica.
5. **P:** ¿Para quién son los anteojos?
   R: Los anteojos son para Eduardo.
6. **P:** ¿Para quién es el llavero?
   R: El llavero es para Carlos.

Extension: Have students describe a recent birthday party, including the gifts given.

Vamos a leer

Enrichment: Have students research the early history of the state of Florida and early Spanish explorers, such as Ponce de León.

El tesoro del *Atocha*

¿Te gusta leer las revistas? Este reportaje en la revista *Bucear* es de una historia interesantísima, el descubrimiento del tesoro del *Nuestra Señora de Atocha.*

Cuando los españoles llegaron a América, encontraron oro y plata en los pueblos de la América Central y la América del Sur. También encontraron perlas y piedras preciosas. Volvieron a España con los barcos llenos de estos tesoros.

Algunos barcos nunca llegaron a España. Se perdieron en el mar en medio de huracanes y el mal tiempo. El *Nuestra Señora de Atocha* es uno de los barcos que desaparecieron. Lleno de monedas de oro y plata y de joyas, se perdió durante un huracán cerca de la Florida en 1622.

Durante más de dos siglos, el *Atocha* quedó en el fondo del mar hasta que Mel Fisher y un grupo de buceadores empezaron a buscarlo. En 1973, encontraron el *Atocha.* En 1985, cuando por fin quitaron la arena del antiguo barco, encontraron un tesoro de millones de dólares.

El tesoro también reveló datos muy importantes para la historia. De los barcos antiguos, aprendemos algo sobre la historia de las Américas. A lo mejor, esta información es el verdadero tesoro del *Atocha.*

This reading is the most complex students have encountered thus far. Have them identify barriers to understanding and then work with them to resolve problems of syntax or meaning. Remind students that they do not have to understand every word in order to understand the main idea and important points. Ask volunteers to summarize the reading in English.

Florida

el Atocha

La cultura y tú

See Unit Plans, Unidad 8, for additional information.

Baja California

Hay dos estados de California que no están en los Estados Unidos. Se llaman Baja California Norte y Baja California Sur. Los dos forman Baja California, en los Estados Unidos de México. (Mira el mapa en la página 44.)

Have students guess the meanings of unfamiliar words from context and confirm their guesses by looking up the words in the Spanish-English Glossary.

Baja California es una tierra de contrastes. El centro de la península es muy árido. Es el desierto. Pero de todos lados están el mar y millas de playas bonitas.

Esta piedra se llama El Arco. El Arco separa el Océano Pacífico del Mar de Cortés. Esta foto es del lado del Pacífico.

Cada año, muchos turistas vienen a Baja California para ver El Arco y, sobre todo, para disfrutar de las playas y de los deportes acuáticos. En el invierno, muchas personas vienen también para ver las ballenas. Cada año las ballenas emigran al sur del norte. Se quedan por unos meses en las lagunas y bahías de Baja California. Las personas vienen de muchos países para estudiar las ballenas y para sacarles fotos.

Have students look at the map of Mexico on page 44 and tell you how they think Baja California got its name.

Unidad

After completing this unit, students should be able to:

- identify and name places and items associated with the country
- talk about past actions by using the preterite tense of the irregular verbs **ir, ser,** and **dar**
- talk about activities by using the preposition **por**
- read a simulated excerpt from a history text about Angel Falls
- read about and discuss a national park in Costa Rica.

The photographs may be used for informal assessment or review:

- ¿Cómo es esa granja?
- Toca las gallinas. ¿De qué colores son?
- ¿Quiénes tienen mochilas? ¿Están contentos o están cansados?
- ¿Cómo es el salto de agua? ¿De qué color es el agua?
- ¿Es bonito el campo? ¿Comieron una merienda las muchachas?

Panorama de vocabulario

Vamos de excursión

la selva tropical

la serpiente

el salto de agua

el puma

el caimán

las abejas

el sendero

There are many synonyms or alternative terms for vocabulary in this unit: **el salto de agua** may also be called **la catarata** or **la cascada;** and **la serpiente** may also be **la culebra.** There are many different species of jungle cat; however, **el puma** and **el jaguar** are the most common terms.

Note: A farm can be called **la granja** or **la finca;** a ranch is **el rancho.** Students may also be familiar with the term **la hacienda,** which refers to an especially large farm or ranch. Alternative words for **el cerdo** include **el puerco, el cochino,** and **el chancho.**

¡Aprende el vocabulario!

A. Hortensia is always stumbling into problems. Her friends tell her to be careful, but danger is her middle name! What do her friends tell her to be careful of this time?

Primero, mira el dibujo. Luego, forma dos oraciones. Sigue el modelo.

Modelo:

Respuesta: ¡Ten cuidado! ¡Hay un puma!

If students cannot guess the meaning of **¡Ten cuidado!** have them look it up in the Spanish-English Glossary.

1.

2.

3.

4.

5.

6.

1. ¡Ten cuidado! ¡Hay un salto de agua!
2. ¡Ten cuidado! ¡Hay un caimán!
3. ¡Ten cuidado! ¡Hay una serpiente!
4. ¡Ten cuidado! ¡Hay un toro!
5. ¡Ten cuidado! ¡Hay unas hormigas!
6. ¡Ten cuidado! ¡Hay unas abejas!

B. Imagine that you and a friend are spending a quiet weekend in the country. What can happen in such peaceful surroundings?

Primero, lee la oración. Luego, escoge una palabra que va con la oración. Por último, escribe la oración. Sigue el modelo.

los árboles	una mochila	comida enlatada
abejas	el sendero	el campo
hormigas	merienda	una granja

Modelo: Es el sábado y estamos en ——.

Respuesta: **Es el sábado y estamos en el campo.**

1. Mi amigo tiene —— en la espalda.
2. Siempre tenemos hambre y llevamos mucha ——.
3. ¡Nos encanta comer debajo de ——!
4. Nuestra —— es muy buena.
5. Nos sentamos y comenzamos a comer, pero pronto vemos cuatrocientas ——.
6. Corremos rápido por ——
7. ¡Pero vienen seiscientas ——! Vuelan rápido y nos pican.
8. Vamos a —— para llamar a nuestros papás. Preferimos ir a casa en un coche.

Have students guess or look up the meaning of **nos sentamos** and **pican**.

1. una mochila
2. comida enlatada
3. los árboles
4. merienda
5. hormigas
6. el sendero
7. abejas
8. una granja

Extension: Have students write about recent or past experiences in the country. Allow them to use the present or the preterite tense.

Enrichment: Students may enjoy illustrating the story and putting it into a Big Book. You may also type the story in sentence strips for practice in sequencing events.

◐ C. Gregorio and his sister are spending the weekend on a farm. Help him describe what they see and do.

Primero, lee las oraciones. Luego, completa las oraciones con las palabras apropiadas. (No vas a usar todas las palabras.) Sigue el modelo.

el cerdo	el gallo	una mochila
una vaca	la granja	un toro
las hormigas	unos becerros	las gallinas
un árbol	los pollitos	unos gansos

Modelo: Mi hermana y yo pasamos el fin de semana en —— de nuestros tíos.

Respuesta: **Mi hermana y yo pasamos el fin de semana en la granja de nuestros tíos.**

Students should automatically combine **a** with the definite article; however, you may wish to use sentence 4 to remind them of the **al** contraction.

1. ¡Qui-qui-ri-quí! —— nos despierta a las cinco de la mañana.
2. Mi tía y yo damos comida a ——. Ellas nos dicen "clo-clo."
3. Me encantan ——. ¡Son tan pequeños y amarillos!
4. Mi hermana le da comida a ——. ¡Es bajo y grande y come mucho!
5. Al mediodía almorzamos en el campo. Llevamos la comida en ——.
6. —— blancos nadan en un lago pequeño.
7. Hay —— lejos de nosotros. La leche que tomamos viene de ella.
8. —— siguen a su mamá. Ellos juegan en el campo.
9. Mi hermana me grita. Hay —— grande y peligroso muy cerca de nosotros.
10. Ella y yo subimos rápido a ——. Allí pasamos una hora.

1. El gallo
2. las gallinas
3. los pollitos
4. al cerdo
5. una mochila
6. Unos gansos
7. una vaca
8. Unos becerros
9. un toro
10. un árbol

After students have completed the exercise, ask volunteers to read the story aloud.

D. Choose a partner and interview your partner about camping or a weekend trip. It can be a real or imaginary experience. Then switch roles.

Escoge a un compañero de clase. Primero, haz cinco preguntas. Luego, contesta las preguntas de tu compañero. Lee el ejemplo. If students need help in thinking of questions and answers, brainstorm a list of places and activities with the class and write it on the chalkboard.

TÚ: ¿Adónde prefieres ir de excursión?

ALUMNO: Prefiero ir a una selva tropical.

TÚ: ¿Por qué?

ALUMNO: Porque me gusta ver los animales de la selva.

TÚ: ¿Cuál es tu animal favorito?

ALUMNO: Me encantan las serpientes.

TÚ: ¿No tienes miedo de las serpientes?

ALUMNO: ¡No! Me gusta estudiar las serpientes. Son muy interesantes.

TÚ: ¿Sacas fotos de la selva tropical y de las serpientes?

ALUMNO: ¡Sí! Tengo muchas fotos. ¿Quieres ver unas?

Extension: Have students report the results of their interviews to the class.

La muchacha se divierte mucho en un salto de agua en Costa Rica. ¿Te bañaste alguna vez en un salto de agua?

Enrichment: Have students work in pairs to make up a story about the girl in the photo.

Los sonidos del idioma

La entonación

Escucha y repite.

sofá	lápiz	rápido
camión	azúcar	pájaro
autobús	carácter	música
ladrón	difícil	fáciles

Compare **casa** with **sofá; comenzar** with **azúcar; trabajo** with **rápido.**

1. El autobús se paró frente al almacén.
2. Este lápiz es útil para escribir la respuesta difícil.
3. Los pájaros vuelan rápido en el viento norteño.
4. El policía describió el carácter del ladrón fácilmente.

You may wish to state the following rules and then ask students why these words are exceptions to the rules:
1. If a word ends in a vowel, **n** or **s**, the second to the last syllable receives the stress.
2. If the word ends in a consonant (not **n** or **s**), the last syllable receives the stress.

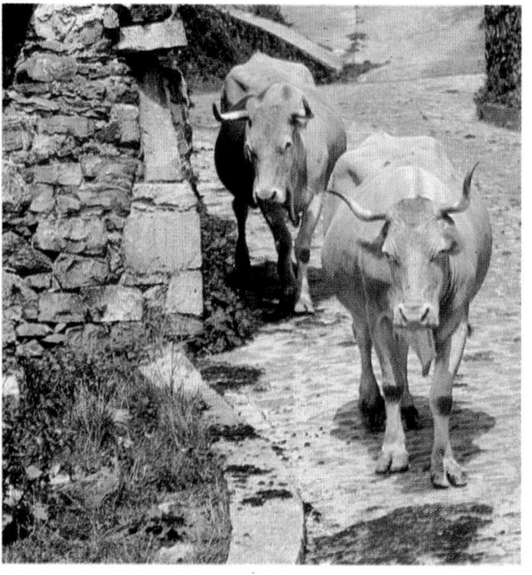

Este pueblo está en el campo.
¿Qué hay en la calle?

Este salto de agua se llama Iguazú.
Está en la América del Sur.

Usando el español

Using Irregular Verbs to Talk about Past Actions

Rule: The verbs **ir** and **ser** have the same irregular forms in the preterite. The forms of **dar** are like **-er** and **-ir** verbs, but without accents.

Study the following chart of three irregular verbs: **ir, ser,** and **dar.**

	ir	ser	dar
yo	**fui**	**fui**	**di**
tú	**fuiste**	**fuiste**	**diste**
él / ella / usted	**fue**	**fue**	**dio**
nosotros (-as)	**fuimos**	**fuimos**	**dimos**
vosotros (-as)	**fuisteis**	**fuisteis**	**disteis**
ellos / ellas / ustedes	**fueron**	**fueron**	**dieron**

Why is the preterite tense easy to remember for the verbs **ir** and **ser**? Are all the forms alike or different?

Even though **dar** ends in **-ar,** are its preterite forms like **-ar** verbs or like **-er** and **-ir** verbs?

[The preterite tense for both **ir** and **ser** is the same. All the forms are the same. / The preterite forms of **dar** are like **-er** and **-ir** verbs.]

Practice reading the following questions and answers:

Pregunta: ¿Adónde **fuiste** el verano pasado?
Respuesta: **Fui** a las selvas de Costa Rica.

Pregunta: ¿Quién te ayudó con el experimento?
Respuesta: Julio me ayudó. **Fue** mi asistente.

Pregunta: ¿Qué le **dieron** ustedes a la Srta. Millán?
Respuesta: Le **dimos** tres pollitos para su clase de ciencias.

How observant are you?

Which example uses the preterite of **ir**? How can you tell?

Which example uses the preterite of **ser**? How can you tell?

Is context important in knowing which verb is being used?

[The first uses the preterite of **ir.** You can tell from the context. The second uses the preterite of **ser.** You can tell from the context. Yes, context is the only clue to which verb is being used.]

¡Vamos a practicar!

A. Your friend is a reporter for the newspaper. He's interviewing you about where you and your classmates went on vacation.

Primero, lee las palabras. Luego forma una pregunta y una respuesta. Sigue el modelo.

Have students work in pairs to ask and answer the questions.
1. **P:** ¿Adónde fueron . . . ? / **R:** Fueron al río.
2. **P:** ¿Adónde fue . . . ? / **R:** Fue a las montañas.
3. **P:** ¿Adónde fuiste? / **R:** Fui a la playa.
4. **P:** ¿Adónde fueron . . . ? / **R:** Fueron al lago.
5. **P:** ¿Adónde fue . . . ? / **R:** Fue a la Argentina.
6. **P:** ¿Adónde fue . . . ? / **R:** Fue a España.

Modelo: Horacio (la selva)
Respuesta: **P: ¿Adónde fue Horacio?**
R: Fue a la selva.

1. Marta e Inés (el río)
2. Ramón (las montañas)
3. tú (la playa)
4. Chemo y Luis (el lago)
5. Evita (Argentina)
6. Camilo (España)

B. Imagine that your class play was last night. How well do you and your friends remember the parts you played?

Primero, lee las palabras. Luego, haz una oración con una forma de **ser.** Sigue el modelo.

You may wish to assign this activity as homework.

1. Pilar y Raúl fueron los maestros.
2. Esteban fue el aeromozo.
3. Andrea y yo fuimos los pilotos.
4. Tú fuiste el enfermero.
5. Ana fue la secretaria.
6. Eva y Tonio fueron los bomberos.

Modelo: Salvador / policía

Respuesta: **Salvador fue el policía.**

1. Pilar y Raúl / maestros
2. Esteban / aeromozo
3. Andrea y yo / pilotos
4. Tú / enfermero
5. Ana / secretaria
6. Eva y Tonio / bomberos

Explain to students that if the sentences were about professions, the definite article would be dropped.

C. Iris has just celebrated her birthday. What did everyone give her?

Primero, lee la pregunta y la frase entre paréntesis. Luego, completa la pregunta y contesta la pregunta con una oración completa. Sigue el modelo.

Modelo: ¿Qué te —— Salvador? (flores exóticas)

Respuesta: **P:** **¿Qué te dio Salvador?**

R: **Me dio flores exóticas.**

Have students work in pairs to ask and answer the questions.

1. ¿Qué te —— Pilar y Raúl? (unos casetes de música)
2. ¿Qué te —— Esteban? (un cartel de España)
3. ¿Qué te —— nosotros? (una torta de chocolate)
4. ¿Qué te —— Ana? (una mochila nueva)
5. ¿Qué te —— Eva y Tonio? (un disco compacto)

1. dieron / Me dieron . . .
2. dio / Me dio . . .
3. dimos / Me dieron . . .
4. dio / Me dio . . .
5. dieron / Me dieron . . .

Extension: Ask students what friends and family members gave them for their last birthday.

D. Mateo went on a trip to a tropical rain forest. Help him finish his report on the experience.

Primero, lee la oración. Luego, completa la oración con la forma apropiada de la palabra entre paréntesis. Sigue el modelo.

Modelo: El agosto pasado, mi familia y yo —— a una selva tropical. (ir)

Respuesta: **El agosto pasado, mi familia y yo fuimos a una selva tropical.**

1. Un día, yo —— con el Sr. López en helicóptero. (ir)
2. El Sr. López —— piloto. (ser)
3. Aterrizó el helicóptero cerca de un río. Bajamos y —— por un sendero. (ir)
4. El Sr. López me —— un mapa. (dar)
5. Él buscó un salto de agua. Yo —— su asistente. (ser)
6. Dos caimanes en el río me —— mucho miedo. (dar)

1. fui
2. fue
3. fuimos
4. dio
5. fui
6. comieron

Extension: Have students write out the complete sentences. Then have them use context to decide which words are forms of **ir** and which are forms of **ser**.

Este árbol muy grande está en la Argentina. ¿Fuiste tú a la Argentina alguna vez?

Using por **to Talk about Actions**

Rule: You can use **por** to talk about when something happened and how long it lasted and to show that something was done or given in exchange for something else.

Study the picture and read the paragraph below it. Notice three different uses of the word **por.**

Ask volunteers to read the paragraph aloud. Have students use the context of the passage and the illustration to guess the meaning of **el granjero.**

Ayer **por** la mañana, Arturo y yo fuimos a una granja. Ayudamos al granjero. Les dimos comida a las gallinas, a los cerdos y a las vacas. **Por** dos horas, trabajamos mucho. El granjero nos pagó diez dólares **por** nuestro trabajo. Le dimos las gracias **por** el dinero. **Por** la tarde, volvimos a casa y ¡nos bañamos!

In the paragraph, find two examples of **por** that indicate when something happened. Find one example of **por** that indicates how long something lasted. Find two examples of **por** that show that something was given in exchange for something else.

[When something happened: **ayer por la mañana** and **por la tarde.** How long something lasted: **por dos horas.** Exchange: **nos pagó diez dólares por nuestro trabajo** and **le dimos las gracias por el dinero.**]

Extension: Ask students to think of classroom situations in which they have heard you use **por** (e.g., **Vamos a leer por diez minutos. Te doy las gracias por tu ayuda. Mañana por la mañana, vamos a cantar.**).

¡Vamos a practicar!

A. Estela is taking a survey of her classmates to find out when they studied yesterday. How do her classmates respond?

Primero, lee la pregunta. Luego, mira el dibujo y contesta con **por la mañana, por la tarde** o **por la noche.** Sigue el modelo.

Modelo:  Bernardo, ¿cuándo estudiaste?

Respuesta: **Estudié por la mañana.**

Make certain students understand the times of day indicated by the pictures.

1. Rita, ¿cuándo estudiaste?

   1. Estudié por la tarde.

2. Juan y Julio, ¿cuándo estudiaron?

   2. Estudiamos por la noche.

3.  Olga y Tomás, ¿cuándo estudiaron?

   3. Estudiamos por la mañana.

4. 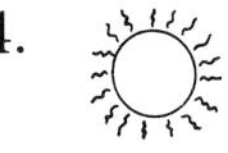 Hugo, ¿cuándo estudiaste?

   4. Estudié por la tarde.

Extension: Ask students when they did their homework yesterday.

B. Now Estela wants to know how long they studied.

Primero, lee la pregunta. Luego, contesta con el tiempo entre paréntesis. Sigue el modelo.

1. Estudié por tres horas.
2. Estudiamos por veinte minutos.

Modelo: Bernardo, ¿cuánto tiempo estudiaste? (una hora)

Respuesta: **Estudié por una hora.**

3. Estudiamos por una hora y media.
4. Estudié por dos horas.

1. Rita, ¿cuánto tiempo estudiaste? (tres horas)

2. Juan y Julio, ¿cuánto tiempo estudiaron? (veinte minutos)

3. Olga y Tomás, ¿cuánto tiempo estudiaron? (una hora y media)

4. Hugo, ¿cuánto tiempo estudiaste? (dos horas)

C. Nicolás hasn't learned that it's not polite to ask people how much they paid for something. What does he ask? How do his friends answer?

Primero, lee las palabras y forma una pregunta. Luego, contesta con el precio entre paréntesis. Sigue el modelo.

Modelo: la mochila ($20)
Respuesta: **P: ¿Cuánto pagaste por la mochila?**
R: Pagué veinte dólares.

Students may work in pairs and alternate asking and answering questions.

1. los discos ($17)
2. el collar ($25)
3. la camisa ($8)
4. las bolsas ($11)
5. el llavero ($1)
6. los casetes ($16)

See Unit Plans, Unidad 9, for answers to exercise C.

D. When was the last time you worked to earn some money?

Primero, lee las preguntas. Luego, escribe las respuestas. Lee el ejemplo.

Preguntas Ask volunteers to read their sentences aloud.

1. ¿Cuándo trabajaste: por la mañana, por la tarde o por la noche?
2. ¿En qué trabajaste?
3. ¿Cuánto tiempo trabajaste?
4. ¿Qué recibiste por tu trabajo?

Enrichment: Ask students to write want ads for jobs. They should include the time the job is offered, the number of hours to be worked, and the amount of money to be paid for the job.

Modelo:
1. Trabajé el sábado por la tarde.
2. Ayudé a mi papá a limpiar el garaje.
3. Trabajé por cuatro horas.
4. Recibí cinco dólares por mi trabajo.

E. Imagine that you are at a flea market. You have brought some items you want to exchange. What will you trade with Alfredo and Gloria?

Primero, escribe una lista de cinco cosas. Luego, lee las listas de Alfredo y Gloria. Por último, escribe cinco oraciones. Sigue el modelo.

Alfredo	Gloria
3 discos compactos	2 camisetas cómicas
2 carteles	3 casetes
1 mochila	4 novelas
1 lancha plástica	1 collar plástico
4 sombrillas	2 llaveros

Modelo: **1.** Gloria, te doy un brazalete por un collar.
2. Alfredo, te doy un salvavidas por una mochila.

Enrichment: Students may enjoy setting up a flea market in the classroom in order to exchange goods (or pictures of goods) with each other.

¡A divertirnos!

Un proverbio

Help students guess the meaning of the proverb from the illustration. You may wish to have them deduce the infinitive form of **dejes (dejar)** and look it up. Ask students to describe situations in which the proverb might apply.

No te dejes dar gato por liebre.

Vamos a leer

El salto Ángel

You may wish to practice stating and writing numbers in the thousands before presenting this activity.

En la escuela, aprendes muchas cosas sobre la historia de tu país. En Venezuela, los alumnos estudian la historia de su país y, a veces en sus libros de historia, leen sobre un piloto estadounidense que descubrió algo muy interesante en la selva de Venezuela.

First have students read the text quickly, scanning for clues to the subject. Then have them read the text carefully and summarize (in English or Spanish) the main points.

En el año 1937, Jimmy Angel, un piloto estadounidense, voló su pequeño avión, el "Flamingo," sobre la selva venezolana. Desde el aire, él vio el salto de agua más alto del mundo. El salto Ángel tiene 3.212 pies de altura.

Jimmy Angel voló muy cerca del salto de agua para medir su altura, pero el motor de su pequeño avión falló y aterrizó en medio de la selva. Después de caminar varios días por la selva, llegó a un pueblo pequeño de indios que lo llevaron a la ciudad más cercana.

El "Flamingo" quedó abandonado junto al salto. En el año 1970, el gobierno de Venezuela mandó a un grupo de personas a buscarlo y traerlo hasta Caracas, la capital de Venezuela, donde ahora está en un museo aéreo.

If parts of the text act as barriers to understanding, help students determine the cause of a barrier (e.g., the meaning of a word) and resolve the problem by using dictionary or deductive skills.

El salto Ángel en Venezuela es el salto de agua más alto del mundo.

El avión de Jimmy Angel, ahora en el museo aéreo de Caracas.

La cultura y tú

See Unit Plans, Unidad 9, for additional information.

El Bosque Nuboso de Monteverde

Costa Rica es un país muy variado. Tiene playas en la costa Atlántica y la costa Pacífica y, en el centro del país, hay montañas muy altas y la selva.

Enrichment: Costa Rica is known for its extensive system of national parks and its varied climate. Have students research Costa Rica, its national park system, and its different regions.

El Bosque Nuboso de Monteverde es uno de los parques nacionales de Costa Rica. El gobierno lo creó en 1973. Está en los montes Tibarán en la parte central de Costa Rica. El Bosque Nuboso es una selva tropical, con un clima muy húmedo. En los meses de febrero y marzo, llueve cada cuatro a seis días, con una acumulación de doce pulgadas al mes. En abril, llueve cada tres días, con una acumulación de treinta y cinco pulgadas de lluvia.

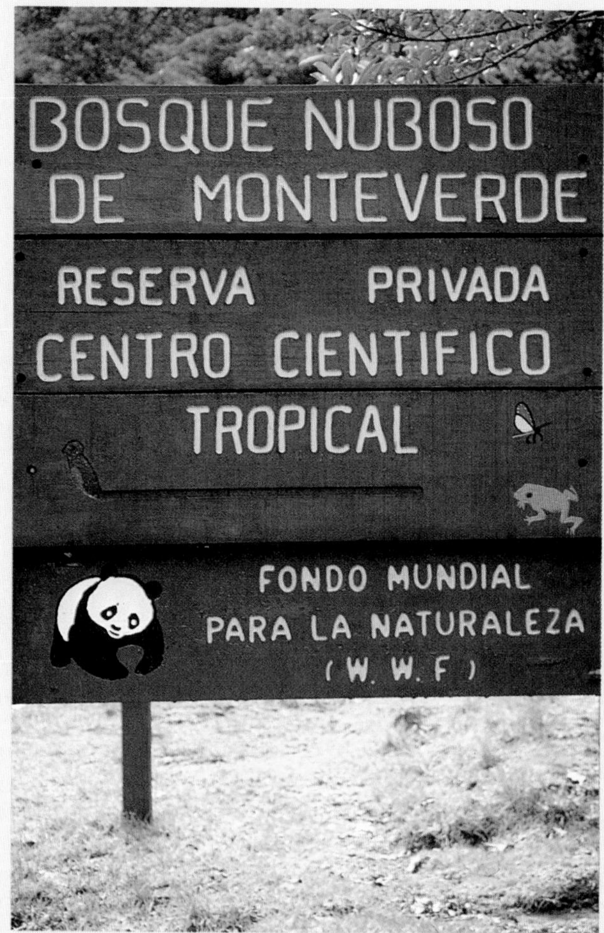

En ciertas estaciones, casi nunca puedes ver el sol en esta selva. Se llama el Bosque Nuboso porque muchas veces hay nubes en la selva. Cuando no hay nubes, puedes ver el Océano Pacífico a cincuenta millas al oeste y el Océano Atlántico a ochenta millas al este desde el punto más alto de la selva.

Muchos animales muy interesantes y bonitos viven en el Bosque Nuboso de Monteverde. Aquí viven pájaros y otros animales que sólo pueden vivir en la selva. Este sapo muy raro vive el el Bosque Nuboso. Como ves, él puede subir a los árboles.

Tercer repaso

Have volunteers role-play the conversation after students are familiar with it.

A. Una conversación entre amigos

LIDIA: ¿Adónde fuiste ayer?

PEDRO: Fui a la playa. Nadé y tomé el sol.

LIDIA: ¿Usaste la crema de broncear?

PEDRO: ¡No! Las cremas son para las muchachas.

LIDIA: ¿Buscaste conchas en la arena?

PEDRO: No, no las busqué. Busqué a las muchachas bonitas y bronceadas.

LIDIA: ¿Las encontraste?

PEDRO: Sí, las encontré.

LIDIA: ¿Qué pasó?

PEDRO: Pues . . . me miraron y corrieron al otro lado de la playa.

LIDIA: ¡No me digas! ¿Por qué?

PEDRO: Es que . . . me quemé mucho. Caminé como una langosta. ¡Les di miedo!

LIDIA: ¡Ahora sabes para qué sirve la crema de broncear!

Ask students if they have ever been so sunburned they looked like lobsters.

Preguntas

1. ¿Adónde fue Pedro?
2. ¿Qué buscó en la playa?
3. ¿Qué encontró en la playa?
4. ¿Adónde corrieron las muchachas?
5. ¿Por qué corrieron?

Extension: Have students write two more questions about the conversation.

B. ¿Y tú?

What did you do last summer?

Lee y contesta las preguntas en tus palabras.

1. ¿Fuiste a la playa el verano pasado?
2. ¿Qué te gusta hacer en la playa?
3. ¿Tomaste una merienda con tus amigos?
4. ¿Qué te gusta hacer cuando vas al campo?
5. ¿Fuiste a una granja el verano pasado?
6. ¿Qué animales te gustan en una granja?
7. ¿Fuiste a una selva tropical?
8. ¿Qué te gusta hacer en una selva tropical?
9. ¿Hay peligro en las selvas? ¿Qué es peligroso?
10. ¿Cuál es tu animal favorito de las selvas?

Enrichment: Have students write a paragraph on a trip they took or an activity they enjoyed last summer.

Extension: Ask four volunteers to be the "talk show" guests and one volunteer to be the interviewer. Students may use the questions for the interviews. Encourage additional questions from the "audience."

¿Fuiste a pasear en barco de vela el verano pasado? ¿Cuántos barcos hay en la foto? ¿Cómo es el mar? ¿Hay olas grandes?

Answers to Preguntas, p. 232
1. Pedro fue a la playa.
2. Buscó a las muchachas bonitas y bronceadas.
3. Encontró a muchachas bonitas y bronceadas.
4. Las muchachas corrieron al otro lado de la playa.
5. Corrieron porque Pedro caminó como una langosta.

C. Una excursión a las tiendas

Adela and her friends went shopping yesterday. How did she describe their trip? You may wish to assign this activity as homework.

Primero, lee la oración. Luego, completa la oración con la forma apropiada de la palabra entre paréntesis. Sigue el modelo.

Modelo: Por la mañana —— a una tienda. (ir)
Respuesta: **Por la mañana fui a una tienda.**

1. Ayer mis amigas y yo —— de compras. (ir)
2. Yo —— un collar bonito en la joyería. (comprar)
3. —— siete dólares por el collar. (pagar)
4. Elena y Mireya —— a la tienda de discos. (correr)
5. Ellas —— comprar casetes y discos compactos. (pensar)
6. Los casetes —— muy caros. (ser)
7. Y un disco compacto —— diez dólares. (costar)
8. Al mediodía nosotras —— en un restaurante. (almorzar)
9. El camarero no nos —— buen servicio. (dar)
10. Nosotras no le —— una propina. (dar)

1. fuimos
2. compré
3. Pagué
4. corrieron
5. pensaron
6. fueron
7. costó
8. almorzamos
9. dio
10. dimos

CH. Ahora ... ¡tú!

Have you been shopping with friends lately? Choose a partner and talk about a recent shopping trip. Have volunteers present their conversations to the class.

Escoge a un compañero de clase. Prepara una conversación. Escribe por lo menos diez preguntas y respuestas. Si necesitas ayuda, lee las oraciones de la actividad C y piensa en algunas preguntas que puedes hacer.

D. Una entrevista parcial

During his radio show, Geraldo Ríos is interviewing the famous photographer Hernán Playa. The static is so bad, you can only hear the answers. What are the questions?

Primero, lee la respuesta. Luego, escribe la pregunta para la respuesta. Sigue el modelo. Do a few more examples with the class before assigning this activity as homework.

Modelo: Volví de la selva la semana pasada.

Respuesta: **P: ¿Cuándo volvió usted de la selva?**

1. Fui a la selva para sacar fotos.
2. Sí, saqué muchas fotos.
3. Le di las fotos al director del zoológico.
4. Sí, viví en una granja el año pasado.
5. Trabajé con los toros.
6. Sí, fue un trabajo peligroso.
7. Pasé una semana en la granja.
8. Salí porque no me gustó levantarme temprano.

Wording may vary.
1. ¿Por qué fue usted a la selva?
2. ¿Sacó muchas fotos?
3. ¿A quién le dio las fotos?
4. ¿Vivió en una granja el año pasado?
5. ¿Con qué trabajó?
6. ¿Fue un trabajo peligroso?
7. ¿Cuánto tiempo pasó usted en la granja?
8. ¿Por qué salió?

E. ¿Qué les preguntas a los fotógrafos?

Imagine that you will interview the photographers who took the pictures on this page. What questions will you ask them?

Escribe por lo menos tres preguntas para hacerle a cada fotógrafo. You may wish to choose a photo and brainstorm a few questions with the class before assigning this activity as homework.

1. 

2. 

3. 

4. 

F. Estela está confundida

Estela went shopping and is so proud of her purchase, she can't stop talking about it. Unfortunately she doesn't know when to use **por** and when to use **para.** Help her out.

Primero, lee la oración. Luego, completa la oración con **por** o **para.** Si necesitas ayuda, mira las páginas 207 y 225.

1. Necesité un regalo (por, para) el sábado.
2. El regalo fue (por, para) Jaime.
3. Le compré un llavero (por, para) todas sus llaves.
4. Fui a la tienda (por, para) la mañana.
5. Busqué el llavero (por, para) una hora.
6. Pagué cinco dólares (por, para) el llavero.

1. para
2. para
3. para
4. por
5. por
6. por

G. ¿Cuál te gusta?

What are your preferences? Choose one item from each group. Then choose a partner and ask and answer questions about what you like.

Primero, escoge tu cosa favorita de cada grupo. Luego, con un compañero de clase, conversa sobre sus gustos. Lee el modelo.

Modelo: A. ¿Cuál te gusta, este disco o aquel disco?
B: Me gusta ese disco. A ti, ¿cuál te gusta?
A: Me gusta aquel disco.

Have volunteers create more sample conversations for the class.

1. 

3. 

2. 

4. 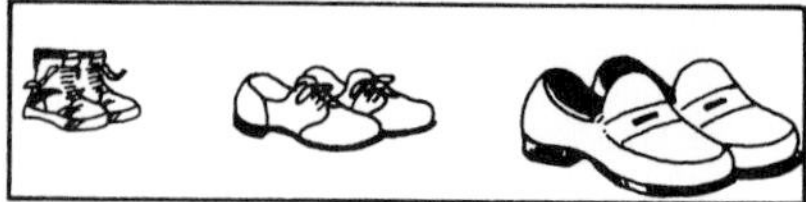

H. En el buzón

Guillermo has sent you some photos of his vacation. He didn't have time to write you a letter, so he wrote some information on the back of each picture.

Lee los párrafos y contesta las preguntas.

Have students read the paragraphs for comprehension before answering the questions.

Fuimos a la playa. Saqué fotos de estos pelícanos. Volaron muy cerca de la playa. ¿Sacaste tú algunas fotos en tus vacaciones? ¿Miraste los animales?

Fuimos de compras en una joyería. El vendedor no nos habló mucho. Compré un collar para mi mamá. ¿Qué compraste en tus vacaciones?

Mi tío Víctor nos invitó a su granja por un día. ¡Qué miedo me dio este toro! ¿A ti te dan miedo los toros? ¿Fuiste a una granja el agosto pasado?

Extension: Have students write different imaginary postcards using the photos on this page.

Unidad 10

After completing this unit, students should be able to:

- name different sports and the people who participate in them
- make comparisons by using the irregular forms of **bueno** and **malo** **(mejor, peor)**
- describe something emphatically by adding the absolute superlative endings **(-ísimo, -ísima)** to adjectives
- read about and discuss the popularity of soccer in Spanish-speaking countries and the importance of the World Cup tournament.

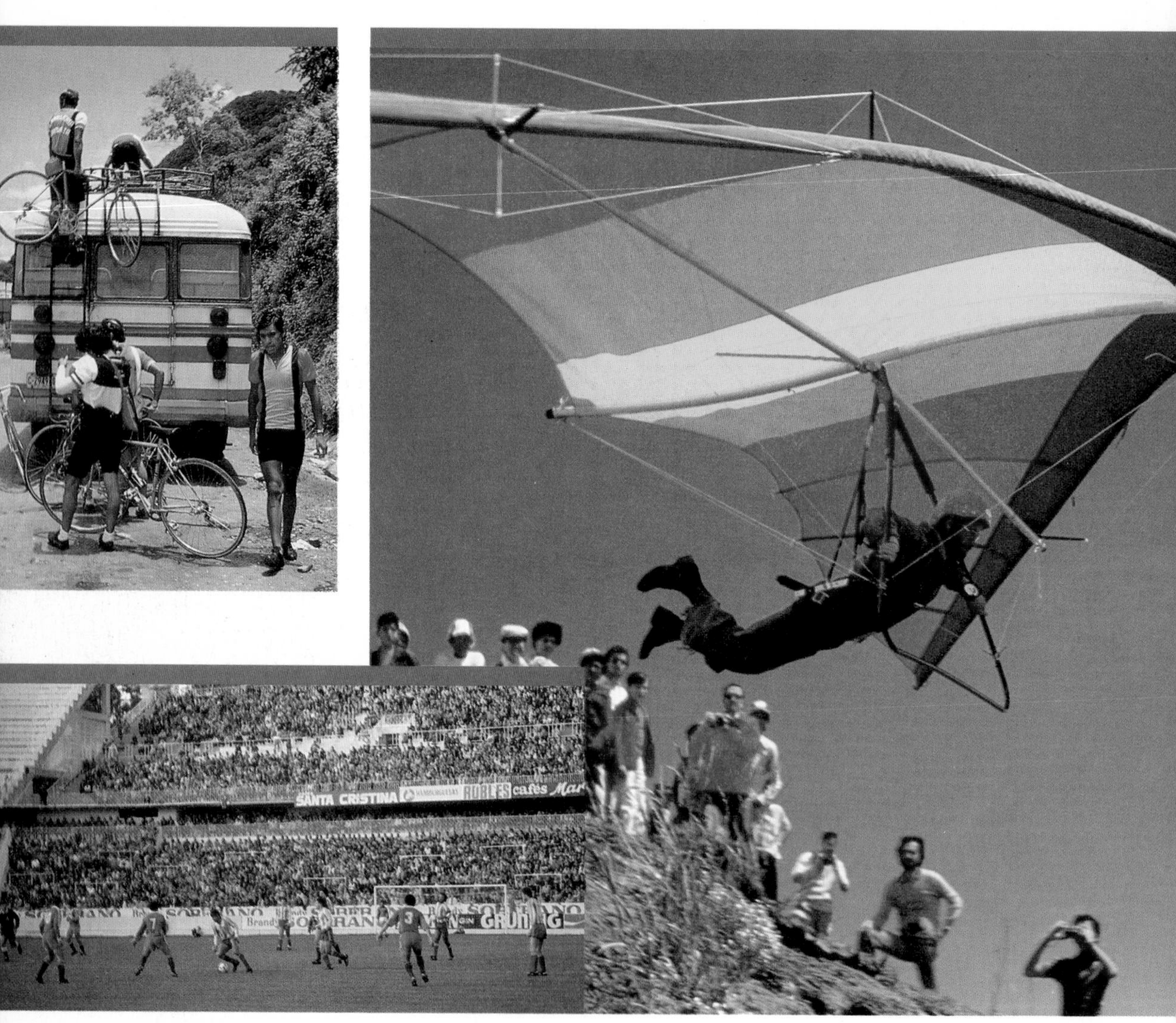

The photographs may be used for informal assessment or review:

- Señala a unos espectadores. ¿Qué hacen los espectadores?
- ¿Qué ganó la joven?
- ¿Qué hacen los ciclistas?
- ¿Vuela el hombre? ¿Participaste en este deporte peligroso el año pasado?
- ¿Fuiste a un estadio la semana pasada? ¿Por qué?

Panorama de vocabulario

Vamos a ver los deportes

gritar

los espectadores

el salto de altura

perder

ganar

la pista

una carrera

Give examples of the verbs used in context and help students conclude that **ganar** and **gritar** are regular **-ar** verbs and that **perder** is a stem-changing verb in the present tense but regular in the preterite.

You may wish to read aloud the following "story" as though a sports announcer were broadcasting the event.

Tenemos una carrera emocionante. La pista está seca y dura. Los atletas están corriendo muy rápido. Los espectadores gritan a sus atletas favoritos. Vamos a ver . . . ¡Javier gana la carrera! Ganó fácilmente. Los otros atletas perdieron y ahora están tristes. ¡Fue la carrera más emocionante del año!

Use examples from athletic events in your school or examples from recent regional and national competitions to present the term **la campeona,** as contrasted with **el campeón.**

los boxeadores

el boxeo

los ciclistas

el ciclismo

los alpinistas

el alpinismo

el boliche

In Spain, **jugar a los bolos** is used for **el boliche.**

la natación

el trofeo

In South America, mountain climbing is **el andinismo** and mountain climbers are **andinistas**—after the Andes Mountains.

¡Aprende el vocabulario!

A. Jorge and Pedro are going to the Olympics! They know exactly which events they want to watch. What will they see?

Primero, mira el dibujo. Luego, contesta la pregunta **¿Qué van a ver?** Sigue el modelo.

Modelo:

Respuesta: Van a ver el salto de altura.

1. Van a ver el boxeo.
2. Van a ver el ciclismo.
3. Van a ver la carrera.
4. Van a ver la gimnasia.
5. Van a ver la natación.
6. Van a ver la lucha libre.

1.

3.

5.

2.

4.

6.

Extension: Continue by asking students if they like to watch the sports pictured in the exercise (e.g., **¿Te gusta ver las carreras?**).

B. Which do you prefer, being a spectator or a participant?

Primero, lee el nombre del deporte. Luego, expresa si prefieres ser espectador o prefieres participar. Sigue el modelo.

Modelo: las carreras en pista
Respuesta: **Prefiero ser espectador (espectadora).**
[Prefiero participar.]

1. la lucha libre
2. el boliche
3. la natación
4. el salto de altura
5. el alpinismo
6. la gimnasia
7. el boxeo
8. el ciclismo

Answers will vary. Encourage students to express their opinions by adding to the answers (e.g., **No me gusta la lucha libre. Juego al boliche todos los sábados.**). Point out that **prefiero** comes from the infinitive **preferir**.

C. Porfirio Pomposo thinks he knows everything. Sometimes he makes the most outrageous statements. Of course, he's usually wrong!

Primero, lee la oración. Si la oración es correcta, escribe **sí** en un papel. Si la oración es incorrecta, cambia la oración para hacerla correcta. Sigue los modelos.

If necessary, do the first two sentences with the class to make sure students understand what is expected of them.

Modelo: A los ganadores les gusta perder.
Respuesta: **A los ganadores les gusta ganar.**
[A los ganadores no les gusta perder.]

Modelo: Los boxeadores participan en el boliche.
Respuesta: **Los boxeadores participan en el boxeo.**

See Unit Plans, Unidad 10, for answers to exercise C.

1. El campeón recibe una medalla de bronce.
2. Necesitas una bicicleta para practicar el alpinismo.

3. A veces los ganadores reciben un trofeo.
4. Tienes que ser muy atlético para la gimnasia.
5. Los alpinistas practican su deporte en el mar.
6. Si sabes nadar, puedes participar en la lucha libre.
7. Los ciclistas necesitan tener piernas fuertes.
8. Si eres boxeador, practicas en una pista.
9. Los espectadores nunca gritan.
10. Tienes que perder todas las carreras para ser campeón.

You may wish to assign this activity as homework after completing it orally in class.

D. We all know that exercise is important for good health. What are your exercise habits?

Primero, lee cada pregunta. Luego, escribe la respuesta en una hoja de papel.

1. ¿Practicas un deporte? ¿Cuál?
2. ¿Prefieres ser espectador o prefieres participar en los deportes?
3. ¿Cuál es tu deporte favorito?
4. ¿Qué deporte practicas en el verano?
5. ¿Cuál practicas en el invierno?
6. ¿Participas en un deporte con tu familia? ¿En cuál?
7. ¿Prefieres los deportes de verano o los deportes de invierno? ¿Por qué?
8. ¿Tienes una medalla o un trofeo? ¿En qué?
9. ¿Juegas con un equipo? ¿Cuál?
10. ¿Qué es más difícil, ganar o perder?

Extension: Have students choose three or four questions and practice interviewing each other. Have them take notes and write reports on the interviews. The written reports can be assigned as homework.

Los sonidos del idioma

Las consonantes: **tr**

Escucha y repite.

trofeo	contrato	entra
triste	estrecho	pupitre
truco	Patricia	teatro
triunfar	eléctrico	patrón

1. Hoy entregan los trofeos en el teatro.
2. El electricista está triste con ese contrato.
3. Patricia trae la pintura para los pupitres.
4. Tres tristes tigres comen tres tristes platos de trigo.

Students should strive for a single-tap sound of **ere** in the **tr** combination. Be alert to a tendency to pronounce the letter **r** as the English **r.**

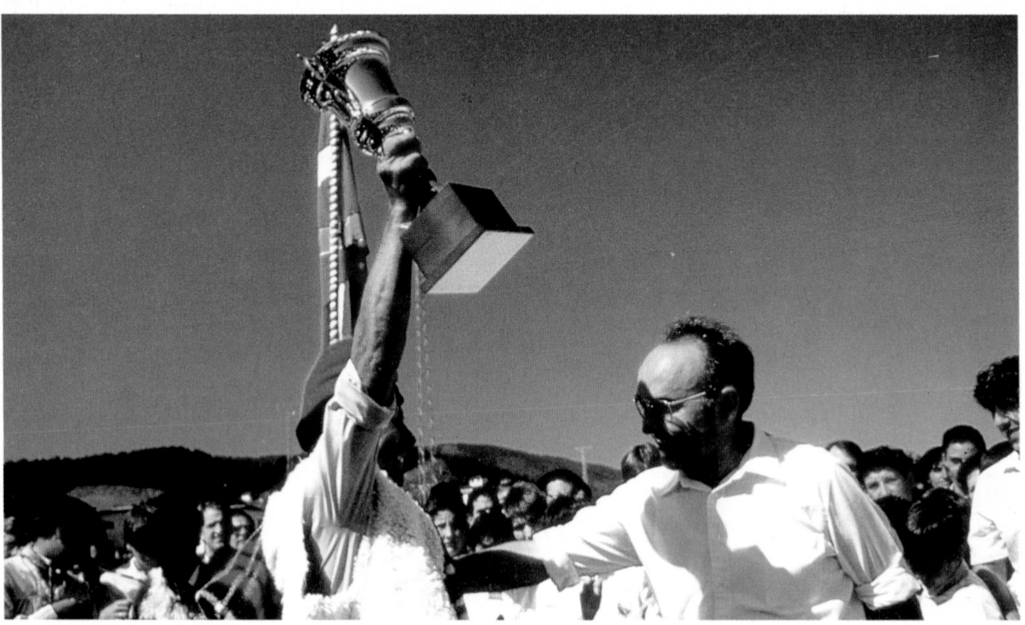

¿Qué gana el campeón?

Have students make up a brief conversation between the champion and the judge **(el juez)**.

Usando el español

Making Comparisons

Rule: To say one person or thing is better or worse than another, you use **mejor que** or **peor que.** To compare more than two, you use **el (la) mejor,** or **el (la) peor.**

Study the pictures and read the sentences below them.

Yo soy **buena** en gimnasia.

Rosa es **mejor que** yo.

Inés es **la mejor.**

Have volunteers read the sample sentences aloud. Make sure the class understands the degrees of comparison.

Recall comparisons you have made using **más . . . que** and **el** or **la más.** Does the adjective **bueno** stay the same or does it change for each degree of comparison? Do you use the word **más**?

[The adjective **bueno** changes to the word **mejor.** No, you do not use the word **más.**]

Study the following chart.

	Comparative	Superlative
bueno (-a)	mejor . . . que	el (la) mejor
malo (-a)	peor . . . que	el (la) peor

You may wish to use examples and exercises from Unidad 9 of *Ya converso más* to review the regular degrees of comparison.

Practice reading the following sentences:

1. Juana es **mala** en matemáticas. Luisa es **peor que** Juana. María es **la peor.**
2. Hugo es **bueno** en historia. David es **mejor que** Hugo. Paco es **el mejor.**
3. Estas fresas son **buenas.** Esas fresas son **mejores.** Aquellas fresas son **las mejores.**

Help students note that **mejor** and **peor** do not change in the feminine, but the superlative form uses **el** and **la** to indicate gender.

How does the word **mejor** change when it refers to more than one? How would **peor** change in the plural form?

[The word **mejor** changes to **mejores** when it refers to more than one. **Peor** would change to **peores** in the plural.]

¡Vamos a practicar!

A. Celia loves to listen to her aunts and uncles trying to outdo one another. If one is bad, the other is worse! If one is good, the other is better!

Primero, lee la oración. Luego, forma otra oración con **mejor . . . que** o **peor . . . que.** Sigue el modelo.

Extension: Have students work in pairs to create other comparisons.

Modelo: Soy bueno en el boliche.
Respuesta: **¡Soy mejor en el boliche que tú!**

1. Soy buena en la natación.
2. Soy malo en el alpinismo.
3. Soy mala en la gimnasia.
4. Soy bueno en el ciclismo.

1. ¡Soy mejor en la natación que tú!
2. ¡Soy peor en el alpinismo que tú!
3. ¡Soy peor en la gimnasia que tú!
4. ¡Soy mejor en el ciclismo que tú!

B. Celia's grandparents usually win all the arguments, though.

Primero, lee las oraciones. Luego, completa la tercera oración con **el (la) mejor** o **el (la) peor.** Sigue el modelo.

Have students answer according to the gender of the names in each group of sentences.

Modelo: Hugo es bueno en boliche. David es mejor. Pero, yo soy ——. ¡Gané un trofeo!

Respuesta: **Pero, yo soy el mejor.**

1. la mejor.
2. el peor.
3. la peor.
4. el mejor.

1. Carmen es buena en las carreras. Elena es mejor. Pero, yo soy ——. ¡Gané una medalla de oro!

2. Jaime es malo en lucha libre. Paco es peor. Pero, yo soy ——. ¡Perdí el campeonato!

3. Éster es mala en el salto de altura. Marta es peor. Pero, yo soy ——. ¡Perdí una medalla de bronce!

4. Enrique es bueno en boxeo. Miguel es mejor. Pero, yo soy ——. ¡Gané el campeonato!

◐ C. Jorge Luis is new in your area. Help him find the best places, things, and people. You may wish to assign this activity as homework.

Primero, lee las oraciones. Luego, forma otra oración con **el (la) mejor** o **los (las) mejores.** Sigue el modelo.

Modelo: Me dicen que estos gimnasios son buenos.

Respuesta: **Sí, pero esos gimnasios son los mejores.**

1. Me dicen que estos teatros son buenos.

2. Me dicen que esta clase es buena.

3. Me dicen que estas pistas son buenas.

4. Me dicen que estos médicos son buenos.

5. Me dicen que este restaurante es bueno.

6. Me dicen que estas zapaterías son buenas.

1. Sí, pero esos teatros son los mejores.
2. Sí, pero esa clase es la mejor.
3. Sí, pero esas pistas son las mejores.
4. Sí, pero esos médicos son los mejores.
5. Sí, pero ese restaurante es el mejor.
6. Sí, pero esas zapaterías son las mejores.

After students complete the exercise, ask volunteers to read the statements and answers as brief conversations.

D. A reporter from **El Preguntón Nacional** wants to know your opinion about people, places, and things.

Lee y contesta las preguntas en tus palabras.

1. En tu opinión, ¿cuál atleta es el mejor?
2. ¿Cuál atleta es el peor?
3. En tu opinión, ¿qué restaurante es el mejor?
4. ¿Qué restaurante es el peor?
5. En tu opinión, ¿qué hamburguesa es la mejor?
6. ¿Qué hamburguesa es la peor?
7. En tu opinión, ¿qué programa de televisión es el mejor?
8. ¿Qué programa de televisión es el peor?

Extension: Have students use these questions to interview each other. They may write reports on their interviews and present them to the class.

Students should use the visual clues to guess the meaning of the expression **mejor tarde que nunca.**

¡A divertirnos!

Have students draw pictures of different situations that would illustrate the expression.

Una expresión sabia

Emphasizing the Nature of Things

Rule: The ending **-ísimo** gives an adjective the same meaning as **muy** ——.

Study the following pictures and read the sentences below them. What ending can you use to say that something is "very . . ."?

Have volunteers read the sample sentences aloud.

Este jugo es **muy bueno.** ¡Es **buenísimo**!

Esta historia es **muy importante.** ¡Es **importantísima**!

Los problemas son muy **difíciles.** ¡Son **dificilísimos**!

Estas sillas son muy **duras.** ¡Son **durísimas**!

What ending can you add to **bueno** to make it mean **muy bueno**? What ending can you add to **importante** to make it mean **muy importante**? What ending can you add to **difíciles** to make it mean **muy difíciles**? What ending can you add to **duras** to make it mean **muy duras**?

[You can add the ending **-ísimo.** You can add the endings **-ísimo** or **ísima.** You can add the ending **-ísimos.** You can add the ending **-ísimas.**]

Study the following "equations":

alto	−	o	+	ísimo	=	altísimo
alta	−	a	+	ísima	=	altísima
altos	−	os	+	ísimos	=	altísimos
altas	−	as	+	ísimas	=	altísimas

Demonstrate the "equations" on the chalkboard by writing an adjective, erasing the final vowel, and adding **-ísimo** or **-ísima.**

fácil			+	ísimo	=	facilísimo
fácil			+	ísima	=	facilísima
fáciles	−	es	+	ísimos	=	facilísimos
fáciles	−	es	+	ísimas	=	facilísimas

What do you do before you add **-ísimo** or **-ísima** to an adjective that ends in a vowel? [You drop the final vowel before adding **-ísimo** or **-ísima.**]

What do you do before you add **-ísimo** or **-ísima** to an adjective that ends in a consonant? What happened to the accent over the **a** in **fácil** when **-ísimo** was added?

[You simply add the **-ísimo** or **-ísima** ending to the adjective. The accent over the **a** in **fácil** is dropped.]

Not all adjectives can be changed this way. The following are examples of some that can.

alto	**altísimo**	duro	**durísimo**
bajo	**bajísimo**	importante	**importantísimo**
delgado	**delgadísimo**	interesante	**interesantísimo**
generoso	**generosísimo**	difícil	**dificilísimo**
blando	**blandísimo**	fácil	**facilísimo**
cansado	**cansadísimo**	nervioso	**nerviosísimo**

¡Vamos a practicar!

A. Josefina always exaggerates. Whenever you say something, she always exaggerates it. What does she say?

Primero, lee la oración. Luego, cambia la oración. Sigue el modelo.

1. ¡Esta novela es malísima!
2. ¡Estos asientos son durísimos!
3. ¡Este hombre es delgadísimo!
4. ¡Estas fresas son buenísimas!
5. ¡Esta mujer is bajísima!
6. ¡Estos niños son generosísimos!

Modelo: Esta película es buena.

Respuesta: **¡Esta película es buenísima!**

1. Esta novela es mala.
2. Estos asientos son duros.
3. Este hombre es delgado.
4. Estas fresas son buenas.
5. Esta mujer es baja.
6. Estos niños son generosos.

Extension: Continue by making statements and having the class respond with a superlative (e.g., **La clase de español es interesante. ¡La clase de español es interesantísima!**).

B. A reporter is taking a survey of how students feel about their classes. How do you respond?

Answers will vary. You may wish to assign this activity as homework.

Primero, lee el nombre de la clase. Luego, escoge una palabra de la lista para describir la clase. Por último, escribe una oración. Sigue el modelo.

Extension: Have students role-play a dialogue between a reporter asking questions about classes and a student.

Modelo: la historia

Respuesta: **La historia es interesantísima.**

1. las ciencias
2. el inglés
3. la salud
4. la geografía
5. el español
6. las matemáticas

facilísimo.......................... dificilísimo

interesantísimo............... aburridísimo

C. You have been asked to participate in an opinion poll. For each category, name one thing you like or don't like and another thing you like or don't like very much.

Primero, lee las categorías. Luego, escribe dos oraciones. Lee el modelo. (Si necesitas ayuda, lee las listas de palabras.)

Categorías

1. Los libros
2. Los deportes
3. Las clases
4. Los programas de televisión

Modelo: **1.** a. Los libros de aventuras son interesantes.
b. Las novelas son interesantísimas.
2. a. El ciclismo es fácil.
b. El boliche es facilísimo.

Etcétera.

Extension: Ask volunteers to chart their classmates' opinions and present the results to the class.

importante	difícil	aburrido
interesante	bueno	fascinante
fácil	malo	emocionante

¿Son estas cosas buenísimas para tu salud?

Ask students: **¿Qué es buenísimo para la salud? ¿Qué es malísimo?**

¡A conversar!

La locura por ganar

LUPE: ¡Ay! Soy mala en todos los deportes.

RUDY: ¡No es cierto! Tú eres buena en muchos deportes. Por ejemplo, eres buena en la natación.

LUPE: ¡Mentiras! Amalia es mejor que yo y Berta es la mejor.

RUDY: Pues, eres buena ciclista. Ganaste una medalla.

LUPE: Sí, pero gané una medalla de bronce. Celia ganó la de plata y Enrique ganó el trofeo. Los dos son mejores que yo.

RUDY: Lupe, tú no quieres ser buena en los deportes; tú quieres ser la mejor. ¿No sabes que es más importante jugar bien?

LUPE: Sí, pero es más divertido ganar. Es aburridísimo perder.

RUDY: ¡Ay, Lupe, tú sí eres la mejor en locura! ¡Te doy una medalla de oro por estar muy loca!

Enrichment: Hold a class discussion about attitudes toward winning and **la locura por ganar.**

Preguntas

Encourage students to give complete answers.

1. ¿Quién es mejor que Lupe en la natación?
2. ¿Es buena ciclista Lupe?
3. ¿Quién ganó un trofeo?
4. En realidad, ¿qué quiere ser Lupe?
5. ¿Por qué Rudy le va a dar una medalla de oro a Lupe?

1. Amalia y Berta son mejores que Lupe en la natación.
2. Sí, Lupe es buena ciclista. Ganó una medalla.
3. Enrique ganó el trofeo.
4. Lupe quiere ser la mejor en los deportes.
5. Rude le va a dar una medalla por estar muy loca.

Continue by asking more questions about the conversation.

¡Conversa tú!

1. ¿Eres bueno en los deportes?
2. En general, ¿te gusta participar en los deportes? ¿Por qué?
3. ¿Es aburridísimo perder? ¿Tiene razón Lupe?
4. ¿Qué es más importante—correr bien o ganar la carrera?
5. ¿Qué piensas de la locura por ganar?
6. ¿A quién le quieres dar un trofeo por ser el mejor amigo?

Have students use the questions to interview each other. You may wish to have volunteers present the results of their interviews to the class.

Enrichment: Have students research the results of the most recent Pan American Games or world championships and present the results to the class.

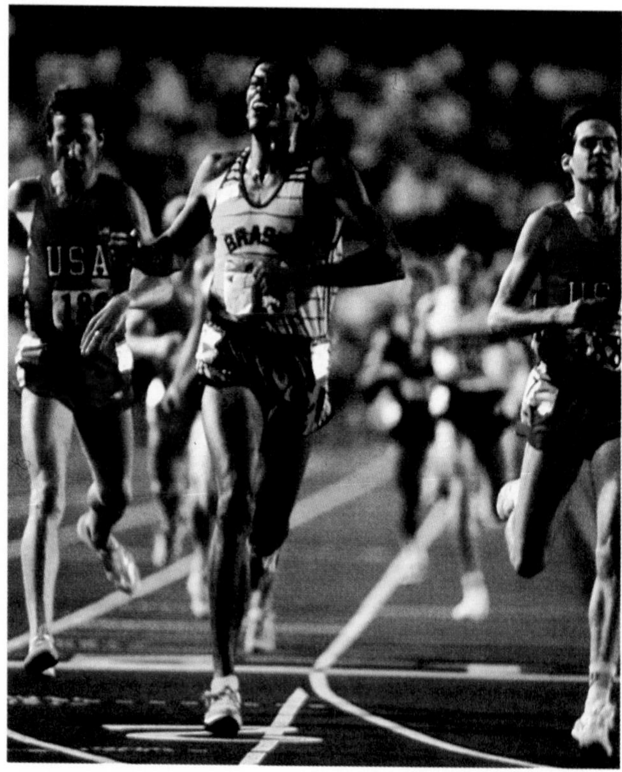

¿Va a ganar la carrera este hombre?

La cultura y tú

See Unit Plans, Unidad 10, for additional information.

El deporte más popular

¿Cuál es el deporte más popular de los Estados Unidos? ¿Es el fútbol americano? ¿Es el béisbol? En los países hispanos, el fútbol es el deporte más popular. A las personas de todas edades les gusta mirar los partidos profesionales de fútbol.

Aquí los espectadores compran billetes en el estadio para ver a su equipo favorito.

Cada cuatro años los mejores equipos nacionales de los países hispanos y de los países por todo el mundo juegan en un torneo que se llama la Copa Mundial. El equipo ganador es el mejor del mundo.

Enrichment: Many Spanish-language television stations broadcast soccer games. Have students watch part of a soccer game on a Spanish-language channel at home and discuss what they saw in class.

Pero a las personas les gusta ser jugadores y no sólo espectadores. Después de la escuela o en los fines de semana, muchos jóvenes juegan al fútbol con sus equipos.

If you have the facilities available, record part of a soccer game on a Spanish-language station and show it in class.

Unidad

11

After completing this unit, students should be able to:

- ▶ name people and activities associated with the performing arts
- ▶ use irregular verbs to give affirmative and negative familiar commands or instructions
- ▶ talk about past actions using the preterite tense of the irregular verbs **decir** and **traer**
- ▶ read about and discuss a musical instrument from Venezuela and a folk dance from Mexico.

The photographs may be used for informal assessment or review:

- ► Toca una orquesta. ¿Cómo es la orquesta?
- ► ¿Cómo son los bailarines españoles? ¿Llevan trajes bonitos?
- ► ¿Cómo es el teatro? ¿Asistes mucho al teatro?
- ► ¿Qué tocan los músicos? ¿Hay una guitarra eléctrica?
- ► ¿Te pones ropa elegante para ir al teatro? Muéstrame una foto de personas que llevan ropa elegante.

Panorama de vocabulario

Vamos al teatro

Note: In popular music, **la batería** is used instead of **el tambor.**

Students might be interested in learning other terms related to music: **la sinfonía** (symphony), **la banda** (band), **el conjunto** (musical group), **la trompeta** (trumpet), **el trombón** (trombone), **el saxofón** (saxophone), **el xilófono** (xylophone).

Enrichment: Have students research the origins of some words for musical instruments. This may lead to a class discussion of how languages evolve and borrow from one another.

Point out to students the spelling change in the plural of **actriz** (i.e., **actrices**). Have students name other words that have this spelling change (e.g., **lápiz, lápices; vez, veces; pez, peces**).

You may wish to teach other words related to the theater: **la comedia** (comedy), **el drama** (drama, play), **la tragedia** (tragedy), **el programa de variedades** (variety show). You may write these categories on the chalkboard and have students list the people who might be involved in each one.

asistir al teatro

reírse

aplaudir

llorar

Point out that **asistir, llorar,** and **aplaudir** are regular verbs; **reírse** is irregular.

Note: Traditionally in Spain, there have always been two theater performances: the "afternoon" show at 7:30 P.M. and the "evening" show at 10:30 P.M.

¡Aprende el vocabulario!

A. The Méndez family is very talented. Everyone is involved in the theater or in music.

Primero, lee la oración y mira el dibujo. Luego, completa la oración. Sigue el modelo.

Modelo: La Sra. Méndez es  .

Respuesta: **La Sra. Méndez es actriz.**

1. el clarinete
2. el tambor
3. actor
4. el piano
5. el violín
6. bailarina
7. la guitarra
8. cantante

1. El Sr. Méndez toca  .

2. Luis toca  .

3. Jaime es  .

4. Olga toca   .

5. José toca  .

6. Iris es .

7. Paco toca  .

8. María es  .

Extension: Ask students if they play musical instruments or take part in school performances. Have them make up rebus sentences about themselves and their friends or classmates.

B. Ernestina is trying to tell you about some people she knows, but she can't remember the names of their jobs. Help her out.

Primero, lee la oración. Luego, escribe una oración con la palabra correcta. Sigue el modelo.

Modelo: Pedro trabaja en la televisión y habla muy bien.
Respuesta: **Es locutor.**

1. El Sr. Pardo lee la música y trabaja con la orquesta, pero no toca un instrumento.
2. Jorge sabe cantar muy bien.
3. Pablo y Juan tocan el tambor.
4. A Rosa le encanta hablar y tiene un programa de radio.
5. José baila muy bien.
6. Aurelia hace un papel en una obra de teatro.

1. Es director.
2. Es cantante.
3. Son músicos.
4. Es locutora.
5. Es bailarín.
6. Es actriz.

Extension: Have students make up riddles for each other. They may give a description or the name of a famous entertainer and challenge classmates to guess what the person does.

A este muchacho le gusta mucho la música. Cada día practica con su violín. ¿Tocas tú un instrumento? ¿Te gusta la música?

C. Angélica has taken her notebook to the school talent show. She wants to remember everything that happens. Unfortunately, she doesn't remember all the words she needs.

Primero, lee la oración. Luego, escoge la palabra o las palabras que van con la oración. Sigue el modelo.

Modelo: Esta noche voy a (hacer, asistir) al teatro.
Respuesta: **Esta noche voy a asistir al teatro.**

1. La orquesta
2. Los músicos
3. llorar
4. aplauden
5. cantantes
6. reírse

1. (La orquesta, La actriz) toca música bonita.
2. (Los actores, Los músicos) tocan muy bien.
3. Empiezo a (llorar, reírme) cuando tocan una canción muy triste.
4. Después de la canción, las personas (lloran, aplauden) mucho.
5. Luego vienen dos (cantantes, bailarines) para cantar canciones españolas.
6. También son muy divertidos los tres bailarines cómicos. Las personas comienzan a (sentarse, reírse).

D. Your local newspaper has asked you to write a review of a play, concert, or television program you have seen.

Piensa en una obra de teatro, un concierto o un programa de televisión. Escribe por lo menos cinco oraciones. Primero, lee el modelo.

Enrichment: Collect students' reviews for a classroom Big Book.

Modelo: Acabo de ver "Un día en la playa." Asistí al teatro con mi mamá. Es una obra de teatro muy buena. Tino Torres hace el papel de Marcos, el cantante. ¡El Sr. Torres es el mejor actor del mundo! Algunas veces me hace llorar. Otras veces me hace reír. Después de la obra, todas las personas aplaudieron mucho.

Before doing this exercise, choose a TV program or film that all or most of the students have seen.

Ask questions about the actors, the story, the music, etc., to elicit information and opinions.

Los sonidos del idioma

Las consonantes: La **x**

Escucha y repite.

éxito	sexto
excelente	reflexión
examen	máximo
extranjero	saxófono

In most cases, the consonant **x** may be pronounced as it is in English. In some regions, however, **x** has the sound of **s**, as in **especial**.

Extension: Have students find examples of the letter **x** pronounced as a **j** (i.e., **México, Oaxaca, Ximena**).

1. El éxito del saxofonista fue máximo.
2. Silvia dio un excelente examen en el sexto grado.
3. El extranjero vive en el extremo sur de Extremadura.
4. Sixto tiene gustos extraños y extravagantes.

Help students guess the meaning of **traje** in this context as "costume."

Los bailarines son de San Antonio, en Texas. Llevan trajes muy bonitos.

Extension: Have students write three questions about the photo for their classmates to answer.

Usando el español

Giving Commands and Instructions

Rule: The familiar command forms of the following verbs are irregular in both the affirmative and the negative: **poner, tener, venir, decir, hacer, ir, salir,** and **dar.**

In the following pictures and sentences are examples of some commands.

Pon la silla aquí, por favor.

¡**No pongas** la silla sobre el gato!

Haz el vestido más pequeño, por favor.

¡**No hagas** el vestido tan pequeño!

Have volunteers read the sample sentences aloud. Students should use the visual cues to understand the meanings of the commands.

Poner and **hacer** are irregular verbs. Would you say their familiar command forms are regular or irregular? [Their familiar command forms are irregular.]

Study the following command forms of some irregular verbs.

	Affirmative	Negative
poner	**pon**	no **pongas**
tener	**ten**	no **tengas**
venir	**ven**	no **vengas**
decir	**di**	no **digas**
hacer	**haz**	no **hagas**
ir	**ve**	no **vayas**
salir	**sal**	no **salgas**
dar	**da**	no **des**

Have volunteers read the sample sentences aloud, with feeling.

Practice reading examples of these commands in sentences:

1. **Pon** tus libros en la mesa. ¡No los **pongas** sobre mis cartas!
2. **Ten** cuidado con el vaso de cristal. Es delicadísimo.
3. No **tengas** miedo del monstruo, Pepito. Es una película nada más.
4. ¡**Ven** acá, Jorge! Quiero hacerte una pregunta importante.
5. Siempre **di** la verdad. Nunca **digas** mentiras.
6. ¡No **salgas** por esa puerta! Acabo de pintarla.
7. No **vayas** al concierto. El concierto es malísimo.
8. **Dame** la mano, Paquita. Hay mucho tráfico.
9. **Hazles** la pregunta ahora. ¡**Hazla** ahora mismo!
10. ¡**Dime** el secreto! Lo quiero saber.

How observant are you?

In sentences 8, 9, and 10, where does the indirect object go when you use it with an affirmative command? In sentence 9, where does the direct object go when you use it with an affirmative command?

In sentence 1, where does the direct object go when you use it with a negative command? Do you connect it to the negative command to make one word?

[The indirect object is connected to the affirmative command. The direct object is connected to the affirmative command. / In a negative command, the direct object goes before the verb. No, you do not connect it to the negative command to make one word.]

¡Vamos a practicar!

A. Josué is the student director of the school play. He loves to give orders. What does he tell the actors and actresses to do?

Primero, lee la oración y la palabra entre paréntesis. Luego, escribe la oración. Sigue el modelo.

Modelo: Rita, (poner) los vasos en aquella mesa.
Respuesta: **Rita, pon los vasos en aquella mesa.**

1. Hugo, (venir) al centro.
2. Sara, (salir) por la puerta a la izquierda.
3. Inés, (ir) a la puerta.
4. Samuel, (poner) el teléfono cerca de Rita.
5. Inés, (decir) las palabras.
6. Hugo, (hacer) la pregunta.
7. Samuel, (tener) miedo de Hugo.
8. Sara (dar) una vuelta al sofá.

1. Hugo, ven al centro.
2. Sara, sal por la puerta a la izquierda.
3. Inés, ve a la puerta.
4. Samuel, pon el teléfono cerca de Rita.
5. Inés, di las palabras.
6. Hugo, haz la pregunta.
7. Samuel, ten miedo de Hugo.
8. Sara, da una vuelta al sofá.

Extension: Have students repeat the exercise, this time making all the commands negative.

B. All day long, people have told you what not to do. What have they been saying?

Primero, lee la oración. Luego, completa la oración con la forma apropiada de la palabra entre paréntesis. Sigue el modelo.

Modelo: No —— los zapatos sucios sobre la mesa. (poner)
Respuesta: **No pongas los zapatos sucios sobre la mesa.**

1. No les —— helados a los niños. (dar)
2. No me —— una mentira. (decir)
3. No —— afuera después de las seis. (salir)
4. No —— miedo de hablar en público. (tener)
5. No —— al cine con tus amigos. (ir)
6. No —— al gimnasio sin tus zapatos. (venir)
7. No les —— preguntas a personas que no conoces. (hacer)
8. No —— los pies sobre el pupitre. (poner)

1. des
2. digas
3. salgas
4. tengas
5. vayas
6. vengas
7. hagas
8. pongas

Extension: Have students change the commands in the exercise to the affirmative.

C. Sra. Cambia can't seem to make up her mind today. She says one thing and then she says something else two seconds later!

Primero, lee la oración. Luego, cambia la oración a la forma negativa. Por último, escribe la oración. Sigue los modelos. You may wish to assign this activity as written homework after presenting it in class.

Modelo: Hazle la pregunta a Juan.
Respuesta: **No le hagas la pregunta a Juan.**

Modelo: Ven a mi escritorio.
Respuesta: **No vengas a mi escritorio.**

Extension: Have students choose partners and create conflicting commands.

1. Dame tu cuaderno.
2. Ponlo en mi escritorio.
3. Dime la respuesta.
4. Hazme una pregunta.
5. Ven a la pizarra.
6. Sal del salón de clase.
7. Ve a la oficina.
8. Ten miedo del examen.

1. No me des tu cuaderno.
2. No lo pongas en mi escritorio.
3. No me digas la respuesta.
4. No me hagas una pregunta.
5. No vengas a la pizarra.
6. No salgas del salón de clase.
7. No vayas a la oficina.
8. No tengas miedo del examen.

D. Your friends need your advice. What do you tell them?

Primero, lee las oraciones. Luego, escribe una oración. Sigue el modelo.

Answers will vary. Encourage students to make their answers as complete as possible.

Modelo: **Pepita:** Me dan miedo las películas de ciencia ficción.

Respuesta: **No tengas miedo de las películas. [¡No vayas a esas películas! Ve a otras películas.]**

1. **Víctor:** No comprendo la lección.
2. **Rosalba:** Estoy cansada. No quiero ir a la fiesta.
3. **Federico:** No me gusta salir por la noche.
4. **Susana:** No sé qué hacer. Si le digo la verdad, Amalia va a llorar.
5. **Lucho:** No sé qué hacer. Si le doy el regalo a José ahora, no voy a tener nada que darle para la fiesta.
6. **Ana:** Si voy al concierto, mis papás van a estar muy enojados. Pero, quiero ir al concierto.

Possible answers:
1. ¡Hazle preguntas a la maestra!
2. ¡No me digas esto! ¡Ven a la fiesta, por favor!
3. ¡Pues, no salgas!
4. ¡No le digas la verdad a Amalia!
5. ¡Dale el regalo ahora!
6. ¡Diles a tus papás que vas a volver a casa muy temprano!

Talking about Your Actions

Rule: **Traer** and **decir** are irregular in the preterite tense. The endings for both verbs are the same. The **e** changes to an **i** in the stem of **decir** in the preterite.

Study the conjugations of **decir** and **traer** in the preterite tense. Are their forms regular or irregular in the preterite?

Have students look up **decir** and **traer** in the Appendix and compare the preterite forms to the present-tense forms.

Decir

Singular		Plural	
yo	**dije**	nosotros (-as)	**dijimos**
tú	**dijiste**	vosotros (-as)	**dijisteis**
él / ella / usted	**dijo**	ellos / ellas / ustedes	**dijeron**

Traer

Singular		Plural	
yo	**traje**	nosotros (-as)	**trajimos**
tú	**trajiste**	vosotros (-as)	**trajisteis**
él / ella / usted	**trajo**	ellos / ellas / ustedes	**trajeron**

What do these two verbs have in common in the preterite tense?
[Their endings are the same.]

Practice reading the following questions and answers:

Have volunteers read the sample questions and answers aloud.

Pregunta: ¿Qué te **dijo** Rafael?
Respuesta: Me **dijo** que hay un examen mañana.

Pregunta: ¿Qué **trajeron** los Vásquez al teatro?
Respuesta: **Trajeron** sus binoculares.

Pregunta: ¿Qué les **dijeron** ustedes a los músicos?
Respuesta: Les **dijimos** que nos gustó el concierto.

¡Vamos a practicar!

A. Your friends are painfully honest. What did they tell the performers after the show?

This activity may be assigned as homework.

Primero, lee la pregunta. Luego, lee la frase y contesta la pregunta. Sigue el modelo.

Modelo: Luis, ¿qué le dijiste al músico?
(que no me gustó la música)
Respuesta: **Le dije que no me gustó la música.**

1. Alicia, ¿qué le dijiste a la actriz?
(que no me gustó la obra de teatro)
2. Pepe y Marcos, ¿qué le dijeron a la cantante?
(que no nos gustó la canción)
3. Juanita, ¿qué le dijiste al bailarín?
(que no me gustó el baile)
4. Berta y Diana, ¿qué le dijeron al locutor?
(que no nos gustó el programa)

1. Le dije que no me gustó la obra de teatro.
2. Le dijimos que no nos gustó la canción.
3. Le dije que no me gustó el baile.
4. Le dijimos que no nos gustó el programa.

Extension: Ask students to repeat something they said to a friend or family member earlier in the day (e.g., **Le dije a mi mamá que voy a ir al gimnasio a las cuatro.**).

B. The class picnic was last weekend. What did everyone bring? Ask them and find out.

Lee las palabras y forma una pregunta y una respuesta. Sigue el modelo.

Modelo: Francisco (la comida enlatada)

Respuesta: **P: Francisco, ¿qué trajiste?**

R: Traje la comida enlatada.

1. Lupe y Elena (los sándwiches de jamón y queso)
2. Antonio y Alonso (diez galones de limonada)
3. Catalina (cuatro manteles y veinte tenedores)
4. El Sr. Murillo y la Srta. Cano (un abrelatas y tres tortas)
5. Esteban (las manzanas y las naranjas)

1. P: Lupe y Elena, ¿qué trajeron?
   R: Trajimos los sándwiches de jamón y queso.
2. P: Antonio y Alonso, ¿qué trajeron?
   R: Trajimos diez galones de limonada.
3. P: Catalina, ¿qué trajiste?
   R: Traje cuatro manteles y veinte tenedores.
4. P: Sr. Murillo y Srta. Cano, ¿qué trajeron?
   R: Trajimos un abrelatas y tres tortas.
5. P: Esteban, ¿qué trajiste?
   R: Traje las manzanas y las naranjas.

Extension: Ask students what they brought for lunch today.

Esta orquesta es pequeña. ¿Tocaste tú un instrumento en una orquesta alguna vez? ¿Fue pequeña la orquesta? ¿Qué trajiste a los conciertos?

Extension: Have students imagine that they are the leader of a band. As the leader, they should ask the musicians if they brought their instruments. Students may role-play the leader and musicians.

C. How organized are you and your classmates? Did you bring everything you need to Spanish class?

Primero, escribe cinco oraciones sobre las cosas que trajiste a la clase. Luego, lee la lista de un compañero de clase. Pregúntale qué trajo a la clase. Por último, contesta las preguntas de tu compañero sobre lo que trajiste tú a la clase.

Extension: Have students tell the class what their partners brought to class.

D. Imagine that yesterday your teachers were trying to recruit you for school activities. What did you tell the teachers?

Primero, lee la pregunta. Luego, contesta la pregunta en tus palabras. Sigue el modelo.

Modelo: El maestro te preguntó: ¿Quieres cantar en un programa de variedades?

Respuesta: **Le dije que no quiero cantar. [Le dije que sí. Canto muy bien.]**

Answers will vary. Accept responses that contain the correct form of **decir.**

1. La maestra te preguntó: ¿Quieres tocar los tambores en la orquesta?
2. El maestro te preguntó: ¿Quieres ser locutor (locutora) del programa de variedades?
3. El maestro te preguntó: ¿Quieres hacer un papel en la obra de teatro?
4. La maestra te preguntó: ¿Quieres ser cantante en el programa de música?
5. La maestra te preguntó: ¿Quieres bailar en el programa de variedades?

Encourage students to elaborate upon their answers (e.g., **Le dije que no. No sé tocar los tambores, pero sí toco el violín.**).

¡A conversar!

María, la gran actriz

Have volunteers role-play the dialogue for the class.

PAPÁ: Dime, María, ¿qué te dijo tu maestro hoy?

MARÍA: Me dijo que voy a hacer el papel de la mamá en el drama de la escuela.

PAPÁ: ¡Felicitaciones! Pero, ¿sabes hablar como una madre de familia?

MARÍA: Sí, papá. Es facilísimo.

PAPÁ: A ver . . . Dame un ejemplo.

MARÍA: (*como mamá*) ¡No pongas los pies en los muebles! ¡Ven acá y saca la basura! ¡No me digas tonterías! ¡Ten cuidado, niña!

MAMÁ: (*entrando en la sala*) ¿A quién estás hablando, María?

MARÍA: A nadie, mamá. Sólo estoy haciendo el papel de una madre de familia.

MAMÁ: María, las madres nunca hablan así . . . Ahora, sube a tu cuarto y haz tus tareas antes de la cena.

MARÍA: (*a su papá*) ¿No te dije? ¡Hago el papel perfectamente!

Preguntas

Encourage students to answer in complete sentences.

1. El maestro le dijo que va a hacer el papel de la mamá (en el drama de la escuela).

1. ¿Qué le dijo el maestro a María?
2. ¿Qué piensa María del papel que va a hacer?
3. Según María, ¿qué dicen las madres de familia?
4. ¿Quién entra en la sala?
5. ¿Qué le dice la mamá sobre el papel?
6. ¿Cómo hace el papel María?

2. María piensa que es facilísimo hacer el papel.
3. Según María, las madres de familia dicen: ¡No pongas los pies en los muebles! (etc.)
4. La mamá de María entra en la sala.
5. La mamá le dice que las madres nunca hablan así.
6. María hace el papel perfectamente.

¡Conversa tú!

Enrichment: Have students write a paragraph about an instrument they play, a play they have taken part in, or an experience at a concert or a play.

1. ¿Haces un papel en una obra de teatro?
2. ¿Cuántas veces al año asistes al teatro?
3. ¿Prefieres llorar o reírte?
4. ¿Eres actor o músico? ¿Conoces a un actor o a un músico?
5. ¿Tocas un instrumento en la banda o la orquesta? ¿Qué tocas?

Have students find more expressions that use **hacer** in the dictionary. They may enjoy creating pictures to illustrate the expressions.

¡A divertirnos!

Adivina los modismos

1. Haz tu maleta.
2. Haz tu cama.

1. Haz ——.

2. Haz ——.

La cultura y tú

See Unit Plans, Unidad II, for additional information.

Enrichment: Bring a **cuatro** or other traditional Latin American instruments to class. Allow students to examine and play the instruments.

Canciones y bailes

La música es parte de la vida diaria en los países latinos. Cada país tiene instrumentos diferentes que son parte de su folklore.

El cuatro es un instrumento típico de Venezuela. Un cuatro es una guitarra pequeña con sólo cuatro cuerdas, muy similar al "ukulele" de Hawai. En Puerto Rico y la República Dominicana también se usan los cuatros pero son un poco diferentes.

Esta muchacha de la foto toca un cuatro de Venezuela. Para aprender a tocar el cuatro no hay que estudiar música. Casi siempre se aprende "de oído". Esto quiere decir que para aprender, escuchas y miras a una persona que toca un cuatro y luego practicas. Hay manuales para aprender a tocar el cuatro que te enseñan dónde poner los dedos de la mano izquierda para formar los tonos. También te enseñan cómo mover la mano derecha para tocar los ritmos diferentes.

Una vez que aprendes los tonos y cómo mover la mano, puedes tocar muchas canciones diferentes.

Los viejitos

"Los viejitos" es un baile típico mexicano del estado de Michoacán al oeste de la ciudad de México. Allá, la gente baila "los viejitos" en las celebraciones especiales y los festivales religiosos.

"Los viejitos" es un baile cómico. Los bailarines actúan como viejitos que no pueden caminar bien, pero al mismo tiempo son muy atléticos. Los bailarines saltan y hacen acrobacias siguiendo la música. La gente se divierte mucho mirando a los bailarines.

Enrichment: Los viejitos is a complicated dance. You may wish to teach the class a simplified version of a dance such as the **merengue.**

Los bailarines casi siempre son hombres vestidos con la ropa típica del hombre del campo: huaraches, un sarape, un sombrero y un bastón. También usan una máscara rosada para hacer el papel de una persona muy vieja.

Unidad 12

After completing this unit, students should be able to:

- ▶ name things associated with emergencies and ask for help in an emergency
- ▶ talk about past actions using the preterite tense of the irregular verbs **tener, estar, andar,** and **hacer**
- ▶ describe actions by using adverbs that end in **-mente**
- ▶ read a humorous short story
- ▶ read about and discuss medical services in rural areas of Peru and a special group of doctors from the United States.

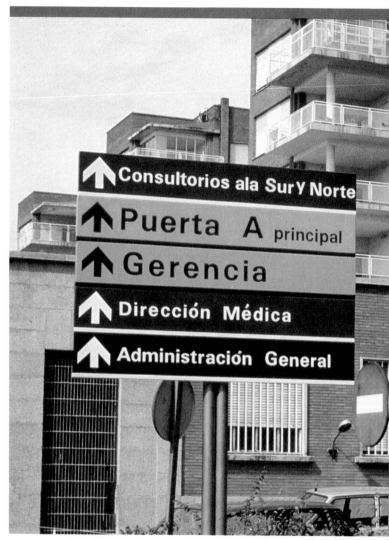

The photographs may be used for informal assessment or review:

- ► Mira la foto al pie de la página 280. ¿Con quién hablan esas personas?
- ► ¿Cómo vas a la recepción de enfermos en este hospital?
- ► ¿Cómo es el hospital? ¿Es moderno? ¿Es grande? ¿Cómo sabes?
- ► ¿Está enfermo el muchacho? ¿Cómo sabes?
- ► Señala una ambulancia. ¿Cuándo necesitas una ambulancia? ¿Estuviste alguna vez en una ambulancia?

Panorama de vocabulario

Note: Another way to say **tener tos** is **toser,** a regular **-er** verb; another way to say **estar enfermo** is **enfermarse,** a regular **-ar** reflexive verb.

Necesitamos ayuda

Students may be interested in learning the verbs **inyectar** and **hacer** or **poner una inyección,** as well as the verbs **atender** and **cuidar.**

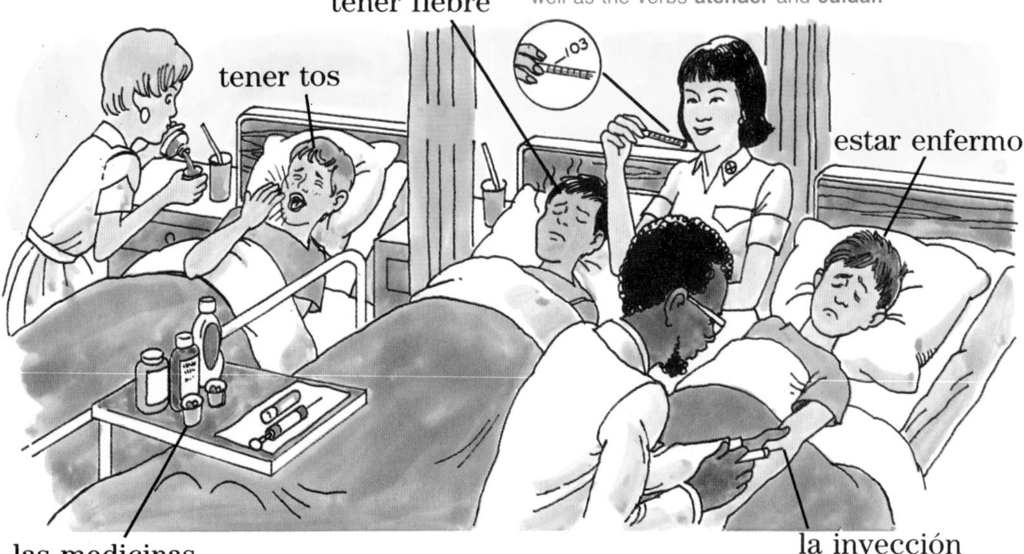

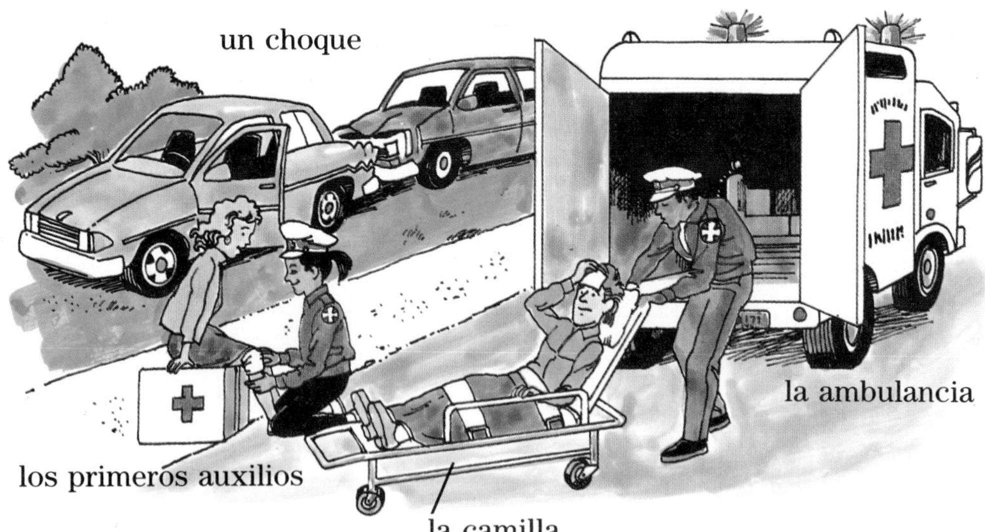

In Spanish there is no equivalent term for paramedic. Often the Red Cross **(la Cruz Roja)** provides ambulance and initial medical services. An alternative term for **un choque** is **un accidente.**

You may wish to review **doler, tener dolor,** and **tener gripe** with this unit.

The feminine form of **el ladrón** is **la ladrona;** the active verb is **robar.** Point out that students should use **tener** as the model for **detener.**

Review words related to fires such as **apagar el incendio** and **los bomberos.**

There are several synonyms for **el extintor: el extinguidor de incendios, el matafuego, el apagaincendios.**

¡Aprende el vocabulario!

A. What a crazy day! Everyone seems to have an emergency.

Primero, mira el dibujo. Luego, lee y completa las oraciones. Sigue el modelo.

Modelo: En una esquina, hay —— entre dos automóviles.

Respuesta: **En una esquina, hay un choque entre dos automóviles.**

1. Hay —— cerca de los automóviles.
2. Una mujer está en ——. Ella va al hospital.
3. Los médicos le dan —— antes de llevarla al hospital.
4. En otra esquina, hay —— pequeño en una cesta.
5. El dueño de una tienda usa —— para apagarlo.
6. También, ¡hay —— en el banco!
7. Dos —— corren del banco con mucho dinero.
8. El cajero grita "¡——!"

1. una ambulancia
2. una camilla
3. los primeros auxilios
4. un incendio
5. un extintor
6. un robo
7. ladrones
8. Auxilio *or* Socorro

Extension: Continue by asking questions (e.g., **¿Dónde hay un incendio? ¿Qué tiene el dueño de la tienda?**).

B. Hipolito is such a hypochondriac. He always thinks he is sick. What problems does he think he has today?

Primero, lee la oración. Luego, completa la oración con la palabra o las palabras apropiadas. Sigue el modelo.

medicinas	enfermo
tos	la camilla
una ambulancia	fiebre
una inyección	auxilios

Modelo: ¡Ay de mí! Estoy malísimo. Estoy muy ——.
Respuesta: **Estoy muy enfermo.**

1. Tengo una temperatura de cien grados. Tengo ——.
2. No puedo hablar mucho porque tengo ——.
3. Necesito muchas ——.
4. Quiero ir al hospital en ——.
5. Voy a acostarme en ——. Estoy muy débil y no puedo caminar.
6. No estoy bien, pero no quiero ——. Tengo miedo porque siempre me duele el brazo.

1. fiebre
2. tos
3. medicinas
4. una ambulancia
5. la camilla
6. una inyección

Extension: Students may enjoy role-playing this exercise. They may convert it into a dialogue between Hipolito and a disbelieving friend.

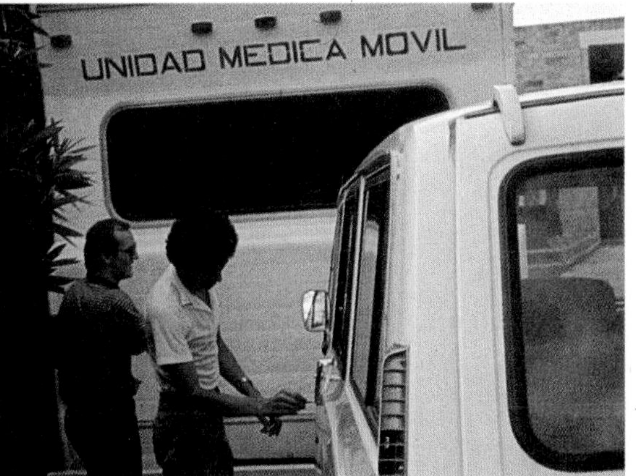

¿Cuándo tienes que llamar una ambulancia? ¿Qué trae la ambulancia?

Ask students to find a synonym for **la ambulancia** on the page. [In the photograph: **Unidad médica móvil.**]

◐ C. Marisa loves to make up riddles. Try to solve a few of them.

Primero, lee la pregunta. Luego, lee la lista y escoge la respuesta. Sigue el modelo.

medicinas	un incendio	un extintor
en ambulancia	¡Auxilio!	los primeros auxilios
al ladrón	una alarma de incendios	detenerlo

Modelo: ¿Qué usas para llamar a los bomberos?
Respuesta: **una alarma de incendios**

1. ¿Cómo van los enfermos al hospital?
2. ¿A quién detiene la policía si hay un robo?
3. ¿Qué usas para apagar un incendio?
4. ¿Qué necesitas cuando tienes fiebre y tos?
5. ¿Qué va a hacer el policía con el ladrón?
6. ¿Qué dices si hay un incendio?

1. en ambulancia
2. al ladrón
3. un extintor
4. medicinas
5. detenerlo
6. ¡Auxilio!

Extension: Have students make up questions for the two terms in the list not used in the activity (**los primeros auxilios** and **un incendio**).

● D. Imagine that you and your classmates are writers for a TV show. Prepare a scene for the next episode.

Con tus compañeros de clase, escoge una emergencia. Prepara una conversación entre tres o cuatro personas. Luego, presenta la conversación a toda la clase.

Emergencias

1. Un robo en la joyería
2. Un incendio en la tienda de discos
3. Un choque en una esquina entre un autobús y un coche caro
4. Una persona está enferma en el Hotel Tosemucho

If students need help getting started, brainstorm lists of possible characters for each situation and the vocabulary each would use.

Los sonidos del idioma

La unión de sonidos

Escucha y repite.

la alarma	mi abuelo	las ambulancias
de español	tu estante	los estudios
los senderos	mucho interés	unas uvas
en noviembre	buena idea	unos obreros

1. Mi abuelo de España vuela en avión.
2. La educación es importante en noviembre.
3. Este año su hermana anda a la escuela.
4. Unos obreros ayudan a la policía a detener al ladrón.

If students are adept at following the models on the Lesson Cassette, they should have no problem with linking sounds in Spanish. Have them follow the curves with their fingers as they repeat the words and sentences.

Esta entrada al hospital es para las urgencias. ¿Hay una urgencia ahora?

Usando el español

Talking about the Past

Rule: **Tener, estar,** and **andar** have irregular stems in the preterite. Except for the **yo** and **él** forms, they have the same endings as regular **-er** and **-ir** verbs, without the written accents.

Study the conjugations of three verbs in the preterite tense: **tener, estar,** and **andar.** (The verb **andar** has the same meaning as **caminar.**)

Have students find charts of these verbs in the Appendix and compare the preterite forms to the present-tense forms.

	tener	estar	andar
yo	**tuve**	**estuve**	**anduve**
tú	**tuviste**	**estuviste**	**anduviste**
él / ella / usted	**tuvo**	**estuvo**	**anduvo**
nosotros (-as)	**tuvimos**	**estuvimos**	**anduvimos**
vosotros (-as)	**tuvisteis**	**estuvisteis**	**anduvisteis**
ellos / ellas / ustedes	**tuvieron**	**estuvieron**	**anduvieron**

What do the conjugations of the three verbs in the preterite tense have in common? Would you say the verbs are regular or irregular in the preterite tense?

[The conjugations of all three verbs have the same endings. Their preterite stems have **uv** in them. The verbs are irregular in the preterite tense.]

Practice reading the following questions and answers: Have volunteers read the sample questions and answers aloud.

Pregunta: ¿Dónde **estuviste** durante el incendio?
Respuesta: **Estuve** muy lejos del edificio.

Pregunta: ¿Dónde **anduvieron** ustedes ayer?
Respuesta: **Anduvimos** por el parque ayer por la tarde.

Pregunta: ¿El Sr. Campos **tuvo** problemas ayer?
Respuesta: ¡Sí, hombre! ¡Un ladrón le robó el dinero!

Pregunta: ¿Cuándo **estuvo** Minerva en Puerto Rico?
Respuesta: **Estuvo** en Puerto Rico el mes pasado.

¡Vamos a practicar!

A. Where were you last night?

Primero, lee la pregunta. Luego, contesta con **sí** o **no.** Sigue el modelo.

Modelo: ¿Estuviste en la casa de un amigo?
Respuesta: **No, no estuve en la casa de un amigo.**
[Sí, estuve en la casa de un amigo.]

Extension: Repeat the exercise, using the plural to ask where students and their friends were (e.g., **¿Estuvieron en el cine?**). Students may work in pairs to ask and answer these questions.

1. ¿Estuviste en el cine?
2. ¿Estuviste en el almacén?
3. ¿Estuviste en tu dormitorio?
4. ¿Estuviste en la escuela?
5. ¿Estuviste en el teatro?
6. ¿Estuviste en el hospital?

1. Sí, (No, no) estuve en el cine.
2. Sí, (No, no) estuve en el almacén.
3. Sí, (No, no) estuve en mi dormitorio.
4. Sí, (No, no) estuve en la escuela.
5. Sí, (No, no) estuve en el teatro.
6. Sí, (No, no) estuve en el hospital.

B. Lidia's friends have all been sick lately. What did they have?

Primero, completa la pregunta. Luego, contesta con la palabra o las palabras entre paréntesis. Sigue el modelo.

Modelo: Juan Carlos, ¿—— fiebre? (tos)

Have students work in pairs to ask and answer the questions.

Respuesta: **P: Juan Carlos, ¿tuviste fiebre?**

R: No, no tuve fiebre. Tuve tos.

1. Éster, ¿—— dolor de cabeza? (fiebre)
2. Luis y Ana, ¿—— tos? (dolor de espaldas)
3. Rogelio, ¿—— la gripe? (dolor de cabeza)
4. Sr. Luna, ¿—— fiebre? (dolor del estómago)

1. P: Éster, ¿tuviste dolor de cabeza?
   R: No, no tuve dolor de cabeza. Tuve fiebre.
2. P: Luis y Ana, ¿tuvieron tos?
   R: No, no tuvimos tos. Tuvimos dolor de espaldas.
3. P: Rogelio, ¿tuviste la gripe?
   R: No, no tuve la gripe. Tuve dolor de cabeza.
4. P: Sr. Luna, ¿tuvo usted fiebre?
   R: No, no tuve fiebre. Tuve dolor del estómago.

C. Were any of your classmates sick last week? Take a survey.

Escoge a cinco compañeros. Hazles dos preguntas. Luego, escribe las respuestas. Primero, lee el ejemplo.

Modelo: TÚ: Inés, ¿estuviste enferma la semana pasada?

INÉS: No, no estuve enferma.

TÚ: ¿Tuviste algún dolor?

INÉS: Sí, tuve dolor de cabeza por un día.

Respuesta: **1. Inés no estuvo enferma. Tuvo dolor de cabeza un día.**

Extension: Have students pool their results and tell you who was sick last week.

D. How good a detective are you? Read the statements from a witness to an accident. What questions is the witness answering? Answers will vary.

Primero, lee cada respuesta. Luego, escribe la pregunta para la respuesta. Sigue el modelo.

Modelo: Sí, estuve cerca del choque.

Respuesta: **¿Estuvo usted cerca del choque?**

1. Estuve en la esquina al norte del choque.
2. Anduve por la calle Jiménez.
3. Sí, tuve tiempo para ver bien el choque.
4. Unos hombres estuvieron en el parque.
5. Ellos anduvieron por la avenida de la Victoria.
6. El choque tuvo lugar en la esquina de la calle Jiménez con la avenida de la Victoria.
7. Sí, un chofer tuvo mucho dolor.
8. No, el otro chofer no tuvo dolor.

1. ¿Dónde estuvo usted?
2. ¿Por dónde anduvo usted?
3. ¿Tuvo tiempo para ver bien el choque?
4. ¿Quiénes estuvieron en el parque?
5. ¿Por dónde anduvieron?
6. ¿Dónde tuvo lugar el choque?
7. ¿Tuvo mucho dolor un chofer?
8. ¿Tuvo dolor el otro chofer?

Have students guess the meaning of **tener lugar** and confirm their guesses by looking in the Spanish-English Glossary.

Enrichment: Have students make posters to remind people to fasten their seatbelts. Possible phrases include: **Es la ley. Abróchate el cinturón.** / **Eviten** (Avoid) **accidentes. Abróchense los cinturones.**

¿Estuviste en un choque de automóviles alguna vez? ¿Abrochaste el cinturón? ¿Es importante abrocharse el cinturón?

Extension: Have students write "eyewitness" reports about a real or imaginary accident.

Talking about What You Have Done

Rule: The verb **hacer** is irregular in the preterite. Its stem changes from **hac-** to **hic-** (**hiz-** in the **él** form) and the endings are not the same as for regular **-er** verbs.

Study the following conjugation of the verb **hacer** in the preterite tense.

Ask students if **hacer** is regular in the present tense.

Hacer

Singular		Plural	
yo	**hice**	nosotros (-as)	**hicimos**
tú	**hiciste**	vosotros (-as)	**hicisteis**
él / ella / usted	**hizo**	ellos / ellas / ustedes	**hicieron**

Do you form the preterite tense of **hacer** by adding regular **-er** endings to the stem of the infinitive? Are all the forms of **hacer** irregular in the past tense? Which form has a different spelling? Which letter changes?

[You do not form the preterite by adding regular **-er** endings to the stem. All the forms of **hacer** are irregular. The **él (ella/usted)** form has a different spelling. The **c** changes to **z.**]

Practice reading the following questions and answers:

Have volunteers make up other sample questions and answers.

Pregunta: ¿Qué **hizo** Rodrigo ayer?
Respuesta: No **hizo** nada. Miró la televisión todo el día.

Pregunta: ¿Adónde fuiste el mes pasado?
Respuesta: **Hice** un viaje a Santo Domingo.

Pregunta: ¿Les gustó la película?
Respuesta: No sé. **Hicimos** fila por una hora. ¡Nunca entramos al cine!

¡Vamos a practicar!

A. Poor Edilberto missed a day of school because of his bad cough. He wants to know what people did while he was sick.

Primero, lee el nombre o los nombres. Luego, forma una pregunta. Sigue el modelo.

This activity may be assigned as homework.
1. ¿Qué hicieron ayer?
2. ¿Qué hiciste ayer?
3. ¿Qué hiciste ayer?
4. ¿Qué hizo usted ayer?
5. ¿Qué hicieron ayer?
6. ¿Qué hicieron ayer?

Modelo: Carlitos

Respuesta: **¿Qué hiciste ayer?**

1. Manuel y Timoteo
2. Gloria
3. Saúl
4. el Sr. Cueva
5. la Sra. Ibáñez y la Srta. Pérez
6. Inés y Rodolfo

Extension: Have students answer the questions.

B. The salsa concert sold out quickly. Hundreds of people stood in line for nothing! Who stood in line the longest?

Have students work in pairs to ask and answer the questions.

Primero, forma una pregunta con el nombre o los nombres. Luego, contesta la pregunta con el tiempo entre paréntesis. Sigue el modelo.

Extension: Ask students to describe the longest time they had to wait in line for something.

Modelo: Hernán (15 minutos)

Respuesta: **P:** **¿Por cuánto tiempo hiciste fila?**

R: **Hice fila por quince minutos.**

1. P: ¿Por cuánto tiempo hiciste fila?
   R: Hice fila por una hora.
2. P: ¿Por cuánto tiempo hicieron fila?
   R: Hicimos fila por tres horas.
3. P: ¿Por cuánto tiempo hiciste fila?
   R: Hice fila por diez minutos.
4. P: ¿Por cuánto tiempo hizo usted fila?
   R: Hice fila por media hora.

1. Linda (una hora)
2. Susana y Roberto (tres horas)
3. Pepe (10 minutos)
4. la Sra. López (media hora)

C. Some days you seem to spend all your time in line! Where did you stand in line this week? How long did you stand in line? Why did you stand in line?

Primero, escoge cuatro lugares. Luego, para cada lugar, contesta las preguntas. Lee el modelo.

Lugares

la escuela	el cine	el auditorio
el supermercado	el estadio	el museo
el gimnasio	el comedor	el restaurante

Preguntas

1. ¿Dónde hiciste fila?
2. ¿Por cuánto tiempo hiciste fila?
3. ¿Por qué hiciste fila?

Extension: Have students compare their answers to see what place causes the longest waiting time and why. Ask students for suggestions to shorten their waiting time.

Modelo:
1. Hice fila en el comedor.
2. Hice fila por cinco minutos.
3. Hice fila para comprar el almuerzo.

Help students combine all three answers into one sentence (e.g., **En el comedor hice fila por cinco minutos para comprar el almuerzo.**).

Estas personas esperan fuera del hospital. Quieren ver al médico. La última vez que fuiste a ver al médico, ¿hiciste fila? ¿Tuviste miedo?

Describing Actions

Rule: To form an adverb from most adjectives, you add the ending **-mente** to the feminine singular form of the adjective.

Study the pictures and read the sentences below them.

La película fue aburrida. El tiempo pasó **lentamente.**

Después de la película, salimos **rápidamente** del cine.

Look at the words in heavy black letters. These words are helping to describe, or modify, the verbs in the sentences. Words that modify verbs are called adverbs.

Which adverb tells you how the time passed? Which adverb tells you how the group left the movie theater? Do both of these adverbs have the same ending? What is it?

[**Lentamente** tells you how the time passed. **Rápidamente** tells you how the group left the movie theater. Yes, both of these adverbs have the same ending: **-mente.**]

Practice using the adverbs by asking questions: **¿Cómo pasó el tiempo el viernes pasado? ¿Cómo saliste de la escuela el viernes pasado? ¿Cómo andas cuando está lloviendo? ¿Cómo andas cuando hace sol?**

Write students' answers on the chalkboard and ask for volunteers to draw an arrow from the adverb to the word it modifies (the verb).

Compare the following lists of adjectives and adverbs. Notice the endings of the adjectives and then notice the letter before the ending **-mente** in the adverbs.

rápido	**rápidamente**	general	**generalmente**
lento	**lentamente**	fácil	**fácilmente**
correcto	**correctamente**	difícil	**difícilmente**
frecuente	**frecuentemente**	usual	**usualmente**
triste	**tristemente**	feliz	**felizmente**

Demonstrate the making of an adverb on the chalkboard. Write an adjective that ends in **-o,** erase the **o** and add an **a,** and, finally, add **-mente.**

How do you change an adjective that ends in **-o** to make an adverb that ends in **-mente**? [You change the **-o** to **-a** and add **-mente.**]

How do you form an adverb with **-mente** from an adjective that ends in the letter **-e**? [You add the ending **-mente.**]

How do you make an adverb that ends in **-mente** from an adjective that ends in a consonant? [You add the ending **-mente.**]

Practice reading the following questions and answers:

Have volunteers read the sample questions and answers aloud. Make sure students understand the function of the adverbs in the sentences.

Pregunta: ¿Cómo saliste en el examen?
Respuesta: Salí bien. Contesté todas las preguntas **correctamente.**

Pregunta: ¿Qué haces los sábados por la mañana?
Respuesta: **Generalmente** juego al béisbol con mis amigos.

Pregunta: ¿Quién ganó la carrera?
Respuesta: Julia la ganó. Corrió **rápidamente.**

Pregunta: ¿A qué hora te levantas los domingos?
Respuesta: **Frecuentemente** me levanto a las ocho.

¡Vamos a practicar!

A. Olivia is proud of her friends. She has written a note about each one in her photo album. How does she describe what they do?

Primero, mira el dibujo y lee las oraciones. Luego, escoge una palabra para completar la oración. Sigue el modelo.

Modelo:

Miguel es atlético. Corre ——.

Respuesta: Corre rápidamente.

1. Contesta las preguntas correctamente (*or* fácilmente).
2. Pinta cuadros fácilmente.
3. Pasa los días felizmente.

1.

Rosa es inteligente. Contesta las preguntas ——.

2.

Pepe es artístico. Pinta cuadros ——.

3.

Ema es simpática. Pasa los días ——.

tristemente	correctamente	difícilmente
rápidamente	felizmente	fácilmente

Extension: Have students make up sentences using the adverbs they did not use in the answers (e.g., **Hugo no comprende la lección. Contesta las preguntas difícilmente.**).

B. **Olivia has given you a good idea! You have decided to describe your friends, too!** Answers will vary. You may wish to create some sample sentences with the class before assigning this activity as homework.

Primero, piensa en cinco amigos. Luego, escribe una o dos oraciones sobre cada amigo. Si necesitas ayuda, contesta las preguntas. **Enrichment:** Include students' descriptions in a Big Book. Encourage them to bring in pictures or draw their own illustrations.

1. ¿Es generoso tu amigo? ¿Te da cosas frecuentemente?
2. ¿Es simpático tu amigo? ¿Pasa las horas felizmente?
3. ¿Es impaciente tu amigo? ¿Hace las cosas rápidamente?
4. ¿Es honesto tu amigo? ¿Siempre te habla francamente?
5. ¿Cómo está tu amigo generalmente? ¿Está cansado? ¿Está nervioso? ¿Está contento? **Extension:** Volunteers may present their descriptions to the class.

Ask students to state the moral of the story.

¡A divertirnos!

Extension: Have students create their own illustrated fables. These may be collected for a classroom Big Book.

Cuenta una fábula

Have students write paragraphs telling the fable of the tortoise and the hare. Students may enjoy comparing their versions of the story.

Describe la carrera entre la tortuga y la liebre.

C. Imagine that you are being interviewed for the school newspaper. First you have to answer some questions about your habits.

Primero, lee la pregunta. Luego, contéstala con una de las palabras entre paréntesis. Sigue el modelo.

Modelo: ¿Asistes al teatro?
(frecuentemente—raramente)

Respuesta: **Sí. Asisto al teatro frecuentemente. Me gusta ver a los actores.**
[No. Asisto al teatro raramente. Las obras de teatro son aburridas.]

1. ¿Estudias mucho los fines de semana?
(usualmente—raramente)
2. ¿Cómo haces tus tareas?
(fácilmente—difícilmente)
3. ¿Cómo pasas tu tiempo libre?
(felizmente—tristemente)
4. ¿Practicas los deportes?
(generalmente—raramente)
5. ¿Llegas a la escuela a tiempo?
(frecuentemente—raramente)
6. Si vas a llegar tarde, ¿cómo corres a la escuela?
(rápidamente—lentamente)

Answers will vary. Sample responses are given here:
1. Sí, usualmente estudio mucho los fines de semana. Me gustan mis clases.
2. Las hago difícilmente. No me gustan las tareas.
3. Lo paso felizmente porque tengo muchos amigos.
4. Sí, generalmente practico los deportes. Soy muy atlético.
5. No. Raramente llego a la escuela a tiempo. Vivo muy lejos de la escuela.
6. Si voy a llegar tarde, corro a la escuela rápidamente.

Enrichment: Have students prepare "celebrity profiles" of themselves by completing the following sentences:
1. El tiempo pasa rápidamente cuando yo . . .
2. El tiempo pasa lentamente cuando yo . . .
3. Frecuentemente me gusta . . .
4. Raramente me gusta . . .

Students may include a picture of themselves on the profile. Display the profiles on the bulletin board or include them in a classroom newsletter.

Vamos a leer

Un cuentito cómico

Una tarde tuve que ir a la tienda para comprar unas cosas. Apenas llegué cuando noté mucho humo. El humo salió de unas ventanas del segundo piso de la tienda. Rápidamente entré a la tienda.

—¡Socorro! ¡Hay un incendio! —grité al dueño de la tienda.

—¿Cómo sabes? —me preguntó el dueño.

—Sale muchísimo humo del segundo piso.

El dueño continuó tranquilamente con su trabajo. Yo lo miré con la boca abierta.

—¿No va a llamar a los bomberos?

—¡Claro que no! —exclamó el dueño. —Mi familia vive en el apartamento del segundo piso. Mis hijos sólo están aprendiendo a cocinar. Además, mi esposa tiene cinco extintores por si acaso. La única cosa que se está quemando . . . ¡es la cena!

Have students read the passage first for general meaning and to guess the meanings of unfamiliar words. Then have them look up the words they still do not know in the Spanish-English Glossary and reread the story.

Ask students to give examples of direct dialogue (i.e., what the characters say) in the story. Ask them to state how direct dialogue is punctuated in the story (i.e., with dashes) and then compare that punctuation with punctuation in English.

La cultura y tú

See Unit Plans, Unidad 12, for additional information.

El Proyecto Perú

¿Qué haces cuando estás enfermo? A lo mejor, vas a ver al médico y él te da medicinas. Si tienes un problema más grave, puedes ir al hospital.

Para una persona en las regiones rurales del Perú, no es tan fácil encontrar ayuda. Hay muchos pueblos pequeños en las altas montañas de los Andes donde no hay hospitales, y muchas veces no hay médico. En estas áreas, hay sanitarios, personas que no son médicos, pero sí pueden dar primeros auxilios.

Las personas del pueblo de Anta están muy contentos cuando llegan los médicos.

Para ayudar a la gente de estas regiones, unos médicos y enfermeros estadounidenses formaron un grupo—el Proyecto Perú. El líder del grupo es el doctor Miguel Vásquez, un médico peruano que vive en California. El Proyecto Perú va al Perú cada año. Las personas del proyecto llevan medicina y equipo médico. Van a los pueblos pequeños de los Andes y ayudan a la gente enferma. También enseñan nuevas técnicas médicas a los sanitarios.

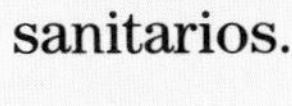

Enrichment: Many organizations provide medical aid and services in Central and South America. Have students write to some of these organizations for information and share their findings with the class.

La gente hace fila para ver a los médicos del Proyecto Perú.

Unidad

13

After completing this unit, students should be able to:

- ▶ name people, places, and activities related to the post office
- ▶ talk about past actions using the preterite tense of the irregular verbs **poder, poner,** and **saber**
- ▶ use knowledge of verb conjugations to select and use the present-tense and preterite-tense forms of the verb **oír**
- ▶ read about and discuss an alternative means of communicating between countries by shortwave radio.

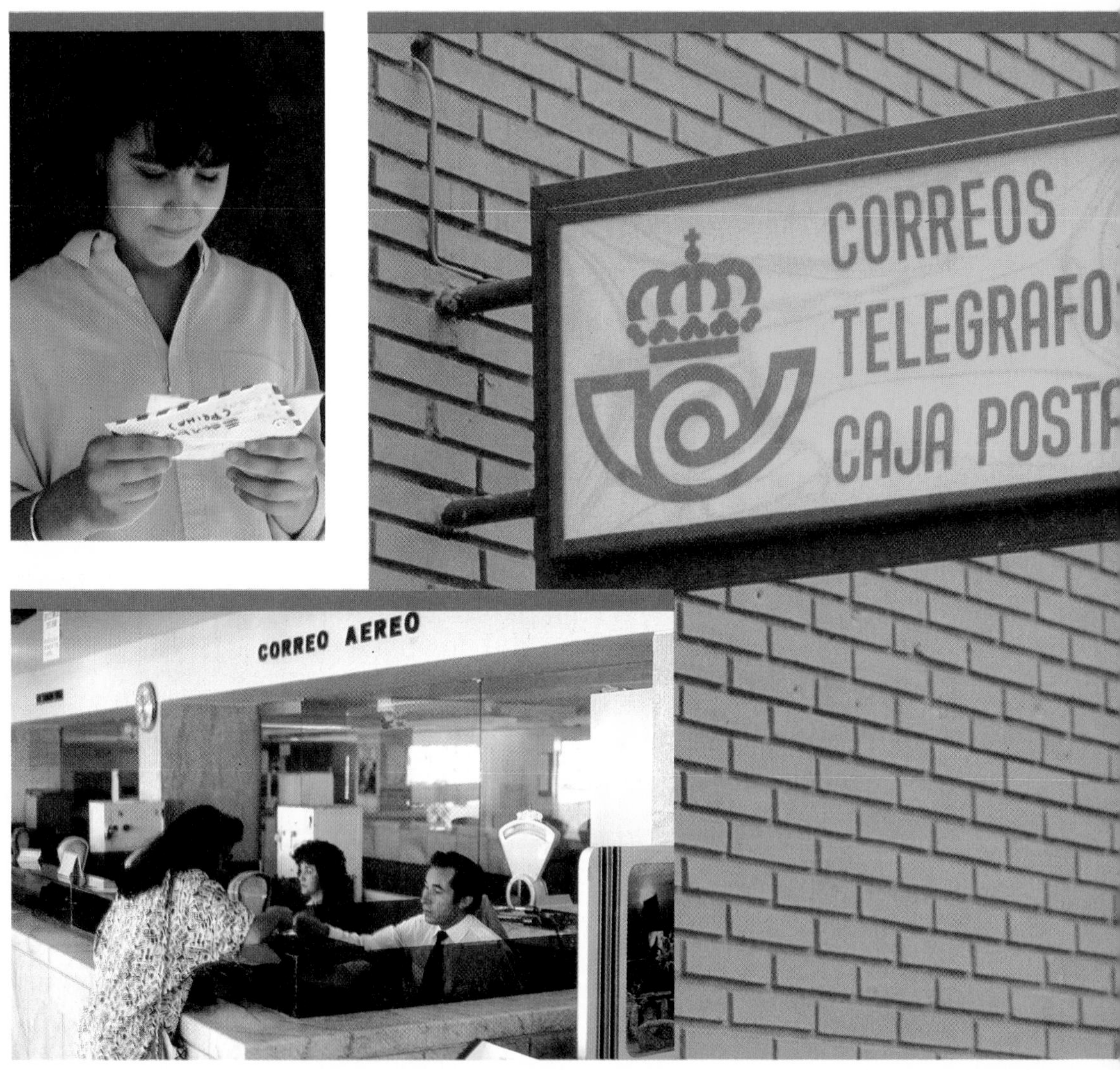

The photographs may be used for informal assessment or review:

- ► Mira la foto a la izquierda. ¿Qué lee la muchacha?
- ► ¿Cómo es el buzón? ¿De qué color es?
- ► ¿Quién está trabajando en la sección de correo aéreo? ¿Hay alguien que quiere mandar una carta o un paquete?
- ► Mira al pie de la página 303. ¿Es moderno este edificio de correos? ¿Es grandísimo el edificio?

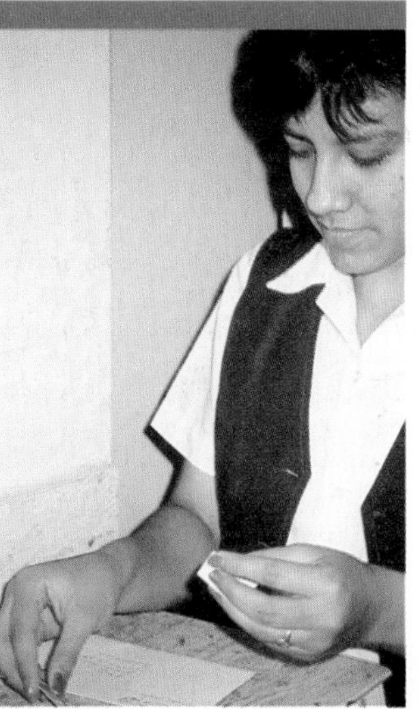

Panorama de vocabulario

Vamos al correo

la carta

el sobre

la dirección

envolver

las estampillas

el paquete

Point out that students should use **volver** as the model for using **envolver.**

Note: Las estampillas are called **los sellos** in Spain and **los timbres** in Mexico.

Students may be interested in learning that a post office box is **el apartado postal.** In Spanish-speaking countries, people use **por correo aéreo** and **por avión** interchangeably.

Enrichment: Have students contact the local post office and find out the procedure for sending a package to Spain or Central and South America.

¡Aprende el vocabulario!

A. Ana is spending some time in Perú and goes to the post office for the first time. What happens?

Primero, mira el dibujo. Luego, lee la oración. Por último, completa la oración. Sigue el modelo.

Modelo: Hay mucho ——.

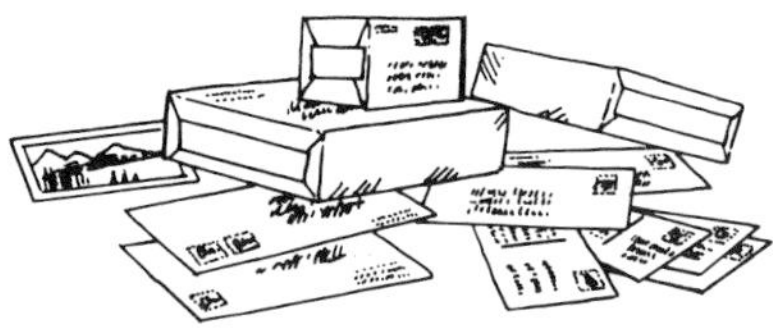

1. estampillas
2. una carta
3. la dirección
4. El sobre
5. un paquete
6. el agente de correo
7. la cartera
8. Manda (*or* Echa al correo)

Respuesta: **Hay mucho correo.**

1. Ana quiere comprar ——.

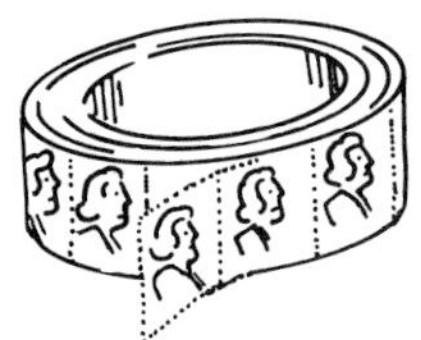

2. Lleva —— a sus padres.

3. Escribió —— claramente.

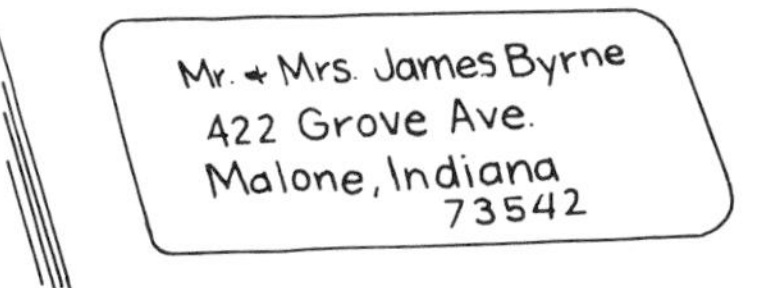

Mr. + Mrs. James Byrne
422 Grove Ave.
Malone, Indiana
73542

4. —— es grande.

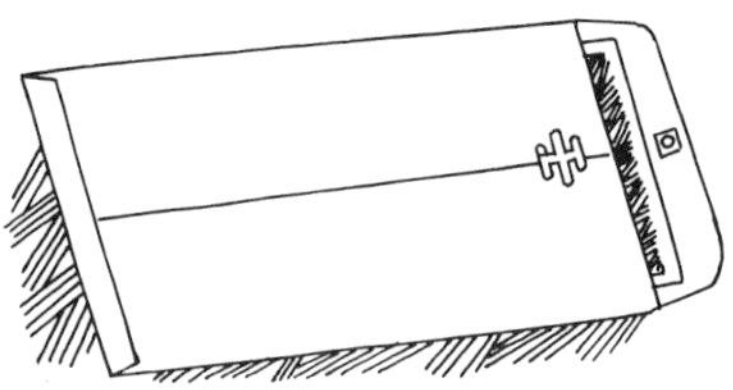

Extension: Have students make up rebus sentences, using illustrations on the vocabulary cards (Unidad 13, *Teacher's Resource and Activity Book*).

5. Tiene —— también.

7. Ve a ——.

6. Habla con ——.

8. —— unas tarjetas postales también.

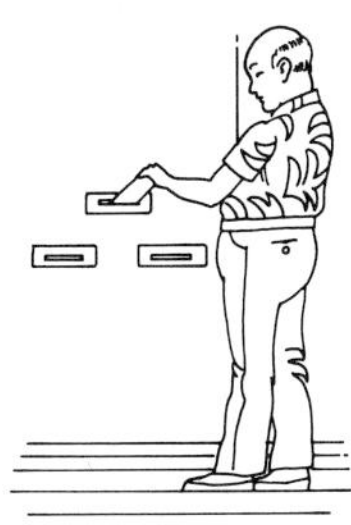

B. Esteban is mailing a letter for the first time. He has a lot of questions about the post office.

Primero, lee la pregunta. Luego, contesta la pregunta y escribe una oración completa. Sigue el modelo.

Modelo: ¿Vende estampillas la agente de correo?

Respuesta: **Sí, la agente de correo vende estampillas.**

See Unit Plans, Unidad 13, for answers to exercise B.

1. ¿Necesitas poner estampillas para mandar una carta?
2. ¿Puedo enviar mi perro por correo aéreo?
3. ¿Va la carta fuera del sobre?
4. El cartero vende sobres, ¿verdad?
5. ¿Tengo que envolver el paquete para enviarlo por correo?
6. ¿Tienes que escribir una dirección en el sobre?

Extension: Have students think of three or four more questions Esteban might ask. This activity can be assigned as homework after completing the exercise orally in class.

C. Make up a conversation between two friends who meet at the post office. First, one person asks all the questions and the other answers. Later, switch roles.

Escoge a un compañero de clase. Primero, haz cinco preguntas. Luego, contesta las preguntas de tu compañero. Lee el ejemplo. Ask for a volunteer to read the sample conversation with you.

TÚ: ¡Hola, José! ¿Qué haces aquí?

ALUMNO: Quiero enviar un paquete a mi hermana.

TÚ: ¿Dónde está tu hermana?

ALUMNO: Estudia este año en México y quiero mandarle un libro.

TÚ: ¿Cómo lo mandas?

ALUMNO: Lo mando por correo aéreo. Tiene que llegar pronto. El viernes es su cumpleaños.

TÚ: ¿Y quién envolvió el paquete tan bien?

ALUMNO: Yo siempre envuelvo los paquetes que mandamos por correo.

TÚ: ¿Me das la dirección de tu hermana? Quiero mandarle una carta.

ALUMNO: ¡Claro! Aquí está en el paquete. La puedes escribir.

Extension: Have volunteers present their conversations to the class. Encourage them to use props such as boxes, envelopes, address books, etc.

¿Qué puedes comprar en estas ventanillas? A veces, ¿mandas paquetes en el correos?

Los sonidos del idioma

La entonación

Escucha y repite.

As students listen to the Lesson Cassette, have them put their thumbs up as the speaker's voice rises and thumbs down as the speaker's voice falls.

¿Cómo está la sopa?	La sopa está caliente.
¿Qué dice Juan?	Juan dice que sí.
¿Dónde está el hotel?	Está al otro lado.
¿Cuándo vas a México?	Salgo mañana.
¡Qué maravilla!	¡Es estupendo!
¡Hola, María!	¡Adiós, Eduardo!

El hombre necesita estampillas para su carta. ¿Cómo quiere mandar la carta?

As students progress in the language, they will realize that just as accents change from region to region, so do patterns of intonation, according to what we want to communicate.

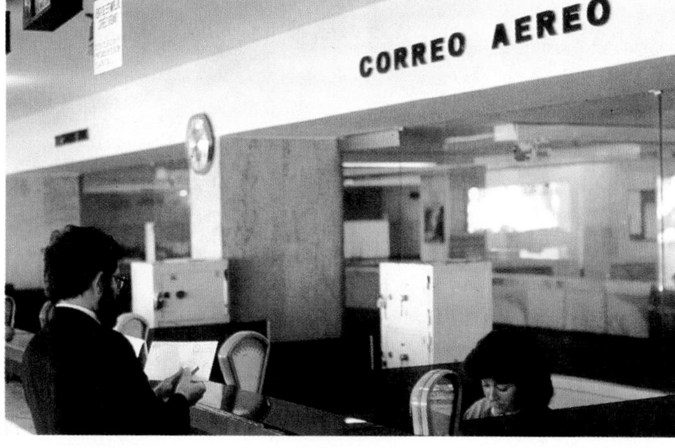

En el correos, hay buzones para mandar cartas por todo el mundo.

Usando el español

Using More Irregular Verbs

Rule: **Poder, poner,** and **saber** change their stems in the preterite tense. They add the endings **-e, -iste, -o, -imos,** and **-ieron.**

Study the following chart. What do the verbs **poder, poner,** and **saber** have in common in the preterite tense?

	poder	**poner**	**saber**
yo	pude	puse	supe
tú	pudiste	pusiste	supiste
él / ella / usted	pudo	puso	supo
nosotros (-as)	pudimos	pusimos	supimos
vosotros (-as)	pudisteis	pusisteis	supisteis
ellos / ellas / ustedes	pudieron	pusieron	supieron

How do the stems of **poder** and **poner** change in the preterite tense? How does **saber** change in the preterite tense?

[The stem of **poder** becomes **pud-**; the stem of **poner** becomes **pus-.** Saber changes its stem to **sup-** in the preterite and adds the same endings as **poder** and **poner.**]

Ask students if these verbs are regular in the present tense. You may wish to review the present-tense conjugations of these verbs by incorporating exercises from *Ya converso más:* **poner,** Unidad 5; **poder,** Unidad 7; and **saber,** Unidad 9.

Practice reading the following questions and answers:

Have volunteers read the sample questions and answers aloud.

Pregunta: ¿Pudiste ver la película?

Respuesta: No, no la pude ver. Tuve que envolver unos paquetes.

Pregunta: ¡Hijos! ¿Dónde pusieron las estampillas?

Respuesta: Las pusimos en tu escritorio, papá.

Pregunta: ¿Supieron la mala noticia? Perdimos el campeonato.

Respuesta: Sí, supimos. ¡Qué lástima!

Pregunta: ¿Por qué no pudo abrir el garaje el Sr. Corona?

Respuesta: Porque puso las llaves dentro del coche. Luego, ¡cerró la puerta del garaje!

Pregunta: ¿Supiste la buena noticia? Contesté correctamente todas las preguntas en el examen.

Respuesta: No, no supe. ¡Felicitaciones!

You may point out that in the preterite tense, the meaning of **saber** changes slightly to "to learn of" or "to find out." Have students guess the meaning of **noticia** from context. Native speakers often use the singular form of **noticia** to mean "news."

Este señor no tiene que ir al correos para mandar su carta. La última vez que mandaste una carta, ¿fuiste al correos o la pusiste en un buzón?

In some regions, **correos** is used instead of the singular **correo.**

¡Vamos a practicar!

○ A. Alicia has had to do everything alone this week. She wants to know why her friends couldn't do anything with her.

Primero, lee las palabras y forma una pregunta. Luego, forma una respuesta de las palabras entre paréntesis. Sigue el modelo. Have students work in pairs to ask and answer the questions.

Modelo: Eugenia / poder / ir al cine
(tuve que estudiar)

Respuesta: **P: Eugenia, ¿por qué no pudiste ir al cine?**
R: No pude ir porque tuve que estudiar.

See Unit Plans, Unidad 13, for answers to exercise A.

1. Ricardo / poder / asistir al teatro
(tuve que escribir un reporte)

2. Manolo y Raquel / poder / ir a la fiesta
(tuvimos que limpiar el garaje)

3. Sra. Enríquez / poder / leer mi historia
(tuve que ayudar al director de la escuela)

4. Patricia / poder / ir al almacén
(tuve que mandar un paquete por correo)

◐ B. The Fulano family is not known for being neat. Sra. Fulano found out that her relatives are paying her a surprise visit! The house is a mess! Where did everyone put things? Have students work in pairs to ask and answer the questions.

Primero, completa la pregunta con la forma apropiada de **poner.** Luego, escribe la respuesta con las palabras entre paréntesis. Sigue el modelo.

Modelo: Iris, ¿dónde —— los sobres?
(debajo del sofá)

Respuesta: **P: Iris, ¿dónde pusiste los sobres?**
R: Los puse debajo del sofá.

1. Paco y Pepe, ¿dónde —— los paquetes? (dentro del ropero)
2. Samuel, ¿dónde —— los platos sucios? (dentro del horno)
3. Enriqueta, ¿dónde —— las novelas? (detrás del sillón)
4. Verónica y Victoria, ¿dónde —— la aspiradora? (en el garaje)

You may wish to assign this activity as homework.

1. pusieron / Los pusimos dentro del ropero.
2. pusiste / Los puse dentro del horno.
3. pusiste / Las puse detrás del sillón.
4. pusieron / La pusimos en el garaje.

Extension: Have students role-play a similar situation in the classroom. Follow up by asking where they put things before the guests arrived.

◐ C. Your school team has won the state championship! Make sure everyone knows about it.

Primero, lee el nombre o los nombres y forma una pregunta. Sigue el modelo.

Modelo: Humberto

Respuesta: **Humberto, ¿supiste las noticias? ¡Ganamos el campeonato!**

1. el Sr. Armendáriz
2. Mónica
3. Lupita y Teresa
4. Óscar
5. la Srta. Garza
6. Hugo e Ignacio

Correct answers must include the following forms of **saber**:
1. supo
2. supiste
3. supieron
4. supiste
5. supo
6. supieron

D. Over the centuries, students have developed some pretty creative excuses for not doing their homework. How creative are you and your classmates?

Primero, lee la conversación. Luego, escoge a dos o tres compañeros de clase para escribir su propia conversación.

SRA. LUNA: ¿Por qué no hicieron sus tareas? ¿Fernando?

FERNANDO: No pude escribir las respuestas. Me dolieron los dedos toda la noche.

JUANITA: Yo sí hice las tareas. Antes de salir de la casa, las puse en mi bolsa. Pero en el autobús, un ladrón altísimo me robó la bolsa.

SRA. LUNA: ¿Y tú, Eduardo?

EDUARDO: No pude hacer las tareas porque no supe las respuestas.

Extension: Have volunteers present their conversations to the rest of the class. The class may vote on whether or not to accept the excuse.

¡A divertirnos!

Students should use the visual clues to understand the expression. Ask students to think of other situations in which the expression might apply.

Una expresión astuta

Esa cartera sabe más que Merlín.

Talking about What You Hear

Rule: The forms of **oír** in both the present and the preterite tense are irregular.

Study the pictures and read the sentences that contain forms of **oír.**

Have volunteers read the sample sentences aloud.

¡**Oigo** un ruido! ¿Es un ladrón?

¡**Oyes** el viento! No hay nada fuera de la casa.

Help students use visual clues to deduce the meanings of the forms of **oír.**

Anoche, **oí** un ruido fuera de la casa. ¡Qué miedo tuve!

Por fin, mis amigos **oyeron** el ruido también. ¡Fue un perrito!

In the top row, the verb **oír** is in the present tense. Would you say that **oír** is regular or irregular in the present tense? [**Oír** is irregular in the present tense.]

In the bottom row, the verb **oír** is in the preterite tense. Would you say that **oír** is regular or irregular in the preterite tense?

[**Oír** is irregular in the preterite tense.]

You may wish to introduce this presentation by explaining to students that as they progress in Spanish, they will often want to use verbs they have not learned in their textbooks. They must rely on dictionaries and other reference books to learn about the verb and the forms they want to use.

If you look for an irregular verb in a dictionary or reference book, you may find all the forms of the verb for all its tenses or you may find just the tenses in which its forms are irregular. You must then choose the form of the verb that fits what you want to say or write.

If you were to look up **oír,** you might find its forms listed in the following way:

Present: oigo, oyes, oye, oímos, oís, oyen
Preterite: oí, oíste, oyó, oímos, oísteis, oyeron

Imperative: oye, no oigas

Infinitive: oír **Gerund:** oyendo

Have students look up other irregular verbs in the classroom dictionary to see how the irregular forms are listed.

From what you have learned about the conjugations of verbs, you can figure out which form of the verb you need. What is missing from the conjugations that you are used to seeing in the charts in your textbook? Do you need the subject pronouns to know which form to choose?

[The pronouns are missing from the conjugations. No, the subject pronouns are not necessary.]

Practice answering the following questions:

1. What form of **oír** would you use to talk about what you hear now?
2. What form of **oír** would you use to talk about what you and your friends heard last night?
3. What form would you use to ask your friends what they heard yesterday?
4. What form would you use to ask a friend if he or she heard a noise?
5. What do you think the word **imperative** means? How would you tell a friend to hear something?

1. oigo
2. oímos
3. oyeron
4. oíste
5. The word **imperative** means a command. ¡Oye!

Practice the forms of **oír** by calling out a subject pronoun and having students answer with the appropriate verb form.

¡Vamos a practicar!

A. Cristina and her friends are having a slumber party. Does everyone hear a noise outside?

Have students work in pairs to ask and answer the questions.

Primero, lee el nombre o los nombres y forma una pregunta. Luego, contéstala con **sí** o **no.** Sigue el modelo.

Modelo: Lucía (sí)

Respuesta: **P: Lucía, ¿oyes un ruido?**

R: Sí, oigo un ruido.

You may wish to assign exercises A and B as written homework after students have completed them orally in class.

1. Anita y Carla (sí)
2. Marisela y Berta (no)
3. Carmenza (sí)
4. Mamá (no)

1. P: oyen / R: oímos
2. P: oyen / R: oímos
3. P: oyes / R: oigo
4. P: oyes / R: oigo

B. The next morning at the breakfast table, they talk about what they heard. Do they all agree on what the noise was?

Primero, forma una pregunta con el nombre o los nombres. Luego, contéstala con las palabras entre paréntesis. Sigue el modelo.

Modelo: Lucía (sí / el perro)

Respuesta: **P: Lucía, ¿oíste el ruido?**

R: Sí, oí el ruido. Fue el perro.

1. Anita y Carla (sí / el viento)
2. Marisela y Berta (no / nada)
3. Carmenza (sí / el gato)
4. Mamá (no / nada)

1. P: oyeron / R: Sí, oímos el ruido. Fue el viento.
2. P: oyeron / R: No, no oímos el ruido. No fue nada.
3. P: oíste / R: Sí, oí el ruido. Fue el gato.
4. P: oíste / R: No, no oí el ruido. No fue nada.

◐ C. The public address system wasn't working at school yesterday. Juan wants to know if he has to repeat yesterday's announcements today.

Primero, lee el nombre o los nombres. Luego, escribe una pregunta. Sigue el modelo.

Modelo: Nina y José

Respuesta: **¿Oyeron los anuncios ayer?**

1. el Sr. Méndez
2. Celia
3. Iris y Clara
4. Tú
5. la Srta. Balboa
6. Marcos

1. ¿Oyó los anuncios ayer?
2. ¿Oíste los anuncios ayer?
3. ¿Oyeron los anuncios ayer?
4. ¿Oyó los anuncios ayer?
5. ¿Oyó los anuncios ayer?
6. ¿Oíste los anuncios ayer?

◐ D. Juan wants to know if the system is working well now. How have people answered his questions? What does he write down?

Primero, lee las oraciones. Luego, completa las oraciones con las formas apropiadas de **oír.** Sigue el modelo.

Modelo: Ayer, Paco no —— los anuncios. Ahora los —— bien.

Respuesta: **Ayer, Paco no oyó los anuncios. Ahora los oye bien.**

1. oyeron / oyen
2. oíste / oyes
3. oyeron / oyen
4. oyó / oye
5. oyó / oye

1. Ayer, las secretarias no —— los anuncios. Ahora los —— bien.
2. Ayer, tú no —— los anuncios. Ahora los —— bien.
3. Ayer, la Sra. Márquez y el Sr. Baroja no —— los anuncios. Ahora los —— bien.
4. Ayer, Guillermo no —— los anuncios. Ahora los —— bien.
5. Ayer, Rosalinda no —— los anuncios. Ahora los —— bien.

Extension: Ask students what announcements they heard over the loudspeaker or on the radio yesterday.

¡A conversar!

Invitados sin invitación

Have volunteers read the conversation aloud.

ALBA: ¿Oíste lo que le pasó a Gloria?

SAÚL: No, no lo oí. Dime.

ALBA: Anoche ella puso la mesa para las cuatro personas de su familia. Pronto sus tíos llegaron de visita. Claro que ella puso la mesa para dos personas más.

SAÚL: ¿Y qué?

ALBA: ¡Espera, espera! Ellos se sentaron a comer. Pronto llegaron sus abuelos de visita. Claro que ella puso la mesa para dos personas más.

SAÚL: Ya son . . . ¡ocho personas!

ALBA: Todos comenzaron a comer a las siete y media. De repente, llegaron de visita sus cinco primos de California.

SAÚL: Claro que puso la mesa para cinco personas más.

ALBA: ¡No, hombre! ¡No pudo darles de comer a trece personas! Así que toda la familia salió a cenar en un restaurante.

Preguntas

1. ¿De quién hablan Alba y Saúl?
2. ¿Cuántas personas hay en su familia?
3. ¿Quiénes llegaron?
4. ¿Qué hizo ella?
5. ¿Adónde salió el grupo? ¿Por qué?

Encourage students to give complete answers:

1. Hablan de Gloria.
2. Hay cuatro personas en su familia.
3. Llegaron sus tíos, sus abuelos y sus cinco primos de California.
4. Ella puso la mesa para las personas que llegaron.
5. El grupo salió a comer en un restaurante. Gloria no pudo darles de comer a trece personas.

¡Conversa tú!

1. ¿Anoche quién puso la mesa en tu casa?
2. ¿A veces llegan personas a tu casa sin invitación?
3. Si es la hora de comer, ¿qué haces con los invitados?
4. Generalmente, ¿sales a cenar con tus invitados?
5. ¿Qué pudo hacer Gloria sin salir de su casa? ¿Pudo pedir la comida por teléfono?

Extension: Have students make up a conversation between themselves and an uninvited guest.

Cultural Note: In Spanish-speaking countries, it is not unusual for family and friends to drop by unexpectedly. The attitude is one of sharing what you have, whether it is a little or a lot.

¿Cuándo escuchas la música?
¿La oyes bien?

¿Qué puedes oír en la calle de una ciudad?
¿Hay muchos ruidos?

La cultura y tú

See Unit Plans, Unidad 13, for additional information.

Nos comunicamos con el mundo

¿Conoces a alguien que vive en un país de habla española? Quizás le mandas cartas por el correo. ¿Sabes que hay otras maneras de comunicarse con otros países? Puedes escuchar o mirar mensajes de países de habla española en tu propia casa.

¿Escuchas la radio? Es probable que sí. Para los programas locales, la gente a veces escucha las noticias en la banda que se llama AM y la música en la banda FM. También, hay bandas que se especializan en la recepción de emisoras muy distantes. Se llaman bandas de onda corta. Muchos países mandan programas de radio a otros países por medio de las bandas de onda corta. Si quieres escuchar estos programas, puedes aprender mucho de otros países.

También puedes mirar programas en español en la televisión. En muchas ciudades de los Estados Unidos, hay canales de televisión que presentan programas en español. En estos canales puedes ver programas cómicos, películas, telenovelas y noticias locales y mundiales—todo en español. Así, con tu televisor y tu radio, tienes muchas oportunidades para estar en contacto con el mundo de habla española, ¡desde tu propia comunidad!

Unidad 14

Unidad 14 contains activities to be used as a final, year-end review of *¡Nos comunicamos!*

The photographs may be used for informal assessment or review:

- ► Señala a las personas que están en la playa. ¿Qué hacen ellos?
- ► ¿Quién pide ayuda?
- ► Muéstrame un paso de peatones. ¿Hay muchas personas o pocas personas que cruzan la calle?
- ► ¿En qué viajan los pasajeros?
- ► ¿Cómo es el barco? ¿Dónde está, en el océano o en el río?

A. Una conversación entre amigos

Have volunteers role-play the conversation.

BETO: ¡Cuántos trofeos! ¿Todos ustedes practican los deportes?

EVA: Sí. Mi hermano ganó este trofeo de oro el año pasado. Fue el mejor en gimnasia.

BETO: ¿Y esa medalla de plata?

EVA: Mi hermana la ganó. Fue muy buena en ciclismo.

BETO: ¿Y aquel trofeo grande?

EVA: Lo ganó mi mamá. Su equipo ganó el campeonato de boliche.

BETO: ¿Quién ganó la medalla de oro?

EVA: Mi papá la ganó hace muchos años. Fue el mejor en la lucha libre.

BETO: ¿Y aquel pequeño trofeo de plástico?

EVA: Yo lo recibí el invierno pasado. Mis papás me lo dieron. ¡Soy la mejor en hablar por teléfono!

Extension: Have students scan the conversation to find additional information not covered in the **Preguntas.** Ask them to write at least two or three more questions about Eva's family.

Preguntas

1. ¿Quién ganó el trofeo de oro?
2. ¿Quién es bueno en ciclismo?
3. ¿Qué ganó la mamá de Eva?
4. ¿Quién ganó la medalla de oro? ¿Por qué?
5. ¿Por qué recibió Eva un trofeo de plástico?

1. El hermano de Eva ganó el trofeo de oro.
2. La hermana de Eva es buena en ciclismo.
3. La mamá de Eva ganó un trofeo grande.
4. El papá de Eva ganó la medalla de oro. Fue el mejor en la lucha libre.
5. (Lo recibió porque) es la mejor en hablar por teléfono.

Ask students to form conclusions based on the information in the conversation:

1. ¿Cómo es la familia de Eva?
2. ¿Es atlética Eva?
3. ¿Tiene Eva muchas amigas?
4. A la familia de Eva, ¿es importante ganar?

B. ¿Qué opinas?

Catalina Salazar is a sports announcer who has some definite opinions. What do you think? Do you agree with her? State your opinions.

Primero, lee las oraciones. Luego, escribe tu opinión.

1. Los jóvenes de hoy son los peores en deportes. Answers will vary.
2. Es mejor ganar que perder.
3. Todos los atletas tienen que practicar sus deportes los siete días a la semana. La práctica es importantísima.
4. El boxeo es mejor que la gimnasia.
5. La natación es facilísima, pero el boliche es dificilísimo.
6. Los deportes son más importantes que los estudios. No puedes ganar un trofeo por ser el mejor alumno.
7. Participar es mejor que mirar. Los espectadores no son importantes.
8. Todos los atletas profesionales son inteligentísimos.

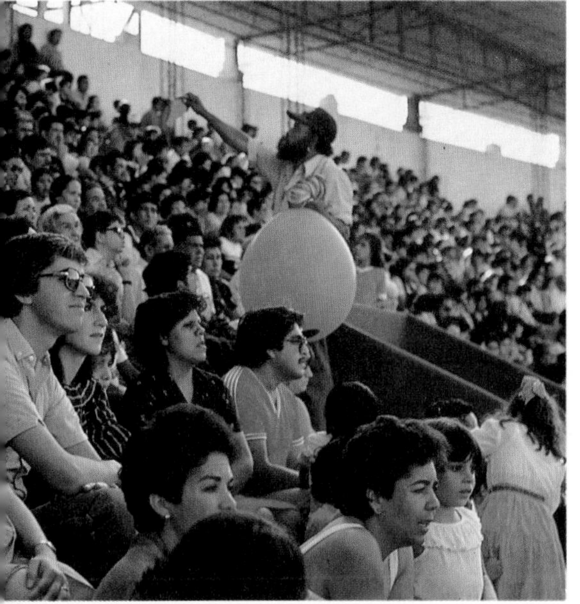

Have students compare their answers to determine whether the class is in agreement on their opinions.

Es mejor ser atleta que ser espectador. ¿Qué opinas?

C. Actividades después de clases

After school, the students are as active as they are during school hours. Everywhere you go, you hear coaches, conductors, and directors giving instructions. What do they say?

Primero, lee la oración. Luego, completa la oración con la forma apropiada de la palabra entre paréntesis. Sigue el modelo.

Modelo: No —— miedo del salto de altura. (tener)
Respuesta: **No tengas miedo del salto de altura.**

1. ¡No le —— el trofeo al espectador! (dar)
2. No —— tarde al campeonato. (venir)
3. No —— del auditorio. (salir)
4. No le —— eso a Samuel todavía. (decir)
5. No —— tu violín en el piso. (poner)
6. No —— tanta prisa de comenzar la canción. (tener)

1. des
2. vengas
3. salgas
4. digas
5. pongas
6. tengas

Extension: Have students repeat the exercise, this time giving the positive commands. Students may enjoy making up more commands a coach or a conductor might give.

CH. Pepito está en las nubes

Pepito's head always seems to be in the clouds. All day long, people have to tell him what to do. He's too busy daydreaming!

Primero, lee las palabras. Luego, forma una oración. Sigue el modelo. This activity can be assigned as homework.

Modelo: hacer fila en la entrada
Respuesta: **Pepito, haz fila en la entrada.**

1. Pepito, ven a la oficina.
2. Pepito, no pongas los pies aquí.
3. Pepito, di la respuesta.
4. Pepito, pon los papeles en la mesa.

1. venir a la oficina
2. no poner los pies aquí
3. decir la respuesta
4. poner los papeles en la mesa

5. hacer el dibujo en colores

6. ir a la biblioteca

7. no dar el libro a Juan

8. no ir al gimnasio ahora

5. Pepito, haz el dibujo en colores.
6. Pepito, ve a la biblioteca.
7. Pepito, no le des el libro a Juan.
8. Pepito, no vayas al gimnasio ahora.

D. Una excursión con la clase

Hortensia has written about a field trip to the theater. However, instead of writing in the past tense, she wrote in the present tense. Help her out.

Primero, lee la oración. Luego, cambia cada palabra en letras negras a la forma apropiada. Sigue el modelo.

Modelo: Ayer **vamos** al Teatro Colón.
Respuesta: **Ayer fuimos al Teatro Colón.**

1. **Tenemos** que estar en el teatro a las dos y media.
2. **Ando** muy rápido para llegar a tiempo.
3. **Hacemos** fila para entrar al teatro.
4. Los actores nos **dicen** mucho sobre la obra de teatro.
5. **Traigo** mi cuaderno para escribir la información.
6. No **puedo** escribir muy rápido.
7. **Estamos** en el teatro por dos horas.
8. El director nos **dice** muchas cosas interesantes.

1. Tuvimos
2. Anduve
3. Hicimos
4. dijeron
5. Traje
6. pude
7. Estuvimos
8. dijo

E. Ahora . . . ¡tú!

Did you go on a field trip or have a special visitor? Write a report for the class bulletin board.

Escribe por lo menos ocho oraciones sobre algo que hiciste durante el año.

Have students work in pairs to write about a field trip or a visitor you had for Spanish class. You may wish to brainstorm a list of questions about the activity to help students get started.

F. Una película de ciencia ficción

Imagine that you have just seen a science fiction film. What happened?

Primero, mira el dibujo y lee las oraciones. Luego, completa las oraciones con la forma apropiada de la palabra entre paréntesis. Sigue el modelo.

Modelo:

1. pudo / tuvo
2. puso
3. tuvo / supo
4. anduvieron / pudo

El camarero (traer) dos vasos a la mesa. Los (poner) entre el hombre y la mujer.

Respuesta: **El camarero trajo dos vasos a la mesa. Los puso entre el hombre y la mujer.**

1.

La mujer no (poder) tomar la limonada. Todo el día (tener) dolor de cabeza.

2.

El hombre tomó las limonadas y (poner) los vasos en la mesa.

3.

En un instante, él también (tener) dolor de cabeza. No (saber) porqué.

4.

Los dos (andar) a la salida. De pronto el hombre no (poder) caminar bien.

5. hizo / oyeron
6. oyó / supo

5.

El hombre (hacer) un ruido.
Todas las personas lo (oír).
Corrieron del restaurante.

Extension: Have students write a paragraph about a movie they have seen. They may illustrate a scene from the movie.

6.

El hombre cambió mucho. No (oír) el grito de la mujer. ¿Quién (saber) qué le pasó al hombre?

G. ¿Supiste las noticias?

Señora Oyetodo knows everything about everybody. This time, though, people heard the news before she did.

Primero, lee la pregunta y complétala con una forma de **saber.** Luego, forma una oración con las palabras entre paréntesis. Sigue el modelo.

Modelo: Horacio, ¿—— las noticias?
(sí / oír / ayer)

Respuesta: **Horacio, ¿supiste las noticias?**
Sí, las oí ayer.

1. Marta, ¿—— las noticias?
(sí / oír / esta mañana)
2. Esteban y Olga, ¿—— las noticias?
(sí / oír / anoche)
3. Sr. Campomar, ¿—— las noticias?
(sí / oír / la semana pasada)
4. Srta. Sol y Sra. Fuentes, ¿—— las noticias?
(sí / oír / ayer por la tarde)

You may wish to assign this activity as homework. Have students work in pairs to ask and answer the questions.

1. P: Marta, ¿supiste las noticias?
R: Sí, las oí esta mañana.
2. P: Esteban y Olga, ¿supieron las noticias?
R: Sí, las oímos anoche.
3. P: Sr. Campomar, ¿supo usted las noticias?
R: Sí, las oí la semana pasada.
4. P: Srta. Sol y Sra. Fuentes, ¿supieron ustedes las noticias?
R: Sí, las oímos ayer por la tarde.

Extension: Have students think of similar situations and create brief skits.

H. Lee un folleto

Have students read the brochure first for general meaning. Help them guess the meanings of unfamiliar words from context.

In 1988 Hurricane Gilbert almost destroyed Cancún, a popular Mexican resort. After everything was repaired and restored, it was necessary to entice visitors back to the resort. A travel brochure might have looked like the following.

Ask comprehension questions about the brochure (e.g., **¿Cuál es la temperatura usual en Cancún? ¿Dónde está Cancún?**).

Ven a Cancún

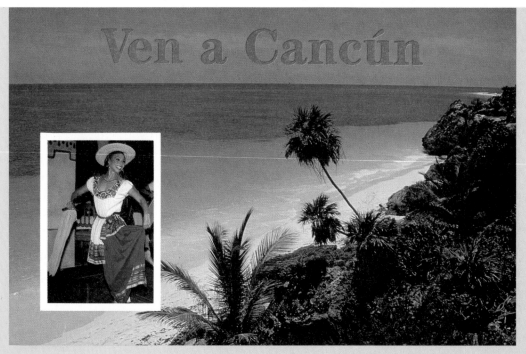

¡Piensa en Cancún para tus próximas vacaciones! Casi todos los días el sol del Caribe calienta nuestras lindas playas. La temperatura usual es de 82 grados Fahrenheit.

Anda por las millas y millas de playas hermosas. Cancún es una isla en el mar Caribe, situada en la costa de la península de Yucatán, en México. Por todos lados, puedes ver las olas tranquilas del mar.

¡No te vas a aburrir en Cancún! Puedes alquilar un barco de vela o aprender a bucear. Nuestros instructores te pueden enseñar en muy poco tiempo.

También puedes encontrar los regalos perfectos. Ve de compras en las tiendas. Los vendedores te atienden con una sonrisa.

Si tienes hambre, prueba la comida sabrosísima en nuestros restaurantes. ¡Nuestro servicio es excelentísimo!

Si quieres conocernos mejor, puedes aprender mucho sobre nuestra cultura. Visita las ruinas mayas de Tulúm, Chichén Itzá o Uxmal. Mira los edificios antiguos y aprende algo sobre la cultura de los indios mayas. Tenemos excursiones cada día a la península.

Llega a conocer nuestra cultura folklórica. Nuestros bailarines son los mejores. Puedes apreciar los vestidos tradicionales y escuchar la música folklórica. ¡No seas tímido si los bailarines te invitan a bailar!

Visita nuestras comunidades y habla con las personas. Si quieres, puedes ser nuestro amigo, no solamente un turista.

Puedes llegar a Cancún fácilmente. Si viajas en coche, hay puentes entre la península y la isla. Si viajas en avión, puedes llegar a nuestro aeropuerto moderno y conveniente.

¡Habla con tu agente de viajes hoy! ¡Ven a visitarnos en Cancún! ¡Nos vemos pronto!

Enrichment: Have groups of students send for information about various vacation resorts in Spanish-speaking countries.

I. Inventa una conversación

How would a travel agent persuade a customer to visit Cancún? What features would be of interest to travelers? Choose a partner and make up a conversation between a travel agent and a customer.

Con un compañero, prepara una conversación sobre un viaje a Cancún. Si necesitas ayuda, lee las páginas 330 y 331.

Ask for volunteers to present their conversations to the class.

J. En tus palabras

Imagine that you and your family went to Cancún and did many of the activities mentioned in the travel brochure. What was your trip like?

Lee y contesta las preguntas.

Answers will vary. Have students use the questions to interview each other.

1. ¿Qué hiciste en las playas?
2. ¿Aprendiste a bucear? ¿Fue fácil o difícil aprender a bucear?
3. ¿Te gustaron las playas? ¿Por qué?
4. ¿Cómo fueron los vendedores?
5. ¿Qué compraste? ¿Para quién compraste regalos?
6. ¿Dónde comieron ustedes? ¿Cómo fue la comida?
7. ¿Cómo fue el servicio en los restaurantes?
8. ¿Cuándo fuiste de excursión a las ruinas?
9. ¿Fuiste tímido o bailaste con los bailarines?
10. ¿Cómo viajaste a Cancún?

Enrichment: Some people think that when they visit a foreign country, they can break all the rules of polite behavior. Other people think that when they travel to another country, they are guests in that country and should observe all the rules of polite behavior. Hold a class discussion of these attitudes. Have the class research the expression "the ugly American."

K. ¿Qué haces tú?

What do you do in different situations?

Lee las oraciones y la pregunta. Luego, escoge una palabra de la lista y contesta la pregunta. Sigue el modelo.

Modelo: Estás en un sendero y ves un caimán. ¿Cómo corres?
Respuesta: **Corro rápidamente.**

You may wish to assign this activity as homework after presenting it in class.

1. Es el día de tu cumpleaños. Tus amigos te dan una fiesta. ¿Cómo pasas la tarde?
2. Estás en el cine. No te gusta la película. ¿Cómo sales del cine?
3. Vas al gimnasio todos los días. Te gusta practicar los deportes. Por lo general, ¿cuándo vas al gimnasio?
4. Hoy te levantaste muy temprano. No tienes prisa porque no quieres llegar temprano a la escuela. ¿Cómo caminas a la escuela?
5. Casi nunca vas al teatro. Ayer fuiste al teatro para ver una obra de misterio. Por lo general, ¿cuándo vas al teatro?

lentamente	usualmente	frecuentemente
raramente	rápidamente	felizmente

Answers will vary.
1. Paso la tarde felizmente.
2. Salgo rápidamente.
3. Voy al gimnasio frecuentemente.
4. Camino lentamente.
5. Voy raramente.

Usualmente, ¿vas de compras en el mercado al aire libre?

L. Una fiesta con preguntas

You're having a wonderful party. Unfortunately, one of your guests had to bring along a nosy little sister.

Primero, lee la pregunta. Luego, contéstala con **sí** o **no.** Sigue el modelo.

Students may enjoy role-playing the nosy little sister and the annoyed host.

Modelo: ¿Conoces a mi hermana? (sí)

Respuesta: **Sí, la conozco.**

1. ¿Invitaste a mi hermana? (sí)
2. ¿Invitaste a tus maestros? (no)
3. ¿Pusiste los discos en tu cuarto? (sí)
4. ¿Trajiste la torta a la mesa? (sí)
5. ¿Oíste mi canción? (no)
6. ¿Miraste los programas de televisión esta mañana? (no)
7. ¿Pusiste tus camisas nuevas en tu ropero? (sí)
8. ¿Me invitaste a mí? (no)

1. Sí, la invité.
2. No, no los invité.
3. Sí, los puse en mi cuarto.
4. Sí, la traje a la mesa.
5. No, no la oí.
6. No, no los miré.
7. Sí, las puse en mi ropero.
8. No, no te invité a ti.

You've decided that enough is enough! You'll tell her so many answers that she will run out of questions!

Primero, lee la oración. Luego, complétala con **me, te, le, nos** o **les.** Sigue el modelo.

Modelo: No, a ti no —— voy a dar mis regalos.

Respuesta: **No, a ti no te voy a dar mis regalos.**

1. No, a mi cantante favorito no —— escribí una carta.
2. No, a mis amigos no —— gusta la música clásica.

1. le
2. les

3. No, mis padres no —— dieron un coche para mi cumpleaños.
4. No —— hago preguntas porque no quiero escuchar tus respuestas.
5. No, a nosotros no —— duele la cabeza.
6. No, el presidente no —— mandó una tarjeta de cumpleaños.

3. me
4. te
5. nos
6. me

LL. Haciendo preparaciones

The Ruiz family is getting ready to go on vacation. Sra. Ruiz is telling her family what must be done before they can leave.

Lee las palabras y las frases entre paréntesis. Luego, escribe una oración con **Hay que . . .** Sigue el modelo.

Modelo: ¿las cartas? (echar al correo)

Respuesta: **Hay que echarlas al correo.**

Have students guess the meaning of **hay que** from context. Ask what other expression they know that has the same meaning.

1. ¿las estampillas? (poner en los sobres)
2. ¿la basura? (sacar de la cocina)
3. ¿el auto? (lavar bien)
4. ¿las ventanas? (cerrar bien)
5. ¿los billetes? (comprar en la agencia de viajes)
6. ¿las cuentas? (pagar hoy)
7. ¿los paquetes? (envolver y mandar por correo)
8. ¿el equipaje? (poner en el auto)

1. Hay que ponerlas en los sobres.
2. Hay que sacarla de la cocina.
3. Hay que lavarlo bien.
4. Hay que cerrarlas bien.
5. Hay que comprarlos en la agencia de viajes.
6. Hay que pagarlas hoy.
7. Hay que envolverlos y mandarlos por correo.
8. Hay que ponerlo en el auto.

Extension: Have students think of other chores that must be done before leaving on a trip.

M. Todo el mundo estuvo confundido

There must have been a full moon last night! No one can remember the correct order in which they did things. Help them out.

Primero, lee las oraciones. Luego, escríbelas en el orden correcto. Sigue el modelo.

You may wish to assign this activity as homework.

Modelo: La Sra. Gutiérrez

a. Compré carne y legumbres.
b. Caminé al supermercado.
c. Volví a mi apartamento.

Respuesta: a. **Caminé al supermercado.**
b. **Compré carne y legumbres.**
c. **Volví a mi apartamento.**

1. El Sr. Mendoza
a. Salí de la casa.
b. Encontré un gato en el árbol.
c. Oí un ruido.

2. Raimundo e Isabel
a. El avión aterrizó.
b. Fuimos al aeropuerto.
c. Saludamos a nuestros primos.

3. Pacha y Eduardo
a. Contestamos sus preguntas.
b. Gritamos al policía.
c. Miramos un robo.

4. Juanita
a. Me dio unas medicinas.
b. Estuve enferma.
c. Fui al médico.

1. a. Oí un ruido.
b. Salí de la casa.
c. Encontré un gato en el árbol.
2. a. Fuimos al aeropuerto.
b. El avión aterrizó.
c. Saludamos a nuestros primos.
3. a. Miramos un robo.
b. Gritamos al policía.
c. Contestamos sus preguntas.
4. a. Estuve enferma.
b. Fui al médico.
c. Me dio unas medicinas.

Extension: Have students make up other sentences about a crazy evening.

N. Una conversación entre hermanos

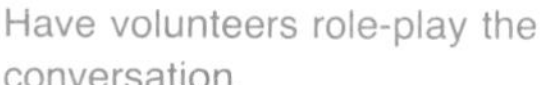
Have volunteers role-play the conversation.

SARA: ¿Qué estás haciendo, Pepe?

PEPE: Estoy escribiendo un reporte para la clase de español.

SARA: ¿Para cuándo necesitas el reporte?

PEPE: Lo tengo que escribir para el lunes.

SARA: Pero hoy es sábado. Ya escribiste por dos horas.

PEPE: Sí. Es un reporte largo.

SARA: ¡No estudies tanto! Es importante jugar también. Los juegos son buenos para la salud.

PEPE: ¿Por qué me dices esto? Eres mi hermana. Raramente piensas en mi salud.

SARA: Es que . . . Quiero jugar al boliche, pero papá no me permite ir sola.

PEPE: Ahora comprendo. Bueno, te doy dos horas de jugar al boliche por una hora de ayuda con mis tareas.

SARA: ¡Está bien! ¡Me ganaste!

Extension: Students may scan the conversation to find information not covered in the Preguntas. Have them write at least two more questions.

Preguntas

1. ¿Qué está haciendo Pepe?
2. ¿Para cuándo es el reporte?
3. ¿Por cuánto tiempo estudió?
4. ¿Qué le dice Sara sobre los juegos y la salud?
5. ¿Qué va a hacer Sara?

1. Pepe está estudiando.
2. El reporte es para el lunes.
3. Estudió por dos horas.
4. Sara le dice que los juegos son buenos para la salud.
5. Sara va a jugar al boliche y después, va a ayudar a Pepe con sus tareas.

Questions will vary. You may wish to choose another photo and brainstorm a few questions with the class, then have them write questions for 5 of the photos as homework.

Ñ. Tú eres periodista

Imagine that you're a reporter for **la Revista Mundial** and you have traveled to all the places in the pictures. What questions did you ask people in each place?

Primero, mira la foto. Luego, escribe dos o tres preguntas sobre cada foto. Lee el modelo.

Modelo:

Respuesta:

1. **Señora, ¿cuántas maletas trajo usted?**
2. **¿Recibió todo su equipaje?**
3. **¿Por cuánto tiempo va a viajar en este país?**

1.

Madrid, España

2.

Bogotá, Colombia

3.

Yucatán, México

4.

Quito, Ecuador

5.

San Francisco, California

8.

Caracas, Venezuela

6.

Barcelona, España

9.

Córdoba, España

7.

Lima, Perú

10.

La Pampa, Argentina

Extension: Have students pair up and answer each other's questions as the people in the pictures might answer.

O. Hay que saber los datos

As a reporter for **la Revista Mundial,** you need to have your facts straight about what you write. Answer your editor's questions. (You may need to look at a map.)

You may wish to assign this activity as homework.

Lee y contesta las preguntas. Sigue el modelo.

Modelo: ¿Dónde está el Perú? ¿Está al norte o al sur de Chile?
Respuesta: **El Perú está en la América del Sur. Está al norte de Chile.**

See Unit Plans, Unidad 14, for answers to activity O.

1. ¿Dónde está Colombia? ¿Está al este o al oeste de Venezuela?
2. ¿Dónde está Guatemala? ¿Está al norte o al sur de México?
3. ¿Dónde está España? ¿Está al norte o al sur de Francia?
4. ¿Dónde está el Ecuador? ¿Está al este o al oeste del Brasil?
5. ¿Dónde está Puerto Rico? ¿Está al este o al oeste de la República Dominicana?
6. ¿Dónde está Panamá? ¿Está al norte o al sur de Cuba?

Extension: Have students role-play the conversation between editor and reporter. They may use a map to ask more questions.

P. ¿Qué hizo la periodista?

The editor for **la Revista Mundial** is curious about the daily routine of his reporters while they're on assignment. How did ace reporter Luisa Llanos answer his questions?

You may wish to assign this activity as homework.

Primero, lee la pregunta. Luego, contéstala con las palabras entre paréntesis. Sigue el modelo.

Modelo: ¿A qué hora te despertaste cada día?
(a las cinco y media de la mañana)
Respuesta: **Me desperté a las cinco y media de la mañana.**

See Unit Plans, Unidad 14, for answers to activity P.

1. ¿A qué hora te bañaste cada día? (a las seis menos cuarto)
2. ¿Tomaste el desayuno todos los días? (té y un pan dulce)
3. ¿Cuántas horas trabajaste cada día? (ocho horas al día)
4. ¿Cómo viajaste en las ciudades? (en autobús y en el metro)
5. ¿A qué hora almorzaste cada día? (a la una en punto)
6. ¿A veces comiste una merienda? (a las cinco y media)
7. ¿Cuántas horas escribiste cada día? (seis horas al día)
8. ¿A qué hora te acostaste cada noche? (a las once y media)

Answers will vary. Have students use the questions to interview each other. Encourage them to think of additional questions.

Q. ¿Y tú?

Now the editor wants to know your daily routine.

Lee y contesta las preguntas en tus palabras.

1. ¿A qué hora te levantas?
2. Usualmente, ¿qué usas, la bañera o la ducha?
3. ¿Qué haces primero, tomas el desayuno o te pones la ropa?
4. Por lo general, ¿almuerzas rápidamente o lentamente?
5. ¿A qué hora te acuestas?
6. ¿Te duermes inmediatamente?

El hombre se peina antes de salir de la casa. Usualmente, ¿a qué hora te peinas por la mañana?

R. ¿De qué te ríes?

Arnulfo is writing a report about what makes people laugh. He looked up the verb **reírse** and found the conjugations. Now he needs your help in choosing the correct forms for his report.

Primero, lee la información sobre **reírse.** Luego, escoge la forma apropiada para completar cada oración. Sigue el modelo.

Have students look up **reírse** in the classroom dictionary and compare the entry to the one on this page.

Present: me río, te ríes, se ríe, nos reímos, os reís, se ríen

Preterite: me reí, te reíste, se rió, nos reímos, os reísteis, se rieron

Imperative: ríete, no te rías

Modelo: Generalmente, las personas —— de cuentos cómicos.

Respuesta: **Generalmente, las personas se ríen de cuentos cómicos.**

1. Algunos programas de televisión son muy cómicos. Mi familia y yo siempre —— de esos programas.
2. Mi amigo Ignacio es muy cómico. Yo —— de él todo el tiempo.
3. Ayer, Ignacio se puso unos anteojos muy cómicos. Todos los alumnos —— de él.
4. Aun la maestra —— de Ignacio con los anteojos grandísimos.
5. El director de la escuela oyó el ruido y entró en el salón. Él no ——. Nos dijo que tenemos que ser más serios.
6. ¡Pobre Ignacio! No pudo controlar la risa. Él —— más de la situación y de la cara tan seria del director.
7. El director le dijo: "¡No ——!" Luego, cerró la puerta bien fuerte.
8. Todos nosotros —— del director y también de Ignacio.

1. nos reímos
2. me río
3. se rieron
4. se rió
5. se rió
6. se rió
7. te rías
8. nos reímos

S. Una encuesta cómica

Take a survey of your classmates to find out what they laugh at. Do they laugh at jokes, at funny TV programs, or at comical people?

Primero, escoge a diez compañeros de clase. Luego, hazles la pregunta **¿De qué te ríes?** Por último, escribe las respuestas. Lee el modelo.

You may wish to remind students that they can look at the conjugations on page 342 for help.

Modelo: TÚ: ¿De qué te ríes? ¿Te ríes de los chistes, de los programas cómicos o de las personas cómicas?

IRIS: Generalmente, me río de los chistes.

Respuesta: 1. Iris se ríe de los chistes.

Extension: After students have completed the activity, have volunteers poll the class to find out what makes people laugh. This information, along with illustrations cut out of old magazines and newspapers can be the basis of a bulletin-board display or a Big Book.

¡A divertirnos!

Un proverbio cómico

El último que se ríe, se ríe más fuerte.

Students should use the visual clues to understand the meaning of the proverb. Have students illustrate other situations in which the proverb might apply. Some may be able to tell of events in their own lives to which the proverb would apply.

Pronouns and Adjectives

Subject Pronouns

Singular	Plural
yo	nosotros, nosotras
tú	vosotros, vosotras
él	ellos
ella	ellas
usted	ustedes

Direct Object Pronouns

Singular	Plural
me	nos
te	os
lo	los
la	las

Indirect Object Pronouns

Singular	Plural
me	nos
te	os
le	les

Reflexive Pronouns

Singular	Plural
me	nos
te	os
se	se

Demonstrative Adjectives

Singular		Plural	
Masculine	Feminine	Masculine	Feminine
este	esta	estos	estas
ese	esa	esos	esas
aquel	aquella	aquellos	aquellas

Possessive Adjectives

Singular		Plural	
mi	nuestro, nuestra	mis	nuestros, nuestras
tu	vuestro, vuestra	tus	vuestros, vuestras
su	su	sus	sus

Verbs

Regular Verbs

-ar Verbs: Model **hablar**

	Present	Preterite
yo	hablo	hablé
tú	hablas	hablaste
él, ella, usted	habla	habló
nosotros (-as)	hablamos	hablamos
vosotros (-as)	habláis	hablasteis
ellos, ellas, ustedes	hablan	hablaron

Gerund: hablando Familiar command: ¡habla! ¡no hables!

-er Verbs: Model **comer**

	Present	Preterite
yo	como	comí
tú	comes	comiste
él, ella, usted	come	comió
nosotros (-as)	comemos	comimos
vosotros (-as)	coméis	comisteis
ellos, ellas, ustedes	comen	comieron

Gerund: comiendo Familiar command: ¡come! ¡no comas!

-ir Verbs: Model abrir

	Present	Preterite
yo	abro	abrí
tú	abres	abriste
él, ella, usted	abre	abrió
nosotros (-as)	abrimos	abrimos
vosotros (-as)	abrís	abristeis
ellos, ellas, ustedes	abren	abrieron

Gerund: abriendo   Familiar command: ¡abre! ¡no abras!

Stem-Changing Verbs

o to ue: Model probar

	Present	Preterite
yo	pruebo	probé
tú	pruebas	probaste
él, ella, usted	prueba	probó
nosotros (-as)	probamos	probamos
vosotros (-as)	probáis	probasteis
ellos, ellas, ustedes	prueban	probaron

Gerund: probando   Familiar command: ¡prueba! ¡no pruebes!

e to ie: Model pensar

	Present	Preterite
yo	pienso	pensé
tú	piensas	pensaste
él, ella, usted	piensa	pensó
nosotros (-as)	pensamos	pensamos
vosotros (-as)	pensáis	pensasteis
ellos, ellas, ustedes	piensan	pensaron

Gerund: pensando   Familiar command: ¡piensa! ¡no pienses!

u to **ue:** Model **jugar**

	Present	Preterite
yo	juego	jugué
tú	juegas	jugaste
él, ella, usted	juega	jugó
nosotros (-as)	jugamos	jugamos
vosotros (-as)	jugáis	jugasteis
ellos, ellas, ustedes	juegan	jugaron

Gerund: jugando Familiar command: ¡juega! ¡no juegues!

e to **i:** Model **servir**

	Present	Preterite
yo	sirvo	serví
tú	sirves	serviste
él, ella, usted	sirve	sirvió
nosotros (-as)	servimos	servimos
vosotros (-as)	servís	servisteis
ellos, ellas, ustedes	sirven	sirvieron

Gerund: sirviendo Familiar command: ¡sirve! ¡no sirvas!

Irregular Verbs*

Dar

	Present	Preterite
yo	doy	di
tú	das	diste
él, ella, usted	da	dio
nosotros (-as)	damos	dimos
vosotros (-as)	dais	disteis
ellos, ellas, ustedes	dan	dieron

Gerund: dando Familiar command: ¡da! ¡no des!

*Not all of the forms and tenses in these charts have been taught for all the verbs listed. They are provided here for your reference.

Decir

	Present	Preterite
yo	digo	dije
tú	dices	dijiste
él, ella, usted	dice	dijo
nosotros (-as)	decimos	dijimos
vosotros (-as)	decís	dijisteis
ellos, ellas, ustedes	dicen	dijeron

Gerund: diciendo Familiar command: ¡di! ¡no digas!

Estar

	Present	Preterite
yo	estoy	estuve
tú	estás	estuviste
él, ella, usted	está	estuvo
nosotros (-as)	estamos	estuvimos
vosotros (-as)	estáis	estuvisteis
ellos, ellas, ustedes	están	estuvieron

Gerund: estando Familiar command: ¡está! ¡no estés!

Hacer

	Present	Preterite
yo	hago	hice
tú	haces	hiciste
él, ella, usted	hace	hizo
nosotros (-as)	hacemos	hicimos
vosotros (-as)	hacéis	hicisteis
ellos, ellas, ustedes	hacen	hicieron

Gerund: haciendo Familiar command: ¡haz! ¡no hagas!

Ir

	Present	Preterite
yo	voy	fui
tú	vas	fuiste
él, ella, usted	va	fue
nosotros (-as)	vamos	fuimos
vosotros (-as)	vais	fuisteis
ellos, ellas, ustedes	van	fueron

Gerund: yendo Familiar command: ¡ve! ¡no vayas!

Oír

	Present	Preterite
yo	oigo	oí
tú	oyes	oíste
él, ella, usted	oye	oyó
nosotros (-as)	oímos	oímos
vosotros (-as)	oís	oísteis
ellos, ellas, ustedes	oyen	oyeron

Gerund: oyendo Familiar command: ¡oye! ¡no oigas!

Poder

	Present	Preterite
yo	puedo	pude
tú	puedes	pudiste
él, ella, usted	puede	pudo
nosotros (-as)	podemos	pudimos
vosotros (-as)	podéis	pudisteis
ellos, ellas, ustedes	pueden	pudieron

Gerund: pudiendo Familiar command: ¡puede! ¡no puedas!

Poner

	Present	Preterite
yo	pongo	puse
tú	pones	pusiste
él, ella, usted	pone	puso
nosotros (-as)	ponemos	pusimos
vosotros (-as)	ponéis	pusisteis
ellos, ellas, ustedes	ponen	pusieron

Gerund: poniendo Familiar command: ¡pon! ¡no pongas!

Querer

	Present	Preterite
yo	quiero	quise
tú	quieres	quisiste
él, ella, usted	quiere	quiso
nosotros (-as)	queremos	quisimos
vosotros (-as)	queréis	quisisteis
ellos, ellas, ustedes	quieren	quisieron

Gerund: queriendo Familiar command: ¡quiere! ¡no quieras!

Saber

	Present	Preterite
yo	sé	supe
tú	sabes	supiste
él, ella, usted	sabe	supo
nosotros (-as)	sabemos	supimos
vosotros (-as)	sabéis	supisteis
ellos, ellas, ustedes	saben	supieron

Gerund: sabiendo Familiar command: ¡sabe! ¡no sepas!

Ser

	Present	Preterite
yo	soy	fui
tú	eres	fuiste
él, ella, usted	es	fue
nosotros (-as)	somos	fuimos
vosotros (-as)	sois	fuisteis
ellos, ellas, ustedes	son	fueron

Gerund: siendo   Familiar command: ¡sé! ¡no seas!

Tener

	Present	Preterite
yo	tengo	tuve
tú	tienes	tuviste
él, ella, usted	tiene	tuvo
nosotros (-as)	tenemos	tuvimos
vosotros (-as)	tenéis	tuvisteis
ellos, ellas, ustedes	tienen	tuvieron

Gerund: teniendo   Familiar command: ¡ten! ¡no tengas!

Traer

	Present	Preterite
yo	traigo	traje
tú	traes	trajiste
él, ella, usted	trae	trajo
nosotros (-as)	traemos	trajimos
vosotros (-as)	traéis	trajisteis
ellos, ellas, ustedes	traen	trajeron

Gerund: trayendo   Familiar command: ¡trae! ¡no traigas!

Venir

	Present	Preterite
yo	vengo	vine
tú	vienes	viniste
él, ella, usted	viene	vino
nosotros (-as)	venimos	vinimos
vosotros (-as)	venís	vinistels
ellos, ellas, ustedes	vienen	vinieron

Gerund: viniendo   Familiar command: ¡ven! ¡no vengas!

Reflexive Verbs

Model lavarse

	Present	Preterite
yo	me lavo	me lavé
tú	te lavas	te lavaste
él, ella, usted	se lava	se lavó
nosotros (-as)	nos lavamos	nos lavamos
vosotros (-as)	os laváis	os lavasteis
ellos, ellas, ustedes	se lavan	se lavaron

Gerund: lavándome, lavándote, lavándose;
lavándonos, lavándoos, lavándose
Familiar command: ¡lávate! ¡no te laves!

Many verbs can become reflexive verbs. You simply use the verb forms for those verbs and add the reflexive pronouns. The following are examples:

dormirse: me duermo, te duermes, se duerme;
nos dormimos, os dormís, se duermen

despertarse: me despierto, te despiertas, se despierta;
nos despertamos, os despertáis, se despiertan

Countries and Nationalities

	El país	La gente
la	Argentina	el argentino, la argentina
	Belice	el beliceño, la beliceña
	Bolivia	el boliviano, la boliviana
el	Canadá	el canadiense, la canadiense
	Colombia	el colombiano, la colombiana
	Costa Rica	el costarricense, la costarricense
	Cuba	el cubano, la cubana
	Chile	el chileno, la chilena
el	Ecuador	el ecuatoriano, la ecuatoriana
	El Salvador	el salvadoreño, la salvadoreña
	España	el español, la española
los	Estados Unidos	el estadounidense, la estadounidense
	Guatemala	el guatemalteco, la guatemalteca
	Honduras	el hondureño, la hondureña
	México	el mexicano, la mexicana
	Nicaragua	el nicaragüense, la nicaragüense
	Panamá	el panameño, la panameña
el	Paraguay	el paraguayo, la paraguaya
el	Perú	el peruano, la peruana
la	República Dominicana	el dominicano, la dominicana
el	Uruguay	el uruguayo, la uruguaya
	Venezuela	el venezolano, la venezolana

	Otros lugares	La gente
el	África	el africano, la africana
el	Brasil	el brasileño, la brasileña
	Francia	el francés, la francesa
	Haití	el haitiano, la haitiana
	Portugal	el portugués, la portuguesa
	Puerto Rico	el puertorriqueño, la puertorriqueña

Los números

1	uno	**19**	diez y nueve	**41**	cuarenta y uno	**71**	setenta y uno
2	dos	**20**	veinte	•		•	
3	tres	**21**	veinte y uno	•		•	
4	cuatro	**22**	veinte y dos	•		•	
5	cinco	**23**	veinte y tres	**49**	cuarenta y nueve	**79**	setenta y nueve
6	seis	**24**	veinte y cuatro	**50**	cincuenta	**80**	ochenta
7	siete	**25**	veinte y cinco	**51**	cincuenta y uno	**81**	ochenta y uno
8	ocho	**26**	veinte y seis	•		•	
9	nueve	**27**	veinte y siete	•		•	
10	diez	**28**	veinte y ocho	•		•	
11	once	**29**	veinte y nueve	**59**	cincuenta y nueve	**89**	ochenta y nueve
12	doce	**30**	treinta	**60**	sesenta	**90**	noventa
13	trece	**31**	treinta y uno	**61**	sesenta y uno	**91**	noventa y uno
14	catorce	•		•		•	
15	quince	•		•		•	
16	diez y seis	•		•		•	
17	diez y siete	**39**	treinta y nueve	**69**	sesenta y nueve	•	
18	diez y ocho	**40**	cuarenta	**70**	setenta	**99**	noventa y nueve
						100	cien

101	ciento uno	**400**	cuatrocientos, cuatrocientas
105	ciento cinco	**500**	quinientos, quinientas
110	ciento diez	**600**	seiscientos, seiscientas
150	ciento cincuenta	**700**	setecientos, setecientas
199	ciento noventa y nueve	**800**	ochocientos, ochocientas
200	doscientos, doscientas	**900**	novecientos, novecientas
300	trescientos, trescientas	**1000**	mil

Hay doscientos alumnos en la escuela.
Hay trescientas sillas en el auditorio.
Hay cuatrocientas cincuenta uvas en la caja.
Hay novecientos veinte y cinco bolígrafos.
Hay mil quinientas cerezas en la mesa.

Glossary
Spanish–English

The Spanish-English Glossary contains the vocabulary words you learn in each unit, as well as the other words that appear in your readings. When a definition is followed by a number, the number stands for the unit in which it is taught.

Some entries—that is, words and definitions—have abbreviations in them to help you learn more about the words. A complete list of the abbreviations follows this introduction.

Some nouns are not regular and you need extra information about them. For example:

lápiz, el (*m.*, *pl.*: **lápices**) pencil

The information in parentheses tells you that **lápiz** is a masculine word (*m.*) and that when you talk about more than one pencil (*pl.*, the plural form), you change the **z** to **c** and add **-es.**

Descriptive words, or adjectives, are given in the masculine singular form and are followed by the feminine singular ending in parentheses:

bajo (-a) short

Some verbs have changes in the stem when you use their forms:

acostarse (ue) to lie down, to go to bed

The letters in parentheses tell you that the letter **o** in the stem changes to **ue.** If you need to see a model of the stem-changing verb, you can look in the appendix of verbs. Also, if a verb is irregular, you will find the abbreviation (*IR*) following the verb.

Sometimes you will find words that are used in only one form in the textbook, such as commands in the exercise instructions. These words have abbreviations that will help you learn more about them:

haz (*com.; inf.:* **hacer**) make; ask

The abbreviations tell you that **haz** is a command form (*com.*) and it comes from the infinitive (*inf.*) of the verb **hacer.**

Abbreviations

adj.	adjective	*IR*	irregular
adv.	adverb	*m.*	masculine
com.	command	*pl.*	plural
f.	feminine	*prep.*	preposition
inf.	infinitive	*s.*	singular

a

a to; at; personal *a*
¿A cuántos (kilómetros)? . . . How many (kilometers) away . . . ?
a lo mejor maybe, perhaps
a tiempo on time (2)
a veces sometimes
a ver let's see
abandonado (-a) abandoned
abeja, la bee (9)
abierto (-a) open (4)
abrelatas, el *(m.)* can opener
abrigo, el coat
abrir to open
abuela, la grandmother
abuelo, el grandfather
abuelos, los grandparents
aburrido (-a) bored; boring (5)
acá here
¡Ven acá! Come here!
acabar to end, to finish
acabar de + *inf.* to have just . . .
acaso perhaps; by chance
por si acaso just in case
acostarse (ue) to lie down, to go to bed
acrobacia, la acrobatics
actividad, la *(f.)* activity
actor, el actor (11)

actriz, la (*f., pl.:* **actrices**) actress (11)
actuar to act, to behave
acuático (-a) aquatic
el esquí acuático waterskiing (8)
acuerdo, el agreement
ponerse de acuerdo to come to an agreement
acumulación, la (*f., pl.:* **acumulaciones**) accumulation
adelante ahead (6)
además furthermore, besides
adentro inside
adivinanza, la riddle
adivinar to guess
¿adónde? (to) where?
aéreo (-a) air, aerial
la línea aérea airline (2)
el correo aéreo airmail (13)
aeromoza, la (*f.*) flight attendant (2)
aeromozo, el (*m.*) flight attendant (2)
aeropuerto, el airport (2)
aerotaxi, el (*m.*) "air taxi"
afuera outside
agencia, la agency (1)
la agencia de viajes travel agency (1)
agente, el *or* la agent (1)
el (la) agente de viajes travel agent (1)
el (la) agente de correo postal clerk (13)
agosto August
agua, el (*f.*) water
ahora now
ahora mismo right now
ahorrar to save (4)
aire, el (*m.*) air
al aire libre in the open air, outdoors
ajedrez, el (*m.*) chess
al (a + el) to the; at the; in the
(tres) veces al día (three) times a day
alarma, la alarm
la alarma de incendios fire alarm (12)
alcaldía, la city hall (5)
alfombra, la rug
algo something
alguien somebody, someone
algún some, any
algún día someday
alguna some, any
almacén, el (*m., pl.:* **almacenes**) department store
almohada, la pillow
almorzar (ue) to lunch, to eat lunch (7)
almuerzo, el lunch
alpinismo, el mountain climbing (10)
alpinista, el *or* la mountain climber (10)
alquilar to rent
alto (-a) tall
alto (*adv.*) high, high up
altura, la height
—— pies de altura —— feet in height
el salto de altura high jump (10)
alumna, la (*f.*) student, pupil
alumno, el (*m.*) student, pupil
allá there
allí there
amarillo (-a) yellow
ambulancia, la ambulance (12)

amiga, la *(f.)* friend
amigo, el *(m.)* friend
andar to walk (12)
animal, el *(m.)* animal
anoche last night
anteojos, los sunglasses (8), eyeglasses (8)
antes de before
antiguo (-a) old (3); antique; ancient
anuncio, el announcement
año, el year
apagar to put out
apartamento, el apartment (5)
apenas as soon as
aplaudir to applaud, to clap (11)
apreciar to appreciate, to enjoy
aprender to learn
apropiado (-a) appropriate
aquel *(m.)* that (way over there) (8)
aquella that (way over there) (8)
aquellas those (way over there) (8)
aquellos those (way over there) (8)
aquí here
árbol, el *(m.)* tree (9)
arduo (-a) arduous, difficult
área, la area
arena, la sand (8)
arepa, la corn griddle cake
argentino (-a) Argentine
árido (-a) arid, dry
arte, el *(m.)* art
artículo, el article
artístico (-a) artistic
ascensor, el *(m.)* elevator (3)
así so, thus, in this way
  ¡Así es la vida! Such is life!
  nunca (hablan) así never (talk) in this way
asiento, el seat (2)
asistente, el *or* la assistant
asistir to attend (11)
aspiradora, la vacuum clearner
astronauta, el *or* la astronaut
astuto (-a) astute, clever
atender (ie) to wait on
aterrizar to land (2)
atleta, el *or* la athlete
atlético (-a) athletic
atrás behind (6)
aun even
aún still, yet
autobús, el *(m.)* bus
autógrafo, el autograph
automóvil, el *(m.)* automobile
auxilio, el aid, help (12)
  ¡Auxilio! Help! (12)
  los primeros auxilios first aid (12)
avenida, la avenue
aventura, la adventure
avión, el *(m., pl.:* **aviones***)* airplane (2)
¡Ay! Oh!
  ¡Ay de mí! Oh my!
ayer yesterday (7)
  ayer por la mañana yesterday morning (7)
  ayer por la tarde yesterday afternoon
ayuda, la help (12)
ayudar to help
azteca *(adj.)* Aztec (ancient civilization of Mexico)

azúcar, el *(m.)* sugar
azul blue

b

bacalao, el codfish
bahía, la bay
bailar to dance
bailarín, el *(pl.:* **bailarines)** *(m.)* dancer (11)
bailarina, la *(f.)* dancer (11)
baile, el *(m.)* dance
bajar to go down; to get out of (a vehicle)
bajo (-a) short (height)
balcón, el *(m., pl.:* **balcones)** balcony
baloncesto, el basketball
ballena, la whale
banco, el bank (4)
banda, la band (music); band (radio)
la banda de onda corta shortwave band
bañarse to bathe (oneself), to take a bath (3)
banẽra, la bathtub (3)
baño, el bath
barato (-a) inexpensive, cheap (7)
barbacoa, la barbecue
barco, el boat, ship
el barco de vela sailboat (8)
barrer to sweep
bastón, el *(m., pl.:* **bastones)** cane, walking stick
basura, la trash, garbage
batidora eléctrica, la electric mixer
batir to beat, to whip
beber to drink
becerro, el calf (9)
béisbol, el *(m.)* baseball
belleza, la beauty
beso, el kiss
biblioteca, la library
bibliotecario, el *(m.)* librarian
bicicleta, la bicycle
bien well, fine; very, quite
bien caliente very hot
billete, el *(m.)* ticket (1); bill (money) (4)
binoculares, los binoculars
bisabuelos, los great-grandparents
blanco (-a) white
blando (-a) soft (3)
blusa, la blouse
boa, la boa
boca, la mouth
boina, la beret
boliche, el *(m.)* bowling (10)
bolígrafo, el ballpoint pen
bolsa, la purse (7)
bombero, el *(m.)* fire fighter
bonito (-a) pretty
bordado, el embroidery
bota, la boot
botón, el *(m., pl.:* **botones)** button
boxeador, el *(m.)* boxer, fighter (10)
boxeo, el boxing (10)
brazalete, el *(m.)* bracelet (7)
brazo, el arm
bronce, el *(m.)* bronze (10)
una medalla de bronce bronze medal (10)

bronceado (-a) suntanned (8)
broncear to tan, to get a suntan
buceador, el *(m.)* diver
bucear to go scuba diving (8)
buen good (before a *m. s.* noun)
bueno (-a) good (10); well, O.K.
¡Qué bueno! Great!
buitre, el *(m.)* vulture
buscar to look (for)
buzón, el *(m., pl.:* **buzones**) mailbox

C

caballo, el horse
cabeza, la head
cada each, every
caer to fall
café, el *(m.)* coffee
cajera, la *(f.)* bank teller (4)
cajero, el *(m.)* bank teller (4)
caimán, el *(m., pl.:* **caimanes**) alligator (9)
calcetines, los *(m., s.:* **calcetín**) socks
calendario, el calendar
calentar (ie) to warm
caliente hot (3)
calor, el *(m.)* heat
Hace calor. It's hot. (weather)
calle, la *(f.)* street
cama, la bed
camarera, la waitress (4)
camarero, el waiter (4)
cambiar to change; to exchange
camilla, la stretcher (12)
caminar to walk; to hike; to go, to travel
camión, el *(m., pl.:* **camiones**) truck
camisa, la shirt
camiseta, la T-shirt
campeón, el *(m., pl.:* **campeones**) *(m.)* champion (10)
campeona, la *(f.)* champion
campeonato, el championship
campo, el country, countryside (9)
canal, el channel (television)
canción, la *(f., pl.:* **canciones**) song
cansado (-a) tired (5)
cantante, el *or* la singer (11)
cantar to sing
caos, el *(m.)* chaos, confusion
capital, la *(f.)* capital
cara, la face
caracol, el *(m.)* snail (8), shell (8)
carácter, el *(m., pl.:* **caracteres**) character, personality
¡Caramba! Wow! Darn!
carne, la *(f.)* meat
caro (-a) expensive (7)
carrera, la race (10)
carretera, la highway
carta, la (postal) letter (13)
cartel, el *(m.)* poster
cartera, la *(f.)* mail carrier (13)
cartero, el *(m.)* mail carrier (13)
casa, la house
en casa at home
casete, el *(m.)* cassette (tape) (7)
casi almost
casi no hardly

castillo, el castle
catarata, la waterfall
categoría, la category
(se) cayó *(pret.; inf.:* **caerse**) (it) fell down
celebración, la *(f., pl.:* **celebraciones**) celebration
celebrar to celebrate
cena, la supper, dinner
centavo, el cent
centro, el downtown; center
cepillarse to brush (oneself)
cerca de near, close to
cercano (-a) near; neighboring
cerdo, el hog, pig (9)
cerrado (-a) closed (4)
cerrar (ie) to close, to shut (1)
  cerrar con llave to lock
cesta, la wastebasket
ciclismo, el cycling (10)
ciclista, el *or* la cyclist (10)
ciencia ficción, la science fiction
ciencias, las science
cierto (-a) certain; true
cine, el *(m.)* movie theater
cinturón, el *(m., pl.:* **cinturones**) belt (7)
ciudad, la *(f.)* city (5)
civilización, la *(f., pl.:* **civilizaciones**) civilization
claramente clearly
clarinete, el *(m.)* clarinet (11)
claro clearly
  ¡Claro! Of course!
  ¡Claro que no! Of course not!
clase, la *(f.)* class
clásico (-a) classic
clo-clo cluck-cluck
club, el *(m.)* club
cocina, la kitchen
cocinar to cook
cocinera, la *(f.)* cook
coche, el *(m.)* car
coherente coherent
coleccionar to collect
colegio, el high school (6)
colorido (-a) colorful
collar, el *(m.)* necklace (7)
comedor, el *(m.)* dining room
comenzar (ie) to begin, to start (1)
comer to eat
cómico (-a) funny, comical
comida, la food
  la comida enlatada canned goods (9)
como like, such as; as
¿cómo? how? what?
  ¿Cómo es? What is . . . like?
cómodo (-a) comfortable (2)
compacto (-a) compact
compañera, la *(f.)* companion, partner
compañero, el *(m.)* companion, partner
  el compañero de clase *(m.)* classmate
comparar to compare
compartir to share
completar to complete, to finish
completo (-a) complete
comprar to buy (7)
comprender to understand
computadora, la computer
comunidad, la *(f.)* community
con with

concierto, el concert
concha, la seashell (8), conch shell (8)
conductor, el *(m.)* driver
confundido (-a) confused (5)
conocer to know (a person); to get acquainted with, to know (a place) (5)
conserje, el *or* la janitor
contacto, el contact
contar to count; to tell (a story, joke)
contento (-a) content, happy
contestar to answer
contraste, el contrast
contrato, el contract
controlar to control
conveniente convenient
conversación, la *(f., pl.:* **conversaciones**) conversation
conversar to converse, to talk
copa, la cup
  la Copa Mundial World Cup (soccer tournament)
copia, la copy
correctamente correctly (12)
correcto (-a) correct (12)
correo, el post office (13); mail (13)
  el correo aéreo airmail (13)
correr to run
corroer to corrode
corto (-a) short
cosa, la thing
costa, la coast
costar (ue) to cost (1)
crear to create
crema, la cream, lotion
  la crema de broncear suntan lotion (8)
cristal, el *(m.)* crystal
cruzar to cross
cuaderno, el notebook
cuadra, la block (length between two streets) (6)
cuadrado (-a) squared
  una milla cuadrada a square mile
cuadro, el painting, picture
¿cuál? *(pl.:* **¿cuáles?**) what? which (one)?
cuando when
¿cuándo? when?
¿cuánta? ¿cuánto? how much?
¿cuántas? ¿cuántos? how many?
cuarto, el room
  el cuarto de baño bathroom
cuarto, el quarter
  a la una y cuarto at a quarter past one
cuatro, el a small guitar, like a ukulele (Venezuela)
cubrir to cover
cuenta, la bill (4); check (in a restaurant) (4)
cuento, el story
cuerda, la string (of a guitar)
cuestionario, el questionnaire
cuidado, el care, caution
  con cuidado carefully
  ¡Cuidado! Be careful!
  ¡Ten cuidado! Be careful! (9)
cuidar to take care of
culpable guilty
  el culpable the guilty party
cultivar to cultivate, to grow
cumpleaños, el *(m., s.)* birthday
cumplir to reach (age)
  cumplir (catorce) años to have one's (fourteenth) birthday

ch

chica, la girl
chico, el boy
chino (-a) Chinese
chiste, el joke
chistoso (-a) funny
chocolate, el *(m.)* chocolate
choque, el *(m.)* collision, crash (12)

d

dar *(IR)* to give (4)
  dar de comer to feed
  dar la mano to shake hands (4)
  dar las gracias to thank (4)
  dar miedo to scare
  dar una vuelta a . . . to go around . . .
dato, el fact
de of; from; at; in
  de noche at night
  de oído by ear
  de repente suddenly
  ¿De veras? Really?
  de visita for a visit
debajo de under, underneath
débil weak
decidir to decide
decir *(IR)* to say (2); to tell (2)
  Ellas dicen que no. They say no.
dedo, el finger
dejar to allow, to let
  no te dejes dar don't let yourself be given
del (de + el) from the; of the
delgado (-a) thin, slim
delicado (-a) delicate
delicioso (-a) delicious
dentista, el *or* la dentist
dentro de inside
deporte, el *(m.)* sport
derecha, la right (direction)
  a la derecha to the right, on the right
derecho straight (direction)
desaparecer to disappear
desayuno, el breakfast
descansar to rest, to relax (1)
describir to describe
descripción, la *(f., pl.:* **descripciones**) description
descubrimiento, el discovery
descubrir to discover
desde from
deseo, el desire
desierto, el desert (1)
despacio *(adv.)* slowly (6)
despegar to take off (airplane) (2)
despertar (ie) to awaken, to wake up (another person)
despertarse (ie) to wake up
después afterwards, later
después de after
destino, el destination
destruir to destroy
detener *(IR)* to arrest (12)
deuda, la debt
día, el *(m.)* day
diario (-a) daily
dibujo, el drawing, picture
diente, el *(m.)* tooth
diferente different

difícil difficult
difícilmente with difficulty (12)
dinero, el money
dirección, la *(f., pl.:* **direcciones**) direction; address (13)
director, el *(m.)* principal; conductor (11)
directora, la *(f.)* principal; conductor (11)
disco, el (phonograph) record (7)
el disco compacto compact disc (7)
disfrutar to enjoy
distante *(adj.)* distant
distinto (-a) different
divertido (-a) fun, enjoyable
divertirse (ie) to enjoy (oneself), to have fun
doblar to turn (a corner)
dólar, el *(m.)* dollar
doler (ue) to hurt, to ache
dolor, el *(m.)* pain
domingo Sunday
dominó, el dominoes
don Don (title of respect for an older man)
donde where
¿dónde? where?
doña Doña (title of respect for an older woman)
dormir (ue) to sleep
dormirse (ue) to fall asleep (3)
dormitorio, el bedroom
drama, el play, drama
ducha, la shower (3)
dueño, el *(m.)* owner
dulce, el *(m.)* sweet, candy
durante during
duro (-a) hard (3)

e

e and (used before words beginning with **i** or **hi**)
echar al correo to mail (13)
edad, la age
edificio, el building (5)
el edificio de apartamentos the apartment building (5)
educación, la *(f.)* education
EE.UU. abbreviation for **los Estados Unidos**
ejemplo, el example
ejercicio, el exercise
el the
él he
electricista, el *or* la electrician
eléctrico (-a) electric, electrical
elegante *(adj.)* elegant
ella she
ellas they; them (*f.* group)
ellos they; them (*m.* or *m.* and *f.* group)
embarcación, la *(f., pl.:* **embarcaciones**) embarkation
la tarjeta de embarcación boarding pass
emergencia, la emergency
emisora, la broadcasting station
emoción, la *(f., pl.:* **emociones**) emotion
¡Qué emoción! What excitement! How exciting!
emocionante moving, exciting
empezar (ie) to begin
empleo, el employment

en in; on; at; by; of, about
¿En qué trabajaste? What work did you do?
en vez de instead of
pensar en to think about
encantar to enchant, to delight
Me encantan las serpientes. I love snakes.
enciclopedia, la encyclopedia
encontrarse to meet, to run into; to be found, to find onseself (6)
encuesta, la survey
enero January
enfermera, la *(f.)* nurse
enfermería, la nurse's office
enfermero, el *(m.)* nurse
enfermo, el *(m.)* sick person
enfermo (-a) sick, ill (12)
enlatado (-a) canned (9)
la comida enlatada canned goods (9)
enojado (-a) angry (5)
enseñar to teach
entrada, la entrance
entrar to enter, to go in; to start
la semana que entra this coming week
entre between, among
entre paréntesis in parentheses
entregar to deliver, to give out
entrevista, la interview
enviar to send
envolver (ue) to wrap up (13)
equipaje, el *(m.)* luggage (2)
equipo, el team; equipment
esa that (8)
esas those (8)
escaleras, las stairs
escoger to choose, to select
escríbeme *(com., inf.:* **escribir**) write me
escribir to write
escritorio, el desk
escuchar to listen (to)
escuela, la school
escultura, la sculpture (5)
ese *(m.)* that (8)
esnórkel, el *(m.)* snorkel
esos those (8)
espagueti, el *(m.)* spaghetti
espalda, la back
español, el *(m.)* Spanish (language)
español (-a) Spanish
especial special
especializarse to specialize
espectador, el *(m.)* spectator (10)
espectadora, la *(f.)* spectator (10)
espejo, el mirror
esperar to wait (for)
esposa, la wife
esquí acuático, el *(m.)* waterskiing (8)
esquiar to ski
esquina, la (street) corner (6)
esta this (8)
estacionamiento, el parking lot
estadio, el stadium (5)
estado, el state
estampilla, la stamp (13)
estante, el *(m.)* bookcase
estar *(IR)* to be
estas these (8)
este, el *(m.)* east (6)
este *(m.)* this (8)
estómago, el stomach

estos these (8)
estrecho (-a) narrow
estudiar to study
estudio, el study
estupendo (-a) stupendous, awesome
etcétera et cetera
examen, el *(m., pl.:* **exámenes**) exam; examination
un examen médico medical examination
examinar to examine
excelente excellent
exclamar to exclaim
excursión, la *(f., pl.:* **excursiones**) excursion, outing (9)
ir de excursión to go on an outing
éxito, el success
exótico (-a) exotic
experimento, el experiment
expresión, la *(f., pl.:* **expresiones**) expression
extintor, el *(m.)* (fire) extinguisher (12)
extranjero, el *(m.)* foreigner (11)
extraño (-a) strange
extravagante extravagant
extremo, el extreme

f

fábula, la fable
fácil easy
fácilmente easily (12)
faltar to be lacking, to be missing
¿Qué falta? What is missing?
fallar to fail
familia, la family
famoso (-a) famous
farmacia, la pharmacy
farol, el *(m.)* streetlight, street lamp (6)
fascinante fascinating
favor, el *(m.)* favor
por favor please
favorito (-a) favorite
¡Felicitaciones! Congratulations!
feliz *(pl.:* **felices**) happy (12)
felizmente happily (12)
feo (-a) ugly
festival, el festival
ficción, la *(f., pl.:* **ficciones**) fiction
fiebre, la *(f.)* fever (12)
fiesta, la party
fila, la line (2)
hacer fila to stand in line (2)
fin, el *(m.)* end
el fin de semana weekend
por fin finally, at last
flor, la *(f.)* flower
flotar to float
folklórico (-a) folkloric, folk
fondo, el bottom
forma, la form
formar to form, to make up
fortaleza, la fortress
foto, la *(f.)* photo
fotografía, la photograph
fotógrafo, el photographer
francamente frankly
francés, el *(m.)* French (language)
francés, (-esa) French
frase, la *(f.)* phrase

frecuente frequent (12)
frecuentemente frequently (12)
frente, el *(m.)* front
frente al (almacén) across the street from (the department store)
fresa, la strawberry
el helado de fresas strawberry ice cream
fresco (-a) fresh
frío (-a) cold (3)
frontera, la border, boundary
frustración, la *(f., pl.:* **frustraciones***)* frustration
frustrante *(adj.)* frustrating
fruta, la fruit
fue *(pret.; inf.:* **ser***)* (it) was
fuente, la *(f.)* fountain (5)
fuera de outside
fuerte strong
las olas están fuertes the waves are rough
fútbol, el *(m.)* soccer
fútbol americano, el football
futuro, el future

g

galón, el *(m., pl.:* **galones***)* gallon
galleta, la cookie
gallina, la hen (9)
gallo, el rooster (9)
ganador, el *(m.)* winner (10)
ganador (-a) winning
ganar to win (10)
ganso, el goose (9)
garaje, el *(m.)* garage
gasolinera, la gas station
gastar to spend (4)
gato, el cat
gaucho, el gaucho (Argentine cowboy)
gelatina, la gelatin
general general (12)
generalmente generally (12)
generoso (-a) generous
gente, la *(f.)* people
geografía, la geography
gimnasia, la gymnastics (10)
gimnasio, el gymnasium
gobierno, el government
golfo, el gulf
Gracias. Thank you. Thanks.
grado, el grade, degree
grande big, large
granja, la farm (9)
granjero, el *(m.)* farmer
gripe, la *(f.)* influenza, flu
gritar to shout, to yell (10)
grueso (-a) fat, stout
grupo, el group
guapo (-a) handsome, attractive
guitarra, la guitar (11)
gustar to please, to be pleasing
gusto, el taste

h

habitación, la *(f., pl.:* **habitaciones***)* (hotel) room (3)
habla, el *(f.)* speech
de habla española Spanish-speaking

hablar to talk, to speak
hablar por teléfono to talk on the telephone
hacer *(IR)* to do (2); to make (2)
Hace calor. It's hot. (weather)
hace muchos años many years ago
Hace sol. It's sunny.
Hace . . . tiempo. The weather is. . .
hacer fila to stand in line
hacer la cama to make the bed
hacer la maleta to pack the suitcase
hacer un papel to play a part (11)
hacer un viaje to take a trip (2)
hacer una pregunta to ask a question
hacia toward
hambre, el *(f.)* hunger
hamburguesa, la hamburger
hasta until; to; even
¡Hasta luego! See you later!
Hasta pronto. See you soon.
hasta (Caracas) to (Caracas)
hay *(inf.:* **haber)** there is; there are
hay de todo there's some of everything
hay que + ***inf.*** it is necessary to. . .
haz *(com., inf.:* **hacer)** make; ask
haz una pregunta ask a question
helado, el ice cream
el helado de fresas strawberry ice cream
helicóptero, el helicopter
hermana, la sister
hermano, el brother
hermoso (-a) beautiful, lovely
héroe, el heroe
hijo, el son
hijos, los children
historia, la history
histórico (-a) historic
hoja de papel, la sheet of paper
¡Hola! Hello! Hi!
hombre, el *(m.)* man
honesto (-a) honest
hora, la hour; time
horario, el schedule (2); timetable (2)
hormiga, la ant (9)
horno, el oven
horrible horrible
horror, el *(m.)* horror
¡Qué horror! How dreadful!
hospital, el *(m.)* hospital
hotel, el *(m.)* hotel (3)
hoy today
huaraches, los *(m.)* sandals (Mexico)
huevo, el egg
huipil, el *(m.)* loose shirt with embroidery (Mexico)
húmedo (-a) humid (climate)
humo, el smoke
huracán, el *(m., pl.:* **huracanes)** hurricane

i

idea, la idea
idioma, el *(m.)* language
iglesia, la church (5)
impaciente impatient
impermeable, el *(m.)* raincoat
importante important
incendio, el fire (12)
incómodo (-a) uncomfortable (2)

incorrecto (-a) incorrect
indio, el Indian
inglés, el *(m.)* English (language)
inmediatamente immediately
inocente innocent, simple
instante, el *(m.)* instant, moment
instrucción, la *(f., pl.:* **instrucciones**) instruction
instructor, el *(m.)* instructor
instrumento, el instrument
inteligente intelligent
interés, el *(m., pl.:* **intereses**) interest
interesante interesting
interior, el *(m.)* inside, interior
internacional international
interrupción, la *(f., pl.:* **interrupciones**) interruption
inventar to make up, invent
invierno, el winter
invitación, la *(f., pl.:* **invitaciones**) invitation
invitado, el guest
invitar to invite
inyección, la *(f., pl.:* **inyecciones**) injection, shot (12)
ir *(IR)* to go
  ir a + *inf.* to be going to
  ir a pie to go on foot, to walk
  ir de compras to go shopping
  ir de excursión to go on an outing (9)
  ir de pesca to go fishing
irse *(IR)* to go away; to leave
isla, la island
izquierda, la left
  a la izquierda to the left, on the left

j

¡Ja, ja! Ha, ha!
jabón, el *(m., pl.:* **jabones**) soap (3)
jamón, el *(m., pl.:* **jamones**) ham
jardín, el *(m., pl.:* **jardines**) garden
jaula, la cage
jinete, el *(m.)* rider (on a horse)
joven, el *or* la *(m., f., pl.:* **jóvenes**) young man or young woman
joya, la jewel (7)
joyera, la *(f.)* jeweler (7)
joyería, la jewelry store (7)
joyero, el *(m.)* jeweler (7)
juego, el game
  el juego electrónico video game
jueves Thursday
jugador, el *(m.)* player (game or sport)
jugar (ue) to play (3)
  jugar a . . . to play (game or sport)
jugo, el juice
juicio, el trial
junto a *(prep.)* next to
juntos (-as) together

k

kilogramo, el kilogram
kilómetro, el kilometer (6)

l

la the; her (2); it (2)
lado, el side
ladrón, el (*m., pl.:* **ladrones**) robber, thief (12)
ladrona, la (*f.*) robber, thief (12)
lago, el lake (1)
laguna, la lagoon
lámpara, la lamp
lancha, la motorboat (8)
lápiz, el (*m., pl.:* **lápices**) pencil
largo (-a) long
las the; them (2)
lástima, la pity, shame
 ¡Qué lástima! What a shame! Too bad!
lata, la bore, annoyance
 ¡Qué lata! How boring! What a pain!
latino (-a) Latin
lavar to wash
lavarse to wash (oneself)
le to her; to him; to you (4)
lección, la (*f., pl.:* **lecciones**) lesson
leche, la (*f.*) milk
leer to read
legumbres, las (*f.*) vegetables
lejos far; far away
lejos de far from
lentamente slowly (12)
lento (-a) slow (12)
león, el (*m., pl.:* **leones**) lion
les to them; to you (*pl.*) (4)
letra, la letter (alphabet)
levantarse to get up
libertador, el (*m.*) liberator
libra, la pound (weight)
libre free; available
 al aire libre in the open air, outdoors
 la lucha libre wrestling (10)
libro, el book
líder, el (*m.*) leader
liebre, la (*f.*) hare
limón, el (*m., pl.:* **limones**) lemon
limonada, la lemonade
limpiar to clean; to wash
limpio (-a) clean
lindo (-a) pretty, beautiful
línea, la line
 la línea aérea airline (2)
lista, la list
listo (-a) smart, clever
lo the; him (2); it (2)
 a lo mejor maybe, perhaps
 lo mismo the same (thing)
 lo que what; that which
 lo siento (mucho) I'm (very) sorry
local (*adj.*) local
loco (-a) crazy
locura, la craziness, madness
locutor, el (*m.*) announcer (11)
locutora, la (*f.*) announcer (11)
loro, el parrot
los the; them (2)
 los (Morales) the (Morales) family
lucha libre, la wrestling (10)
luego then, next
lugar, el (*m.*) place
luna, la moon
lunes Monday

ll

llamada, la call
llamar to call
llamar por teléfono to call on the phone
llamarse to be called
llano, el plains
llave, la *(f.)* key (3)
cerrar con llave to lock
llavero, el key chain, key holder (7)
llegada, la arrival (2)
llegar to arrive (2)
lleno (-a) full
llevar to take, to carry; to lead; to wear
llorar to cry (11)
llover (ue) to rain
lluvia, la rain

m

maestra, la *(f.)* teacher
maestro, el *(m.)* teacher
mal *(adv.)* not well; badly, poorly
maleta, la suitcase (2)
malo (-a) bad (10)
mamá, la mother, mom
mandar to send (13)
mandar por correo to send by mail (13)
mano, la *(f.)* hand
manta, la blanket (3)
mantel, el *(m.)* tablecloth
manual, el *(m.)* manual, instruction book
manzana, la apple; (square city) block (6)
mañana, la morning
mañana *(adv.)* tomorrow
mapa, el *(m.)* map
mar, el *(m.)* sea (8)
maravilla, la marvel, wonder
¡Qué maravilla! How wonderful!
mariposa, la butterfly
marrón *(pl.:* **marrones***)* brown
martes Tuesday
más more; most
más de more than (number)
más . . . que more . . . than
máscara, la mask
matemáticas, las mathematics
máximo (-a) maximum
maya *(adj.)* Mayan (ancient civilization of Mexico and Central America)
mayor *(adj.)* major, principal
me me (2); myself; to me (4)
medalla, la medal (10)
la medalla de bronce bronze medal (10)
la medalla de oro gold medal (10)
la medalla de plata silver medal (10)
medianoche, la *(f.)* midnight
médica, la *(f.)* doctor
medicinas, las medicine (12)
médico, el *(m.)* doctor
médico (-a) medical
medio, el middle
medio (-a) half
las seis y media six-thirty
mediodía, el *(m.)* noon, midday

medir (i) to measure
mejor better (10); best (10)
a lo mejor maybe, perhaps
el (la) mejor the best (10)
mejor que better than (10)
mi mejor amiga my best friend
menos less; to, of (time)
a las tres menos veinte at twenty minutes to three
por lo menos at least
mensaje, el *(m.)* message
mentira, la lie
menú, el *(m.)* menu (4)
mercado, el market
el mercado al aire libre open-air market (5)
merienda, la snack (9)
mes, el *(m.)* month
mesa, la table
métrico (-a) metric
metro, el subway (5)
mexicano (-a) Mexican
mi, mis my
mí me
¡Miaou! Meow!
miedo, el fear
miércoles Wednesday
migrar to migrate
milla, la mile
una milla cuadrada a square mile
minuto, el minute
mirar to look (at), to watch (2)
¡mire! look! (formal command)
mismo (-a) same
ahora mismo right now
de la misma manera que in the same way that
lo mismo the same (thing)
mochila, la backpack (9)
modelo, el model, example
moderno (-a) modern (3)
modismo, el a word or group of words that has a special meaning, idiom
moneda, la coin (4)
monetario (-a) monetary, of money
monstruo, el monster
montaña, la mountain (1)
montar a caballo to ride on horseback
monte, el *(m.)* mountain
monumento, el monument (5)
mover (ue) to move
muchacha, la girl
muchacho, el boy
mucho *(adv.)* a lot
mucho (-a) much, a lot of
muchos (-as) many
muebles, los *(m.)* furniture
mujer, la *(f.)* woman
mundial *(adj.)* world, of the world
la Copa Mundial World Cup (soccer tournament)
mundo, el world
museo, el museum (5)
música, la music; *(f.)* musician (11)
musical musical
músico, el *(m.)* musician (11)
muy very

n

nacional *(adj.)* national
nada nothing; not . . . anything
nada más that's all, just

nadar to swim
nadie nobody, no one
naranja, la orange (fruit)
natación, la *(f.)* swimming (10)
naturaleza, la nature
necesitar to need (3)
negativo (-a) negative
negro (-a) black
nervioso (-a) nervous (5)
neutral neutral
nevar (ie) to snow
ni neither; nor
niño, el boy
no no, not
¡No corras! Don't run!
noche, la *(f.)* night
nombre, el *(m.)* name
norte, el *(m.)* north (6)
norteño (-a) northern
nos us (2); ourselves; to us (4)
nosotras we; us (*f.* group)
nosotros we; us (*m.* or *m.* and *f.* group)
nota, la note
noticias, las news (13)
novela, la novel
noviembre November
nube, la *(f.)* cloud
nublado (-a) cloudy
nuestro (-a) our
nuevo (-a) new
número, el number
nunca never

O

o or
obra de teatro, la play (11)
obrero, el *(m.)* worker
observar to observe
océano, el ocean
octubre October
oeste, el *(m.)* west (6)
oficial *(adj.)* official
oficina, la office
ofrecer to offer
oído, el ear
de oído by ear
oigo *(inf.:* **oír***)* (I) hear
oír *(IR)* to hear (13)
ola, la wave (8)
opinar to think (as an opinion)
opinión, la *(f., pl.:* **opiniones***)* opinion
oportunidad, la *(f.)* opportunity
oración, la *(f., pl.:* **oraciones***)* sentence
orilla, la bank (of river)
oro, el gold (10)
una medalla de oro gold medal (10)
orquesta, la orchestra (11)
os to you; you (*pl.* used in Spain)
oso, el bear
el oso polar polar bear
otro (-a) another; other

p

paciente, el *or* la patient
pagar to pay (1)
página, la page
país, el *(m.)* country
pájaro, el bird
palabra, la word
  en tus palabras in your own words
palacio, el palace
palito, el little stick
panorama, el *(m.)* panorama, scene
papa, la potato
papá, el *(m.)* father, dad
papás, los *(m.)* parents
papel, el *(m.)* paper; part, role
  hacer un papel to play a part (11)
paquete, el *(m.)* package (13)
par, el *(m.)* pair
para by (8); for (8); in order to (8); to
  ¿para qué? what for? why? (8)
  ¿para quién? for whom? (8)
parada de autobús, la bus stop
pararse to stop
parcial *(adj.)* partial
pared, la *(f.)* wall
paréntesis, los *(m.)* parentheses
  entre paréntesis in parentheses
parque, el *(m.)* park
párrafo, el paragraph
participar to participate
partido, el game, match (sport)
pasado (-a) past, last (7)
  la semana pasada last week (7)
pasajera, la *(f.)* passenger (2)
pasajero, el *(m.)* passenger (2)
pasar to pass; to happen; to spend (time)
  pasar la aspiradora to vacuum
  pasar las vacaciones to spend (one's) vacation (1)
  ¿Qué pasa? What's happening?
  ¿Qué te pasa? What's happening with you? What's wrong?
pasear to ride
pasillo, el hall, hallway
paso, el crossing
  el paso de peatones pedestrian crosswalk (6)
patinar to skate
patio, el patio
patria, la country, nation
patrón, el *(m., pl.:* **patrones**) patron
peatón, el *(m., pl.:* **peatones**) pedestrian
  el paso de peatones pedestrian crosswalk (6)
pedir (i) to ask for, to request (3)
peinarse to comb (one's hair)
peine, el *(m.)* comb
película, la movie; film (camera)
peligro, el danger (8)
peligroso (-a) dangerous
pelo, el hair
península, la peninsula
pensar (ie) to plan; to think
  pensar en to think about
  pensar + *inf.* to plan (to do something)
pensión, la *(f., pl.:* **pensiones**) small hotel or inn

peor worse (10); worst (10)
el (la) peor the worst (10)
peor que worse than (10)
pequeño (-a) small, little
perder (ie) to lose (10)
perderse (ie) to be (or get) lost (6)
perdido (-a) lost
perfectamente *(adv.)* perfectly
periodista, el *or* la reporter
perla, la pearl
permitir to permit, to allow
pero but
perro, el dog
persona, la person
personal *(adj.)* personal
peruano (-a) Peruvian
pesca, la fishing
peso, el peso (currency of several Spanish-speaking countries)
piano, el piano (11)
picar to sting
pie, el *(m.)* foot
ir a pie to go on foot, to walk
___ **pies de altura** ___ feet in height
piedra, la stone, rock
las piedras preciosas precious stones, gems
pierna, la leg
piloto, el *or* la pilot (2)
pintar to paint
pintura, la paint; painting
piña, la pineapple
piso, el floor
pista, la track (running) (10)
pizarra, la chalkboard
plan, el *(m.)* plan
planchar to iron
planta, la plant
plástico (-a) plastic
plata, la silver (10)
una medalla de plata silver medal (10)
platillo, el saucer
plato, el plate; dish
playa, la beach (1)
plaza, la plaza, town square (5)
población, la *(f., pl.:* **poblaciones***)* town; population
¡Pobrecita! Poor thing!
¡Pobrecita de Paquita! Poor little Paquita!
poco *(adv.)* little
un poco de a little bit of
pocos (-as) few
poder (ue) *(IR)* to be able; can (1)
poema, el *(m.)* poem
policía, el or la police officer
polvo, el dust
pollito, el chick (9)
pollo, el chicken
poner *(IR)* to put
poner la mesa to set the table
ponerse *(IR)* to put on (oneself)
ponerse de acuerdo to come to an agreement
ponerse la ropa to get dressed
por for (9); during (9); in (9); through; at; by
por eso that's why
por favor please
por fin finally, at last
por hora per hour
por la mañana during, in the morning (9)
por lo menos at least
por medio de by means of

por la noche during, in the evening (9); during, at night (9)
por la tarde during, in the afternoon (9)
¿por qué? why?
por si acaso just in case
por último (*adv.*) finally, last
porque because
posibilidad, la (*f.*) possibility
postal (*adj.*) postal, post
practicar to practice
práctico (-a) practical
precio, el price
precioso (-a) precious
preferir (ie) to prefer
pregunta, la question
preguntar to ask
preparar to prepare, to make
presentar to present
prima, la (*f.*) cousin
primavera, la spring
primero (*adv.*) first
primero (-a) first
los primeros auxilios first aid (12)
primo, el (*m.*) cousin
prisa, la hurry
probable (*adj.*) probable
es probable que sí it's probably so
probar (ue) to try; to taste
problema, el (*m.*) problem
profesional (*adj.*) professional
programa, el (*m.*) program
prohibir to prohibit (8)
se prohibe (nadar) (swimming) is prohibited (8)
pronto (*adv.*) soon
propina, la tip (4)
propio (-a) (one's) own
proverbio, el proverb
provincia, la province
próximo (-a) next
proyecto, el project
público, el public
pueblo, el town, village
puente, el bridge
puerta, la door; gate (at airport) (2)
puerto, el port
pues well
pulgada, la inch
puma, el (*m.*) puma, cougar (9)
punto, el point; dot
en punto on the dot, sharp (time)
pupitre, el (*m.*) (student) desk

q

que that; who; than
¿qué? what? which?
¿Y qué? So what?
¡qué! what! how!
quedar to be (located) (6)
quedarse to remain, to stay
quemado (-a) sunburned (8)
quemar to burn
querer (ie) to want
querido (-a) dear
queso, el cheese
¿quién? ¿quiénes? who?
¿con quién? with whom?
¡Qui-qui-ri-quí! Cock-a-doodle-doo!
quitar to take away, to take off
quitar el polvo to dust

quitarse to take off (oneself)
quitarse la ropa to get undressed
quizá, quizás perhaps, maybe

r

radio, el radio (set)
radio, la radio (programs, broadcasts)
escuchar la radio to listen to the radio
rápidamente *(adv.)* rapidly, quickly (12)
rápido *(adv.)* quickly, fast (6)
raramente *(adv.)* rarely
raro (-a) rare
rato, el while, awhile
ratón, el *(m., pl.:* **ratones***)* mouse
razonable *(adj.)* reasonable
realidad, la *(f.)* reality
en realidad really, in reality
recepción, la *(f., pl.:* **recepciones***)* reception
recibir to receive, to get
recoger to pick up
reflexión, la *(f., pl.:* **reflexiones***)* reflection
refrigerador, el *(m.)* refrigerator
regalado(-a) given (as a gift)
regalo, el gift (7)
regatear to barter, to bargain (for a price)
región, la *(f., pl.:* **regiones***)* region
reina, la queen
reírse *(IR)* to laugh (11)
religioso (-a) religious
reloj, el *(m.)* watch, clock
repetir (i) to repeat
repite *(com.; inf.:* **repetir***)* repeat
reportaje, el *(m.)* report (in a newspaper or magazine)
reporte, el *(m.)* report
respirar to breathe
respuesta, la answer
restaurante, el *(m.)* restaurant (4)
resultar to result; to produce an effect
retrato, el portrait
reunión, la *(f., pl.:* **reuniones***)* meeting
revelar to reveal
revista, la magazine
río, el river (1)
rió *(pret.; inf.:* **reír***)* (he, she, you) laughed
risa, la laughter
ritmo, el rhythm
rizado (-a) curly (hair)
robo, el robbery (12)
roedor, el *(m.)* rodent
rojo (-a) red
romántico (-a) romantic
ropa, la clothes
ropero, el clothes closet
rosado (-a) pink
rubio (-a) blond(e)
ruido, el noise (13)
¡Qué ruido! How noisy!
ruina, la ruin
las ruinas ruins
rural *(adj.)* rural, outlying

S

sábado Saturday
sabana, la savanna, treeless plain
sábana, la sheet (3)
saber *(IR)* to know
saber + *inf.* to know how to
saber más que Merlín to be very wise, clever
¿Supieron (las malas noticias)? Did you hear (the bad news)? (13)
sabio (-a) wise
sabroso (-a) delicious, tasty
sacar to take out (7)
sacar fotos to take photos
saco, el sack, bag
sala, la living room
salida, la departure (2)
salir *(IR)* to leave, to depart; to turn out
¿Cómo saliste en el examen? How did you do on the exam?
salón, el *(m., pl.:* **salones**) (large) room
el salón de clase classroom
saltar to jump
salto, el jump
el salto de altura high jump (10)
salto de agua, el waterfall (9)
salud, la *(f.)* health
saludar to greet
saludo, el greeting
Saludos a todos. Greetings to everybody.
salvavidas, el *(m.)* life preserver, lifesaver (8)
sandalia, la sandal (7)
sándwich, el *(m.)* sandwich
sanitario, el medical worker (Peru)
sapo, el toad
sarape, el woven blanket (Mexico)
saxofonista, el *or* la saxophone player
saxófono, el saxophone
secar to dry
secarse to dry (oneself)
secretaria, la *(f.)* secretary
secreto, el secret
secundario (-a) secondary
la escuela secundaria secondary school, high school
sed, la *(f.)* thirst
seguir (i) to follow; to continue
según according to
segundo (-a) second
selva, la rain forest (1)
la selva tropical tropical rain forest (9)
semana, la week
la semana pasada last week (7)
la semana que entra this coming week
sendero, el path, trail (9)
sentarse (ie) to sit down
sentir (ie) to regret, to be sorry
señor (Sr.) Mr.; sir (polite address)
señora (Sra.) Mrs.; ma'am (polite address)
señorita (Srta.) Miss
separar to separate
septiembre September
ser *(IR)* to be
serio (-a) serious
serpiente, la *(f.)* serpent, snake (9)

servicio, el service
servir (i) to serve
sexto (-a) sixth
si if
sí yes
siempre always
sierra, la mountain range
siglo, el century
sigue *(com.; inf.:* **seguir**) follow
silla, la chair
sillón, el *(m., pl.:* **sillones**) armchair, easy chair
símbolo, el symbol
simpático (-a) nice, pleasant
sin without, with no
sinagoga, la synagogue (5)
sino but (conjunction)
sistema, el *(m.)* system
sitio, el place, location
situado (-a) located
sobre, el *(m.)* envelope (13)
sobre *(prep.)* about; on, on top of, upon
sobre todo most of all, above all
¡Socorro! Help! (12)
sofá, el *(m.)* sofa, couch
sol, el *(m.)* sun
solamente *(adv.)* only, just
solo (-a) alone
sólo *(adv.)* only, just
sombrilla, la beach umbrella (8)
sonido, el sound
sonrisa, la smile
sopa, la soup
sorprender to surprise
sorpresa, la surprise
su, sus her; his; their; your
subir to climb, to go up; to board, to get in or on (a vehicle)
sucio (-a) dirty
suéter, el *(m.)* sweater
sumar to add, to add up
supermercado, el supermarket (5)
sur, el *(m.)* south (6)

t

también also, too
tambor, el *(m.)* drum (11)
tampoco either, neither
tan so
tan poco so little
tanto (-a) so much
¿Por qué tienes tanta prisa? Why are you in such a hurry?
tarde, la *(f.)* afternoon
tarde *(adv.)* late (2)
tarea, la assignment, homework
tarjeta, la card
la tarjeta de embarcación boarding pass
la tarjeta postal postcard (3)
taxista, el *or* la taxi driver
taza, la cup
te you (2); yourself; to you (4)
té, el *(m.)* tea
teatro, el theater (11)
técnica, la technique
las técnicas médicas medical techniques
techo, el roof
tejer to weave
tejido, el weaving

telar, el loom
teléfono, el telephone
telenovela, la soap opera
televisión, la (*f., pl.:* **televisiones**) television
televisor, el (*m.*) television set
tema, el (*m.*) theme, subject
temperatura, la temperature
temprano (-a) early (2)
tenedor, el (*m.*) fork
tener (*IR*) to have
  ¡Ten cuidado! Be careful! (9)
  tener . . . años to be . . . years old
  tener deseos de to desire, to want
  tener dolor to be in pain, to hurt
  tener fiebre to have a fever (12)
  tener frío to be cold
  tener hambre to be hungry
  tener lugar to take place
  tener miedo to be afraid
  tener prisa to be in a hurry
  tener que + ***inf.*** to have to . . .
  tener razón to be right
  tener sed to be thirsty
  tener tos to have a cough (12)
tenis, el (*m.*) tennis
tercero (-a) third
tesoro, el treasure
ti you
tía, la aunt
tiempo, el time; weather
  a tiempo on time (2)
tienda, la store
  la tienda de discos record store (7)
tierra, la land
tigre, el (*m.*) tiger
tímido (-a) shy, timid
tío, el uncle
tíos, los aunt(s) and uncle(s)
toalla, la towel (3)
tocador, el (*m.*) dresser
tocar to play (an instrument); to touch
todavía still, yet
todo (-a) all
  todo el (zoológico) the whole (zoo)
  todos los días every day
todos (-as) all; everybody
tomar to take; to drink
  tomar el desayuno to eat (have) breakfast
  tomar el sol to sunbathe (8)
  tomarle el pelo a uno to pull someone's hair (to tease)
tomate, el (*m.*) tomato
tono, el tone
tontería, la foolishness, nonsense
torneo, el tournament
toro, el bull (9)
torta, la cake
tortuga, la tortoise
tos, la (*f.*) cough (12)
trabajar to work
trabalenguas, el (*m.*) tongue twister
tradición, la (*f., pl.:* **tradiciones**) tradition, custom
traer (*IR*) to bring
tráfico, el traffic
traje, el (*m.*) costume
traje de baño, el (*m.*) bathing suit, swimsuit
tranquilamente calmly
tranquilo (-a) calm, tranquil
trapeador, el (*m.*) mop
tren, el (*m.*) train
trigo, el wheat
triste sad (12)
tristemente (*adv.*) sadly (12)
triunfar to triumph

triunfo, el triumph
trofeo, el trophy (10)
trompeta, la trumpet
tropical tropical (9)
truco, el trick
tú you
tu, tus your
tubo, el tube
  el tubo esnorkel snorkel tube
turismo, el tourism
turista, el *or* la tourist (3)

U

último (-a) last
  por último (*adv.*) finally, last
un, una a, an
único (-a) only
unidad, la (*f.*) unit
  la unidad monetaria monetary unit
unos, unas some, a few; any
urgencia, la emergency
usar to use
usted you (used when addressing adult)
ustedes you (*pl.*)
usual usual (13)
usualmente (*adv.*) usually (13)
útil useful
uva, la grape

V

vaca, la cow (9)
vacaciones, las (*f., s.:* **vacación**) vacation
valle, el (*m.*) valley (1)
variado(-a) varied
variedad, la (*f.*) variety
  el programa de variedades variety show
varios (-as) several
vaso, el glass; vase
vela, la sail
vendedor, el sales clerk
vender to sell
venir (ie) (*IR*) to come
  ¡Ven acá! Come here!
ventana, la window
ventanilla, la small window (at a counter) (4)
ver to see
  a ver let's see
verano, el summer
veras, las truth, reality
  ¿De veras? Really?
verbo, el verb
verdad, la (*f.*) truth
verdadero (-a) real, true
verde green
vestido, el dress
vez, la (*f., pl.:* **veces**) time
  a veces sometimes
  ¿Cuántas veces a (la semana). . . ? How many times a (week) . . . ?
  en vez de instead of
viajar to travel (1)

viaje, el *(m.)* trip (1)
la agencia de viajes travel agency (1)
el (la) agente de viajes travel agent (1)
hacer un viaje to take a trip (1)
viajera, la *(f.)* traveler (1)
viajero, el *(m.)* traveler (1)
vida, la life
viejitos, los little old men (folk dance, Mexico)
viejo (-a) old
viento, el wind
viernes Friday
violín, el *(m.)* violin (11)
visita, la visit
de visita for a visit
visitar to visit
viuda, la widow
vivir to live
vocabulario, el vocabulary
vocal, la *(f.)* vowel
volar (ue) to fly (2)
volcán, el *(m., pl.:* **volcanes***)* volcano (1)
volibol, el *(m.)* volleyball
volver (ue) to return, to come back, to go back (8)
vosotras you (*pl.* used in Spain; *f.* group)
vosotros you (*pl.* used in Spain; *m.* or *m.* and *f.* group)
vuelo, el flight (2)
vuelta, la turn
dar una vuelta a . . . to go around . . .

y

y and
¿Y qué? So what?
ya already
yo I

z

zanahoria, la carrot
zapatería, la shoe store (7)
zapatero, el shoemaker (7)
zapato, el shoe (7)
zoológico, el zoo (5)

English-Spanish Word List

The following list contains the English equivalents of the active vocabulary in *¡Nos comunicamos!* For reference, the unit in which the Spanish word is taught is given in parentheses.

able, to be poder (1)
actor el actor (11)
actress la actriz (11)
address la dirección (13)
ahead adelante (6)
airline la línea aérea (2)
airmail el correo aéreo (13)
airplane el avión (2)
airport el aeropuerto (2)
alligator el caimán (9)
ambulance la ambulancia (12)
angry enojado (-a) (5)
announcer el locutor, la locutora (11)
ant la hormiga (9)
apartment building el edificio de apartamentos (5)
applaud, to aplaudir (11)
arrest, to detener (12)
arrival la llegada (2)
arrive, to llegar (2)
ask (for), to pedir (3)
asleep, to fall dormirse (3)
at night por la noche (9)
attend, to asistir (11)

backpack la mochila (9)
bank el banco (4)
bank teller el cajero, la cajera (4)
bathe, to bañarse (3)
bathtub la bañera (3)
be, to estar, ser (1); quedar (6)
be able, to poder (1)
beach la playa (1)
beach umbrella la sombrilla (8)
Be careful! ¡Ten cuidado! (9)
bee la abeja (9)
begin, to comenzar (1)
behind atrás (6)
belt el cinturón (7)
best el (la) mejor (10)
better mejor (10)
bill (currency) el billete (4)
blanket la manta (3)
block (street) la cuadra, la manzana (6)
bowling el boliche (10)
boxer el boxeador (10)
boxing el boxeo (10)
bracelet el brazalete (7)
bronze el bronce (10)
bull el toro (9)
buy, to comprar (7)
by (deadline) para (8)

calf el becerro (9)
canned goods la comida enlatada (9)
cassette el casete (7)
champion el campeón, la campeona (10)
check (bill) la cuenta (4)
chick el pollito (9)
church la iglesia (5)
city la ciudad (5)
city hall la alcaldía (5)
clap, to aplaudir (11)

clarinet el clarinete (11)
close, to cerrar (1)
closed cerrado (-a) (4)
coin la moneda (4)
cold frío (-a) (3)
collision el choque (12)
come back, to volver (8)
comfortable cómodo (-a) (2)
compact disc el disco compacto (7)
conductor (music) el director, la directora (11)
confused confundido (-a) (5)
corner (street) la esquina (6)
correctly correctamente (12)
cost, to costar (1)
cough, to have a tener tos (12)
country, countryside el campo (9)
cow la vaca (9)
crosswalk el paso de peatones (6)
cry, to llorar (11)
cycling el ciclismo (10)
cyclist el (la) ciclista (10)

dancer el bailarín, la bailarina (11)
danger el peligro (8)
departure la salida (2)
desert el desierto (1)
difficulty, with difícilmente (12)
do, to hacer (2)
drum el tambor (11)

early temprano (2)
easily fácilmente (12)
east el este (6)
eat lunch, to almorzar (7)
elevator el ascensor (3)
envelope el sobre (13)
expensive caro (-a) (7)
extinguisher (fire) el extintor (12)
eyeglasses los anteojos (8)

fall asleep, to dormirse (3)
farm la granja (9)
fast rápido (6)
fever, to have a tener fiebre (12)
fire el incendio (12)
fire alarm la alarma de incendios (12)
fire extinguisher el extintor (12)
first aid los primeros auxilios (12)
flight el vuelo (2)
flight attendant el aeromozo, la aeromoza (2)
float, to flotar (8)
fly, to volar (2)
follow, to seguir (3)
for para (8); por (9)
found, to be encontrarse (6)
fountain la fuente (5)
frequently frecuentemente (12)

generally generalmente (12)
gift el regalo (7)
give, to dar (4)
go, to ir (1)
gold el oro (10)
goose el ganso (9)
guitar la guitarra (11)
gymnastics la gimnasia (10)

happily felizmente (12)
happy contento (-a) (5); feliz (12)
hard duro (-a) (3)
hear, to oír (13)
Help! ¡Socorro! ¡Auxilio! (12)
help la ayuda (12)
hen la gallina (9)
her la (2); le (4)

high jump el salto de altura (10)
high school el colegio (5)
him lo (2); le (4)
hot caliente (3)
hotel el hotel (3)

in (time of day) por (9)
inexpensive barato (-a) (7)
it lo, la (2); le (4)

jewel la joya (7)
jeweler el joyero, la joyera (7)
jewelry store la joyería (7)

key la llave (3)
key chain el llavero (7)
kilometer el kilómetro (6)
know, to saber (13)

lake el lago (1)
land, to aterrizar (2)
last week la semana pasada (7)
late tarde (2)
laugh, to reírse (11)
leave, to salir (2)
letter (mail) la carta (13)
life preserver el salvavidas (8)
look, to mirar (2)
lose, to perder (10)
lost, to be (*or* get) perderse (6)
luggage el equipaje (2)

mail el correo (13)
mail, to echar al correo, mandar por correo (13)
mail carrier el cartero, la cartera (13)
make, to hacer (2)
me me (2); me (4)
medal la medalla (10)
medicine las medicinas (12)
menu el menú (4)
mile la milla (6)
modern moderno (-a) (3)
monument el monumento (5)
motorboat la lancha (8)
mountain la montaña (1)
mountain climber el (la) alpinista (10)
mountain climbing el alpinismo (10)
museum el museo (5)
musician el músico, la música (11)

necklace el collar (7)
need, to necesitar (3)
nervous nervioso (-a) (5)
news la(s) noticia(s) (13)
north el norte (6)

old antiguo (-a) (3)
on time a tiempo (2)
open abierto (-a) (4)
open-air market el mercado al aire libre (5)
orchestra la orquesta (11)
outing, to go on an ir de excursión (9)

package el paquete (13)
passenger el pasajero, la pasajera (2)
path el sendero (9)
pay, to pagar (1)
piano el piano (11)
pig el cerdo (9)
pilot el (la) piloto (2)
plan to, to pensar + *inf.* (1)
play (theater) la obra de teatro (11)
play, to (game or sport) jugar (a) (3)
play a role, to hacer un papel (11)

plaza la plaza (5)
postal clerk el (la) agente de correo (13)
postcard la tarjeta postal (3)
post office el correo (13)
prefer, to preferir (4)
prohibited, it is se prohibe (8)
puma el puma (9)
purse la bolsa (7)
put in the mail, to echar al correo (13)

race la carrera (10)
rain forest la selva (1); la selva tropical (9)
rapidly rápidamente (12)
receive, to recibir (1)
record (album) el disco (7)
record store la tienda de discos (7)
rest, to descansar (1)
restaurant el restaurante (4)
return, to volver (1)
river el río (1)
robber el ladrón, la ladrona (12)
robbery el robo (12)
room (hotel) la habitación (3)
rooster el gallo (9)
run, to correr (1)
sad triste (5)
sadly tristemente (12)
sailboat el barco de vela (8)
sand la arena (8)
sandals las sandalias (7)
save, to ahorrar (4)
say, to decir (2)
schedule el horario (2)
scuba diving, to go bucear (8)
sculpture la escultura (5)
sea el mar (8)
seat el asiento (2)
see, to ver (2)
send, to (mail) mandar por correo (13)
serpent la serpiente (9)
serve, to servir (3)
shake hands, to dar la mano (4)
sheet la sábana (3)
shell la concha, el caracol (8)
shoe el zapato (7)
shoemaker el zapatero, la zapatera (7)
shoe store la zapatería (7)
shot la inyección (12)
shout, to gritar (10)
shower la ducha (3)
sick, to be estar enfermo (-a) (12)
silver la plata (10)
singer el (la) cantante (11)
slow despacio (6)
slowly lentamente (12)
snack la merienda (9)
snail el caracol (8)
soap el jabón (3)
soft blando (-a) (3)
south el sur (6)
spectators los espectadores (10)
spend (money), to gastar (4)
spend (time), to pasar (1)
sport el deporte (10)
square block (street) la manzana (6)
stadium el estadio (5)
stamp la estampilla (13)
stand in line, to hacer fila (2)
street corner la esquina (6)
street lamp el farol (6)
stretcher la camilla (12)
subway el metro (5)
suitcase la maleta (2)
sunbathe, to tomar el sol (8)
sunburned quemado (-a) (8)
suntan lotion la crema de broncear (8)

suntanned bronceado (-a) (8)
supermarket el supermercado (5)
swimming la natación (10)
synagogue la sinagoga (5)

take a trip, to hacer un viaje (2)
take off, to (airplane) despegar (2)
take out, to sacar (7)
taste, to probar (1)
tell, to decir (2)
thank, to dar las gracias (4)
that ese, esa, aquel, aquella (8)
theater el teatro (11)
theater, to attend the asistir al teatro (11)
them los, las (2); les (4)
these estos, estas (8)
think, to pensar (1)
this este, esta (8)
those esos, esas, aquellos, aquellas (8)
ticket el billete (1)
tip la propina (4)
tired cansado (-a) (5)
tourist el (la) turista (3)
towel la toalla (3)
track (running) la pista (10)
trail el sendero (9)
travel, to viajar (1)
travel agency la agencia de viajes (1)
travel agent el (la) agente de viajes (1)
traveler el viajero, la viajera (1)
tree el árbol (9)
trip el viaje (1); la excursión (9)
trophy el trofeo (10)

uncomfortable incómodo (-a) (2)
us nos (2); nos (4)
usually usualmente (12)

valley el valle (1)
violin el violín (11)
visit, to visitar (1)
volcano el volcán (1)

waiter el camarero (4)
waitress la camarera (4)
walk, to andar (12)
waterfall el salto de agua (9)
waterskiing el esquí acuático (8)
wave la ola (8)
west el oeste (6)
win, to ganar (10)
window la ventanilla (4)
worse peor (10)
worst el (la) peor (10)
wrap, to envolver (13)
wrestling la lucha libre (10)

yesterday ayer (7)
yesterday morning (afternoon) ayer por la mañana (la tarde) (7)
you te, lo, la, los, las (2); les (4)

zoo el zoológico (5)

Index